THE PARENTING QUIZ

1 Your baby won't stop crying. The first thing to try is:

a) post it back to the hospital refund

b) offer it a Kit Kat

c) look for hairline cracks on check the electricals

d) wear one of those deerhu furry flaps you can tie ove

2 A dressing-gown is:

a) only to be worn over pyja

b) attractive all-day before-fi

c) too much trouble if you h the cord.

Plea
date s
can b

3 Sleep deprivation can lea osing your:

vocabulary

nind

c) short-term . . . thingie

d) "What?"

4 You'll only have time t ear one arti cle of c g a day. To

⇨

7 Tinky Winky is:

a) a terrific name for a child's private parts, right up until they leave home

b) sailor slang for semaphore messages

c) a bit of a nancyboy and that's the way we like 'em

d) an 8-year-old rapper from Launceston.

8 The parenting anthem is:

a) "I Will Survive" by Gloria Gaynor

b) "Insomnia" by Faithless

c) that lullabies compilation in the glove box with peanut butter on the underside

d) "I Mashed the Pumpkin, But I Did Not Fool the Fussy One" sung to the tune of "I Shot the Sheriff, But I Did Not Shoot the Deputy" by Mr Bob Marley.

9 When a child weighs approximately twenty kg, a safe car restraint should:

a) be buckled up by someone in a less cranky mood than me

b) come in a late-model Mercedes provided by the government

c) be constructed entirely from plastic dinosaurs that go "Raaarghhh"

d) be slightly less expensive than an aircraft carrier.

10 Discipline:

a) shmisipline

b) should be consistent, persistent and performed by trained robots

c) shut up

d) should never be humiliating or confusing to the parent.

11 What's the worst thing to say when you're dropping your child off at creche?

a) "We think of lice as our special little friends."

b) "Christ on a STICK, I could do with another vodka."

c) "Is this the child-care centre?"

d) "If I'm not back by 7 or so, sweetie, make your own way home."

12 Reassuring phrases for your child can include:

a) "Don't worry, personality isn't always genetic."

b) "Don't worry, body shape isn't always genetic."

c) "It's true, the Prime Minister does look like a boiled turnip."

d) "When you're 18 you can leave."

13 You think fathers who look after their own children are:

a) fictitious

b) marvellous, really quite marvellous

c) married to vicious, godless, feminist, selfish, hairy harridans

d) seahorses.

14 "Controlled crying" is:

a) when you can sob without getting snot on your face

b) a method whereby parents can cry for five minutes at a time, for efficiency reasons

c) when you cry and you look like the guy in that Scream painting, but no tears come out

d) usually recommended by people who are not in your house at 8.20 pm.

15 Sex is:

a) something done by people whose photos are in *Hello* magazine

b) "Huh? Wha . . . er . . . the . . . (snonk) *zzzzzzzzzzzzzz.*"

c) over

d) ova.

16 The most important thing is:

a) love

b) trust

c) thinking of your child as your friend

d) not starting to order the vodka by the keg.

17 Children's clothes should always be:

a) designed to make kids look like demented Italian supermodels in their thirties

b) made of plastic wipe-down materials

c) able to withstand being machine washed with knives and tumble dried in temperatures exceeding 32,000 degrees Celsius

d) partly removed from under the bed before being placed on child.

18 The dog and the kid have both thrown up in the car at the same time. You:

a) pull over safely to the kerb and scream into a pillow

b) pull over safely to the kerb and hose down the inside of the vehicle

c) thank your lucky stars you don't own the car

d) pull over safely to the kerb, calmly exit the vehicle, go to the airport and fly to Antigua.

Answers Oh, who the hell knows? We're all trying to make this up as we go along.

KAZ COOKE

The Rough Guide to

BABIES
AND
TODDLERS

The essential guide to caring for babies and toddlers

CREDITS AND PUBLISHING INFORMATION

Designed by Sandy Cull © Penguin Group (Australia)
Kazza font created by Kaz Cooke, digitalised by DiZign Pty Ltd
Typeset in 10/15 pt Stone Serif by Post Pre-press Group/Dan May, Rough Guides
Printed in Singapore by SNP Security Printing
Edited by: Pauline Savage and Andrew Lockett
Proofreading: Amanda Jones
Production: Rebecca Short and Vicky Baldwin

Rough Guides Reference
Editors: Peter Buckley, Tracy Hopkins, Matt Milton, Joe Staines, Ruth Tidball
Director: Andrew Lockett

First published as *Kidwrangling* by Penguin Group (Australia) 2003

This edition first published March 2009 by Rough Guides Ltd:
80 Strand, London WC2R 0RL
www.roughguides.com
mail@roughguides.com
Distributed by the Penguin Group:
Penguin Books Ltd, 80 Strand, London WC2R 0RL

576 pages; includes index

ISBN 978-1-84836-026-6

A catalogue record for this book is available from the British Library

1 3 5 7 9 8 6 4 2

CONTENTS

PaRt 2: ToDDLeRs 225

PaRt 3: PaReNtiNg 279

PaRt 4: stuff

acknowledgements

This book is dedicated to my mother, for all the kindnesses she showed me as a small girl and for doing the best she could even though when I was four I told the greengrocer she had a beard on her bottom.

Many professionals and brilliant amateurs (that means us, parents) helped with this book and I thank them from stopping my head from exploding (although it was a close-run thing). Here are just a few others who need special thanks for fact-checking, research and other invaluable service to this book: paediatricians Dr Jenny Royle, Dr Michael Harari, Dr Michael Rice, Dr Martin Ward Platt and paediatric infectious diseases specialist Dr Nigel Curtis, obstetrician Dr Len Kliman, midwives Cathryn Curtin and Melanie Dunlop, parenting educator Gina Ralston, child psychologist Frances Thomson Salo, physical development specialists Dr Katie Heathershaw and Dr Elizabeth Waters, lactation consultant Margaret Callaghan, children's dieticians Beth Martino and Jenny Taylor, nanny Anna Daffy, editor Pauline Savage, publisher and editor Andrew Lockett, aides and allies Geoffrey Leonard, Violet Leonard, Julie Gibbs, Lesley Dunt, Peg McColl and all the medical and other advisors on the predecessor to this book, *The Rough Guide to Pregnancy and Childbirth*.

iNTRO

The information in this book is not meant to be taken instead of individual, professional medical advice. Nor is it a good substitute for a nutritional diet. The book will, however, prop up a sash window when you're not using it.

What should I do when the baby cries? What do babies eat? Is it like having a puppy? What's a good present for a 2-year-old's birthday? What do I do when my toddler behaves like a supermodel? What do kids need to know before they go to school? Which is better: staying at home or using child care? Is immunization dangerous? Is that a Marmite stain on my forehead? Will I get to a hairdresser before my first-born turns 6?

Have a cup of tea and take the load off, we'll get to all that.

A lot of the people who read my book *The Rough Guide to Pregnancy and Birth* wrote to me and said, "WHERE'S THE SEQUEL?! HURRY UP YOU DEMENTED SLATTERN, I NEED TO KNOW WHAT TO DO NEXT!", which was quite rude but I understand they were sleep deprived and needed to know which end to put the nappy on. So I started to research what a parent needed or might want to know in the first five years.

The book ended up being fairly huge. (It also took a while because I had a toddler of my own, and I don't know whether you've heard but toddlers can be a tad time-consuming.) Please don't be appalled by the size of the book. Don't think "Oh MY GOD, I need to know all THIS?" because you won't.

Don't be freaked out by the "Health" chapter, for example. It's full of lurgies your kid might catch, but it's practically impossible for kids to have all of them – and certainly not at the same time!

Some people say we shouldn't need a book to help us look after our kids – that we should follow our "instincts" like animals, who are automatically proficient parents. This is piffle. (Sometimes lionesses eat their own cubs, for heaven's sake.) We're not born with parenting instincts, we develop them.

> *"Some animals are lovely, and we can learn a lot from watching them, but as role models and guides to personal hygiene they're the dregs."* DAME EDNA EVERAGE, *VANITY FAIR*, FEBRUARY 2002

Anyway you don't need to know everything at once. Knowing only some things at a time is perfectly fine in the parenting department. If you're starting with a baby, it's years before you'll need any preschool info: this book should last you about three years. As you go on you'll almost certainly need less info so that's why the toddler part is shorter than the baby bit. And then there's a whole bunch of other subjects that can apply to more than one age group, such as dummies, health, food, immunization, siblings, parenting philosophy, safety and lots more, which you can look up in the last two parts of the book when it takes your fancy.

The Rough Guide to Babies and Toddlers is designed to help the people who are madly in love with their babies and just need some nipple advice, as well as the people who haven't a clue what to do with a small person and keep accidentally folding nappies into attractive swan shapes and putting them in the freezer. And to help all the parents and carers in between. The whole book is for dads as well as mums, even though there's a special "Dads" chapter (see p.305) and there isn't much you can teach them about how to breastfeed.

It's a book designed to be used by busy parents who want information given as succinctly as possible. So if you try to read it in sequence like a novel, you may come across a few repeated facts because mostly we expect people to be looking up "toddler development", "party ideas for

2-year-olds" or "gastro" in the Index or the Contents list as they need things. Don't think we were asleep at the wheel – we left in some repetition in case you only read one or two chapters.

This is not a parenting-guru book that represents one theory or the ideas of one person. I'm no expert, with a brilliant, one-size-fits-all theory. All parents and all children are different so wherever possible a number of solutions are given and there are pointers to further help. I didn't write this book because I had all the answers – I wrote it because I had to go looking for them.

Most of the quotes you'll see scattered in this book are from the parents (mainly mums) who responded in a survey done during research for the book, in which I asked a number of questions about being a parent. More than 900 people responded, and I'm grateful to everyone who gave generously of their time. The survey wasn't in the least designed to be scientific or produce statistics; instead it provided a rich source of helpful hints, a base of advice from the real experts, and the feeling that we're not in this parenting caper alone. The quotes are on selected topics, not every one, because unfortunately the survey questions couldn't go on forever.

Most chapters in *The Rough Guide to Babies and Toddlers* include a "More Info" section at their end, which includes book recommendations, and the phone numbers, websites and addresses of services you can go to for further advice or research. The part called "Extra Resources" at the end of the book has other important services and contacts.

Don't be slow to get professional help: it's what we have now instead of a tribal society full of wise women. Right at the end of your phone line are networks of specialists in all sorts of baby-related businesses. I think I rang about half of them three times each when I was a new mother, so don't be shy.

Many of the books I've suggested are, by their nature, specialized, but your local bookshop will order them for you, and at the same time you and your child can get used to browsing in bookshops. (I've given the publishing details of the copies reviewed, but there may be newer editions available for some now – always get the latest edition.) A lot of the books should also be available at your local library, which needs your support.

Although *The Rough Guide to Babies and Toddlers* is pro-kid, it is also very much on the side of parents and carers. You can't do or be everything your child wants (otherwise they'd be eating Easter eggs every day for breakfast and you'd be dressed as a giant penguin).

This book doesn't make a big deal – or any sort of a deal – about different family structures or parents' sexuality because that's largely irrelevant to being a good parent. Here's a round-up of possible family groups parents might be in or their child might encounter as they make friends: Mum, Dad and the kid; Mum, Step-dad and nine kids; Grandma and kids; Step-mum, Dad, Dad's brother Ron and kids; Mum, Mum's girlfriend, kids and offsite Dad; Dad, Dad's girlfriend, kids and offsite Mum; Mum and kids in a flat and an aunty next door; Mum and the kid, with Dad and Dad's boyfriend offsite; Mum and the kid in a shared house with some friends and their kids.

The only thing that's relevant to the child in all these possibilities is that they're in a safe and loving home. Especially when they're under 5, kids just assume their home is normal ("Yes, my father sleeps with a cardboard cut-out of Barbra Streisand and he supports West Ham." "Jeez! Mine farts like a tractor.") I mean, why should kids know what one gets up to in the privacy of one's room with a tin of golden syrup and a photo of the Duke of Edinburgh? Okay, that's just me.

So I'm not going to bang on about all these different types of families except to say it's always worth remembering that sole parents – who don't have someone to share custody with – have a harder time than shared-custody parents.

Some people complain that "Books never tell you how much you'll love your children". No – you can make that serendipitous, wonderful discovery for yourself. This book is supposed to help you with just about everything else.

I hope you'll find *The Rough Guide to Babies and Toddlers* reassuring, informative and easy to read. I hope it becomes your friend, helps you to feel calmer and more confident about being a parent, and provides lots of fun on the way. If not, I plan to have a tantrum.

— kaz

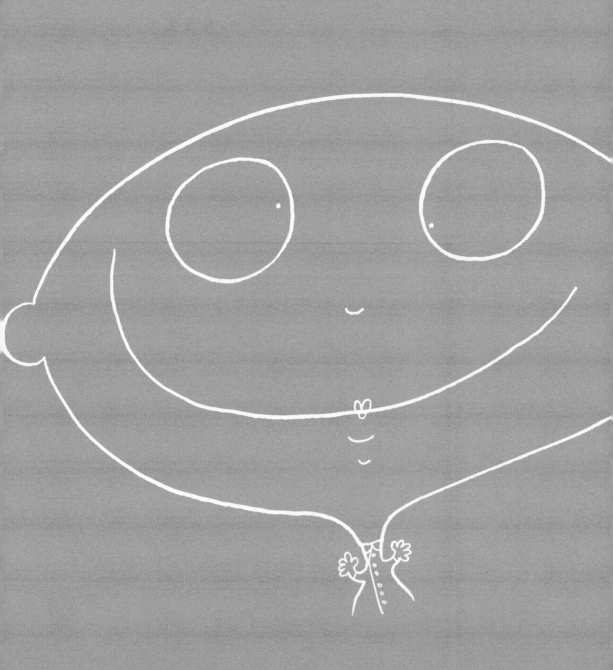

1

BaBies

IF YOU'RE READING *PART 1: BABIES*, YOU MIGHT ALSO BE INTERESTED IN CHAPTERS IN OTHER PARTS OF THE BOOK.

iN THe BeGiNNiNG

So, you're home. Now what? If you had enough brain cells left you'd be wondering why everyone makes you babyproof the house, because here's this wee, tiny, curly-up creature wrapped like takeaway fish and chips, who lies in whatever position you put them in and does nothing but blink, eat, poo, yell and sleep, not necessarily in any order – and who isn't all that chatty.

hello!

useful THiNGS to KNOW iN THe fiRSt DaYS

You don't have to know everything straight away
In fact you'll never know everything. You're starting a new, important job for which you have no qualifications. Treat yourself at least as kindly as you would a work-experience Girl Guide on the space shuttle, and accept that you'll be learning as you go.

Don't expect your baby to be the life of the party
Newborns shouldn't even really be out of the womb – they just come out because otherwise they wouldn't fit down the "birth canal" (oh please, can we start calling it

a vagina again now?). So they're not like baby giraffes, who are up running around an hour after the birth. (Which is probably just as well, frankly.) Newborn babies literally don't know where they are, sleep a lot, cry a lot and need to fill their tiny tummies at irregular or regular intervals (like every two to four hours – closer to four if you're lucky).

Babies like baby talk

They like burbly-urbly, slightly high-pitched talk – and the voice of their mum, and any other voice they've heard during their time inside or are getting to know on the outside. Even though a baby can't speak or fully understand, hearing you talk to them is great for their own fun and development. If you feel weird talking to them, describe what you're doing as you go about the day, tell them things that are going to happen or even sing silly songs. You'll be surprised how much babies understand from your tone of voice. And a sudden or loud noise will frighten them – they'll need a cuddle and some soothing words to calm down.

Babies love an animated face to go with life's chat

Make close-up surprised and delighted faces and smile as you chat (as long as they're not too tired, in which case if they could they'd tell you to naff off). You're their major source of visual entertainment. In the first few weeks newborns can see about the distance from their mother's breast to her face. They'll love you making wildly interesting faces, with mobile eyebrows – but not from the other side of the room.

Babies love a heartbeat

(Well, they've been soothed by their mum's for months.) Being cuddled against a chest can comfortingly remind babies of those floaty times on the inside.

You will probably never be this tired or clueless again

This is good news. I am not kidding you, it all gets better from here. Don't listen to gloomy nincompoops who say each stage of childhood has its own vastly worrying concerns (pause for violin music so you can take notice of their tragic lives): the new-ness and the sleeplessness set this time apart. The more communicative your child becomes, the easier it is to be a parent.

Let your baby know you understand it's all a bit freaky

Everything is new to babies: imagine landing on a planet where nothing, not even air or shapes or colours, is like anything you've experienced before. Imagine you've never felt anything on your skin or digested food – no wonder babies cry sometimes, especially at the end of the day. It must be so much to take in. Talk to them in a soothy, explainy, "It's okay, darling" sort of way when they seem discombobulated.

Your baby doesn't know which cry means what yet, either

After a while you may be able to tell whether your baby is having a little cry or is really distressed, whether they are hungry or just have something that feels wet and odd coming out of their bottom, or whether their tummy hurts while trying to digest all that brand-new milk. I reckon if you've exhausted possible reasons for crying (they're hungry, wet, pooey, cold, hot, overtired or have indigestion: see the "Crying" chapter), then they've probably got a case of understandable, non-specific, I'm-not-used-to-the-world freak-out. All you can do is try to be comforting and as bouncy-rocky as a womb, and share the crying baby around as much as possible so if you go mad you all go mad together. You can get so worried about solving the crying it only occurs to you months later that some of it may have been unsolvable.

Babies are born with personalities

People who have a lot to do with babies know that some of them are placid and some are cranky, and some are intense and some are incredibly alert. If your baby is clean, comfy, cuddled and well fed and still cries, it isn't a reflection on what sort of parent you are. A crying baby may be much more a reflection on what sort of baby you've had. (Or what sort of baby they are TODAY.)

You don't have to let go of your baby yet

Sometimes in the early days you hardly want to let your baby go to anyone else's arms, let alone out of your sight. That's okay. (Conversely you may have an immediately social or laid-back baby who is happy to be passed around, and you don't mind a bit. Do what feels right.)

Never force anyone to hold the baby if they're clearly uncomfortable or frightened of dropping them – there's a lifetime of cuddles coming for family and friends.

Let them sit down on the couch and have the baby on their knee if they feel safer doing that. But don't push it: there's no point making everyone tense.

As the weeks go on you'll know which people you feel happy to let hold or even look after your baby while you go to the shops or have a quiet moment.

HOW TO PICK UP A NEWBORN BABY

This info is for everyone, but especially new mums and those dads who might think being female automatically means you know how to pick up a very new baby – it's just practice and you can be as good at it as any mum. (Many men actually have a major advantage with their bigger hands.)

In the first weeks just make sure that when you pick up the baby you pick up the whole baby so there aren't any bits (head, arms, legs) dangling unsupported over the edges.

The most important part to be careful of, especially in the first two months, is the baby's neck. That oversized baby head is so heavy for the little-baby neck, and the neck muscles have to be developed and trained.

As with almost everything you do with your baby, tell them when you are going to pick them up or put them down. This is also how they start learning to anticipate and communicate. They'll get to understand and not be too startled.

GOOD THINGS TO DO FOR A NEWBORN BABY

* Start a baby scrapbook.

* Plant a tree against which to measure your child's growth – perhaps a photo in front at each birthday would be fun to take. (If you're not green-fingered, plant a spare just in case.)

* Write a letter to your baby to be opened when they're grown up.

* Pick a nice newborn photo, run off a heap of copies, stick a stamp, an address and the baby's name on the back and send it to friends and rellies. Nobody should expect prose at a time like this.

* Put your bubba's hands and feet into some non-toxic water-based poster "paint" and gently make some "paw prints". They'll only be this small for about a minute.

When you pick your baby up, slide your arm along the bub's back until your hand is supporting the head and neck and try to lift them in one steady movement (all early jerks should be accompanied by a soothing apology).

HOW TO HOLD A NEWBORN BABY

Once you've picked them up, you can go horizontal: transfer the baby to the crook of your other arm so that the head is cradled in your elbow and the body supported along your forearm. Or you can go vertical: pick the baby up gently, continually supporting the head and neck, and hold them so that the little head peeks over your shoulder.

Keep supporting the head and neck at all times until the baby has full control of them (usually at about 6 weeks old). Don't forget that babies love to be held close and to hear your heartbeat. Another thing you can do is sit down, put both your feet flat on the floor and lay the baby tummy up, with their head and neck supported by your knees and their feet in your lap.

HOW TO TOUCH A NEWBORN BABY

Gentle, stroking motions will probably soothe your baby. For centuries people have been touching and massaging babies without having to take lessons in baby massage or read books about it so don't feel you have to do anything special. Skin-to-skin contact between baby and carers, like cuddles and chat, is known to improve baby happiness and health, and it can help you fall in love with your baby.

Tell your baby when you're going to touch them. You can lay them on their back on the floor (to avoid a fall from a table), then sit down and lean forward to stroke them. Make sure your core is strong, your tummy is held in and your back is braced. (This is no good after a Caesarean obviously because it will be too painful.) Or try sitting in a chair and putting the baby in a basket on the table – with a rule that you never take your hand off them or wander away when they're up high. Babies also love to lie skin to skin on a bare chest. (For more on baby massage techniques see "More Info" at the end of the chapter.)

WRaPPiNG a NeWBORN BaBy

Almost all newborns like to be firmly wrapped; it helps them feel snug (as they were in the womb) and to drift off to sleep. Many of the "slings" and wrap-around baby carriers work on the same principle. (This is often referred to by the hilariously biblical term "swaddling".) In summer you can use a square (or rectangle) of muslin or cotton. In winter you can use heavier cotton or wool if it's not scratchy. Written instructions can be confusing, so ask your midwife to show you how to do it, and which weight of fabric to use so your baby doesn't get too hot – midwives are wrap artists. See "More Info" for further web resources. Usually by, say, 4 months old a baby will wriggle too much to be kept in their package and you can abandon the wrapping, either straight away or slowly, whatever the baby seems to prefer. Don't start to wrap a baby after 4 months and don't keep a baby wrapped all day: perhaps just for sleep or a winding-down time. Babies, especially those more than a couple of weeks old, need to practise wriggling around a bit, to stretch their arms and legs, and to feel the fresh air on their skin.

It's important not to wrap a baby too tightly or let them overheat so only wrap a lightly dressed baby (vest and nappy).

Like all babies, a wrapped baby should be placed on their back to sleep. A wrapped baby on their side is more likely to roll onto their tum (see p.128 for safe sleeping positions).

more info

BABY-CARE BOOKS

What baby-care books you'll find useful will depend on your own philosophy, and whether one author's method has failed you and it's time to try another. Remember to always get the very latest edition of any baby book so the health and safety information is bang up to date (don't borrow a friend's old copy) – and beware of nasty foreign editions with useless contacts in Vermont or Venezuela.

GOOD THINGS ABOUT BABIES

✶ Their head smells of Baby.

✶ Their tiny starfish hands.

✶ That little hollow at the back of their neck.

✶ Their excellent chubby thighs.

✶ The way they bend time when you're sitting holding them in a quiet place.

✶ They stare at you and you can stare back.

✶ They hold onto your finger.

✶ Their toothless grins.

✶ They have amusing hair or they're bald.

✶ They look kind of Star Trekky.

✶ There's so much potential in such a small package.

✶ They have hilariously short arms.

✶ You can read stuff into their faces: "wise", "bewildered", "flabbergasted".

✶ They mimic facial expressions.

✶ They snore, but not very loudly.

✶ They have a total body response when they're excited.

✶ You are keeping another human alive.

✶ You are creating new love in the world.

✶ The green poo stage doesn't last long.

Secrets of the Baby Whisperer, and The Baby Whisperer Solves All Your Problems,
both by Tracy Hogg with Melinda Blau, Vermilion, 2008
The late Tracy Hogg has many devotees for her suggestions on how to identify your
parenting philosophy and the personality of your baby, and adjust your approach
accordingly. "Secrets" includes "translations" of baby cries and gestures, troubleshooting of
common problems, development milestones, and covers feeding, sleeping, not coping and
more. The more encyclopedic "Problems" covers how to get into a routine, "sleep training",
common problems, crabby babies, food and toddler issues.

The Baby Book
by Dr William Sears and Martha Sears, Thorsons, 2005
Written by the US leaders in attachment, or "baby-centred" parenting philosophy, this
thumping big book recommends "baby wearing" (slings), and rather than sleep time,

"night parenting" (yikes, 24-hour duty?). Humane and realistic, it covers feeding, sleeping, parents' work, development, high-needs babies and other issues up to the age of two. Their much more compact *Fussy Baby Book* helps parents of babies who are "demanding", unpredictable, hyperactive, not keen on sleeping or extra "clingy".

The New Contented Little Baby Book
by Gina Ford, Vermilion, 2006

Ms Ford's an experienced maternity nurse who is confident her strict routines will benefit sleepless or desperate parents, and babies from birth to 1-year old. Ms Ford has added an introduction to answer many of her critics and what she sees as misconceptions about how inflexible or confronting her plans can be. Not for a "go with the flow" parent; whether you're grateful or appalled will depend on your own philosophy.

Jo Frost's Confident Baby Care
by Jo Frost, 2007

Supernanny's let down her bun, taken off the prop glasses and dispensed with the naughty step to show her gentler side to babies and parents. Sensible, useful, chatty advice for the first year covering the lot including babyproofing, nappy changing, when babies get interested in seeing out from the pram, suggested feeding routines and adoption.

WRAPPING A NEWBORN

www.fitpregnancy.com/yourbaby/847
A "baby wrap" slide show.

www.sidsandkids.org/sa/documents/wrappingbrochure.pdf
Baby wrap instructions with photos.

www.youtube.com/watch?v=vMBn-hdA3e8
One of a number of YouTube demonstration videos.

OTHER INFO ON BABIES AND TODDLERS

The Great Ormond Street New Baby and Child Care Book
by Tessa Hilton with Maire Messenger, Vermilion, 2004
A comprehensive reference from the UK's leading children's hospital that starts at conception and takes you to age 5. All the practical info on looking after a new baby, growth and movement, language development, common medical concerns and why play is important.

Your Baby and Child
by Penelope Leach, Dorling Kindersley, 2003
Loads of stuff about development as well as sleeping and crying, up to age 2 and a half. Several mentions of "excreting", as if we're all in nurses school in 1932. Very comprehensive and always focused on the important needs of the baby. The author's "voice" can be a little hard to take, especially if you're exhausted. Sentences like this don't help: "Babies in this age group (6–12 months) cannot have any sleeping difficulties so if there are any problems they are yours, not your baby's."

Complete Baby and Childcare
by Dr Miriam Stoppard, Dorling Kindersley, 2008
Whacking big book with lots of helpful pics from birth to preschool. The rather medical and conservative approach from Dr Stoppard might be what you're looking for. With the occasional superfluous suggestions such as, when dressing a girl baby, "You may prefer more feminine clothes for special occasions" – a bikini and a feather hat, perhaps. Baby boys, we're told, should pop on something "practical as well as smart".

See also: There are some more books on looking after small children under "More Info" at the end of the chapter "Who's the Centre of the Universe". (See p.227)

BOOKS FOR DADS

Many books aimed at dads go through the pregnancy but stop after the birth, as if that's your job done, sunshine. Here's some good ones to help you feel confident about looking after your own baby. See also the "More Info" section in the "Dads" chapter in Part 3.

A Dad's Guide to Babycare
by Colin Cooper, Carol and Brown, 2008
Here's your go-to manual. With pictures! Of dads with babies! Hoorah. Practical stuff about feeding, holding, equipment and how to behave around a bub. Thoughtful stuff about seeing your partner in a new light.

The New Father: A Dad's Guide to the First Year
by Armin A Bott, Mitchell Beazley, 2007
By a US "fatherhood expert". This is the bloke's version of a comprehensive baby-care book, from birth to teeth, with feelings, conflicts, and work hours thrown in.

BABY WEBSITES

These tend to have a lot of stuff about pregnancy as well as after the birth, and chat rooms galore (and see also the parenting websites in "More Info" at the end of the next chapter, "Your Support Team" – they usually include baby business too). A warning on the web: some of the more obscure sites are set up by single-issue enthusiasts or even fanatics. Information on subjects such as vaccination can be outdated, selectively chosen to support a belief, or plain bonkers. Always check medical info with your GP or health visitor.

www.babyandpregnancy.co.uk
Useful and practical advice about the early days, including unexpected hospital stays, feeding, colic and babyproofing your home.

www.babycentre.com
Huge site covering almost everything to do with babies, and includes articles and advice from baby professionals.

www.babyzone.com

Gigantic US-based website with heaps of question-answering and articles.

www.bbc.co.uk/health

The "Health" section of the BBC's general website has a good, all-round section on parenting, which covers topics like bathing a newborn through to work/life balance.

www.marthastewart.com/baby

Although everything looks too perfect in Hyperhomemaker Marthaland, this is actually a useful site with pics of how to bath a baby and hints on feeding and nursery decoration. Also has parent forums and advice. Other parts of the Martha site have tips on housekeeping and craft activities for kids.

BABY MASSAGE

Baby Massage

by Dr Alan Heath and Nicki Bainbridge, Dorling Kindersley, 2004

Explains why massage is good for a baby, plus lots of pictures showing how to massage and gently stretch your bub's limbs. Contains info on massage for premature babies, newborns, older babies and toddlers, children with special needs, and techniques that may help "colic" (wind stuck inside a baby causing tummy pain), constipation, non-specific cranky crying, teething and dry skin. It also has sensible advice such as don't use nut oils in case your baby has an allergy to nuts, and don't always massage your baby to sleep because when they wake up in the night they can't get themselves back to sleep without another one.

www.iaim.org.uk

The UK branch of the International Association of Infant Massage can put you in touch with trained baby masseurs who can teach you or a group what to do and what to use. Phone 020 8989 9597 or email **mail@iaim.org.uk**.

your support team

You'll be needing a hand, then. Ideally you will have

thought about this before the baby arrives and have lined

up some home help, in particular with the cooking and

cleaning, or a full freezer at least, for the first few weeks.

Some people are lucky enough to have trusted relatives

and friends close by who know what to do with babies.

Your back-up team will probably also include the people

mentioned in the following pages and a few butlers

and footmen if you've

married well.

midwives and Breastfeeding consultants

If you're given conflicting advice about the baby in hospital, pick a midwife you like and only listen to that one, or employ an independent midwife, or a "doula" (someone to help you with breastfeeding and baby care in the first little while at home). After you've left hospital, you will still be under midwife care for another month. They should visit you at home at least every few days to check over you and the baby and to offer advice.

Whilst many hospitals do have a specially trained midwife to deal with breastfeeding issues, the reality is that many others can still be unsupportive of the whole idea. If you do need more advice and encouragement than is being offered, breastfeeding counsellors (or shall we call them Bosom Ladies?) can be contacted via the National Childbirth Trust, the La Leche League, the Association of Breastfeeding Mothers, or the Breastfeeding Network (see "More Info" at the end of the "Bosoms" chapter).

Health visitors

Health visitors are employed by local councils and one should visit you when you come home from hospital (and even if you haven't been to hospital) to see how you're going and if they can help with anything such as breastfeeding. This is when you will be given your "red book", or Personal Child Health Record, in which all medical information about your baby will be documented. After your midwife care has ended, the health visitor will either continue to visit you at home or you can visit your local health centre or doctor's surgery, where they will run a weekly clinic for weighing the baby, giving immunizations and general advice. Some also offer classes for new parents covering topics such as baby massage, dental care and sleeping. It's often the best way to meet new mums in your area. The contact is especially important when so many women have such a short time in hospital and go home – aieeeee! – without a manual, or experienced friends or relatives to help.

If you're not contacted by a health visitor in the fortnight after the birth, find out the number for your nearest health centre and ask them to come and see you. You should be able to ring your local health visitor with queries at any time. If your local centre is only open part-time and you need help RIGHT NOW, call a 24-hour support helpline (see the contact details given in "More Info" at the end of this chapter).

The health centre services can be literally lifesaving. Incidentally, if your local council or the government tries to scale them back in your area, ring the people concerned and explain you will NEVER vote for their party again IN YOUR LIFE unless they maintain or upgrade the services.

Regular appointments will get you out of the house and talking to somebody who understands what you're going through. If you're coping well it's fun, and if you don't feel you're coping they should be both sympathetic and helpful. These health visitors see a lot of babies, and most of them are a real encyclopedia of reassuring, indispensable baby knowledge. They're an on-tap reality check.

Health visitors can give the impression that statistics are important because they're required to keep them. But baby measurements don't matter a bit. Unless the results are very unusual or your baby isn't putting on weight, don't take any notice of them (look up "weight" in the index).

Several women who responded to the survey undertaken for this book said that health visitors insisted that they persevere with breastfeeding even though they were having a great deal of trouble and their baby was losing weight. This is a situation that needs strong, swift action: either a great deal of help from one of the breastfeeding support services or a move onto baby formula bottlefeeding (see the "Bottles" chapter).

Try to avoid personality clashes. One local health visitor I encountered had all the optimism of Eeyore and all the sensitivity of a house brick. She was brusque rather than briskly comforting. She was dismissive of worries rather than reassuring. If she answered the phone at the local clinic when I rang, I'd hang up and make an appointment with my doctor or, if I could, I'd call back on another day to see the health visitor I liked and trusted. If necessary, go to your next nearest centre. These weeks and months are too important to deal with someone who rubs you up the wrong way.

your general practitioner (gp)

Now you have a bub at home you'll be needing a local doctor. If you're living in an area where there are very few kids and the waiting room is full of octogenarians, find out who's the nearest doctor who sees most of the kids. This GP will be experienced, and they'll usually know what's "going around". It's always worthwhile finding out who's the parents' favourite. A GP who really listens and thinks laterally is important. A GP who is also a parent of young children can be a bonus, but so can one who specializes in paediatrics. (Many GPs specialize in children these days, others have special interests in women's health or geriatrics.) GPs don't always get it right – a fever and non-specific symptoms could mean so many different things – but one who is thorough, experienced and kind to children is a good start. I know it's harder to have a choice in a rural area: you may need to go to another town if that's possible.

If you feel concerned about your baby's health, always have it checked out. It doesn't matter if there's nothing wrong. It will help get your child used to going to the doctor, and a check-up never hurts. If you're not happy with the outcome, go to another doctor – you'd probably feel more guilty about changing to another hairdresser.

If you can afford it, have health insurance for the adults as well as the kids in the family. It will mean you won't have to wait for an operation for a condition that could make it harder for you to be a parent.

family and friends

Family and friends can be a great source of help or not much cop at all, depending on how used they are to babies and kids. If they're not up to speed on offspring the age of yours, they can help in other ways, such as doing housework and hunter-gathering, provided they're willing and able. Someone who has a child a little older is always helpful as long as their ideas about children are similar to your own. Anyone with much older or grown-up children may be sympathetic and handy for babysitting, but will probably have forgotten the specifics of caring for a small baby or child: you may need lists on the fridge or other reminders to help them. Leaving this book around to be looked up when necessary may be helpful, unless you have a 98-year-old gran who's sure she learned everything she needed to know before 1953. (There's more on carers in the "Child Care, Kindergarten and Preschool" chapter in *Part 3: Parenting*.)

Some family members of course will pop around every few months to wave from the other side of the room but otherwise won't be much actual use. The trick is to recognize the people who'd like to get to know the baby, and learn how to help look after and enjoy the bub as a developing person, and those who are genuinely not interested or are benign onlookers. Which is probably fair enough. To be utterly candid, before I had a baby myself I used to be more interested in people's dogs than their babies.

Godparents or special adult friends can have more defined roles than others. Perhaps they can take the baby for regular outings and have preferred-babysitter privileges.

maternity Nurses and Nannies

If you have some hessian bags full of cash down the back of the couch, or you've saved up for some baby extras, you can hire a maternity nurse, doula, independent midwife or a nanny to help you in the first few weeks. Some will live in, others will do shift work or just come during the day. To find one, try the Yellow Pages or ask friends who've done the same thing. Always check the legitimacy of an agency and personally check the references of the maternity nurse or the nanny (see the "More Info" section below or look up "nannies" in the index).

parents' groups, mothers' groups and playgroups

Your health visitor will give you the contact details for a local group of parents (usually but not always mums), with babies or kids about the same age as yours. Your local library is often a good source of information on local groups and services. These groups can be particularly good for mums who feel isolated and can be great for making friends and reminding you that your feelings and experiences are probably not so unusual (although some parents find parents' groups nothing but a hotbed of judgemental remarks and dull conversation). Children for the first couple of years and even beyond, depending on the kid, really don't play together, but after several months babies are at least interested in looking at each other, and meanwhile you can hang out and chat.

Groups meet in local halls, each other's houses or local parks. Remember to make a shared community space a child-friendly zone – for example, unplug and don't use urns and lock gates to the street.

See "More Info" at the end of the "Baby Development (0 to 1)" chapter.

more info

HELPLINES

Phone counsellors can help when you're feeling at the end of your tether and phone advisers can give you specific practical information. You can call anonymously. Some of them are 24-hour freephone lines or have seven-day daytime access, although since they are often run by charities the situation with any of them can change depending on funding. For help with specific issues such as sleep, excessive crying, or feeding, see the "More Info" sections for the relevant chapters later in this book. For general emotional support you can call Samaritans on 08457 90 90 90 and for emergency medical advice, NHS Direct has a nurse-led service on 0845 46 47.

Parentline Plus

0808 800 2222 (24 hr)

National charity that works with and for parents because, as it says, instructions aren't included. The phone line aims to give support in a non-judgemental, parent-to-parent way. Website parentlineplus.org.uk has helpful message boards and Q&As.

National Childbirth Trust

www.nctpregnancyandbabycare.com

Enquiry line 0300 33 00 770 (Mon–Thurs 9am–5pm, Fri 9am–4pm)

The UK's leading charity supporting parents through pregnancy and the early days with a baby. Nationwide network of branches runs courses for new parents to help them adjust to their new role.

PARENTING WEBSITES

If you like the Internet, you could find these sites useful or reassuring (and see also the baby websites in "More Info" at the end of the preceding chapter, "In The Beginning").

www.badmothersclub.co.uk

A very naughty website, also incorporating bad dads, with high entertainment value, about how parenting's not all beer and skittles. Has good links and includes articles such as "One return trip to Vagina please".

www.brainchildmag.com

Subtitled "The Magazine for Thinking Mothers", this is a US quarterly magazine. Includes essays, forums and personal stories.

www.forparentsbyparents.co.uk

A UK website where parents give advice to each other: there's mums on mums, dads on dads (you know what I mean) and lots on common questions to do with caring for babies.

www.mumsnet.com

Billed as the country's most popular meeting point for parents, this UK site has lists of local groups, product reviews on everything from holidays to recipes. You can create your own profile, start a blog and take part in live web chats.

PARENT SERVICES

Your local health centre or doctor's surgery should always be the first port of call if you are experiencing difficulties. If necessary, they can make referrals for other help available on the NHS. However, the services listed below may also be useful in helping you move on from a bad patch.

While there are many agencies who will find you a nanny (see p.371), fewer can provide you with a specialist maternity nurse with experience in newborn baby care (as opposed to a hard-up newly qualified nanny who needs some extra cash). Make sure you ask if they have relevant experience, particularly if your baby was premature or has special needs. Maternity nurses live in (usually sleeping with the baby) and care for the baby's needs rather than yours, but can be helpful in establishing routines and showing you the basics, useful if you don't have relatives or other help nearby. With doulas, the emphasis is on looking after you, and can offer a more flexible and less intrusive (not to mention cheaper) service.

www.mumszone.co.uk
A site for all parents with a touch of the new age about it. Usual forums, and product and book review, and auction sections.

www.raisingkids.co.uk
Brilliantly comprehensive site offering age-appropriate advice, discussions and parent forums up to and beyond age 13. Access online to a range of specialists for specific questions regarding medical and parenting issues.

www.ukparentslounge.com
Billed as the place to get away from the kids, this site is far from it, with plenty of parenting articles and tips from resident baby-care celebrities Gina Ford, Miriam Stoppard, Jo Frost and Annabel Karmel.

www.parenting.com
Comprehensive website of the US *Parenting* magazine so has lots of resident experts and advertising. Lots of info about sleep, budgeting, cooking and a useful Child Health centre.

British Doulas

www.britishdoulas.co.uk

020 7244 6053

Agency for hiring doulas throughout the UK, useful for vetting what is still an unregulated role in the UK. Can help you decide your requirements and mediate in any difficulties with the doula you may have.

www.doula.org.uk

0871 433 310

Run by the doulas themselves to provide trained but non-medical experienced women to "mother the mother". Takes the pressure off dads, too. Postnatal doulas can be hired for up to eight weeks. Roles are flexible, so website offers a useful list of questions to ask before hiring.

Independent Midwives

www.independentmidwives.org.uk

0845 4600 105

Helps you find a fully qualified independent midwife in your area. Will still support the aims and ideals of the NHS, so it is important to discuss your requirements before hiring a particular midwife. Deep pockets also help.

NEWBORN WORRIES

In the first days our babies are so new to us we hardly recognize them. And they're so teeny tiny and so unlike the big, robust babies crawling around on TV ads smiling, grabbing things and signing modelling contracts. It's easy to stress out about newborns. What follows is some stuff we tend to worry about that is probably, actually, usually okay.

Ask your obstetrician or midwife about any anxiety while you're in hospital, and after you've left bring it up with your obstetrician at your six-weeks-after-the-birth appointment or make an appointment with your health visitor. You're beginning to develop a parent's instincts. If your baby is fine you've learned something and no harm was done. Never be afraid to ask questions.

WORRIES ABOUT HOW THE BABY LOOKS

Because of the birth experience babies may have a squashed or bruised face; puffy, closed or even bloodshot eyes; scrunched-up ears; or a pointy head. Almost all weird-looking stuff disappears quickly: ask your doctor if something worries you.

Foetal position

Babies have been in that womb for so long and have been so cramped at the end that they keep their foetal pozzie for a while, and they like their little hands closed tight. Things gradually uncurl by themselves: you don't need to stretch or pull any bits.

Eyes

GUMMY ONES Squirt on some of your own breast milk (a traditional remedy) or squeeze some sterile saline from the chemist onto clean cotton-wool balls (a new one for each eye) and wipe gently. The problem should clear up: if not, see a doctor.

DRY ONES Little babies sometimes don't cry tears, and sometimes the tear ducts are blocked. These should right themselves in the first few months. Babies should be able to produce tears by about 2 months old.

WANDERY, SQUINTY ONES Babies don't really focus their eyes when they first come out into the world. This should sort itself out by 6 months. If one eye doesn't move from a certain position, see a doctor straight away so that it can be fixed.

CHANGING-COLOUR ONES Some people claim all babies change eye colour in their first year. Utter piffle. And all babies are not born with blue eyes despite what they tell us in lots of Anglo-Saxon textbooks. Some babies change eye colour, some don't.

Skin

BIRTHMARKS Many babies have "stork" marks, a red, rash-like mark on the forehead, eyelids and back of the neck. (The idea that a stork's beak made the marks dates from the days when people pretended babies were brought by storks to avoid any mention of s-e-x. Can you believe it?) The stork marks are visible blood vessels close to the skin and usually fade quickly. But they can hang around or "reappear"

REASONS TO GET MEDICAL HELP WITH A NEWBORN

Call an ambulance on 999 if:

✱ the baby has difficulty breathing or has stopped breathing

✱ the baby has a convulsion

Go to the doctor if:

✱ the baby seems to have a fever and/or is distressed or floppy and uninterested

✱ there are signs of dehydration (dry, pinched skin; sunken eyes and fontanelle; fewer wet nappies than usual; dark, stinky wee)

✱ the baby has been repeatedly vomiting

✱ the baby seems in pain or otherwise screams for a long time no matter what you do

✱ the baby suddenly doesn't want breast or bottle

✱ there's something that looks yucky or pussy oozing or coming out of somewhere

✱ there's something you haven't seen before such as a rash or lump

✱ the baby has a wheezy cough

✱ you are worried about anything

See also the "Health" chapter in *Part 4: Stuff.*

as the blood vessels bulge away harmlessly when a kid holds their breath, yells a lot or is hot or stressed. I've heard of some that last until towards the end of primary school or perhaps longer, despite some books saying that they all disappear in the first months.

Some babies of Asian heritage or dark skin are born with bluish grey pigment spots on their buttocks, back and sometimes arms and legs. These spots fade.

Other birthmarks can be more permanent, although most are removable by laser treatment later in life if that's important to the child. You should talk about the marks with your doctor and have them identified. If in doubt, get your GP to give you a referral to a paediatric skin specialist.

NAPPY RASH   This is usually caused by wee or poo irritating the skin under a nappy. Wash everything off with a baby wipe or a cotton-wool ball soaked in a bot-cleaning lotion or water, pat or air dry and apply a barrier or nappy-rash cream. Disposable nappies are less likely to cause nappy rash. (For more on all this see the "Bottoms" chapter.)

CRADLE CAP   You can remove this rather crusty layer on top of a baby's head, but it may keep coming back for a few weeks or even months. Don't ask me why, but they say it's caused by oily, not dry, skin. To get rid of it try a paste of one teaspoon of bicarb of soda and about half a teaspoon of cold tap water. Make the paste a consistency you can apply with a cotton-wool ball. Rub it into the baby's scalp lightly and leave it on for five minutes, then wash the head with baby shampoo. Gently comb through the baby's hair if it is combable or rub the scalp gently to loosen the flakes so they fall off, or wait for them to fall off by themselves. If you only rub them with olive oil, as many recommend, it will get on everything and have to be wiped off. The cradle cap is often over that soft bit of your baby's head, the fontanelle. It's okay to massage it gently.

THRUSH   This is a horrid white rash, usually in the mouth or on the bot, and is caused by a fungus. Try an over-the-counter treatment from a chemist or get your doctor to prescribe a cream.

SPOTS   Little pimples, whiteheads and other spots are pretty standard for babies, and often last for about three months. You just need to make sure they're not insect bites (in which case you'll need to use screens, a mozzie net or another non-chemical strategy in the baby's bedroom) or something else. See your health visitor or a doctor for a diagnosis.

SUCKING BLISTER   Some babies get a small blister on their lip from sucking. It might make the bub a little antsy while feeding, but should heal by itself.

VEINS   The thinner a baby, or the thinner the skin, the more you may be able to see veins or a bluish tinge where the blood vessels are close to the skin.

Private parts

Well, there's nothing very private about a baby's bits, but "genitals" sounds so po-faced, Doctor Weirdy. The festival of hormone production that happens at birth can lead to some rather swollen parts on boy and girl babies, and even a slight, period-like bleed from a baby girl's vagina – just some of her own tiny, tiny womb cells coming away. This will right itself in a few days. If anyone is proud that their son has an enormous pair of testicles they should know it's temporary. And feel free to roll your eyes.

Hair

Some babies have a headful, some have none. Others have baldy patches where their head rests in the cot. The first baby hair sometimes falls right out and is replaced later. Body hair (called lanugo), which is often found on the back and shoulders, is normal and will fall out.

Fontanelle

This is the squishy bit on your baby's head where the skull plates haven't meshed together yet. It makes it easier for your baby's head to go temporarily pointy when coming down the vagina during birth. It will grow over (sadly unlike your vagina in the early days) and you won't notice it in a few weeks' time – although the plates don't fully fuse until the second year of life. The fontanelle requires the same amount of careful handling as the rest of a tiny baby. If it looks higher or lower than the rest of the head, see a doctor: it could be swelling or a sign of dehydration.

Head

Babies' heads are big compared with the rest of them: this lasts well into childhood. Babies who were pulled out with a vacuum device or forceps may have heads that look a bit pointy or dented. Ask your obstetrician how long this is likely to last. It's usually very temporary.

Arms

Yes, well spotted: babies have short arms compared with us.

Heartbeat

Okay, it's got nothing to do with how they look, but you may want to know that babies' heartbeats are faster than adult ones.

Teeth

Apparently some babies are actually born with teeth. Let's hope they keep them to themselves during breastfeeding.

Jaundice

If a baby is jaundiced their skin and the whites of their eyes look a bit yellow. It's just that the liver should have broken down some extra red blood cells by the time bubba was a few days old, but it's going a little slowly. Sometimes the getting-rid-of-the-yellow process is given a kick along in hospital by putting the baby under bright lights. Some experts dispute that this helps, insisting that jaundiced babies sort themselves out in their own good time, which can take days or even weeks. In the maternity wards temporary jaundice is generally considered ho-hum unless the baby is lethargic and not feeding well in which case, a paediatrician should investigate immediately.

Umbilical cord

What a strange little stumpy thing they send you home with on the front of your baby: the blackened remains of the umbilical cord fastened with a plastic, well, peg. It looks absolutely revolting. At some time during the first couple of weeks, perhaps even after a few days, the cord stump will fall off, plastic peg and all. Usually you just clean the tummy button and stump with tepid tap water, and gently pat and air dry afterwards. If there's a bit of blood after the stump falls off, continue cleaning the area in the same way once a day and it should come good in a few days. See your GP if there is pus, or inflamed redness around the area, or it's smelly.

temporary pointy head

stumpy bit

Ears

Don't squirt or poke anything into an ear, including breast milk, a cotton bud or a finger. Ears clean themselves. Ear experts say deafness should be detected as soon as possible so ask if your hospital can do a hearing test before you take your bub home. (For more info look up "ears" and "hearing" in the index.)

worries about measurements

Early days weight loss

Newborn babies are supposed to lose weight. They do it – losing up to about ten percent of their birth weight – in the time after they're born and before your proper milk comes in several days later (see the "Bosoms" chapter for all the guff on milk and getting the hang of breastfeeding). Coincidentally at the time the milk comes in you sometimes have a big, weepy hormonal crash. (Helpful, isn't it?) So worrying about whether your baby has lost too much, and scampering about with your bosoms akimbo trying to make up the loss quick smart, is just going to cause you stress. Medical staff and midwives really shouldn't say anything about your baby losing weight unless it's really a problem, and it so rarely is. Mentioning it just leads to thousands of parents worrying and women wondering if their baby is fading away and it's their fault.

Multiple birth babies, because they have to share the womb, and premmie babies are often at the lower weight end. The biggest babies are usually boys.

Most babies are back to their birth weight in a week or two.

Weight and length

I know that midwives and health visitors have to weigh and measure babies but unfortunately, instead of resulting in a public health tool that reassures parents, this tends to produce graphs and lines and sets of numbers for people to worry about. Remember that the charts are often out of date and are a poor guide to the weight gain of any individual baby, notably breast fed babies as the charts were predominantly constructed from data on formula fed children. If your baby is diagnosed as "failing to thrive", you may have to change your approach to feeding. Apart from that the numbers are just facts that nurses write down. They're not nearly as interesting as what sort of personality your baby is developing.

Some babies are darling roly-polies with dimply buttocks, others can be surprisingly lean yet healthy: this is mainly a matter of genes. It doesn't necessarily bear any relation to their eventual grown-up size and shape – although it is sometimes exactly that, an indicator of a child's natural body. As long as the baby is not distressed, lethargic or undernourished, weight is not a problem.

Babies should steadily put on weight – but not so steadily that you need to weigh your baby yourself or constantly have their weight checked. Some weeks there'll be more growth than others. Suddenly going backwards may indicate a problem, but growth spurts are pretty normal. Regular visits to the health visitor will pick up any problems. If your baby is anywhere on the chart they're somewhere in the normal range.

Head size

Don't even think about taking notice of the head circumference measurement unless a nurse or doctor tells you there might be a medical problem (extreeeeemely rare).

WORRieS aBOUT PReMaTURe BaBieS

Bringing home a tiny baby can be awfully daunting – especially after seeing so many tubes and machines doing things to and for your bub in the hospital. Sometimes it can help to be introduced to great, hulky, galumphing teenagers who were once as premmie as your wee baby. Your hospital should have a handbook or at least a pamphlet on premmie babies, which you can take home.

Find out from the doctors whether your baby needs special handling, but don't be afraid to touch your bub, no matter how fragile they seem. Almost constant skin-to-skin contact and soothing, comforting soft songs and voices are known to perk up a premmie baby in the early days. They may have a specially pale or red skin, a distressing thinness and prominent veins, but when they put on weight these will disappear. Very early babies may be covered in the tiny hairs (lanugo) that all babies have in the womb: it's temporary. Your baby may have difficulty with sucking so if breastfeeding isn't possible don't stress.

You mustn't be hard on yourself about being emotional or feeling overwhelmed: after what you've been through that's absolutely normal. Many people feel scared of their premmie babies and daunted by the responsibility. DO get help if you feel that the difficulties are constant and never-ending (see the parent helplines and parent services given in "More Info" at the end of the previous chapter, "Your Support Team", and also "More Info" at the end of this chapter).

Early arrivals can have physical difficulties, including lung trouble and pooing problems, and might always be a smaller size than other kids of the same age. Ask your obstetrician to recommend a paediatrician who specializes in premmie babies.

Make sure you fully understand from midwives and doctors, including your ongoing paediatrician or GP, what to expect. Some premmies never have a problem: it often depends on how premmie they are.

Most of the small sizes in baby clothes may be too big at first. Your baby will soon grow into them, but in the meantime you'll need the softest cotton things you can find: little hats are particularly important to keep a tiny head warm. Many hospitals are given clothes especially made or knitted for premmie babies by wonderful volunteers. Be careful that any wool isn't causing an itch the baby can't tell you about. Most of the large department stores and kid's clothing shops carry a limited range of clothes for premmie babies labelled by weight or somewhat euphemistically "tiny baby": you should be able to order with a credit card over the phone or Internet.

WORRIES ABOUT NEWBORN BEHAVIOUR

Noises
Babies often make odd snorky breathing sounds, just getting used to breathing with their little tubes and lungs. Sneezes, hiccups, grunts and general snonkiness are all perfectly normal.

The baby has slept longer than normal
It's probably just your baby's first big sleep. Most parents know the blind panic, on the first morning the baby misses a night feed and "sleeps through", of racing in to find a hungry but healthy bub. As long as the breathing seems regular and untroubled, and there is no fever, it's almost always best to "let sleeping babies lie". They can be quite cross at being woken up.

Is my baby hurt?

Happily babies are very resilient. Many have been dropped. Usually everything's fine, but of course if you do drop your baby, or they receive a knock, go to the doctor immediately. A baby who's floppy or sleepy after a drop or knock is a worry, and if they can't be roused, stop breathing or have a convulsive fit call an ambulance on 999.

Rough play

Some parents and relatives – often older men – think it's a great idea to throw babies up in the air and catch them: they must be stopped. This shouldn't happen to babies at all until they're at least a year old, and certainly never to newborns, whose brain and eyes can be badly damaged by being rattled about. This is the same damage that can be done by shaking a baby.

Is my baby sick?

You'll find info on gastro, colds, fever and convulsions, in particular, in the "Health" chapter in *Part 4: Stuff* (and you can look these up in the index).

Is my baby too hot?

By this I mean too hot because of the weather, not too hot because of a temperature caused by an illness. Signs of a too-hot baby include crying, a red rash and dehydration. Make sure your baby has lots of fluids on a hot day. (This usually means breast or bottle milk. Some people suggest a few teaspoons of cooled boiled water, while others scoff at the boiled water business: it seems to go in and out of fashion.) To cool down an overheated baby, get their gear off and lay them on the floor or bed, sponge them with tepid water and perhaps use a fan – but not directed right at them – to move air around. The change should be relatively gradual so don't use ice or cold water. A hot bedroom at night can be cooled by air conditioning (if you have a thermostat, about eighteen to twenty degrees Celsius is standard); by wetting towels and hanging them over the edge of the cot; or by using a fan not directly pointed at the baby.

If you are travelling to the tropics with a child who is not used to high temperatures they will need to drink more, be watched more closely (monitor the number of wet nappies) and perhaps be sponged with tepid – never icy – water if they're hot and cross.

Babies in hot countries, especially visitors, are more susceptible to skin problems such as infected scratches, thrush, rashes, impetigo and prickly heat. Don't overdress them.

Is my baby too cold?

Most of the cases of prickly heat don't occur in the tropics, but in cold areas where the babies have been so bundled up to the eyebrows in woollies that they're sweating under all their layers. This particularly happens with bubs who are dressed for the cold outside and then brought into shops or homes that are heated. This is the time when a lambskin underneath the baby in a pram or stroller, with a small rug (polar fleece or woollen) over the top, rather than extra clothes, may help.

Hats are good for keeping a baby warm outside: the general rule is if you need a long-sleeved top, a small baby needs a hat. Remember that while you walk with the pram you're warming up, but not so the baby being wheeled about. Small babies can't run around to warm up, or throw on more clothes, so you need to be aware that a too-cold baby may start out crying but then become very quiet and still.

Cases of hypothermia are rare. One expert puts it like this: "... if babies do get too cold, they get lethargic and don't feed or cry. Anyone would know there's something wrong. Wind-chill is the most obvious problem." According to him, the general rule is that little babies need at least one extra layer than we do to feel comfortable outside. (When they're toddlers and they're on the move they can start having the same number of layers as we do.)

To check how cold your baby is, feel their face: if it's cold, check their tummy, and if it's cold too that's unusual. Warm up a too-cold baby (or toddler or small child) with a hat and direct skin-to-skin contact under rugs pulled around you both, in a warm room – but not directly in front of a heater and not with a hot-water bottle, which is too much heat too suddenly.

A baby's room on a cold night should be kept warm, not hot (at about eighteen to twenty degrees, as mentioned above). Make sure that the room is aired well between sleeps (and that the baby is too!). If it's not possible to heat a baby's bedroom, they need a hat and mittens, appropriate covers (blankets, not a duvet, which can cause overheating and suffocation), and their feet covered with one more layer than adults would have.

WORRies aBOUT SUDDeN iNFaNT DeaTH SYNDROMe (SiDS)

It's normal, but awfully tiring, to keep waking up and creeping next to your baby to check whether they're still breathing. In the past few years there's been a steady drop in the number of babies dying from an unknown cause that makes them stop breathing called sudden infant death syndrome (SIDS). (It used to be called "cot death".) It is believed that the babies who die have a respiratory problem that means they can't fight for air if they have trouble breathing or their mouth or nose is blocked; and of course very young babies are unable to move their bodies at all by themselves. Most SIDS deaths happen before the baby is 6 months old. At about 6 months babies start to move in their sleep, which means they will almost certainly be able to shift to a better position if they can't breathe, unless they have a respiratory problem.

ANTI-SIDS CHECKLIST

* All babies should be put on their back to sleep, not on their tummy. (As babies get older and can move their head to the side themselves and shuffle around changing position in bed – at about 6 months – they might choose to sleep on their tummy themselves. This is usually not a problem.) If your young baby tends to vomit during sleeps, talk to your health visitor about sleep positions. When your bub's lying on their back for a sleep, roll their head to either side, alternating from time to time otherwise a slightly flat-back-of-the-head situation can arise (this usually fixes itself before school starts).

* Avoid overheating. Try to keep the bedroom at a mild, pleasant 18 to 20 degrees Celsius.

* A sleeping baby should never have their face covered, and shouldn't have a duvet or any other puffy paraphernalia such as pillows. They should be firmly, not tightly, tucked in at the bottom of the cot because babies wiggle up, away from where their feet are pointing, when they're asleep. Babies can be "dressed" in a sleeping bag, which is like a grow-suit that ends in a square bag instead of separate feet. Babies in hot climates can drift off in a singlet and nappy, and all babies who like it can be wrapped (from the neck down) in a cotton sheet until they are old enough to wriggle out of them.

The marked drop in SIDS cases is attributed by doctors and researchers to the publicity campaigns warning parents about the risk factors for SIDS. Researchers and doctors now recommend a checklist (below) that emphasizes babies sleeping on their back.

There is no causal link between vaccinations and SIDS and there is no causal link between breastfeeding (or not) and SIDS. Awake babies can be regularly placed on their tummies to help them strengthen their necks and kick against the floor, although some babies hate this so just do it for a minute or two a day until they're cool with it.

One of the UK's leading charities working to prevent sudden infant death and promoting safe baby care is The Foundation for the Study of Infant Death (FSID). They have info and counselling services for grieving parents (for contact details see "Sudden Infant Death Syndrome (SIDS)" in "Extra Resources" at the end of the book).

✱ The baby's mattress should be firm, not something their nose or mouth can sink into. To keep the airflow going and to cut down on the chance of smothering, avoid bumpers (padded cot liners), fluffy toys and similar objects. Babies don't need fluffy toys when they're tiny; they need the comfort of having a parent or carer nearby and on call.

✱ If the baby is sleeping unattended, they should always be in a modern, safety standard cot (see "cots" in the index).

✱ The baby should never be left to sleep unattended in a car, a baby car seat or a pram.

✱ Don't let a baby sleep on a sofa whether someone is there or not.

✱ There should be no smoking by anyone near the baby or inside the home, car or any other environment. The parents of the baby should be non-smokers. If either of the parents smokes, or the mother smoked during pregnancy, the baby should not sleep in their bed. If any parent or carer is drunk or drugged, the baby should not sleep in their bed.

✱ Parents need to keep an eye out for any breathing or rousing problems and see the doctor about them straight away.

WORRi·es aBouT CiRCUMCiSioN

Male circumcision is the removal of part of the penis foreskin with a scalpel. This is usually done in the first few hours or days of a boy's life, without general anaesthetic (babies are almost never given this). It is performed because it is believed a religion requires it; for cultural reasons; because the parents mistakenly think it will be cleaner; or because they want the boy's penis to look like his father's.

Results of the operation include severe pain, shock, hysterical crying and, in some cases, infection and bleeding. Reclaim-the-foreskin groups say circumcision will result in the penis having up to 75 percent less sensation during sex.

Sometimes boys are born with a fusion of the foreskin to the penis that in time will cause pain or friction, requiring surgery to correct it, which is the same procedure as a circumcision. Doctors almost always recommend that babies be 6 months or even older when they have this operation so that they can have anaesthetic. (Evidence is increasing that anaesthetic should be avoided as much as possible with children because of brain cell damage.) There is no other medical reason for circumcision.

Female circumcision is the removal or mutilation of the clitoris, usually with a knife or razor blade, sometimes accompanied by a process called infibulation: the vagina is stitched closed or mostly closed. It is rarely performed in the UK (and then usually by people who are not doctors and because it is believed a religion requires it or for cultural reasons). The aims are that the girl will grow up to be an "acceptable" wife because she is unable to enjoy sex, and that her stitched-up vagina will only be penetrated by her husband.

The results of female circumcision variously include shock, severe pain, mutilation, permanent sexual disability, possibly septic wounds, deep psychological trauma, menstrual and childbirth complications and severe pain with penetrative sex. There is never a medical reason for female circumcision. It is not always illegal as people fear this would result in girls being kept away from doctors. Education is believed to be the strongest factor leading to the decline of female circumcision in some countries.

The practice of male and female circumcision, which causes pain in the most sensitive parts of the body, is widely regarded as unnecessary, outdated and barbarous. Many religious parents who want their son circumcised are now waiting until a general anaesthetic can be safely used or until the child is 18 and old enough to make his own decision. There are growing movements, in all the religions associated with male circumcision, that say the practice is traditional and cultural but not actually required by the rules of these religions. It is not mentioned in the Koran, or in some versions of the story of Abraham (other translations of the Bible have suggested circumcision is a way for Abraham's descendants, the Jewish people, to identify themselves to God).

Worries about feeling angry and frustrated with your baby

Most parents know the inexplicable rage that sometimes comes over you when you're spectacularly tired, you've tried EVERYTHING to make the baby happy but they're still crying. I can remember shouting at my baby to shut up (you don't see that on the nappy ads, do you?), which was just nutty but I was at the end of my rational self. It's not as if it's the baby's fault, and in normal circumstances you'd never take out your frustration on a baby. But in these days of isolation and lack of sleep, your coping skills are sometimes hard to find.

You must not shake or hit the baby. The "Feeling Overwhelmed or Depressed" chapter has suggestions for dealing with your anger and frustration (look up "rage" in the index), but you must immediately get help because the situation will probably happen again, and you'll need a strategy to get you through the next time. (Parent helplines and parent services are listed in "More Info" at the end of the second chapter, "Your Support Team".)

A grab-bag of worries

Strange baby dreams
Remember those strange baby dreams you had when you were pregnant? Dreams are a way of processing what's been going on, and when you have a baby there's a lot going on in your brain at once. (I once dreamed I was panicking in a huge library because my baby was a flat, baby-shaped bookmark and I couldn't remember which book I'd left her in.) Don't take the dreams too literally, and if you're really worried about a recurring or distressing one ask your doctor about seeing a counsellor.

Worries about not being a good parent

Are you doing it "right"? Probably, most of the time, particularly bearing in mind THERE'S NO ONE RIGHT WAY to do everything. You'll learn. It's okay. Nobody knows what to do at first: even people who've been midwives get a shock when the baby is their own and they can't go off shift! And don't forget that magnificent parental motto: near enough is good enough. Chuck away any books or people who make you feel guilty or inadequate. If you're reading this book, you care enough to find out the right things to at least try. So guess what? You're already a good parent.

Fears that something awful will happen to the baby

We all get those. They fade with time. If you find that they're the focus of most of your waking life, see your doctor.

Magazine envy

Well yes, don't the babies in the magazines look adorable! Aren't their clean little nurseries so full of gadgets and pale gingham flouncy French things and perfect furniture and expensive toys! Nobody really lives like that. Magazine people have teams of stylists running around deciding what a baby's room should look like, and many of them have had nothing to do with babies since they were one. If it makes you feel better, use the magazine to light the fire. One homewares mag I read suggested bolting a raffia basket to the top of a chest of drawers for a changing table. (Anyone for hints on how to get liquid poo out of raffia?)

And can celebrity mothers please shut right up? Oh, they're all so radiantly happy and say such stupid things about how sexy they feel with a new baby and how unremittingly marvellous it all is, and never mention their postnatal depression or their 24-hour team of nannies and how they have nothing else to do all day except stomach crunches. Ignore them! And if necessary stick pins in the eyes of their photographs, for they be the Devil.

more info

PREMATURE BABIES

Preemies: The Essential Guide for Parents of Premature Babies
by Dana Wechsler Linden, Emma Trenti Paroli and Mia Wechsler Doron, MD, Pocket
Books, 2000
This is a US book (hence the term "preemies" rather than "premmies"), but much of the
info holds true here.

**The Premature Baby Book: Everything You Need to Know About Your Premature
Baby from Birth to Age One**
by William Sears, Robert Sears, James Sears and Martha Sears, Little Brown, 2004
Also American, this is from the family business of books with an attachment-parenting
philosophy.

www.babycentre.co.uk
From the home page choose "Baby" then "Your Premature Baby". Info on all aspects of
caring for your premmie baby, including feeding and feelings.

www.bliss.org.uk
Helpline: 0500 618140
The premature baby charity BLISS provides family support and information. Includes a
dads' page and message board.

www.preemie-l.org
A US-run website for parents of premmie babies (don't forget when web-surfing and
searching that Americans spell premmies "preemies"). This site has discussions, answers to
common questions, fact sheets and links to other relevant sites.

New mum Health

You and your bub will have a check-up with your GP about six weeks after the birth. (I recommend you wear pasties on your nipples and a sombrero, just to indicate you're doing fine.) While being concerned about your baby, don't forget yourself: you are a child of the universe. Or at least a confused woman in a ludicrous dressing-gown.

...that can't be right, surely?

Recovery from the Birth

Childbirth is still a big health risk for women. Don't be surprised if body and soul take a while to recover from such a stressful event. Even if your experience was relatively easy, your mind and physical self will still need time to heal.

After your baby is born, you have a kind of period (known as the lochia) so that all the blood and tissues from the wall of your uterus, which nourished the baby, can come out. This will go on for two to six weeks, and starts off as a heavy period with some small clots, then gets paler and paler and eventually stops. Don't use tampons because they are more likely to cause an infection as the cervix slowly closes. Tell your obstetrician immediately if the bleeding doesn't happen; it suddenly turns bright red after being paler for a while; there are large clots; or it has a yucky smell. As your uterus contracts to help expel the lining and shrink down to its normal size, you may feel some cramps like period pains.

You should be healing well: any bruising or stitches should be dissolving. If you can, have therapeutic massages. Treat yourself as you would your best friend who's just been through the same thing. For heaven's sake don't be leaping about with a hockey stick trying to prove you can do it all.

Women who have had a difficult labour – or an emergency Caesarean – will probably need to talk and cry about it, and then move on when they are ready. You can do this with your friends and family, mothers' group, midwife, health visitor or a postnatal counsellor at the hospital or one that your doctor can refer you to.

Recovery from a Caesarean

The injuries caused to your body are at least as severe as those caused by a serious car accident: they've cut through about seven layers of your body. Your scar will be itchy and may heal as a ropey line: some say massage with vitamin E will help, some say take vitamin E capsules and others say stuff and nonsense to both ideas. Good, healthy food will speed recovery. Having a Caesarean makes it much harder to look after a baby in the house. You'll need help: ask for it. Go easy on yourself.

Before you leave make sure you find out from the hospital what you can't do: usually no picking up of anything except your baby for six to eight weeks (that includes the shopping and the washing basket); no reaching above your head to lift anything at all; no driving for a few weeks – that sort of thing. Don't tire yourself out. Do half as much each day as you think you "should". You'll be shuffling about from the pain of your wound. Make sure your obstetrician or GP gives you some effective pain relief for the first week or two at home.

NUTRITION

Eat as well and heartily as you can, particularly if you're breastfeeding. Special breastfeeding or "women's" vitamins are probably a good idea, although they're not as well absorbed by the body as nutrients from food: your pharmacist can advise you about reputable brands, or you can carefully read the labels at the supermarket and choose an appropriate one. Basically try to keep up with your body's needs, which will be higher if you're breastfeeding. Have things you can eat in the middle of the night if you get ravenous, snack-monstery feelings: soya milk and a banana perhaps, or cheesy biscuits. Or indeed a block of Toblerone. Sorry. Try to eat different kinds of veggies and fruits every day – don't get stuck on just carrots and courgettes. Try to get some protein in at every meal: cheesy omelette, tuna sandwich, tofu mountain. Rice with protein and veggies is filling and quick, as is a potato or a sandwich. Chicken and veggie soup is sublimely useful. And great hunks of toasty, crusty bread can be dipped into oil and dribbled on a passing sailor.

POSTNATAL FITNESS

Your hospital should have already given you a pamphlet or some sort of information on exercise and physio (and see "More Info" at the end of this chapter). There will be different stuff to do, depending on whether you had a vaginal or a Caesarean delivery. A physiotherapist can help you work out what exercise you can do to recover from a Caesarean. Physiotherapists are listed in the Yellow Pages.

If you take up or resume exercise, it's imperative that you are taught and supervised, initially by a specialist in postnatal exercise, so make absolutely sure the person you choose is not just a general instructor. Take any exercising slowly, with an approved trainer,

SEE YOUR DOCTOR AT ONCE IF

* you have a worry

* anything is swelling up or getting redder

* you have any stinky or yucky discharge from your vagina or your Caesarean wound

* you have a high temperature

* you have any shortness of breath

* you find a lump in a breast (this could lead to mastitis)

* you're depressed

* you're never hungry

or a community group or a class run by someone trained in post-pregnancy yoga or Pilates. Tell the instructor you're recovering from the birth. Do not under any circumstances buy celebrity or supermodel exercise tapes or DVDs.

Sneezy wee

You may have noticed that your pelvic-floor muscles are so weak that you do a little wee if you sneeze or laugh. The pelvic strain is caused during pregnancy by the weight of the baby on your trampoliny pelvic floor.

To avoid a small wee, try tensing, sitting down or crossing your legs before the sneeze or laugh. The only way to really stop it permanently from happening is to tighten your pelvic-floor muscles by exercising them.

You can find your pelvic-floor muscles by "holding on" for a minute before you do a wee, or stopping the wee midstream and then starting again. That's what you need to do without the wee factor: tighten and hold those same muscles for as long as you can, then repeat until you're sick of it.

Current wisdom (which keeps changing) is to do the exercises as often as you can until it's tiring. Some people put red sticker dots around their house and do the exercises every time they see one. (In a similar exercise you can scream every time you see the prime minister on telly. It does nothing for the vagina, but I find it passes the time.) If all else fails, you can buy thin panty pads in case of unscheduled wees, and get a GP's referral to a specialist physio.

Your back

The most important priority for you is to protect your back, especially after a Caesarean (see the "Recovery from a Caesarean" section earlier in the chapter). Your core muscles – your abdominal and lower back area – may now be very weak, leaving you vulnerable to lower back injury or strain.

Core muscles can be built up using specialized yoga, Pilates or other exercises. You must not be doing any abdominals such as sit-ups if your rectus muscle has separated during the pregnancy (a common, hernia-like condition): ask your obstetrician, GP or specialist trainer to check.

Make sure all your equipment such as the baby bath and change table are at a good bench height. Always lift heavy things with bent knees, and squat down instead of bending over for actions such as picking up bub from the floor. (If you have a toddler, squat in front of the stroller to fasten or undo the straps: don't bend forward from your position at the handles behind the stroller.) Your baby is just going to get heavier so start strengthening your back now, or at least avoid injuring yourself.

Resuming sex

A fall in libido is probably a mixture of hormonal changes and wanting a rest for your body, or more sleep, or George Clooney. Many women feel that their body has been through enough, and has enough to do, and want a rest from sex. Some women are worried about what their body looks or feels like now – please believe your partner when they say they still find you sexy. Sex should be mostly about how we feel, not whether we look particularly like Uma Thurman. Otherwise only Uma would be doing it, to herself.

If you don't feel like sex, talk with your partner about why: the best way to keep the relationship working is to talk about your feelings. And work out ways you might become less tired.

If vaginal dryness (caused by an oestrogen drop in breastfeeding women) is a problem, use a lubricant – olive oil is good (you can even use extra virgin!).

Ask your obstetrician when you can have sex again after the birth: usually you're told four to six weeks. (Some blokes say they've been told it's four to six years.)

Contraception

Please use it unless you want to get pregnant again. Breastfeeding is NOT a guarantee you won't get pregnant: some people ovulate in the first few months and get caught out.

Some forms of contraception can have the effect of lowering the libido. Many breastfeeding women are prescribed the Mini Pill as it's less likely than the stronger Pill to cancel out the hormone prolactin and so interfere with the breast milk supply. By the way, women on this sort of contraception should still look out for the symptoms of ectopic pregnancy, which happens when the fertilized egg implants itself outside the uterus (usually in a tube). Symptoms, which tend to occur at about six weeks, may include abdominal pain, either on one side of the abdomen or more generalized and which come and go; spotting or bleeding; dizziness, faintness, paleness and sweating; nausea and vomiting; sometimes shoulder pain; and sometimes a feeling of pressure in the bum.

Please have condoms near the bed and use them if you suddenly get frisky unless you're just so fine with the idea of two kids under 3 (or more if you have twins!). Talk to your GP about contraceptive options.

mum's weigHt

While you might be feeling proud about every weight gain of your baby, and loving kissing every funny, pudgy baby roll on their thighs, you might be feeling the exact

---

COMMON FEELINGS ABOUT SEX

✱ Never again.

✱ I'm too tired.

✱ Leave my body alone: someone's already getting milk out of it and it's recently been inhabited. I want it to myself for a while.

✱ I may have sex again if I ever want another child.

✱ I can't see the point now I've had a baby.

✱ It's fine with me as long as you don't wake me up.

---

opposite about yourself – well, unless you're one of those mums who snaps back to pre-pregnancy weight without thinking about it.

Mums who have trouble keeping weight ON after pregnancy, and especially those who want to breastfeed yet keep losing weight so much they can't keep up a milk supply and feel rundown, need to see a nutritionist at their hospital or their GP to get help to maintain a weight-gaining, nutritional diet.

Right. Put on a lot of weight during pregnancy? Can't believe what you look like now? Stuffed if you know how to start getting it off?

1 Don't read women's magazines with stories about celebrities who are the shape of lollipops with gravity-defying bosoms a week after the birth. They're freaks. Rich, pampered, freaky freakified freaks who are just a little too on the freaky side. And this is no time to be concerned about what some A-lister you'll never meet did with her arse.

2 Banish all full-length mirrors from the house. Either put them in the shed or tack some dark fabric over them. You won't be needing them for a while.

3 Search through your clothes and make a big space in your wardrobe for the stuff you can wear right now – maternity, stretch, wrap, whatever. Just make it so every morning you're not searching through clothes you can't wear to get to things you can.

4 You are officially not permitted to worry about your weight for at least four months after the birth unless your obstetrician tells you you have a serious health problem that must be addressed by weight loss in that time.

5 Exercise. You need to be fit and strong to do the things a mum has to. Don't think of exercise as being only about weight loss. If you are self-disciplined, set yourself some goals and work towards them. Day One: walk around the block and sit in the park. Day Two: walk around the block twice. Week Seven: briskly walk one or two km, depending on you. Start at your own pace and work towards being "puffed" for half an hour to an hour every day. Or you might prefer the idea of walking the pram solo while listening to an

I used to be a pear, now I'm a quince

MP3 or other music or enjoying the sounds of nature. Try to avoid traffic and stressful areas if possible. If you've had a Caesarean, make Day One getting to and from the letterbox, and proceed more slowly with the suggested build-up of exercise.

If you'd rather have company, plan to exercise with a friend or join or start a mums' exercise group, which could be part of your mums' group in the neighbourhood. Your group could employ a yoga teacher or personal trainer very cheaply by all pitching in. A trainer could set up a few "circuit" programmes and then you could run them yourselves. (Supervision is always important for new things such as weights and yoga-style exercises.) Or do without by just getting together to walk once, twice, three times a week.

An everyday routine will soon have kilos you won't miss coming off. I know walking quickly is much harder when you have a baby *and* other children. If you can't use a double-decker pram, you can maybe arrange with a friend to mind each other's kids so that you can take it in turns to walk. Or do your exercise before your partner goes to work or after they return, or on your way home from work.

6 Don't even think about dull or fad exercise programmes, such as walking up an down the stairs a berzillion times, because you "can't" leave the house, or ridiculously expensive exercise "machines" bought off daytime telly that look like they're made out of a bike frame and a rubber band and would have your back hurt and your eye out.

Get outside

7 Fresh air, a change of scenery and social interaction are all good blues-busters too.

8 Forget about fad short-term diets with low calories. If you need help to work out a healthy, long-term eating programme, ask your GP for a referral to a nutritionist. (See also "More Info", which follows.)

9 Keep reminding yourself that any sensible weight-loss scheme means that losing a kilo a week, max, is realistic. (It may need to be even less for you – check with your GP.)

PS They say breastfeeding causes weight loss, especially after the first four months of it: this doesn't work for everyone. Don't believe claims such as "Breastfeeding burns 500 calories a day" because (a) it's bollocks and (b) this is no moment to find the time to count calories.

POSTNATAL FITNESS

An Unfit Mother, How to Get Your Health, Shape and Sanity Back After Childbirth
by Kate Cook with Lucy Wyndham-Read, Collins, 2005
Funny, and with an acknowledgment that tiredness is the death of good intentions, this book gives suggestions for simple exercises and healthy and organic eating rather than dieting. She's realistic as to what you can hope to achieve in the early weeks. Includes websites for food delivery, and other nutritional links.

www.acpwh.org.uk
The Association of Chartered Physiotherapists in Women's Health has a useful range of leaflets on postnatal exercise which you can preview and download from the website.

www.babycentre.co.uk
Has postnatal exercise and nutrition tips (search "postnatal exercise"). Other also "Baby Websites" in "More Info" at the end of the first chapter, "In the Beginning". They have fitness sections.

www.postnatalexercise.co.uk
The Guild of Pregnancy and Postnatal Exercise Instructors can help you find a fully qualified instructor in your area. Website also offers book and DVD reviews and gives useful information about breastfeeding and exercise.

Yoga websites **www.bwy.org.uk** and **www.yoga.co.uk** have details of local classes.

MUM'S WEIGHT

The Body Shape Bible
by Trinny and Susannah, Weidenfeld and Nicolson, 2007

It's better to accept your natural shape and post-baby changes you can't do much about than to aim for something unrealistic and feel miserable about never getting there. These two use some rather inelegant language ("tits") and tell you that your basic body shape is "brick" or a "pear" or a "goblet", but then they'll show you how to dress for maximum effect and confidence.

If Not Dieting Then What?
by Dr Rick Kausman, Allen and Unwin, 2004

A book about weight issues and a realistic and self-friendly future.

www.ifnotdieting.com
This is Dr Rick Kausman's website.

BOSOMS

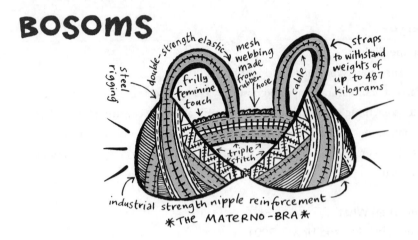

steel rigging

double-strength elastic

mesh webbing made from rubber hose

frilly feminine touch

cable

straps to withstand weights of up to 487 kilograms

triple stitch

industrial strength nipple reinforcement

THE MATERNO-BRA

Whether you're breastfeeding or bottlefeeding (of which more in the next chapter, "Bottles"), remember that a newborn baby is as new to this as you are. Their digestive system has never worked like this before. It may take some time. They've never had air trapped in their insidey bits before, and until they burp that air up or fart it may hurt their tummies – a most unpleasant feeling they never had before they were born. Together you'll work it all out.

WHY BReastfeeding is Recommended (if you can)

Breast milk has so much good stuff in it the scientists haven't even worked out all the benefits yet. Not only is it full of exactly the right combination of vitamins, minerals, fats and other compounds for optimum health, but it also has stuff that boosts a baby's immune system. Literally hundreds of elements are all packaged perfectly to be absorbed properly and quickly by the baby's body. Babies need special fats and cholesterol for growth and development, all of which breast milk has. It's got anti-infection stuff and agents to help digestion, and it doesn't have things in it that a baby's kidneys find hard to process. Many of these components can't be reproduced in formula milk.

delicious!

The current expert line is that babies will get some of breast milk's benefits even if they're only breastfed for a short time, but they will probably benefit fully if they breastfeed for at least six to twelve months.

Good points about breastfeeding

- ★ Breast milk has all the necessary ingredients.
- ★ Breast milk has important health and immune system benefits.
- ★ Breast milk is portable and on tap.
- ★ Breast milk is free.
- ★ Breast milk is always the right temperature.
- ★ There are no hygiene contamination problems.
- ★ Breastfed baby poo smells better than bottlefed baby poo.
- ★ It's very, very rare for a baby to be allergic to breast milk.
- ★ The baby usually doesn't get constipated.
- ★ There's an immense feeling of pride in being able to, just with your own body, keep your baby alive and healthy.

"I am lucky – breastfeeding came very easily to me and is a part of babyhood I savoured, and missed dreadfully once they were weaned. [But] it's your decision alone, and nobody else's business!"
TIFFANY

Possible drawbacks of breastfeeding

- ★ The baby is totally dependent on you: some people love this idea, others don't.
- ★ It can cause problems such as the infection mastitis.
- ★ Breast milk will carry drugs or illnesses from you, which can affect the baby.
- ★ People assume that breastfeeding is a contraceptive.
  For some women this is true for about eighteen months, for others it is never true. If you want to avoid another pregnancy for the time being, make sure you use condoms: you can't be on some of the Pills as the hormones will go through your breast milk to the baby (ask your doctor).
- ★ Your breasts can leak at embarrassing moments.
- ★ If you want someone else to feed the baby, you'll have to express the milk.
- ★ You have to wake up (sometimes barely!) for every night-time feed. In the early days this can be incredibly draining and put you into a brainless, starey state that only gradually, gradually gets better as you start getting more sleep.
- ★ You get short-term memory loss, extreme fatigue and other symptoms such as putting the car keys in the toaster.
- ★ You really need someone to look after you in the first weeks by feeding you nutritious things and taking the housework weight off your shoulders.

"Breastfeeding is something you both need to learn to do."
LIBBY

Dodgy reasons to continue breastfeeding

- ★ Guilt: a feeling that you'll be a lesser mother if you stop.
- ★ Pressure from partner, friends or family.
- ★ You think it will help you lose weight (it depends on the individual: for many people it makes no difference).
- ★ Your baby is more than a year old and wants to wean but you love breastfeeding too much to give up.
- ★ You think it will affect your child's future health or intelligence: there are many factors that come into play for that, not the least of them genetics.

"I ended up doing it to keep my husband happy, even though my son and I would both be in tears trying to get it right."

MOTHER WHO BREASTFED FOR SIX MONTHS

Dodgy reasons to stop breastfeeding

- ★ It didn't work the first time.
- ★ You can't be bothered.
- ★ All your friends have stopped.
- ★ You reckon it would be easier to use bottles (it isn't necessarily).
- ★ Partner or family pressure.

Some reasons why it might not be a good idea for you to breastfeed

- ★ You can't make enough milk to keep your baby growing and happy. Some women don't produce enough prolactin, the hormone that controls the milk supply, so they can't make enough milk for their baby (luckily this is rare, and you could well be able to combine breast- and bottlefeeding).
- ★ Your baby can't suck effectively: some babies have a real problem with learning to suck properly, and a few are never going to get it together.
- ★ The difficulties you have experienced trying to breastfeed are affecting your relationship with your baby, which is more important than your baby's relationship with your bosoms.
- ★ You've tried everything, received help from all sorts of groups and individuals and it still isn't working.
- ★ You are so against the idea of breastfeeding that if you do it you will resent the baby.
- ★ Breastfeeding or its side effects (such as chronic mastitis) are consistently making you ill or depressed.
- ★ You have an illness such as HIV that could be passed to your baby through the breast milk.
- ★ You smoke, drink alcohol or take other drugs: even if you don't do this often, you shouldn't be breastfeeding. Some people have an occasional glass of wine – but even this does affect the baby.
- ★ You've had breast surgery: any kind can make it physically difficult or impossible to breastfeed.

★ You need to be on medication that will go through to the breast milk
and won't be good for your baby, or which interferes with milk production. This is especially true for women who need to be on a high-dose
anti-depressant or anti-psychotic drugs – it's so much better for the baby
to have a happy, sane mother and a lovely bottlefeed.

If you've decided to bottlefeed, tally-ho on to the next chapter, "Bottles".

*"I encountered a lot of opposition when I gave up, but both kids were lactose
intolerant and had to go on lactose-free formula."*
AMANDA

*"I ended up with acute mastitis, a temperature of 42 degrees for four days, and a
hospital stay to have the lumps surgically removed.*
*And still the do-gooders insisted I should feel guilty for not wanting to continue
breastfeeding."*
MUM WHO BREASTFED FOR A MONTH

*"Every woman is capable of breastfeeding her baby and you should try to do
so."* A BOSSY BABY BOOK

"Oh shut up, you bossy baby book!" ME

MEDICATION AND BREASTFEEDING

Many drugs are okay to take while breastfeeding, but
always check with your GP and pharmacist about **any**
medical or herbal preparations, whether prescribed or off
the shelf. Many herbal preparations as well as drugs can
be very dangerous for pregnant or breastfeeding women
because of possible damage to the baby.

   To find out which drugs go through to breast milk
and whether it's a problem for a baby see "More Info" at
the end of this chapter.

the first days

Colostrum

Breast milk doesn't "come in" until three or four days after you've given birth, as your body switches from baby-inside-you hormones to baby-outside-you hormones and pumps out its new, large output of prolactin, allowing your body to make breast milk. But your bub still gets to snack because in the meantime some yellowy stuff called colostrum comes out of your breasts, which is really good for babies (body builders take formulas with animal colostrum in it – euww). Human colostrum's full of antibodies and mysterious ingredients that help the baby's digestive system gear up for a totally new way of ingesting, now that the whole umbilical cord thing is out of fashion.

Newborns lose weight

Your bub will lose some weight before the milk comes in. So despite the fact that people in hospital run around weighing babies all the time and telling you they've lost a few grams, you are not to worry! Unfortunately the impression sometimes given is that babies have to be breastfed, breastfed, breastfed (no pressure) to get that weight back on, creating unnecessary stress for a new mum trying to work out how to breastfeed. Remember nobody used to weigh babies and know about five grams here or there – and your bub is almost certainly fine.

getting started

Most people have some sort of trouble getting started: like anything, breastfeeding takes practice to find a successful technique. After all it's quite possibly the first time you've had to do tricks with your bosoms – and the fact that it's "natural" to breastfeed doesn't mean that knowing how to do it comes naturally. We don't every day see women around us breastfeeding so don't blame yourself if you feel awkward! Most people take a while to get used to breastfeeding.

Mums who've had more than one baby say that breastfeeding depends on the kid: with some it's easy, with others it's hard. It doesn't seem to get easier or harder with each child – it's just the luck of the draw. So you mustn't blame yourself if it's difficult.

All the women I know had some kind of problem, and the ones who went on with it were only really hitting their stride and feeling fully comfortable at about three months: then many went on to breastfeed for a year or more – even the ones who had inverted nipples or painful breast infections. The first month or so will always be the hardest. Expect some hurdles and know you'll usually be able to get over them. If you can't, there's the bottle so don't panic, and always feel you've got the time to have a second or third go at a new technique: your baby won't starve as long as you are under the care of a good breastfeeeding counsellor, health visitor or GP (see the second chapter, "Your Support Team").

There's so much new information to pick up when you're in hospital, don't be afraid to ask a midwife to go over something once more or to sit with you and help you try again. Once you've left hospital, it's almost inevitable you'll need further help or reassurance, especially with hospital stays getting shorter and shorter. It's a guaranteed recipe for getting into a state and results in many women giving up breastfeeding when all they needed was some practical advice.

It's always much better if you can have someone show you, and then just refer to written notes to remind yourself. Often midwives or well-meaning friends and relatives will tell you different things: one will recommend the "American football hold", another will say wait until the baby opens up for a yawn and then whack them on the nipple. Choose one whose approach you like and only listen to them. I ended up getting a breastfeeding counseller and just listened to her, which was the best thing I ever did. My theory usually is, when in doubt make sure you get onto a specialist.

The hospital where your baby was born has an obligation to help you with breastfeeding even if it discharges you before your proper milk comes in (which is appalling). Many are working towards accreditation for UNICEF's Baby Friendly Initiative, a scheme which has established a code for best breastfeeding practice (see "More Info") If a hospital tells you its infant feeding specialist is busy or on holidays or can't come until next week, kick up a stink. If you're too tired, get your mum or your partner or an in-law or a friend to do it. Make enough fuss until it's worth the hospital's while to shut you up by obliging you. Call the head of maternity, the hospital manager, your MP. Put the heat on. Threaten to call the *Today Programme* if you have to. (But don't – it's too stressful.) Other than that, see the list of contacts in "More Info" at the end of this chapter. It's important to get help quickly before it all becomes too difficult, or before a milk-duct blockage becomes a serious mastitis infection.

"I went home on Day Three from a public hospital just when my boobs were lusciously sore and lumpy and me having no idea how to breastfeed. So three weeks was IT." JANE

How often to breastfeed?

Newborn babies usually feed eight to twelve times in a 24-hour period. In the early days you will have to try to muddle through, but to give you an ideal "textbook" situation (I know, I know, we're not textbooks), your aim would be to feed the baby every three to four hours during the day and when they wake and cry during the night – unless they wake every hour or two, in which case they may just be feeling a bit freaked out about not being in the womb and need a rock back to sleep.

Some nutcases say you should feed babies only according to the clock (for example every four and a half hours), no matter how long they cry. This does not account for the needs of individual babies or natural variations in a baby's requirements or growth spurts. On the other hand, although breastfeeding as often as you like in the first weeks will help you build up a constant, replenishing supply of milk, it will leave you a zombie if you wake up every couple of hours to feed the baby.

Try to give a complete feed at intervals of three to four hours rather than get the baby used to snacking or top-ups every two hours. This may be easier after the first three or four weeks. Sometimes a baby may genuinely need a feed in two hours, but often this is just habit – it's impossible to tell but try not to feed every two hours as a regular habit. Be aware that you can get yourself into a vicious circle of feeding your baby little bits too often: you'll need to gradually extend the time between breastfeeds.

I finally worked out my baby wanted a feed pretty much exactly every four hours – which is the case for most babies by the second month (but not all of them!). Despite the fact that a telephone informa-tion-line Bosom Lady told me to feed her if she cried (the baby, not the Bosom Lady), any breast milk dispensed between the four hours was always projec-tile vomited a minute later. I just needed time to get to know my baby, and I was too worried to wait. I didn't know why she was crying and I wanted an answer on the phone NOW.

Sometimes it's just a matter of trying to be calm enough to let things happen. This is a philosophy that has always made me want to repeatedly strike hippies with a cricket bat. (How infuriating that on this issue they are absolutely right. Damn it all to hell.)

> *"Escape from the extremes of scheduled feeding has led some mothers into difficulties with the extremes of demand feeding."*
> **PENELOPE LEACH, *YOUR BABY AND CHILD***

> *"Watch your baby, not the clock."*
> **MARTHA AND WILLIAM SEARS, *THE BREASTFEEDING BOOK***

How long to breastfeed for?

In the early days feeds tend to take between thirty and fifty minutes in total (both bosoms). The time usually gradually reduces. Eventually you'll probably be feeding only seven to ten minutes on each breast.

Incidentally the first weeks are no time to be going "back" to work or becoming the unassisted chief executive officer of a house – even though that's exactly what may be happening to you. If you've chosen to breastfeed you need to allow yourself time and energy to concentrate pretty much solely on that, as well as to get to know your baby, to give yourselves some fresh air and to recover from the birth. Eventually your baby will develop a rhythm of feeds.

Breastfeeding privacy

It's possibly best for everyone in the first few weeks if you leave a crowded room so that you can concentrate fully on breastfeeding and have time alone with your baby. While totally believing breastfeeding should be allowed to happen anywhere, you may find that a quiet corner in another room or a discreetly draped muslin will allow you to avoid having to deal with distracting conversations (for you and the baby), ludicrous disapproving stares or the understandable embarrassment of male relatives, in-laws and friends who don't know where to look because they're trying to be respectful but end up feeling dreadfully uncomfortable.

Learning How to Breastfeed

After a few weeks you'll probably be able to breastfeed upside down on the monkey bars at the local park, but in the beginning you may need to set up a comfort zone at home. Choose a rocking chair or armchair as your breastfeeding HQ. Next to the baby's bed is perfect, especially for middle of the night feeds. Make sure the room is warm. On a side table put a big glass of water or a bottle of water and a glass. You need to drink a lot during the day if breastfeeding, and you'll sometimes feel thirsty during a feed when you can't get up.

You may also want a pencil and notebook if you're recording which breast you need to start on next time, and how long each feed is. You don't need to do this, but I found it quite useful when I was brain dead. (It hadn't actually occurred to me that if the baby fed every four hours I would have to be awake every four hours.) The lack of sleep makes everything harder – including trying to remember which bosom you started with last time. After a while you'll gain confidence and forget to make notes. Later you can look back and laugh at your funny lists with "L 25 min." and "R 17 min." on them.

BREASTFEEDING STATION

cushions for lower back

water

phone

pillow

TV remote

PUMP
(already plugged in)

BABY

table in reach

65

If you're out and need to feed your baby, go to a large mall or department store and use their ladies' lounge or mothers' room; many shopping centres, department stores, museums and other public spaces now have a special breastfeeding area, although this can be little more than a cupboard – or even a toilet, ugghh (well, would you want to eat your lunch there?). The better ones have a quiet section behind a curtain, with a sofa, armchair or special rocking chair to sit on. It remains to be seen how widely the Department of Health's 2008 initiative of "Breastfeeding Friendly" stickers will be taken up by businesses (see "Extra Resources"). Otherwise a corner of a café will do fine, or even a park bench or the car.

"If you're out, plan to be in the bigger shopping centres around feedtimes: these days they have decent parenting facilities at most of them." FIONA

Breastfeeding equipment

You'll need:

- ★ maternity bras – supportive, stretchy, your new size and front-opening
- ★ a lanolin-based nipple cream or one that's okay for a baby to swallow (some people use calendula cream) – ask your chemist
- ★ breast pads – little disposable or washable pads to put in your bra to soak up any leaking milk
- ★ to carry a spare top and bra and spare breast pads in your bag in case you do leak those big, tell-tale wet circles on your front
- ★ pillows to help you support your baby and your back
- ★ hot wheat-filled fabric packs (many are designed for microwave heating) to help the milk come (or used cold to stop your breasts becoming engorged)
- ★ a hand pump in case your nipples are sore – you can express some milk (see the "Expressing Breast Milk" section later in this chapter) and give it in a sterilized teaspoon or bottle.

"Using a U-shaped pillow to support the baby for breastfeeds made it easier." AMY

BREASTFEEDING CHECKLIST

✱ Drink a big glass of water and have another one within reach.

✱ Put a cloth over your shoulder for when you burp the baby.

✱ To bring the baby up to the right level without your getting aching arms, and to help if you've had a Caesarean, put a couple of pillows on your lap and lay the baby on this high, comfy "tray" (while still holding onto them so they don't roll off).

✱ Talk to your baby and explain what you're doing.

✱ Sit up straight.

✱ Find a feeding position for the baby that's comfy for you.

✱ Start on the breast you didn't start with last time or the one that is fuller.

✱ Get your baby to open wide, by tickling their cheek, so that they take a big mouthful of areola as well

as nipple when they latch on.

✱ As your baby opens wide aim your nipple towards the roof of their mouth.

✱ Reattach if the attachment is not a big mouthful, feels wrong or hurts.

✱ Let the baby have as much as they want on the first breast, and then however much they can take on the second.

PS   You don't need to wash or sterilize your nipples after a feed.

How to breastfeed

Basically choose whatever works for you and your baby. Speak to your baby soothingly and encouragingly. Trying to get breastfeeding going can be stressful if the baby is crying with hunger, and I know it can be hard, but a calm attitude will help you both.

Take a few deep breaths. Sit up straight and make sure your lower back is supported. This means you need to bring the bub to your breast rather than hunching over, round shoulered, to deliver the breast to them.

Put a muslin or cloth over your shoulder in case the baby throws up a little during a break or straight after feeding (this is sometimes called "posseting" in the books: I don't know why – probably because they don't want to say "puke").

You can try various feeding positions, including laying the baby sideways on a pillow across your lap, face up, then turning them gently so the bub is facing you and tummy to tummy with you. Another common one involves holding the baby on their side, under your arm and facing your body, then bringing them forward to the nearest breast, as if you're holding a hungry surfboard (this is the "American football hold" or the "French loaf hold" – or any term suggesting carrying something under one arm – that is often referred to). Experiment until you find a position that feels good. Some people prefer to breastfeed lying down, but this seems an unduly restrictive position to have to be in every time. The Department of Health has a useful leaflet on how to position the baby for a breastfeed. (For contact details, see "Extra Resources" at the end of the book.)

Support your baby's body and neck, either with your arm or pillows. Remember that tiny babies can't hold their heads up by themselves.

Start with the breast you didn't start with last time. After a while you may be able to tell by feel which is the fuller one; otherwise jot the info down or put a safety pin on the side to start on next time to remind yourself. If being seen in public with a safety pin above one bosom worries you, why not substitute a priceless ruby brooch in the shape of a small mouse or somesuch?

Tickle your bub's cheek to create the sucking reflex: their mouth will open. Try to get the breast in when the mouth is open wide, wide: if you need a visual idea, go to the supermarket, lurk furtively in the breakfast cereal aisle and look at the curve of the K on the *Special K* packet. Think of your baby's mouth as that K curve. The baby needs to get a big mouthful of areola (the coloured circle around the nipple) as well as nipple, not just to suck on the nipple itself, which will be painful for you. If the baby latches onto only the nipple, slip your little finger into their mouth and gently dislodge it. If you just pull the nipple out, it can really hurt.

BURPING

HOW LONG ON EACH BREAST Let the baby suck for approximately twenty minutes or more on the first breast. Some advisers say there isn't any point in going much over twenty minutes on each breast, but others say a newborn can take up to an hour to get everything they need while they're working up those jaw muscles and swallowing skills. Helpful, ain't it? Some babies suck faster and the milk is squirted out more quickly. (I remember in those first few days it was half an hour each side, and then by three months it was about fifteen minutes.) So it's probably best to be guided by what your baby seems to want to do, and ask for help if you still feel bamboozled. The baby will pull away when they've finally had enough, and then you can burp them (or not) and bung them on the other bosom until they've had enough there.

BURPING A lot of babies don't need to be "burped", and it's unknown in many cultures. If you want to, you can burp or "wind" the baby when they have a rest during the feed and then get back into it. After the feed or between bosoms hold your baby upright, peeking over one of your shoulders, and rock and pat until there's a burp – but don't worry if there isn't one. The theory is that burping stops "wind" from causing tummy pain.

Foremilk, middlemilk and hindmilk

In the first few minutes at the breast the baby gets a big thirst-quenching, tummy-filling squirt of "foremilk", and then, several minutes in, there are other goodies, followed in the middle part of the feed by different stuff, and at the end there's some important fatty, vitaminy elements that babies like and need, sometimes called the "hindmilk". Look, it's not all that scientific, I know, but basically don't worry. This just explains why you don't do only five minutes on each breast, and so you know that over a full day of breastfeeding your bub gets fore-, middle- and hindmilk without your having to measure anything or be concerned. And even if your baby only does five minutes, it's still not panic time – according to some experts eighty to ninety percent of milk volume goes in in the first four minutes on each breast!

> *"It's practically an art form, and takes ages to master."*
> ALEXIS

> *"With both children it worked like a dream – both were keen feeders from the word go."* ANN

Breast-milk supply and demand

Unless you have a problem, the more a baby sucks, the more milk your body will produce. This is how people are able to feed twins, and were able to become "wet nurses" – women who fed other people's babies as well as their own. If you stop breastfeeding for a few days, the milk will "dry up" and you may not be able to get the flow going again, although breastfeeding organisations will help you to try: many mums have been very successful.

Anecdotal evidence suggests that older mums, especially those over 40, may have difficulty with supplying enough milk. At this age the reproductive system is winding down and the body produces fewer eggs, so it makes sense. Women who conceive using scientific methods can also find their body isn't geared up for maximum milk supply.

BREAST SIZE   Bosom size is irrelevant to breastfeeding – even the titchiest ones are up to the task. All breasts get bigger for breastfeeding.

Getting in a state

You're tired, your brain's on strike, your new baby's crying, you're crying, you feel like you're the only woman in the world who can't get her bosoms to do the right thing, and nothing seems to be going right. You feel you might as well start on bottles today, although you're too tired to work out what to do and you'd feel so guilty. But please don't give up without having another shot. You might regret it later. What you need is a fresh eye on the problem. Call someone from one of the breastfeeding support groups or your health visitor; or ring for a personal visit from a breastfeeding counsellor. For heaven's sake, don't mind about calling complete strangers to advise on bosom business: that's what they're for. Then, if you do give up, you will always know you did your best and got the best help you could: there's no shame in that.

And get some sleep: sleep between each feed at night and between some during the day. Take the phone off the hook and put a sign on the door saying not to knock (you might like to photocopy the sign supplied in the "Sleeping" chapter). Or express some milk for someone else to give in a bottle; although some babies are fussy and don't like a teat, most will take it when they're hungry. It's impossible to make rational decisions when you're very sleep deprived.

Perseverance

Everyone bangs on about perseverance but perseverance itself won't get you through. You need perseverance and good technique (as well as no physical problems) or you just keep persevering with something that isn't working. But it's true that, all going well, what feels clunky and by the book at first becomes, simply with repetition and practice, something you can do without even thinking about it.

The other problem with perseverance is that when you're in the middle of a difficult time, every hour seems to drag and every feed can bring new tension and anticipation of pain and trouble. I can remember someone telling me at six weeks that it would all be sorted out by three months, and I wanted to hit them. Three months! They may as well have said 2027, it seemed so far, far away. This is a Babyland situation where you have to take one day at a time, even each hour at a time.

COMMON PROBLEMS

Temporary supply problems

The reasons can include a mum not getting enough fluids and nutritious, filling food; going back to work; being rundown, tired, ill or stressed; smoking; taking some medications (always check the fine print and talk to your doctor and pharmacist about the effects any medication might have on breastfeeding); starting the Mini Pill (and look out for the signs of ectopic pregnancy: see "contraception" in the index); using cabbage leaves too much to reduce engorgement, which can have an adverse effect on supply. Or the baby could be ready to eat stuff and want less milk – some time between four and six months babies show signs of wanting more in the food department.

Home remedies to increase the milk include the rather stinky fenugreek tea or less stinky fenugreek tablets, raspberry-leaf tea or tablets, and blessed thistle herbal tablets, but you must check all these with a breastfeeding counsellor or your GP before using them. Make sure you get a mainstream brand, and read the label to check all the ingredients and additives. Feed your baby more often to encourage the supply, and have good nutrition, REST and lots of fluids.

> *"The best tip I have had for bringing milk in was: while showering direct the shower as close to your nipples as possible and blast them with the warmest water you can stand. Doing this for the first three days of your baby's life seems to help get it going. That and drinking water like there's no tomorrow."* SOPHIE

> *"When at 4 months he started crying for no good reason after every feed I knew something was up. Of course the experts said, 'Just persevere, mother.' Meanwhile he was nearly starving as the quality of my milk decreased. Although health visitors have their place they are not always right."* HELEN

Very zingy or buzzy pain in the breast

This is a normal feeling early on in your breastfeeding career and is caused by your body doing as it should, creating a "let-down" of the milk – and telling you you're full of goodies and ready to go. In the first days you may feel contractions of your uterus while feeding as it shrinks. If you have sharp pains in your breasts or underarm area, especially accompanied by a temperature, you may have a blocked milk duct causing the infection mastitis.

Milk not coming

Try thinking about babies, thinking about your own baby, listening to a baby cry, smelling a baby's head, and/or putting hot flannels on your breasts and drinking lots of water. My friend Miss Kate used to let down her milk in the supermarket if she heard someone else's baby cry. "It's my 'feed the world' reflex", she would say.

Blocked ducts and mastitis

A blocked milk duct may cause a red mark or lump on a breast: treat by pressing warm packs on the spot and massaging the area before and after a feed. Run warm water on it in the shower. If not cleared, it can become mastitis, a quite common infection, which is often accompanied by a temperature and flu-like aches. Treatment includes cold compresses to alleviate pain; warm compresses or a warm hot-water bottle to maintain the flow; painkillers (check with your chemist or GP); keeping the breast empty by offering the bub frequent feeds or by expressing; REST (yes, that means no housework and faffing about); and, in serious cases, antibiotics to clear the infection: the doctor will prescribe one that doesn't harm the baby. If you have mastitis, you must see your doctor. It can lead to high fever, severe pain and unconsciousness.

Cracked, sore nipples

These are almost always caused by the bub not being attached with a big mouthful. It will NOT help to "toughen up" nipples by scouring or pinching them! The only real cure is to get the baby positioned in a different, mouthfully way. This is best done with a breastfeeding counsellor, midwife or health visitor watching you and advising. The most common methods of treating the pain and keeping breastfeeding going are rubbing on naturally based ointments from the chemist; using nipple shields; massaging breast milk into the cracks and sores; briefly exposing your bosoms to sunlight (but most certainly not to sunburn); and resting your nipples from feeding for 24 hours and expressing milk for your baby instead.

Most breastfeeding experts warn against nipple shields, and say only the thinnest silicone ones should be used and only at the beginning of a feed. The conventional wisdom is that they should be used by women with very flat or inverted nipples to make it easier for the bub to get hold of something to suck. Shields can cut down the milk supply a little because they cut down the sensa-

---

A WISH LIST FOR EASY BREASTFEEDING

✷ As much rest as possible.

✷ No other commitments apart from baby, at least for the first six to eight weeks.

✷ A healthy diet.

✷ Extra food. (Everyone I know got the munchies at 4am in the early days.) Soya milk and bananas are good.

✷ No obsession with low-fat products and losing weight – you need fuel for breastfeeding, although you shouldn't be actually gaining weight. Your

protein requirements are higher now than they were in pregnancy.

✷ Lots of fluids – but not coffee, tea or gin.

✷ Support from family and friends.

✷ Perseverance: nearly everyone has early problems to overcome.

✷ Help: even champion breastfeeders can come across temporary problems.

✷ Luck: you need to be one of the people who can do it.

---

tion of the baby sucking, which stimulates the milk supply, but they work well for some people.

Inverted nipples

It may be difficult to coax those shy, inverted suckers out at first, but most people can breastfeed successfully after some initial nipple pain. Breastfeeding counsellors and breastfeeding groups have heaps of hints on how to "pop out" your nipples so the baby can really latch on. The underarm hold is often recommended for women with inverted nipples, and shields and creams are commonly used to try to reduce soreness in the early weeks. According to a friend who had stubborn inverted nipples, medical staff often presume your nipples will just pop out when required, but some people with severe inversion should investigate as much as they can the sorts of techniques or equipment that may help. Don't accept "it will all be fine" if it isn't fine for you, and expect some pain when establishing feeding because your nipples need extra coaxing to come out to play.

> *"Against advice I used nipple shields the entire time. I guess once he got used to this he wouldn't do it any other way."* JOANNE

Thrush

This common fungal infection loves warm, wet areas such as babies' mouths and bots, and mums' breastfeeding nipples. It causes a painful red rash. Your pharmacist will have over-the-counter creams and drops, but the rash should be seen by a doctor.

Painfully full breasts

This is also known as "engorgement". Don't worry, most new mums get this rock-hard, possible-exploding-bosomry feeling while the breasts are trying to find the right amount to keep in readiness for the baby. After a few weeks the bosoms will settle down and feel quite normal in between feeds instead of being all hard and bursty just before each one. As with mastitis, you can relieve the pressure by putting a warm flannel on your breasts and leaning over the bathroom basin to let a bit of milk dribble or squirt into it; conversely a cold (not icy) pack should calm things down. A cabbage leaf cupping each breast is also said to work wonders but if you use cabbage leaves all the time it can reduce your milk supply.

"Cabbages, cabbages, cabbages. Let's be honest, your chest starts to take on the appearance of a bad Renaissance painting by the time your milk starts coming in." TESSA

One breast not behaving

This needs professional help. You can feed with only one breast if you absolutely have to.

Baby pulls away from the breast and cries

There can be a number of causes. "They" say babies may baulk at the taste of your milk if you've had an unexpected curry, onions or garlic – but presumably this doesn't happen in a culture full of that sort of food. Having different tastes in breast milk is a way babies get to know variation. If something you've eaten doesn't agree with them, babies may show distaste but are more likely to have farty problems, indigestion or diarrhoea. Chocolate and citrus upset many newborn babies, according to breastfeeding specialist Margaret Callaghan (see also the later "Crying" chapter).

The baby might have something making their mouth or throat sore. Check for baby health problems such as thrush.

IS MY BABY GETTING ENOUGH BREAST MILK?

A baby should be growing and putting on a certain amount of weight each month (depending on their individual size). This is one of the reasons you go to those regular weigh-ins at a health centre. Babies shouldn't stay the same weight or go backwards between visits.

The other major sign of a problem is screaming or listlessness. Basically a baby who is hungry will tell you by yelling. Unfortunately the baby doesn't know how to yell so specifically that you get the picture immediately. A baby who is really starving will stop yelling and become lethargic.

A young baby should need six to eight nappy changes in a 24-hour period, and have regular poos as well throughout the day (look up "poo" in index).

Babies do go through hungry periods and growth spurts, when they seem to want more, and then the rate drops back a little. If you have any doubts or worries, see your health visitor, a breastfeeding counsellor or your GP, or call a breastfeeding support group.

Some newborns come off the breast at the start or during a feed when they get big squirts of milk (this could be messy so keep a cloth handy). Your supply will sort itself out and your bub will get used to it.

"For lunch in hospital they served coleslaw and I chose not to eat it because I'd been told it caused problems with wind in babies: mine was the only baby in the ward not screaming during the night and I had a midwife ask me what on earth I had done to have the only angelic baby on the ward. When I told her she was amazed. I found the following to cause problems: cabbage, broccoli, onion, cherries, kidney beans, spicy food." MAREE

Your baby may have a blocked nose so can't breathe very well on the breast – in which case try to clear the nose very gently by taking the baby into a steamy (but not hot) bathroom, putting a steam vapourizer (from the chemist) in their bedroom or dabbing some eucalyptus oil on a hanky and waving it under their nose (but not blocking it). A few drops of sterline saline solution from the chemist into the baby's nostrils can also help to clear the congestion, but the administration of it might temporarily distress the bub even more.

The baby could just be so hungry they're cross and confused, or they may be feeling pain caused by a windy tummy, a tooth coming or something else (haven't you developed ESP *yet?*). Use the usual calming techniques, including burping, soothing chat, swaddling and going to a quiet, dim room for a slow, rocking cuddle. Not easy, but you're supposed to stay calm. (Like when they say "relax" just before a smear test – yes, such a soothing atmosphere!)

If your baby continues to pull away and cry, get some advice from your health visitor or a breastfeeding counsellor. (see "More Info" at the end of this chapter).

"I'd advise perseverance. For me it was mastitis and cracked and bloodied nipples early on, but this sorted itself out in due course and the convenience of not having to prepare countless bottles countless times a night is a good trade-off." KARINA

"My GP told me to stop breastfeeding at 3 weeks because I was so tired, so I stopped cold turkey, got blocked milk ducts and mastitis. I ended up in hospital on a drip and sicker than before (when I was just tired). In hospital the midwives encouraged me to go back to breastfeeding even though it hurt like hot pokers and sharp needles being jabbed into my nipples but I went on and we made it to 10 months." JULIA

getting Help With Breastfeeding

Your hospital will have an infant feeding specialist, trained in both breast- and bottlefeeding techniques, but with a duty to promote breastfeeding. Many offer a daily workshop, with a video as well as hands-on instruction. If you miss out on this, your first port of call once you've left hospital should be your midwife or health visitor. They will have had special training in this area, and can check to see if there are any physical problems with your bosoms, but if you find their advice isn't working for you, or their approach isn't as supportive as you'd like, there are other options. There are four specialist charities in the UK, all of which offer an emergency helpline, publications and a website for further information. You don't have to be a member to access the help, although remember that they are funded by donations. All claim to listen, support and offer up-to-date information, rather than "advise". (Details are listed in the "More Info" section at the end of this chapter.)

Probably the best-known of these is The National Childbirth Trust, an independent charity and campaigning group with a mission to promote and support pregnancy, birth and early parenthood. The NCT wants breastfeeding to be part of everyday life, to make it easier to combine breastfeeding with a social and working life, and for women to receive the support they need to breastfeed for as long as they and their baby want. It has been invaluable in addressing the lack of social and cultural support for breastfeeding, particularly for younger women and women from disadvantaged backgrounds. For immediate help it has a Breastfeeding Helpline (see "More Info" at the end of this chapter) where you can talk to a counsellor trained to help you establish and continue breastfeeding. If a phone chat isn't enough, a face-to-face visit can be arranged, either in a local drop-in or at home. It also produces loads of useful books and leaflets to help with breastfeeding. Not as evangelical as some support organizations, it does acknowledge that not all women choose to, or can breastfeed, for a variety of reasons.

The La Leche League is an international charity aiming to help mums breast-feed, with mother-to-mother support and encouragement, and to vigorously promote breastfeeding. While its campaigning function has undoubtedly helped to make strides in international policy, if you're not convinced of your personal growth through breastfeeding then its helpline may not be the best for you.

The Association of Breastfeeding Mothers prefers to say that "Breast is Normal" rather than that overused phrase "Breast is Best", and its information does not discuss the "benefits" of breastfeeding but treats it as the norm against which all other methods should be evaluated. It will help with mixed feeding (breast- and bottlefeeding), although the aim is to give the mother the support needed for her to breastfeed for as long as she wants, and any "disadvantages" are treated as inconveniences to the mother and the family, rather than the baby. Its helpline gets you through to a mother who has breastfed her own baby and has received in-depth training on all aspects of breastfeeding. A home visit may be possible if your local counsellor is close enough.

Likewise The Breastfeeding Network aims to provide a service alongside mid-wives and health visitors for mothers who face challenges in breastfeeding. Its national helpline puts you in touch with a "supporter" for a telephone consultation, or a home visit where possible. Together these last two organizations also act as counsellors for the government-sponsored National Breastfeeding Helpline (see "More Info" at the end of this chapter).

YOUR BREASTFEEDING BODY

What do your bosoms look like?

Breastfeeding boosies can look like a road map of Manchester, with the veins pushed closer to the surface by all the milk ducts and milk in there. Large breastfeeding bosoms hopefully don't get *too* much larger, but expect to go up a full size plus one or two cup sizes. That is, if you start out a 34B you're likely to be a 36C or 36D in a

maternity bra. What that will settle down to after breastfeeding is anyone's guess. Some breasts get smaller than before.

Pregnancy itself makes the breasts bigger – everyone has floppier, softer, less pert and pointy-out breasts afterwards, whether they breastfeed or not. Cosmetic surgeons who want your money call this "deformed". Billions of partners around the world beg to differ and love you and your bits just the same. Celebrities who claim pregnancy made their breasts permanently bigger, firmer and perkier deserve only one reply: liar, liar, pants on fire. And probably bosoms as well if they get too close to a naked flame.

Nipples

Nipples have lots of holes, like a sprinkler, for feeding. The areolae appear darker (they will stay darker forever now) so it's easier for the baby to zero in when the light is dim. Your nipples will stay more prominent.

Some bosomry issues

Partners can find the transformation of breasts from sexual objects to life-giving bosoms needs a little adjusting to. Some of them don't like to hear breasts referred to with new words that relate to babies and children only, such as "booby" (as in "Do you want some booby?"), "boo-boo" or other baby-talk expressions, and prefer to have them more formally referred to (although presumably not as the divinely romantic "fun-bags"). I'm not saying you have to indulge a partner on this one, but I am saying you may need to be sensitive to the issue if it arises. A good indicator of attitude to breastfeeding is gained by "accidentally" squirting your partner with breast milk. Initial shock is fine, but you may have some psychological work to do if, instead of eventually laughing, they freak out and think it's revolting.

Some partners and older kids want to have a taste of breast milk. It won't do them any harm. But don't do it unless you feel comfortable. You may well feel one (or two) recipients is quite enough.

Does breastfeeding make you lose weight?

Yes. No. Depends. Some breastfeeders start to lose weight after three months, some snap back into pre-pregnancy weight within weeks and others hold onto every extra kilo with a white-knuckle grip no matter how much they breastfeed. The best way to lose weight after a baby is slowly, with self-respect, and by walking briskly with the pram. Most of the celebrities who miraculously lose 27 zillion kilos in the first three weeks after pregnancy don't breastfeed. Come to think of it, half of them don't even have a pregnancy, and the other half live on lettuce ends and Peter Stuyvesants.

expressing breast milk

Mums who want to go out or go "back" to work can "milk" themselves with a handheld or electric breast pump that can be hired or bought from chemists or breastfeeding support groups. Do compare prices of pumps, which can be wildly different. If you're going to be expressing milk a lot, get an electric pump. The machine will make a noise (sort of a cross between a sucking noise and a vibrator, from memory, but that can't be right – you'd sound like a porn movie). You can hook yourself up and read while it's rhythmically pulling a nipple into a soft silicone nipple shield attached to a bottle. The electric business seems quite contraptiony, but it's basically very simple. A breastfeeding counsellor or instruction pamphlet should be able to help you learn how to use a hand pump or an electric one. The hand pump can give you a very sore hand from repetitive action. The electric pump is hands-free. Although it's hard not to say "moo". You usually pump both breasts, one after the other, to keep them "even" as you would if you were breastfeeding directly.

Expresso di Breasto

The collected milk can be put straight into a sterilized bottle and then the fridge and warmed for the feed in the next few hours, or poured into a plastic freezer bag that can be frozen and later thawed by someone. Chemists have special sachets for breast milk, which funnel into a bottle when it's time to use them and which you can write the use-by date on. Your baby will need to accept a bottle teat – something many babies reject. Some parents give a bottle of expressed milk a day, or in the night-time to serve the dual purpose of giving mum a rest and getting the baby used to a teat. Some breastfeeding advocates say this can cause "nipple confusion", with the baby not wanting to go back to the breast, which can be harder work to suck on. If you do use a bottle, use one designed to avoid creating bubbles of air (see the next chapter, "Bottles").

Try to build up a store of frozen milk for emergencies – for instance, if one is spilled or you can't get home in time for the next feed. (Always carry breast pads for milk leaks and feel free to squirt some milk out if your breasts get too painful – probably not into the air on a bus but, say, into the basin of a locked bathroom.) Remember that the more you express, the more your breasts will think they need to make extra milk, so don't go overboard and try to fill heaps of bottles, freezer bags or sachets all at once.

Freeze or store the breast milk in single-breastfeed amounts to avoid waste or having to use part of a thawed, second freezer bag or sachet for a feed. The bottles you express into will have markings on the side so you'll know when to stop.

Do label the milk properly and let everyone who uses the freezer understand not to tamper with it. Write "BREAST MILK" and the date you pumped it. You may also like to put a sign on the freezer saying "Keep Freezer closed as much as possible! Breast milk inside!" if it's used by lots of people.

> *"Angus is now 6 months old and while breastfeeding we have listened to [as talking books from the library]* **The Hunchback of Notre Dame,** *a variety of the Brontë sisters' works, lots of Agatha Christie radio plays and Charles Dickens's* **Bleak House."**
> KATE

"Emmerdale can easily be watched in one feeding session when you fast-forward the ads."
KIMBERLEY

Storage times for breast milk

Breast milk should always be immediately put in the fridge after it's been expressed if you're not sure when you'll use it or you're not using it in the next wee while, and especially if you live somewhere hot and humid. Stored expressed milk will "separate", but it's still okay – you just need to shake the bottle gently (turn it upside down once or twice, don't treat it like a cocktail shaker) before giving it to your baby.

Breast milk can usually be kept:

★ at room temperature for six to eight hours
★ in the fridge, stored at the back in the coldest part, for three to five days (they describe this as four degrees Celsius or lower)
★ in a cyclic defrost freezer for two to three months
★ in a self-contained freezer with separate door for three months
★ in a deep freeze (maximum of minus eighteen degrees Celsius) for six months.

You should also remember:

★ if milk has been frozen then thawed at room temperature, use within four hours
★ if milk has been frozen then thawed in the fridge, use within twenty-four hours
★ if milk has been frozen then thawed, do not refreeze
★ once a baby has started on a thawed batch of milk, any left over in the bottle must be thrown away.

These guidelines are conservative – others will give you up to a week to store breast milk in the fridge. Milk that will be used within a day is better off in the fridge than in the freezer because "the antimicrobial properties of human milk are better preserved with refrigeration", the La Leche League says.

Thawing breast milk

★ You can take a batch out of the freezer and leave it in the fridge overnight to thaw.

★ Or you can put the frozen container into a saucepan, bowl or sink of warm water to thaw. Boiling water will curdle the milk and it will be spoiled.

★ Don't use the microwave to thaw or heat breast milk: "research suggests that microwaving changes the immunological and nutrient quality of breast milk", according to some sources.

★ Don't boil your breast milk. The milk should be thawed and brought gradually up to room temperature, and not made any hotter. Some babies are happy to take milk at room rather than body temperature. This is handy if you're out.

Breastfeeding and going back to work

If you want to work outside the home and continue breastfeeding, you'll need to be very organised, and very careful about not getting overtired. Breastfeeding support organizations have lots of hints and info about how to accomplish this. Employers now have an "obligation" to support working mothers who want to breastfeed, and should at the very least provide a place for mothers to express milk so they can lock the door and don't have to be in a toilet. (It's about time!) The Department of Health's leaflet *Breastfeeding and work* outlines what you can expect from your employer.

Breastfeeding twins and bunches of babies

I know it sounds daunting, but lots of people do it and have milk to spare – it's amazing how most women's bodies can keep up with supplying the milk demand, although if your multiple birth was the result of IVF and you are an older mum you may not have the milk supply you would have had when younger.

And if you don't want to do it, here's official permission: you don't have to. It's more important that you're well rested and enjoying your babies and coping well. Anecdotal evidence suggests mums with twins usually give up in the first couple of months or get the hang of it and go on to feed for a year or more.

See the "Multiples" chapter in *Part 4: Stuff*, which has the contact details for the Twins and Multiple Birth Association: they have booklets and can put you in touch with people who have done it or are doing it. The La Leche League website has FAQs (frequently asked questions) and other info about breastfeeding twins or more. (See "More Info" at the end of this chapter.)

DROPPING BREASTFEEDS

As your baby gets older the feeds will become further apart. The first feed to "drop", if you can manage it, is obviously a night-time one. When people say a baby "slept through" they mean the baby stayed asleep from, say, a 10.30 or 11pm feed until, say, 6am. Eventually many mums get down to just a breastfeed in the morning, the time when their breasts are fullest, or perhaps one in the evening as a comfort before the baby goes to sleep (obviously that one can become a hard habit to break).

The chapter "Possible Routines for Babies" has suggested feeding schedules for babies of various ages, which could suit you. Talking at a playgroup to other mums with babies the same age, or to your health visitor, can also help you to establish a routine that fits your and your baby's needs and is adjustable as time goes on. Some babies sleep through as early as 6 weeks old, others at 3 or 4 months, 18 months or later – which is why people seek help (see the "Sleeping" chapter).

WEANING FROM THE BREAST

"I'm still breastfeeding at twenty months much to the disgust of parents/in-laws who have been encouraging me to wean since she was nine months old." NICKI

Everyone who breastfeeds will need to wean their baby – end breastfeeding – eventually. Some experts and people who say "weaning" use it to mean starting on solid foods. This book uses it to mean the end of breastfeeding, or coming off the bottle. (See the "Learning to Eat" chapter for the other business.) Many mums have the luxury of weaning gradually, others have to wean suddenly because of illness or another reason. Some babies wean themselves gradually – or stop suddenly with no warning.

Most mums in the survey undertaken for this book suggested that if you're happy to breastfeed until, say, 10 months or more, wean the baby directly onto a cup. You can buy special ones with lids at the chemist and some supermarkets so that the baby can start with a spout, then progress to a straw and finally to a normal open cup. Older babies and toddlers can also learn to drink from those little "popper" bottles, with pop-up tops like the ones on sports drinks, although you may have to be in charge of the opening and closing. This way you can avoid bottles with teats altogether.

If you know you'll be weaning onto bottles, try beforehand to get your baby used to the artificial teats – and someone else feeding them – by giving a bottle of expressed milk or formula once a day. This is when a companion or a full-time live-in nanny (with her own Rolls-Royce) comes in terribly handy.

The most common reasons given by mums in the survey for weaning their kids were:

- ★ the baby gave up themselves (many mothers described their reaction to this as "horror at the feeling of rejection").
- ★ the baby got teeth and bit a nipple (some breastfeeding encouragers say you just need to say no sharply, but some babies find this simply hilarious).
- ★ the mums reached their breastfeeding goal – most often set at 1 year.
- ★ another baby came along and they didn't want to feed two.

A feeling of "wanting my body back" was mentioned by many.

Expect to have an emotional response to weaning, which may or may not be affected by hormonal changes. Some women feel an aching sense of loss and disappointment, others rejoice in a new-found freedom and independence.

Everyone does it differently. As you'll see, there are a lot of ways to choose from. Do remember that if you wean a baby from the breast before 12 months, you'll need to get them onto formula bottles, not straight onto cow's milk, or they won't be getting everything they need. Any weaning should be done after a chat to your health visitor or GP about how to replace the breast milk.

Self-weaning babies

British kids with parents who care have a fabulously varied and nutritious diet and access to plenty of yummy food and drinks. It's not surprising that many wean themselves. Try not to take it as a rejection or the end of close, good times with your baby.

You're still your baby's most favourite mum of all, and they shouldn't be made to feel they're doing the wrong thing when they tell you they're getting enough nutrition elsewhere and it's time to take your bosoms away. If your baby weans independently, feel exultant – you've done your job brilliantly. Self-weaning can happen as early as 8 or 9 months, although it's most common at about 1 year, but some babies will happily go on breastfeeding into their second year or longer. If you definitely want to continue after 8 or 9 months and your baby loses interest, you may need some strategies to continue (see "More Info" at the end of this chapter for breastfeeding support groups).

When you talk to your health visitor or GP about the self-weaning, they will be able to make sure your baby hasn't temporarily lost interest in breast milk because they have a sore mouth or some other physical cause.

Many babies wean themselves when their mum is pregnant with the next one. This could be due to the supply, the taste or other factors being affected by the mum's different hormones.

"I was devastated when my baby self-weaned very abruptly at 11 and a half months. I wasn't prepared for it at all." JILLIAN

"One day he just thought my breast was the funniest thing he'd ever seen and kept laughing when I tried to give it to him. I can take a hint." JULIE

"My baby self-weaned at 10 months much to my disgust and heartbreak!" FRAN

"We swapped for a tricycle." CHRIS, A GRANDAD

"He got a tooth and two bites later the breastfeeding stopped." LEANNE

"Follow the baby's lead." KELLY

"She cut back to one feed a day herself, eating more food so not wanting the breastfeed." MELANIE

Fast weaning

If you have to wean immediately or relatively quickly (over four or five days) for any reason you may spend a couple of days with rock-hard bosoms, wearing a one-size-too-small sports bra to "bind" them and standing over the basin in the bathroom a couple of times a night with a warm flannel compress, letting out just enough milk from each nipple to stop the painful pressure, but not enough to let your body think it still has to feed a baby.

The danger of fast or sudden weaning, apart from the possible shock all round, is that it leaves the breasts mightily engorged and vulnerable to blocked milk ducts and mastitis, so keep an eye on yourself. To help breasts during sudden weaning:

★ massage any lumpy bits

★ use warm compresses to let a little milk leak out to relieve the pressure

★ use cold cabbage leaves to help relieve engorgement

★ wear a tight bra, or a very tight shirt over a handtowel wrapped around your breasts – the pressure can help to relieve the pain and some milk can leak into breast pads or the towel.

"I expressed in the shower every morning, just enough to take the pressure off. I massaged my boobs during the day to push lumps out. Sometimes I leaked a bit in my bra. It took about ten days to be really comfortable and about three weeks for the milk to totally dry up." FIONA

"Freeze newborn-sized disposable nappies and put one in each bra cup. Initially (30 seconds) it's freezing, but after that it is pure heaven." JOHANNA

"I weaned my son at 4 months when he was admitted for surgery. I told numerous hospital staff (doctors, nurses, nutritionists, etc.) but no one told me how to go about it. I thought you stopped cold turkey. Even when my son was recovering in intensive care he refused a bottle for three whole days before finally giving in. This was the most horrendous way to wean a baby imaginable. I was very distressed (as was my baby) and was left with hard and painfully engorged breasts. No one told me how to relieve my discomfort or even seemed to care." ELIZABETH

Elizabeth's story above is so heartbreaking. It reminds me that we should all keep talking to each other about how we do various aspects of our child caring – not so we can give unsolicited advice with the assumption it will be taken, but to keep discussions going and to keep reminding people there is more than one way of doing something. Nobody should have to go through what Elizabeth did. I'm so sorry she didn't know she could ring any number of parent helplines and services for instant help and support.

Semi-fast weaning

Breastfeeding counsellor Margaret Callaghan says the following method, compared with fast weaning, is much kinder to you, your bosoms and your baby. It involves dropping one feed every four days and replacing it with a bottle feed.

★ On the first day of dropping a feed, express a little bit of milk until you feel more comfortable.

★ On the second day of dropping a feed express a little again if you are not comfortable enough.

★ On the third and fourth days don't express.

★ Then drop another feed, but not one on either side of the first one you dropped.

After the last breastfeed is stopped:

★ express on the first day to comfort level

★ don't express for the next 48 hours

★ express again to comfort level

★ don't express for another three days

★ express again, then don't for the next four days, and so on.

When you get down to only being able to get about 20ml from both breasts in total, you can "leave the rest to nature to reabsorb".

Marg says that when your baby hasn't had any formula before you wean, you're less likely to have the bottle chucked back at you if the first bottles you give them contain expressed breast milk, or half expressed breast milk, half formula. Gradually increase the ratio of formula until your baby's happy to have one hundred percent formula. (For the whole palaver about preparing formula milk see the next chapter, "Bottles".)

"I realised it would be much easier to wean them onto a cup and bypass bottles if I fed them till around 12 to 15 months. There seems to be a crucial point at which you can wean them and they'll forget about breastfeeding altogether, whereas friends who continued till the child was older, say 18 months to 2 years, found that even after they were weaned the kids still wanted to comfort suck."
MERONA

"Be prepared to get really clucky because your hormones go haywire." WENDY

"Have smaller bras ready for the deflation of your boobs."
KIMBERLEY

"After 3 days of not feeding I felt as though I had postnatal blues again and cried for a while – I guess my hormones were settling down. I wasn't expecting this." SARAH

Gradual weaning

Most mums who weaned gradually suggested dropping a daily feed – say, the middle of the day one – for a week, then dropping the late night one, then the evening one, then the morning one. This way you cut down gradually over a few weeks and the supply adjusts without your bosoms getting a fright. Many mums advised only giving the breast on request, apart from a morning or before-bed feed, then phasing those out too.

"All the books tell you to take it slowly ... it still hurts."
EDWINA

"Just before her first birthday I was feeding around four or five times a day. I decided to drop a feed every two weeks starting with breakfast. Instead she had 200ml of cow's milk. Then two weeks later I dropped lunchtime feeds and so on to the dinner feed. By her first birthday she was weaned onto three bottles of cow's milk a day." ALISON

"I weaned his early morning feed at 8 months, his lunchtime feed at 9 months, and his 4 p.m. feed at 12 months, and then his 7 p.m. feed at 13 months." BRENDA

"Try and drop the later feeds – you will still need to do the morning as your breasts will be full. Get Dad to handle bub during a normal feedtime." SUE,

"The cuddles continued, the closeness, the holding, so it was just the menu that changed." MYLEENE

"Unless there is a great rush, drop a feed every 2 weeks." CAROLINE

"I found that introducing a cup or sipper cup to my children at about 9 or 10 months helped them wean." LIBBY

"Basically I needed to have my body back." KATHY

"Late" weaning

Mums tend to agree that if you don't wean by about a year, either by baby's or mother's choice, it becomes much harder later as toddlers start to use the breast for comfort, often demanding a breast to suck or fondle in social situations when they feel a little uneasy and Mum least wants to participate. But of course, some mums are happy to go on and on.

Every mum who breastfeeds a kid old enough to walk, talk, get themselves a sandwich and have a chat on the phone, and tall enough to breastfeed standing up when their mum is sitting down, knows the disapproval and shock this causes. Some relish it and encourage their kid to do it as long as possible. Many regard it as an act of defiance against parents and parents-in-law, who see it as a discipline or social acceptability issue. Others are embarrassed and wish they could find a way to stop.

"Some people found me feeding a 2-year-old who hopped off the nipple to join the conversation quite disconcerting." SARAH

"At 18 months the poor kid was getting bruised cheeks trying to elicit moisture from my little breasts. It was obvious it was time to move on. From 12 months we were down to three to four feeds a day, by 18 months it was down to two a day. She was getting adequate liquid from a cup so it was really gaining the courage to accept my daughter was growing up, and being ready in my head to move to the next stage." LISA

"Cold turkey. He would have gone on until he was 18 given the choice." HELEN

"Don't talk to me about breastfeeding . . . mine was still having her 'booey-boos' at the ripe age of 3 and a half . . . I am very sorry to say that the little buggers make their own minds up before you have a say in it at all." PENNY

"I breastfed all four of my children until they were 2 years or more. I found it a beautiful way of mothering. They all weaned themselves when they were ready. They are all adults now but those years were some of the happiest." MARGARET

more info

MEDICATION AND BREASTFEEDING

www.ukmicentral.nhs.uk

Quick-reference guide for the effects of commonly prescribed drugs on breastfeeding and your feeding baby.

BOOKS ON BREASTFEEDING

Breastfeeding

by Sheila Kitzinger, Dorling Kindersley, 1998

Bask in the bosom of Sheila, birth and English mothering guru. Common-sense, rah-rah breastfeeding advocacy and lots of reassurance. A general reference.

The Breastfeeding Book

by William Sears, MD, and Martha Sears, Little, Brown, 2000

They're really into breastfeeding, but also have a great troubleshooting section, a guide to products (remember it's meant for the US, although a lot is relevant here) and a chapter on mums and babies with "special needs".

Breastfeeding and Bottle-feeding: A Easy-to-Follow Guide
by Naia Edwards, Vermilion, 2008
One of the few books to cover both methods of feeding in one book. Very useful if weaning from breast to bottle. Text has top tips in bite-sized chunks.

NCT: Breastfeeding for Beginners
by Caroline Deacon, Thorsons, 2002
Great little book from The National Childbirth Trust covering all the basics, with practical advice from trained counsellors and answering common questions offering help with expressing breast milk and advice on going back to work.

What to Expect If You're Breastfeeding...and What if you Can't
by Claire Byam-Cook, Vermilion, 2006
Written by a longtime London breastfeeding counsellor with practical advice to get breastfeeding going, and what to do if it just isn't for you. Includes info on feeding twins, expressing and weaning. Tends to be loved by women who've had trouble, and loathed by activists who think everyone should be breastfed.

NCT Breastfeeding tips DVD
Several mums talk about their individual experiences on breastfeeding and show how they overcame their difficulties.
Orders: 0845 8100 100 or www.nctsales.co.uk

BREASTFEEDING HELPLINES

Association of Breastfeeding Mothers
www.abm.me.uk
Helpline: 08444 122 949 (9.30am–10.30pm)
Telephone support from mothers who breastfed. Website offers a small range of leaflets and a noticeboard, as well as email counselling. Lists support groups nationwide.

The Breastfeeding Network

www.breastfeedingnetwork.org.uk

Supporterline: 0844 412 4664 (9.30am-9.30pm, 7 days a week)

Scottish Charity offering nationwide breastfeeding support. Its publications cover useful information such the storage of expressed milk, drugs in breast milk, mastitis and thrush. The website can help locate a breastfeeding centre near you.

La Leche League

www.laleche.org.uk

Helpline 0845 120 2918 (24 hours)

International charity and campaigning organization. Its website expounds on its mission rather than offers solutions to problems, although its online shop has instructional leaflets and DVDs.

National Breastfeeding Helpline

0844 20 909 20 (9.30am–9.30pm)

Government-sponsored helpline staffed by volunteers from the Association of Breastfeeding Mothers and the Breastfeeding Network.

National Childbirth Trust

www.nctpregnancyandbabycare.com

Helpline: 0870 444 8708 (8am–10pm)

Helpline will give immediate advice, or put you in touch with a local breastfeeding counsellor for a personal visit. The extensive website has an in-depth A–Z of common problems, and an online shop for publications and products.

BREASTFEEDING WEBSITES

See also the "Helplines" section above.

www.babyfriendly.org.uk

The website of the UNICEF Baby Friendly Initiative, a worldwide programme to encourage the health services to establish good breastfeeding practices. Lists hospitals and health centres with BFI accreditation. Comprehensive research archive, latest statistics and informative section for parents.

www.breastfeeding.nhs.uk

The official NHS line, but offers a good summary of basic techniques, all the support helplines, and useful links and downloads.

www.breastfeedingmums.com

Extensive site with instructional videos which can be viewed on-line (by "VideoJug", but we won't snigger about that). Blogs, Q & As, community forums with an approachable, non-evangelical tone. (Okay, I sniggered a bit.)

BOTTLES

While accepting that breastfeeding is the best possible start for a baby, it's very important to realize that in a developed country such as the UK, with its public health system and access to fresh, healthy foods, bottlefed kids are on a very good wicket indeed.

BOTTLEFEEDING IS YOUR OWN BUSINESS

If you decide to bottlefeed, for whatever good reason, it's important not to feel guilty about it. This is hard because of the constant pro-breastfeeding fanfaronade. Many studies have shown that kids who were breastfed are statistically less likely to get a range of illnesses, and even that breastfed kids "perform" better (I hope they brought their leotards) in IQ tests – but, to be honest, it very much depends on other factors as well, not least of them genes, lifestyle and access to good medical advice and educa- tion. Who sets the IQ tests and what do they measure? What about studies that don't repeat the result? Who paid for the study? There are too many variables to unravel the reasons for how smart children are. How do you measure intellectual curiosity anyway? Bah, humbug! Many breastfed children have allergies and asthma, and many bottlefed kids are absolutely brilliant.

These statistics are not about your individual baby in your caring family in your environment. If you've given breastfeeding a red-hot go and it doesn't work for you, move on. As I said in *The Rough Guide to Pregnancy and Childbirth*: look at the adults around you. Can you tell who was breastfed and who wasn't?

Good points about bottlefeeding

★ The kid always gets the same thing (breast milk varies in quality and taste according to a mum's health and diet), and you can eat and drink anything you like – curry, onions, a glass of wine – that would otherwise go through to the breast milk.

★ Someone else can feed the baby and enjoy the loving bond and eye contact.

★ You can sleep through the night while someone else gives the night feeds.

★ You know exactly how much the baby has drunk.

★ Babies tend to sleep longer on formula.

★ Your body is now your own again.

★ Most people find it easier to teach a baby to bottlefeed than to get the breastfeeding right.

Drawbacks of bottlefeeding

★ Formula can't supply all the goodies that breast milk does.

★ Formula's harder for the baby to digest because it forms a curd.

★ You have to sterilize bottles and teats.

★ You need to be careful with quantities and measuring, and it's easy to contaminate bottles. (Poor people in developing countries have made up formula with contaminated water or watered it down to save money, with predictably tragic results.)

★ A baby on formula does smellier poo.

★ Going out and travelling require more planning.

★ When you're away you're dependent on local water supplies and need to find somewhere to heat up a bottle.

★ It costs money.

★ It can take trial and error to find a good teat for your baby.

★ Formula is much more likely than breast milk to cause allergic reactions.

★ Bottlefed babies are more prone to constipation.

★ Some babies who are used to the breast reject the artificial teat and refuse the bottle for the first few tries: this is usually overcome by hunger and having someone other than the mum feed the baby. (The theory goes that a baby smells the mum and expects breast, if that's what they're used to, but they're more likely to realise they've never had any bosom action from Dad or Aunty.)

Many people who fear a lack of bonding when forced to give up breastfeeding are thrilled to find that, in the absence of stress and the faff about faulty breastfeeding, bottlefeeding is a tender time that can be spent quietly enjoying the moment, free from pain or worry.

"Don't let anyone make you feel guilty if you can't breastfeed. You can still maintain closeness with your child." WENDY

"I didn't have enough milk for my premmie baby and I was under a lot of pressure from health-care workers for him to put on weight. After realizing that he wasn't thriving at 12 weeks I tried a bottle on him and he looked at me with absolute marvel that I had finally given him a decent meal. It's a shame the breastfeeding wasn't a success as I really enjoyed it and am looking forward to trying again next time. I did find out from this, though, that I will never listen to the advice of people who are not directly involved with my children. I knew my son was hungry but I was told that I should never give up breastfeeding as it's the best thing for children. Didn't I try my best as it was?" AMY

Things you get from bottlefeeding as much as from breastfeeding

★ The baby enjoys the sucking reflex.

★ Intimacy.

★ Bonding with your baby.

★ The feeling that you're sustaining your baby.

★ The knowledge that you're doing your best for your baby and making sure they're as healthy as possible.

"I will not bottlefeed my baby in public because I get disapproving stares from other mothers who feel I am not giving my baby the best source of nutrition. When will society provide information to mothers who can't or choose not to breastfeed their babies?" AUDREY

equipment

Make some space on the kitchen worktop: you're going to need some stuff. A large pharmacy in an area where there are lots of kids should be able to give you good advice about available products. Remember that some shops will only carry one brand, but there are several brands to choose from. Chemists, some supermarkets and some baby shops will have the best range of bottlefeeding paraphernalia, including sterilizers.

Formula

The important thing to know is that there are plenty of people who make squerzillions of dollars out of formula, the upside of which is that they have a lot of employees working for their companies trying to make the best formula and get it as nutritionally close to breast milk as they can, with some extras such as iron supplements. Formulas, obtained at the chemist or supermarket, usually come in a big tin with a plastic pop-off top, a measuring spoon inside and instructions. Generally the tins are divided between formulas for babies under 6 months and those for babies over 6 months. After a year babies tend to come off formula and start to drink cow's milk, or a substitute such as calcium-enriched soy milk if necessary, as their solid food should be providing them with most of the nutrition they need. Toddler "formulas" sold in similar tins are really just vitamin drinks, not the whole nutrition package of a baby formula.

The instructions folded inside or printed on the side of the formula tin will tell you how much you need to give a baby of a certain weight or age (weight is always a better indicator as some babies are wee and premmie, while others are great hulking cuddlers). Follow the instructions carefully.

Some companies do a ready-made liquid formula. It's much more expensive and needs to be used within 24 hours of opening. Travellers or parents on the go may also like to buy formula sachets, which can be added to boiled cold water en route.

DON'T MESS WITH THE FORMULA

You must not try to second-guess dosages. Too little formula powder can result in hunger and distress; too much in an overload of calories and a tummy upset. You are not doing more for your baby by adding more, and babies should never be put on a "diet" of watery formula. Chucking in an extra spoon or putting in less than the recommended amount in the long term can make your baby very ill. Babies on properly prepared formula – or on breast milk – are never too fat. They are supposed to have those lovely jubbly rolls, or not, depending on their individuality.

And you must use a commercial formula made especially for babies. Do not ever try to make up your own formula by using cow's milk or soya or rice milk – or anything else. Your baby's life depends on it: babies have died when people with good intentions have made their own "formulas". It's not like the old days when a Dickensian crone mixed a bit of rice water and flour together to see if a baby could survive long enough to do a spot of chimney sweeping. Millions of babies have been brought up healthy on modern commercial formula. Have a look at the ingredients so you know what a complex lot are going into your baby.

WHICH FORMULA? It doesn't really matter: you can even pick the tin you like the look of best. Just make sure it's for the right weight and age of your baby. If your baby has been diagnosed by a GP or hospital consultant (not by you or a relative) as having an intolerance, you can use a special formula such as a lactose-free one or one based on soya or goat's milk. Ordinary formulas are based on cow's milk, but have a reduced salt content as a baby's kidneys don't cope well with salt. Formula has more iron and vitamin D than breast milk does, but this doesn't make it better than breast milk. (All babies over 6 months old need iron in their "solid" food or formula.) If you are opposed to genetically modified foods, check the label: this is most likely to be relevant to soya-based formulas. There are no animal hormones in formulas as they are destroyed by the manufacturing process.

Bottles

If your baby will need, say, six bottles a day (see the tin instructions), buy those and a couple of spares in case of emergency or loss. Get all the same brand so the parts are interchangeable. There's no point in buying tiny bottles – soon enough you'll be going

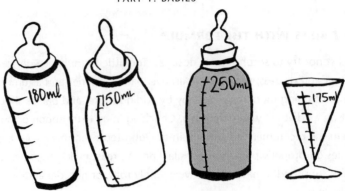

up to 250ml of milk so get the full-sized ones. Buy bottles with a wide neck as these are designed to reduce the air bubbles that can be gulped down and cause tummy aches.

Some research suggests that hot liquids can dramatically increase the amount of a harmful chemical (bisphenol A, known to have hormone-disrupting effects in animals) released by some plastic bottles. British health officials say the bottles are completely safe, although if you are concerned you can look for specially labelled "BPA-free" bottles.

Teats

Check out the age-related teats – there are ones with tiny holes for newborn babies, and ones with bigger holes that allow slow, medium and fast flows, with maximum flow for older babies. Also check teats regularly to make sure they don't have bits falling off, especially after your bub gets teeth. Buy as many teats as bottles plus a few extras.

Sterilizing equipment

You'll need the biggest saucepan or pot to sterilize the bottles, tops, teats and anything else that will touch the formula, plus some tongs to fish them out with. If you're going to be doing this for months or even weeks and you have enough money, buy a plug-in electric steam sterilizer. It looks like a big lettuce spinner and it heats bottles using water vapour to a high enough temperature to kill harmful bacteria. They come out wet, so you need to air dry them as well (a tea towel will be contaminated). Remember too you have to wash up the bottles first with detergent (or clean them in a dishwasher). There are also microwave sterilizers. For travelling or emergencies you can get sterilizing tablets to dissolve in water, but they make things taste nasty and chloriney.

Once a baby starts crawling around and getting a nice supply of immune-system-building germs, there's probably not much point in sterilizing everything that goes into their mouth – but make sure to use very hot water and detergent to wash out all dregs of milk.

Bottlebrush

Use this to scrub all traces of milk out of bottles, tops and teats before they go in the sterilizer.

How to make formula milk

The Department of Health has updated its recommendations for the making up and storing of formula milk. It advises that all feeds are made up fresh, with water at seventy degrees Celsius or hotter, since powdered formula is not sterile and there is a small risk of contamination if formula is then kept. In practice this means boiling a kettle and leaving it to cool for no more than thirty minutes, and throwing any unused formula milk away after two hours. Water needed for a later feed can be put into a sterilized flask or bottle for use in making up fresh formula when required. Since newborns are at increased risk from infection it is better to use commercially sterile liquid ready-to-feed products for premmie or low birth weight babies.

Look on the tin's label to see how many bottles a day your baby will probably need. Keep checking the label as your kid grows because they will need more formula milk. It will still be essential to get the proportions of water and powdered formula right as directed, but your baby will drink more of it – it's not like throwing a good-looking amount of cocoa into a glass of milk and stirring.

★ Sterilize all equipment – if you are using a saucepan for this, the water needs to boil for five (some say ten) minutes.

★ Boil a saucepan of water for making up the formula for five minutes, then let the water cool down.

★ Wash your hands with soap and wipe them on a newly washed towel.

★ When the bottle or bottles are cool enough, take them out of the saucepan or sterilizer, using sterilized tongs.

★ Fill a sterilized bottle with the number of millilitres of freshly boiled water recommended on the formula label (for example, to the 125ml mark).

★ Spoon in the exact amount of formula powder recommended on the label, using the measuring spoon provided. Scoop the powder up and then, without packing it down, level off the top with a sterilized knife. (You can just pour some freshly boiled water over the knife to sterilize it, if you like.)

★ Fit the sterilized teat through the plastic bottle ring using the sterilized tongs, then screw this combo onto the top of the bottle, and snap on the protective see-through bottle cap.

★ Shake the bottle until the formula is well mixed.

★ Immediately put the bottle in the back of the fridge so that it cools down as quickly as possible.

★ Keep all formula powder in the fridge once opened.

★ Warm a bottle just before you serve it. Prepared bottles should only be heated up once.

You might think it's nutty to waste time making up bottles as you need them. Some people have a night-time ritual where they sterilize the used bottles from the day in the six-bottle steamer thingie (which takes 10 minutes or less) or a boiling cauldron of some description. Then they make up the bottles for the next day, plus one with just boiled water in case they need to go out and make one on site somewhere. However, the Department of Health recommends throwing away unused formula milk after two hours so if you want to play safe then you'll have to budget for that extra time on a regular basis and follow their recommendations.

How to warm formula milk

Formula milk should be at body temperature when it's given to your bub – you can check by squeezing a little onto the inside of your wrist. If the milk feels cold, heat it up a little more and test again. If it's too hot, allow it to cool down and test again before giving it to your baby. The milk should be gently warmed up to the right temperature and should never be scalded, cooked or boiled.

The best way to warm formula milk is to place the whole bottle in a saucepan, bowl or sink with hot (not boiling) tap water up to about the level of the milk in the bottle if possible, and then let it sit for a few minutes. Shake the bottle gently or turn it upside down once or twice to distribute heat through the milk, without causing bubbles – or let any bubbles subside before testing.

AVOID THE MICROWAVE Heating a bottle in a microwave isn't a good idea: it can lead to hot spots in the milk. If using a microwave is unavoidable because no hot water is available, make sure the milk is left to stand for a minute, then turn the bottle upside down ten times (rather than shaking it as that will create air bubbles). Test the milk's temperature carefully: the formula should feel tepid, not warm or hot.

Never give a bottle without testing the temperature. It can be a good idea, in case you're ever caught short, to give a baby a bottle that is not really cold but not quite tepid either. If your bub is used to this happening occasionally, it will increase the chances of them accepting a colder bottle, warmed under your arm, in an emergency.

"My firstborn was a premmie and couldn't suck. My milk didn't even 'come in'. Both of my children were lactose intolerant so they had to have a special formula." TRACEY

HOW TO BOTTLEFEED

★ Sit down comfortably, holding your baby in one arm. You may want to "balance" your baby on one or two pillows (holding onto your bub all the time!) to bring them up higher: this can be particularly helpful in the early weeks if you've had a Caesarean.

★ Support the baby's head and neck.

★ Tickle the baby's cheek to make them open their mouth.

★ Hold the bottle on enough of an angle so that milk always totally covers the inside of the teat to make sure the baby is sucking milk and not air.

★ Let the baby suck at their own pace, resting as many times as they'd like during the bottle. (Sucking is hard work when you're new at it, or if your parent has put on a teat with a too-small hole for your size.)

★ Immediately the baby has had the last drop of milk, gently disengage the teat from their mouth with your little finger so they don't suck on air.

★ After a pause in the feed or at the end, put a tea towel or a muslin over your shoulder and, letting it hang down your back in case of a little vomit, hold your baby upright, looking over the covered shoulder, and rock and pat them until there's a burp (or not). The theory is to stop that "wind" from causing pain.

"When I was ready to bottlefeed the twins – for me it was about 3 months – I put each baby in a rocker/bouncer and sat between them with my back resting against the settee and a bottle in each hand and off we went. It took the stress out of listening to one baby cry while I fed the other and it was a real milestone for me."
JENNIFER

"Make it a quiet time to cuddle and enjoy rather than have the TV blasting." SUE

The sleepytime bottle

Older babies who can hold their own bottle still shouldn't be left with one to leisurely suck on when they go to bed. Give the bottle in another room, then put it away. Do something else such as washing your baby's face or reading a story before finally going through the sleepytime ritual in the bedroom. Otherwise when you want to wean your baby, this bottle part of the nummy bedtime tradition will be hard to give up. Bottles that kids carry around and drink over a long time contribute a lot to tooth decay as the milk swishes against the teeth for ages.

"I found my baby slept better through the night as the formula is thicker and fills tummies better." SHARON

Transporting formula milk

Because warm milk is a breeding ground for germy nasties, it's best when you're out or travelling to heat a bottle right before a feed rather than carry a warm one around with you like a Thermos. No more than two hours before you need to use it, take a bottle from the fridge, wrap a bottle in ice or a cool pack from the freezer and a tea towel, with a rubber band around it (you might want something more groovy-looking such as a wine insulator), and place it upright in your handbag or baby bag.

In case of hunger spurts, an accident to the bottle or the original bottle being rejected (if you've already heated it once, you can't reheat it), you could take an extra bottle with just the right amount of sterilized water and add a sachet of formula (according to the sachet instructions) when needed. Because a sachet is always the right amount for a big bottle, pour some of the made-up milk out until it's the right amount if your baby is very young. (A few sachets could be left in the baby bag at all times, just in case.)

You'll get used to asking café kitchens to sit a bottle in a saucepan of hot water for five minutes – always with the cap on to protect the sterilized teat. If people are reluctant (very unlikely), smile sweetly and say "Oh come now, you really don't want this baby screaming with hunger in your café, do you?".

"I would fill a bottle with quite hot (sterilised) water, put the right amount of dry formula into another, wrap the water one in a tea towel, then, while I was shopping, when my son was ready for a bottle the water had cooled to the right temperature. Saved me from having to get a shopkeeper to heat the water for me." KARYN

TROUBLESHOOTING

If you need help with bottlefeeding, your first port of call should be your health visitor. (See also "More Info" at the end of this chapter.)

Constipation

This sometimes happens when bottlefed babies are little or you've just made the switcheroo from breast milk. Also check you're not putting in too much formula powder. A small spoon of sugar in the bottle is an "old wives' cure", and shouldn't be used regularly.

Diarrhoea

This is most likely caused by a tiny speck of unclean milk or other agent contaminating the milk – or it has nothing to do with the milk. Step up your cleaning and sterilizing procedures. Also make sure your formula is not too weak and watery. (Look up "diarrhoea" in the index.)

WEANING FROM THE BOTTLE

As your baby gets close to 1 year old, talk to your health visitor about when's a good time to cut formula milk out.

As when weaning from breast to cup, those baby cups with a detachable spout top, and a straw for later, are good to start your kid on, before they graduate to a cup with one or two handles. It's also not a bad idea to teach your baby to drink from a small bottle of water or juice with a pop-up top, or even from a spill-proof bottle of water, such as still mineral water, that can be resealed. This gives you more options when you're out and about. Don't take milk drinks around with you – they spoil quickly and are more likely to result in hideous cleaning-the-vomit-in-the-hot-car scenarios, not to mention very-bad-bus-incidents.

"I changed from a bottle to a non-spill cup at 18 months (or I'd do it earlier) before they became emotionally attached to the bottle." KATRINA,

"One night she went to sleep without her bottle and didn't wake during the night for it, so I just stopped giving it to her and she didn't miss it." RACHAEL

"My child thought he was a very big boy using a cup, not a bottle." KIM

"By accident I gave the 20-month-old the newborn teat. He threw it at me. I did this again and he did the same thing, so I thought he no longer wanted the bottle, just his cup . . . I finally realized but I had gone this far so I just left him with his cup." HEIDI

It's not necessary to give a child fruit juice if they eat lots of fruit. And juice, because it lacks fibre, shouldn't be substituted for bits of fruit. Juice should usually be diluted with water by fifty per cent as the acid can attack tooth enamel. Watch out for commercial juices in little packs with a straw attached – some are chock-a-block with sugar and many other dubious-sounding things with numbers instead of names (look up "drinks" in the index).

"The more pressure I put on myself to breastfeed the worse I felt, and in the end I put my babies on formula and never looked back." JEANETTE

> *"I was worried to tell the nurse that I had decided to bottlefeed, and she was wonderful."* DONNA

> *"I cried for a year because I 'failed' [to breastfeed] and it was such a waste of energy!"* JOANNE

more info

See "More Info" section on p.92 for books covering bottlefeeding.

messageboards.ivillage.co.uk
Friendly and sympathetic advice from other bottlefeeders. Search on "Bottlefeeding Support". As always, things internetty can get internutty in chatrooms and forums so don't take any advice as gospel and always check their info with your doctor.

www.nhsdirect.co.uk
Gives the medical and emotional factors involved in bottlefeeding.

www.smanutrition.co.uk
Careline: 0845 776 2900
Site for makers of infant formula milk SMA. It has some useful information on the nutritional content of formula milk, and a good outline of bottlefeeding and sterilizing procedures.

Bottoms

Suddenly you need to deal with someone else's
bottom. A baby can go through six to eight
nappies a day (that's nearly sixty a week). A toddler
just before toilet training will have perhaps three to
four a day and, once toilet trained, some kids may
still need one at night until they're 4 or older,
especially if it's a long, cold trip to the loo. About 95
percent of nappied bots in the UK are swathed in
disposable rather than cloth nappies, according to the
Environment Agency. That could be 5000 to 8000
disposables per child in two and a half years.

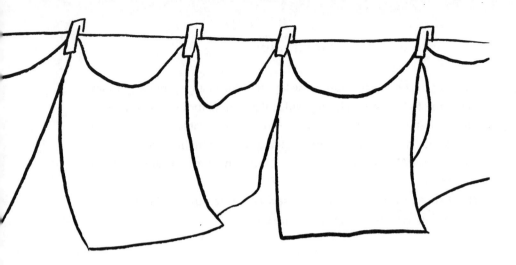

HOW OfteN BaBies wee

All babies are different but generally really new babies wee a lot – often more than 24 times a day in the first six weeks. Most are little wees. A slightly older baby wees in larger amounts about every three hours, in between each feed, and has quite pale wee. If yours doesn't, they could be dehydrated (look up "dehydration" in the index): give them fluids and see a doctor immediately.

CLOtH Nappies

Cloth nappies are usually flat-weave cotton (always used for newborns) or more absorbent towelling.

Good points about cloth nappies
★ They're reusable for first and subsequent kids.
★ They're the cheapest option, after the initial outlay.
★ Clean ones can be thrown over shoulders to catch baby vomits or turned into rags when finished with.

★ They get uncomfortable more quickly so toddlers are more likely to want to use the toilet, although they will still get there in their own time.

★ Nappy-wash services will take away dirties in a sealable bucket each week and reissue you with clean ones, making the cost higher than for disposables (see "More Info" at the end of this chapter to locate a service in your area)

★ The first few weeks of nappy-wash service is sometimes paid for by friends, relatives or colleagues as a present.

Bad points about cloth nappies

★ They require *far* more labour.

★ Soaking and washing them is an unpleasant, tedious task.

★ They need to be washed with antibacterial chemical washing powders and in hot water, and if poo-stained they need bleaching products to look non-skid marked. Polluted water is the by-product. And if they are dried in a dryer, they also use a lot of electricity.

★ They require folding.

★ A couple of days' worth of nappies can become a seething, space-munching, stinky monster in your laundry, which you have to deal with because you're running out of clean ones.

★ It's hard to cope unless you have a whizzbang washing machine and dryer. Although front-loading washing machines use less water and so are better for the environment, they're a lot less suited to soaking and washing loads and loads of nappies, not only because of their lower capacity but also because you usually have to squat down to drag out heavy, wet loads.

★ Cloth nappies are slightly trickier to fasten.

★ They require plastic overpants (sometimes bizarrely called "pilchers") to stop leaks, and these need to be thoroughly rinsed, soaked in something antibacterial, rinsed again and hung out to dry or, in an emergency, towel dried. (It may seem obvious to some, especially those who aren't sleep deprived, but don't put placcy pants in the dryer.) Plastic pants can lead to hotter and rashier bots.

★ If you have to take your washing to a laundrette, I really think using cloth nappies is asking way too much of yourself – most laundrettes won't let you wash them there anyway for health and hygiene reasons.

Choosing cloth nappies

You'll need:

★ about 30 to 35 nappies

★ about six to eight plastic overpants – newborns can dispense with these as their volumes of wee are small

★ a decent supply of paper liners (in some cloth nappy systems)

★ fasteners: either plastic snap-on ones or antique-becoming safety pins

★ rubber gloves

★ a special plastic spatula or brush for scraping off poo

★ two big nappy-soaking buckets with close-fitting lids kids can't get off (to avoid accidental drowning)

★ bleach and antibacterial soaking powder

★ a washing machine with a hot function

★ antibacterial laundry detergent

★ lots of clothes-line space and fine weather or a big clothes dryer (clear the lint after each load because it's a fire hazard)

★ two waterproof undersheets for the cot (one for the wash, one on the bed).

DiSPOSaBLe NaPPieS

Good points about disposables

★ They're stupendously more absorbent so don't need to be changed as often and cause fewer rashes. The nappies' absorbency means wetness is drawn away from the skin.

★ They're much less fiddly to put on than cloth ones.

★ Because the bot stays much drier, the baby sleeps longer.

★ They're ready to go from the packet – no folding required.

★ You don't have to deal with the contents of the nappy – just put it in a plastic bag and bin it. (When the big poos start you're supposed to put the contents in the toilet.)

★ According to the industry itself around eighty percent of a disposable nappy – and its contents – is biodegreadable.

★ The sticky tabs that fasten the nappy can be reused so you can check a nappy quickly and refasten.

Bad points about disposables

★ They're expensive, and cheaper brands are usually not as absorbent.

★ They add hugely to the problem of rubbish. Two and a half billion are sold in the UK each year, contributing two to three percent of household waste, according to the Environment Agency.

★ Most disposable nappies contain chemicals to make them absorbent: the long-term effects of these chemicals next to the skin are unknown.

★ Even buried biodegradable nappies will take hundreds of years to decompose, and the plantations used for the nappy material may be taking the place of old forests.

★ Disposable nappies get more expensive as the baby gets bigger.

★ You have to empty inside bins often as the discarded pooey nappies are stinkeroo, and by the end of the week the outside bin is pretty tough on the nose to say the least; deodorised plastic bags to put dirty nappies in cost extra and add to the waste problem.

★ Because nappies take up so much space on shelves, many small shops don't stock them, and supermarket shelves can be depleted if just four or five parents want the same brand as you do on the same day: you may have to ask an assistant to get you some from the storeroom.

★ You can sometimes see little squishy balls in a wet disposable nappy, that's absorbent crystals leaking out: just wipe them away and change the nappy.

Choosing disposable nappies

You'll need:

★ two packets of the right-sized nappies (the size is marked on the packet). Some brands have different ones for boys and girls – something to do with the spouty effect of a willie no doubt – but in a shopping emergency it's not a big enough difference to matter

★ two waterproof undersheets for the cot (one for the wash, one on the bed).

CHOOSING BETWEEN CLOTH AND DISPOSABLE NAPPIES

A report from the Environment Agency comparing the environmental impact of cloth nappies (both home and commercially laundered) and disposables reached the surprising conclusion that there was very little difference between them. Critics say that the sample on which this was based was too small and based on inaccurate assumptions regarding the behaviour of nappy users (washing at ninety degrees, for example). However, no one can dispute that cloth nappies produce less landfill, and so local authorities in large cities, for example, which are under particular pressure for landfill space, are still promoting the use of cloth nappies with a voucher system or other incentive scheme to be used against your first purchase. Personally I think if you have even a hint of feeling overwhelmed or depressed after having a baby the cloth nappies should be metaphorically the first thing out the window, then the housework. (I don't mean you should live in a tip, just that you should try to lower your standards and get lots of help.)

Your decision will probably be based on your philosophy – all have an environmental impact. It is useless to try to argue that disposable nappies, cloth nappies or more children are good for the environment. But it is also useless to argue that a disposable nappy is anything but a boon to parents and babies. They are far and away better than a cloth nappy and that's why they're now so much more popular. The only two reasons not to use them are philosophical and economic: both very sensible reasons. (See "More Info" at the end of this chapter.)

If you want to use cloth nappies, that's fine – but not a word to individuals, letters to newspaper editors or columns, or calls to radio phone-in about how everyone else should too. No one is in a position to judge what other people need to do to get by and be kinder, more cheerful parents.

It seems to me that women at the most stressful time of their lives shouldn't be taking the blame for environmental pollution, or being turned into drudges because corporations haven't got the biodegradable thing right yet. It's worth thinking about what women (it's almost always women) have to do if they have to use cloth nappies day after day: scrape poo of all colours and descriptions into the toilet; then cart the nappies to the laundry and soak them; then wash them in hot water and washing powder; then drag the heavy, wet nappies out and peg them on the line, praying for good drying weather, or run them through an electricity-sucking dryer; then get them down from the line or out of the dryer; then fold them; and then do it all over again a grizillion times.

One way to rationalize choosing disposables is to say that our water is becoming increasingly precious, whereas we might find a better solution to landfill: oh, I know it's not a perfect solution, but then I'm not a perfect mother. If anyone slags you off about using disposables and ruining the environment, ask them if they'll do the washing. Ask them if they have any idea how much water and how many pesticides are used to make cotton fabric. Then ask them if they ever ride in cars.

If they still give you a hard time, hit them gently on the nose with a rolled-up newspaper, or try a firm, stern, disapproving voice and a water pistol.

And as for those women who wash nappies themselves for years, and I'm utterly serious about this: what's the point of having a New Year's Honours List if they don't get a medal?

WHeN to cHaNge a NaPPy

Change your baby's nappy when you smell the poo or feel the wetness. Check it every now and then, and change it if there's been any action, even if your bub is happy. Nappies should be changed promptly, no matter how super-absorbent they are.

Babies can sometimes do a wee or poo straight after you've changed them: never assume they're dry because you only changed a nappy five minutes ago. A baby, especially one in a cloth nappy, may cry to let you know it's wet and uncomfortable.

A nappy can be changed when a baby is asleep. This prevents the nappy being really wet and nasty when the baby wakes up later.

If you are in someone else's home, double-bag your disposable nappy and take it home with you. Needless to say cloth ones shouldn't be left behind either: peuwww.

How to change a nappy

Keep within reach of the changing table or the bench or table you use for changing nappies:

★ new nappies

★ baby wipes or cotton-wool balls, and other bot-cleaning needs such as baby lotion or tepid water

★ a barrier or nappy-rash cream if required

★ a lined bin or other container for the used nappy

★ clean clothes for the bub.

Lay your bub on the changing table, always keeping a hand on them. Open the soiled nappy and clean the baby's bot with a baby wipe or cotton-wool balls dipped in baby lotion or tepid water. Throw away the baby wipe or cotton-wool balls and put aside the soiled nappy. Pat or air dry the bot. Many people also use baby powder or smear on some babies' barrier or nappy-rash cream before fastening the new nappy. Deal with a pooey cloth or disposable nappy as soon as you're free to do so but don't leave the bub alone on the table while you go to the bathroom, laundry or rubbish bin.

If the baby has done a ballistic poo, give them a bath after a thorough wipe down.

Nappy rash and skin irritations

Nappy rash is most common in older babies who spend long hours at night in nappies. Some people say cloth nappies are better for preventing nappy rash because they allow more airflow, but most people agree disposables draw the irritating wee away from the skin more. Heat and moisture create a great rash environment. An allergy to washing powders may also be a cause of nappy rash.

When washing your bub, use a soap substitute (soap is very drying) on the bot bits; and use baby wipes that contain an oil or lanolin but not alcohol. A barrier or nappy-rash cream will protect the baby's skin from the worst irritation caused by

FREE THE BOTS

Whenever possible – say, when your baby is lying on a rug inside, with a towel folded underneath, or outside under a shady tree or umbrella – let their bot run free and give them a rest from the heat and padded feeling of a nappy. But don't put a baby in direct sunlight because they're likely to end up with sunburn as well as nappy rash (look up "sun care" in the index).

wee. Let the bot run free as much as possible, and be vigilant about changing a nappy as soon as you can after your baby has a wee or poo.

OH my goD, it's someone else's poo

Yes, well, just make sure you don't talk about it to other people unless they ask. There's nothing worse than a parent banging on about their offspring's poo unless it's to another interested or gobsmacked parent, I say. If you must know, here's a rundown (sorry).

- ★ Breastfed newborns can poo six to eight times in 24 hours, and this can go on for up to three months.
- ★ Breastfed babies can happily go a week without a poo, but bottlefed babies have a poo once or twice a day.
- ★ If the baby cries when pooing, the poo is hard, there's blood in the poo or there's any other poo worry, see your health visitor or doctor.
- ★ Breastfed baby poo is that classic orangey "baby poo" colour; surprisingly it doesn't smell too bad.
- ★ I am sorry to say that sometimes baby poo is green, and I don't know why and I'm not going to ask. All I know is it's not a problem and I'm happy to go with that.

★ Bottlefed baby poo is usually bigger, browner and smellier than breastfed baby poo. Constipation is not unusual when you switch to a bottle.

★ See your GP if diarrhoea – frequent, watery poos – goes on for longer than 24 hours. (There's more info in the "Health" chapter in *Part 4: Stuff*; look up "diarrhoea" in the index.)

★ Huge, stinky poo? Your child is now on solids, possibly meat.

Oh, what a charming and whimsical way to end a chapter! Do pass me a martini, Lady Georgina, and we'll stroll down to the ornamental ocean.

MORE iNFO

www.realnappycampaign.com
Helpline 0845 850 0606
Tips for reducing the environmental impact of real nappies, and help sourcing a retailer and nappy-wash service in your area. It does describe home washing as a breeze, though... which isn't true for everyone.

www.which.net
The website of *Which?*, the independent consumers' magazine, has stats on nappies and their effect on the environment (search "Nappies").

www.environment-agency.gov.uk
Access the full report on Life Cycle Assessment on the use of Disposable and Reusable Nappies in the UK. Heavy duty reading.

THROWING UP

Baby books call baby puke "possetting" because it sounds so much more refained, dahling. Usually throwing up happens straight after a feed or in the middle (or during burping). If milk is vomited later, it can be partially digested and smellier. Parents and carers get really used to this and usually have a tea towel or muslin over one shoulder for a year or so.

Most of us have unwittingly gone out with baby puke down our back. And we'll never know how many of the non-initiated we freaked out. A woman once said to me "And then her baby threw up on me and I realised, euwww, that was just in her breast a minute ago. Yuuuuck." If she thinks that's yuck, thank heavens she hasn't had any dealings with green poo.

WHY DO BaBies THROW UP?

A baby usually vomits because all the bits of their digestive system aren't in fool-proof working order yet. Or because they drank too much milk at once (they're still learning how to take the right amount). Repeated throwing up associated with what seems to be a rejection of the milk can indicate an intolerance and in any case can be very tedious for all concerned, so if you're sick of sick see your health visitor or doctor.

iNSOUCiaNt Vomiting

The state of mind of some babies can best be described as la, la, la, happy, happy, enormous vomit, la, la, la, happy, happy. In other words, there is a kind of vomiting the baby doesn't mind in the least, and which poses no threat to anything but your patience, ambitions to wear something without chuck on it and the warranty on the washing machine. It's annoying but not actually a problem for the baby unless they're losing weight because they're vomiting up lots of food (when you hear "food" in relation to a baby under 6 months, it really just means breast milk or formula milk). Most babies vomit a tiny bit when burping.

Some babies also seem to be on a hair-trigger and vomit if they choke slightly on some milk, or later on solids, or someone puts a finger too far into their mouth to check for teething action. It makes perfect sense for babies to be quick to vomit in this way as nature is preventing them from choking. I know a baby who is like that. The only doctor who listened to the mother's warning is the only one who doesn't put a depressor on the baby's tongue to check her throat, and is consequently the only doctor not to get utterly chucked on every time.

BaBies WHO THROW UP a LOT aND CRY (ReFLUX)

Some babies cry a lot or are unsettled – find it hard to get to sleep or stay asleep – because they have a valve problem in their oesophagus that means milk rushes back up from their tum, causing heartburn-like pain. Sometimes it rushes up so regularly that the baby seems to constantly vomit a lot after each feed. This condition is called "reflux", or gastro-oesophageal reflux disease (GORD) to give it its medical term.

It's important to remember that lots of babies throw up a bit after each feed, but it doesn't mean they have reflux. Reflux needs to be medically diagnosed before being treated.

If your baby is diagnosed with reflux, a breastfeeding counsellor can help you learn to feed with the baby held somewhat upright rather than lying down – bottle-feeders can try the upright possie too. A refluxing baby will probably prefer smaller feeds, more often. Medical treatments include thickening agents in formula; anti-vomiting drugs (which seem to be out of fashion due to doubts about whether they make much difference); and heartburn preparations: ask your doctor. (See also "More Info" opposite.)

more info

www.askbootshealth.com
High Street chemist Boots has teamed up with the *British Medical Journal* to bring together all the relevant research on reflux in its health directory.

www.littlerefluxers.co.uk
Snappily named support group for carers. Parent forum and listings of local groups.

www.reflux.org
The gastro-oesophageal reflux site for US parents. Has frequently asked questions, parents' stories, discussion groups and links to other sites.

SLeePiNg

The sleeping habits of a newborn baby are perfectly

logical and sensible – unless you're not a newborn baby,

in which case they're completely and utterly insane. And

luckily temporary. Babies usually wake up when they are

hungry, which is far too often because they have such

tiny tummies. They really should stay in the womb for

longer and do the umbilical thing, but then they'd be too

big to come out in the time-honoured fashion.

Ape babies are carried by parents until they learn

to swing from trees themselves.

The babies can sleep any time

they need to, wake up for a

breastfeed or to check out a

leaf, and then fall asleep

again when it suits

them. Unfortunately

there is no research

on whether this makes the parent apes put the peanut butter in the freezer, sob hopelessly on occasion and sometimes wonder whether they could leave the small apes at a café and get the next flight to Freakoutistan.

your baby's attitude to sleep

All babies are different. Experienced maternity nurses tend to be able to spend some time with a baby and know whether they're a sleepy, placid bub or an alert sort of a little tyke who will always fight sleep. You'll need to get to know these things too because your baby is probably not an exactly average sleeper – so any sleeping strategies from a textbook or "sleep clinic" will have to be tailored to you and your bub, usually by a bit of trial and error and time expenditure.

"I don't want to take a 'nap', goddamnit. I want to SLEEEEEEEP!" ME, AS A NEW MOTHER

newborn sleep facts

Newborn babies will go to sleep just about anywhere. Once they're asleep they're initially very deeply asleep, then they have peaks of being easily roused before going into deeper sleep again.

Some babies are born with a pregnancy-induced pattern of being soothed to sleep while you're walking around (amniotic bouncing) and waking up when you're still (asleep). That's why lots of people end up rocking their baby in their arms, pushing a pram backwards and forwards, borrowing or buying some kind of bouncy, thing for their baby to sleep in during the first few months, or driving around aimlessly in a car trying to get the baby to sleep.

Newborns love to hear a heartbeat. If you don't mind them sleeping in a strap-on baby carrier, you can do other stuff – but this is not the answer if you need to sleep when they do, early on. Do get the best one you can so the weight is distributed properly across your shoulders, back and waist: your baby will get heavier all the time (look up "baby carriers" in the index).

Don't worry about being tight-lippedly strict about routines in the early days. (Come to think of it, that's probably to be avoided at any stage.) But if you want to, it doesn't hurt to start heading towards some sort of pattern to make more sense of your days, as long as you know it goes out the window on the whim of a newborn and almost always in later days if a baby or toddler is sick. (See "More Info" at the end of this chapter, and the "Possible Routines for Babies" chapter.)

Baby Sleep Patterns

In the first 6 months the "average" baby wakes two to three times a night, then between 6 months and 1 year they wake one to two times. Most babies after 6 months will be having one long stretch of sleep, perhaps six to eight hours, and will be getting sufficient milk during the day and evening not to need a night feed. It's good to try to manipulate this long sleep to last until the dawn or early morning feed. Most babies over 6 months will have a morning and afternoon nap, and then just the afternoon nap from whatever age it suits them – say, 10 months, 3 years, 4 years or 5 years. Depends on the kid. Older baby and toddler naptimes usually range from about 45 minutes to two and a half hours. I reckon they often sleep longer when they seem to be having a growth spurt and eating more too. Others have observed that babies learning to crawl get more restless in bed.

What a Baby Needs to get to Sleep

Your baby may need a few or all of the following elements:
   ★ a quiet wind-down time

- ★ a feeling of comfort and safety – often a firm tucking in or swaddling (ask your midwife or health visitor how to wrap a baby for sleep). But don't swaddle a baby who seems to detest it: that's your little individual!
- ★ a dry bottom
- ★ a full tummy
- ★ a ritual – words, pats, music, swaddling
- ★ a blackout blind
- ★ a dim night-light.

"Tips to encourage sleep? Read them the **Financial Times.***"*
TOM

Ritual

Remember, though, that babies can get hooked on the back pat or rub, the soothing music, the dummy, Mum or Dad lying down with them, or a breastfeed or a bottle. This may be fine with you or it may pose difficulties now or later.

SIGNS OF BABY TIREDNESS

✴ droopy eyelids

✴ the slow blinks

✴ stiff and jerky movements, like a clockwork figure

When the baby is a bit older, add:

✴ rubbing their eyes

✴ pulling their earlobes or hair

✴ hyper-style hysteria or aggression

✴ mood swings

✴ clingy behaviour

✴ the long-distance blank stare

✴ whingy and irritable

✴ yawns.

✴ going to bed and getting in (well, you can hope).

DO NOT DISTURB

A bedtime routine for an older baby can include a story, a catchphrase – "Sleep tight, I love you", "Sweet dreams, my little farter" (maybe not) – and a firm but loving exit.

Products

Many baby gear shops have a full range of moses baskets, cribs, travel cots, bassinets (cribs on wheels) as well as other bouncy things for settling a baby, although not necessarily settling them to sleep (the "Equipment" chapter in *Part 4: Stuff* has all the info on safety requirements). Remember that a baby that's used to sleeping only in a bouncy bed will require a few days to adjust to a flat cot.

There are mail-order products and sleep techniques offered on the Internet, but geez, Louise, some of these are as shonky or what? Do be careful about what you send money away for – you're almost certainly better off talking to a real person on the phone or face to face, or getting one of the books mentioned in "More Info" at the end of this chapter.

Sleepy music

Most sleepy music for bubs has a picture of a sleeping baby on the front. Often it comes as two CDs or cassettes, or CDs only. I'm convinced that in about ten years a generation of young adults will be easily and instantly hypnotized by Brahms lullabies. Some say any old drifty classical music will do; others insist the magical ingredient is a beat that's like the human heartbeat. Some babies like the white noise of an electric fan or other machine. A rug or curtains will make a room quieter – fabric soaks up sounds while hard surfaces bounce them around. (See "More Info" at the end of this chapter for some CD titles.)

A blackout blind

It's a big call – I don't usually say anything's essential unless it involves a health or safety issue. But if you want your baby to get as much sleep as possible, my sister-in-law Emma gave me the best tip ever: get yourself a blackout blind or curtain – not just a dark or heavy one, but one that doesn't let in a line or chink of light from outside. (I'd say paint the window black and nail it up, but light and fresh air are good between naps!)

The expensive version involves pelmets on the top and sides of the window, a blackout roller blind, and heavy curtains lined with blackout material on each side to stop light creeping around the edges of the roller blind. For a cheaper version, get a regular roller blind, attach it a little above the glass, put a wooden Venetian blind above that or tack on a wide piece of heavy cardboard as a pelmet – anything to stop light spilling in around the top of the blind. Put loops of masking tape or a pliable adhesive (look, we're not mentioning any brand names but one rhymes with Flootack) around the bottom and side edges of the blind, and stick it to the window frame or wall to cut out all light. Pull curtains across the edges.

A blackout blind means your baby isn't up with the dawn, when the outside light changes, unless you have really loud birds outside or that's when they insist on waking anyway: no doubt it's what lots of humans are programmed to do.

Scottish newborn-nurse Gina Ford also recommends an elaborate curtain system in her *The Complete Sleep Guide for Contented Babies and Toddlers* (see review in "More Info" at the end of this chapter): she is so strict about this that she "will not take a booking unless the nursery has both curtains with a blackout lining and a special blackout roller blind". Ooh, my gawd.

If there's a handyperson in your life, this can make them feel they are con-tributing something crucial. If you haven't a handyperson, use your life savings to get the window covering up to blackout standard. Those extra hours of sleep are worth it.

Kids will usually go to sleep in the afternoon in a dim, not black, room but may wake up earlier if they're in a lighter, unfamiliar place. Take blackout fabric with you when you and your baby are away overnight.

A night-light

Lots of kids like a dim night-light that throws out a consistent light so they can see if they wake up. It also lets you see to feed at night. Don't put it near your baby's head – under the cot, or any other spot where it will be as diffuse as possible, is good. Most hardware shops sell a light (about the size of a double adaptor) which can be plugged into a socket, or look in baby shops for a kiddie-themed one. A dimmer switch can also be used for low light.

make a safe, familiar sleeping place

Subject to safety considerations, your baby's bed in the early days can be your bed, a moses basket, a specially designed carrycot that snaps out of a pram, or a cot. For the first couple of months many people sleep with their baby, who then graduates to a cot. Other babies are still co-sleeping at toddler stage or moving on only when a new baby is taken into the parental bed.

Okay, let's get the stern, rulesy bits out of the way: babies must never be left alone in a car, even if they're sleeping peacefully, in case of overheating or theft. Babies in a locked car can overheat and die in a matter of minutes even on a seemingly mild day – you may be unavoidably delayed. Apart from this, a baby in a car seat can droop their head too far forward – for most babies this won't matter, but a very few can cut off their air supply and not be able to revive.

Always put the baby somewhere safe for naps, such as their own cot: it will be familiar and they may resettle themselves if they wake up rather than be startled, and if you fall asleep or are somewhere else you won't have to worry about them getting lost under, for instance, a sofa cushion.

In case they wriggle into a suffocating position, babies should not be put to sleep and then left alone out of sight in a pram, a stroller, an infant car seat (either in the car outside or brought inside), or a couch or a chair.

It's dangerous to leave a baby sleeping unsupervised in an adult-sized bed: they can become tangled in adult bedding, wedged between the bed and the wall or caught under a pillow; they can also roll out and fall at an earlier age than you think.

Makeshift sleeping environments are dangerous, and the Foundation for the Study of Infant Deaths (FSID) say that it is safest for babies to sleep in a crib or cot, with their feet to the foot of the cot to prevent them wriggling down further under the covers. Don't make adjustments to prams, beds or devices not designed for babies to actually sleep the night in. Follow construction and operating instructions exactly.

Bed safety requirements

It's best to buy a cot that conforms to British Standard EN 716 (look up "cots" in the index). Basically a cot needs to have the bars spaced at the right intervals – not so far apart that a baby can be trapped between them. It should have a tight-fitting mattress. If at all possible get a new mattress made from cotton or another material that "breathes" rather than hard foam. The cot should also have cotton sheets and cotton cellular blankets, but no duvet until the baby is 1 year to 18 months old.

It's better to heat the room a little bit in winter if you can afford it; otherwise use light woollen blankets. A lambskin underneath the baby is a nice idea unless the room gets too hot; they are machine washable (but not meant for the tumble dryer). Cot "bumpers" restrict the flow of air in and around a cot, and babies can get their heads stuck underneath them. Any waterproof undersheet should be a plastic-backed fitted cotton one so the baby doesn't get too hot. Spares of everything are important in case of a washing emergency (although towels can be substituted during a bedding shortage). Babies don't need pillows and they're not recommended until at least 2 years. (Older kids move around so much in bed they're often off the pillow too: it's not a problem.) If you use pillows and other foofery to "dress" the cot and make it look nice, take it all out before the baby goes down to sleep.

CO-SLeePiNg OR SLeePiNg aPaRt

In an effort to snatch as much sleep as possible, parents often choose to sleep with their baby in their bed so they don't have to get up to crying or for breastfeeding (although they need to wake up enough to change nappies). For the same reason (maximizing sleep) many parents choose to have the baby sleeping near the bed in a moses basket or crib. Others have the baby sleep in a separate room and get up whenever summoned by a cry in the night. Any of these options is a legitimate choice. One is not necessarily better than any other, and it is very annoying to have people rudely insisting that you do what they did with their children. The important question is "Which suits *us* better, co-sleeping or sleeping apart?".

Proponents of co-sleeping insist that "babies sleep better" and "mothers sleep better". If you like the idea and this seems to be true for you, then go for it. It certainly seems to make sense, especially for mums who have had a Caesarean, unless someone else gets up and brings them the baby for feeds and cuddles each time. And it must be easier for some single parents.

But in my case if my baby was in the bed I woke up so many times in response to the tiniest snuffle, and had so many experiences of a recurring nightmare in which I had lost her under the duvet, that to continue would have led to madness. I started to sleep better when she was in her own cot, and the nightmare went away. So co-sleeping isn't for everyone. (I recently read, to my surprise, an account of virtually the same recurring dream experienced by another mother: as usual, any thought you have as a parent is unlikely to be unique, no matter what you believe at the time.)

People who go to bed drunk or drugged, smoke or have a disorder that makes them sleep very heavily should not sleep in the same bed as a baby because there is a higher risk of suffocation or sudden infant death syndrome (see the earlier "Newborn Worries" chapter). Some studies show a higher SIDS risk when babies are in another room, some show a greater risk when babies are in bed with a parent, particularly if the babies have a respiratory illness at the time. Co-sleeping or not co-sleeping is still a personal choice that isn't supported one way or the other by medical advice and it depends on your individual situation. A baby's cot or moses basket right next to your bed is a middle ground if you're worried about sleeping too heavily or rolling on the baby. (Co-sleeping fans say parents always sleep lightly enough to wake if this happens – which sounds like a possible recipe for sleeplessness for some.)

An unattended baby in a bed is always at risk even if their parent hops out for only a moment or so.

your young baby wakes constantly

Some babies, especially ones who sleep with their mum, can train themselves to take little bits of milk, often, at the all-night milk bar lying next to them, which means that instead of feeding every few hours, the mum has to wake up every hour or so for snack-time. And some babies are picked up whenever they make a little cry or snuffle during the night, which is quite normal behaviour for babies. Instead wait and see if they'll settle themselves, and always try to soothe them back to Dreamland, with a soft word or ritualized pat. Of course if it's the usual time for a feed, they probably won't settle. Even with their baby in the next room, some mums have to wear earplugs to cut out the little snuffles, grunts, sighs and snorky noises in the night. If the baby definitely needs some-one or is really awake and needing attention, the noise is quite different – and louder. And even through the earplugs most mums hear the sounds first and are out the door before the dad is aware of the slightest noise. Here's a brilliant suggestion I heard: reverse the baby monitor, if you have one, so the baby can hear their parents snoring or chatting (but perhaps not doing erotic folk-dancing practice). This means you can't hear the little grunts and snuffles, but you'll hear them yell out if they really want you.

Developing a pattern for night and day

Help your baby understand daytime and night-time. Night-time feeds should be a sleepy, quiet, darkened affair, with no play and straight back to sleep. Daytime feeds can be animated and chatty, with a play afterwards.

"Never wake a sleeping baby"

Generally it's a good rule. If the baby's asleep, they probably want to be. Certainly never wake a sleeping baby at 2am for their usual feed – this may be the night they drop it! Yes, but what if it's the 11pm feed they sleep through? If you let them stay asleep and go to bed yourself, the baby may wake at 12.30am for a feed. I reckon you should wake the baby up at 11pm, but expect possible dreadful grumpiness.

What if the baby is asleep in the car and you have to go inside? Take the baby. What if you need to move your baby from pram or baby car seat to cot so they can keep sleeping and you can get on with something somewhere else? Put the baby in the cot (or safely on the floor) every time, but try to be so gentle that sleep isn't much disturbed.

Hints for more parental sleep

Sleep when the baby does: forget housework and take the phone off the hook if you need sleep. Of course you need sleep. You have a baby. (Unless you have a 24-hour live-in nanny and a weekend nanny and go to the hairdresser every day to get your hair "do", in which case you wouldn't be reading this book because you'd be getting your 24-hour live-in nanny to read it while you had Tumultuous Mauve painted on your fingernails by someone whose name you don't know.)

You may find yourself getting hysterical when your baby is just a few days old, and sobbing that there's no point in going to sleep if you only have to wake up in two to three hours for another feed. If you're anything like me, you'll be a lot less hysterical if you take all the catnaps you can in those early days.

If you have a partner or flatmate, get them to do half, or some, of the night feeds (using expressed breast milk or formula). Also get them to settle the baby to sleep sometimes so the baby doesn't demand you every time.

I know it seems obvious, but there are some things you can do or not do to get a better sleep. If you sleep better with your baby in the bed, do that; if you sleep more deeply with them elsewhere, do that. Avoid stimulants such as coffee, tea and cigarettes, and a cocaine habit. Drink warm milk with honey in it, have your own rituals such as a warm bath, make your room dark, make rules about other people being quiet if you need to; wear earplugs. Taking sleeping tablets is *not* a good idea for the same reason that you must not sleep with your baby if you're drunk or stoned, and because they will go through to your milk if you're breastfeeding.

You may find you need to readjust to sleeping through the night once your baby decides to!

Daytime Naps

Some people say day sleeptimes shouldn't be unduly quiet so the baby learns to sleep through any noise. Really it depends on the baby. At certain times in their sleep babies can sleep through anything loud, but a sudden noise such as a slammed door will always wake them at other times. You may want to put a sign on the front door asking people not to ring the doorbell or knock (there's a sign on the following page you might like to photocopy). You'll probably need to also ask people if they would call beforehand to get the go-ahead for a visit. And why not unplug the phone when your baby is asleep? The result will be the baby sleeps as long as possible, and so will you. And quite frankly unless you're expecting Johnny Depp to pay a call, what could be more important right now? ("Johnny! Take off your trousers! Now fold that washing!")

Sleeping Through

This is the holy grail: the baby finally drops a feed between 12am and dawn so they sleep through from an hour or so before midnight to six or so in the morning, to take a random example. Be aware that a baby might do this once and then not again for days or weeks. The first sleep through is often a big surprise to the parents, especially a breastfeeding mum with explodey-feeling bosoms. If the baby is old enough to be getting all the milk they need during the day, sleeping through can be encouraged by having a non-lactating person go in to the baby to try to settle them without a feed, although perhaps with some cooled boiled water in a sterilized bottle. (The baby is supposed to think "Oh perlease, water instead of milk, how boring, I'm going back to sleep".) If the baby goes back to sleep without minding, it can herald the start of sleeping through. Your health visitor a book on sleeping (see "More Info" at the end of this chapter) will help you with likely routines at various ages (see also the "Possible Routines for Babies" chapter).

Helping a Baby Learn to go to Sleep By Themselves

Basically your baby will adjust to whatever bedtime or naptime ritual you decide to use. Many people develop one unconsciously, although this might not end up being the most useful one for them; for example, exhausted mum breastfeeds, then baby and mum flake out on the bed together, and so baby only learns to go to sleep when mum is there.

When babies are little you must always go in to comfort them if they cry or call out: only nutty, fundamentalist, baby-disliking theorists would dream of recommending that a baby should be left alone in a cot to cry, without your patting or soothing them, before the age of 6 months. But it is good to be able to comfort a baby back to sleep without picking them up. (Of course they may have done a particularly irritating poop and need to be changed.)

The usually recommended way to help a baby get to sleep on their own is some sort of variation on the following.
- ★ Have some wind-down time.
- ★ Wrap your baby firmly, but not too tightly.
- ★ Pat their back or bot gently, with a slow rhythm, a few times until they're sleepy.
- ★ Place your baby to sleep on their back.
- ★ Give them a dummy if you want to.
- ★ Leave the room before they actually fall asleep.

You can train your baby over time to understand that they are being put to sleep by themselves (always in a darkened room, with a comfy temperature, familiar smells

SHHHHH!
PLEASE

DON'T KNOCK OR RING BELL

BABY ASLEEP

COME BACK LATER
OR
LEAVE MESSAGE IN LETTERBOX

THANKS

© *The Rough Guide to Babies and Toddlers*

and blankies, a comforting back rub and the same catchphrase such as "Nightie-night, possum"), but that you'll return reassuringly if they need you so that they realize they're not being abandoned. The idea is to get the baby to realize that it's safe and fine to go to sleep by themselves in their own bed without your being there, rocking the side of the cot for ages or breastfeeding them to sleep. It will go a long way to setting up good habits that you will be grateful for later.

The key is that after comforting rituals, the baby is left in the room calm, happy, safe, hopefully sleepy, but still awake, and learns how to go to sleep independently without your obvious presence so that if they wake during the night and don't need a feed they can go to sleep again without your help.

Yes, I know it sounds like an impossible dream when you're in the mad, sleep-deprived early weeks. It isn't, but I fully admit I was in a tizz and to get the hang of it had to go to a day-visit sleep clinic at four months, and then we needed to refer to a book to practise. After we learned some patting and settling techniques, our baby could go to sleep herself, knowing that if there was anything wrong she could yell and someone would respond to her.

There is an exultant joy in having a baby who can wake up and then happily settle back to sleep. In our case it eventually took the added assistance of a dummy and a loop tape of classical music, but it worked. (At least until the tape slowed down and started sounding like the Eeyore Boys Choir and then broke.) If you are consistent (and lucky), your baby will be happy with the arrangement too.

Think of it as you and your baby learning together. And if another way suits you, then for heaven's sake use that. It's just that most people eventually don't want to have to rock their baby to sleep or breastfeed every time, or lie down with their toddler until they're asleep and then again if they wake up during the night.

Your health visitor can help you with establishing or altering routines. If you feel the problem is more deep-rooted than this or you're really desperate, or has got too far out of control, you can ask your health visitor or GP for a referral to a specialist sleep clinic (variously called "sleep studies units" or "sleep disorder clinics", which are run as weekly classes or live-in programmes by some NHS hospitals. Some accept self-referrals but there can be a waiting list of around a month. Many more sleep clinics are private, with varying philosophies and approaches – you can self-refer if you're paying yourself. If you have private health insurance, first check out if you are covered for this (sleep "problems" can be subjective). Also look for informal advice on one of the parent forum websites listed in the first and second chapters of this book, and in "More Info" at the end of this chapter, which sometimes helps to put crisis moments in perspective.

"Controlled crying" or "controlled comforting"

Most babies will cry when you're trying to get them to go to sleep by themselves. "Controlled crying" and "controlled comforting" are the terms used for a structured way of getting these babies to sleep without a parent. They're the same thing, only controlled crying sounds a bit scary and controlled comforting is what you want to feel you're doing. It's not recommended that this approach be tried on a baby under 6 months old: talk about it with your health visitor if you're unsure when or how to begin. Basically some time is spent letting the baby cry and some spent comforting them. The aim is to slowly change the sleeping habits of your baby if these are disrupting family life or driving you bonkers.

The approach is to reassure the child that it's time to go to sleep, institute the ritual and then retire to outside the door while they yell at you. Depending on whose theory or book you follow you wait, say, thirty seconds, then go in and reassure them again and resettle them. The next time you stay out for one minute, then progressively make the margin wider – but never longer than five or ten minutes. A baby left to cry for a long time will wind up being very distressed.

While practising this routine, parents will often sit in the corridor looking at their watch, crying and taking turns not to let the other one in until the right number of minutes has elapsed. Sole parents really need someone to help: it's much harder for them, I reckon.

The people who subscribe to the attachment parenting theory (described in the "Parenting Philosophy" chapter in *Part 3: Parenting*) think that controlled crying is cruel because it teaches babies not to expect comforting on demand (look up "attachment parenting" in the index). Others say that babies need help to understand how to put themselves to sleep, that it's kinder to teach them how to go to sleep instead of getting constantly overtired and distressed, and that this can be gradually achieved without actual trauma.

This may be one of those times when you start to learn to distinguish the kinds of crying: heartbreakingly sad, outraged or trying it on (see the next chapter, "Crying"). Sometimes it can be really useful to have the help of an outsider, who can be kind but more dispassionate (and is less shatteringly sleep deprived). Often the attitude of the baby is "Well, all right, I can see the way this is going, I might as well go to sleep". Many people achieve this when they attend a sleep school or parenting centre as a last resort.

The baby can have changed habits in as little as three or four days: possibly three or four traumatic days, with a bit less trauma each passing night until there's none.

The *Secrets of the Baby Whisperer* author and maternity nurse Tracy Hogg doesn't believe in letting babies cry; she takes up to two weeks to train them. She says some-times on the first night a baby will have to be laid back down to sleep many, many, many times, but then it's always less the second night and so on until the problem is solved. (Mind you, those parents in her book had Miss Tracy in their house for days on end helping. So you'll need to be strong when it becomes your time to change a baby's habits.)

You *can* change your baby's habits

No baby's sleeping habit is set in stone: quite often a difficult habit happened by acci-dent. It's important to know you're not stuck with it. Even very ingrained habits can be changed gradually – some within a day or so, some within three weeks. I'm not saying this is easy or that a person should be expected to do it alone. It takes loving firmness and lots of patience. This means the baby will be very cross occasionally but never afraid or desolate: there's a big difference. It means you as a parent have to take control rather than letting chance or a confused baby impose a way of life that doesn't work for you and is therefore not good for the baby either.

"Use an association with sleep other than yourself or any other person, for that matter: sheepskin rug, doll, musical toy. Must be carried everywhere so make sure it's not the size of an elephant." KAREN

"Make sure they're full and if not settled after having a dry nappy pat them on the bottom until their eyes start to droop, and repeat if they stir." ANITA

"For me a baby's sleep routine was when they wanted sleep. The old tired signs of rubbing eyes, yawning and generally getting grumpy work if you can catch them at the right time. But if all else fails be a sucker mum like I was and rock your baby to sleep: you never know, you might like it . . . if your child needs a cuddle or a story or just someone to be there then so be it. Enjoy that. They will only be little for a small amount of time." CHERRIE

"I found putting the newborn into the older siblings' routine to be the best way, especially for afternoon naps and bathtime." TRACEY

"Kids love consistency, consistency, consistency. My baby actually sighs with delight and relief when she is tucked in and usually lets us know (loudly) when we are running behind time." HAYLEY

"Be flexible! Accept from the start there is no such thing as a baby routine . . . Baby Number 1 slept from 6 pm to 5 am from 6 weeks and still needs 10 hours' sleep at age 6. But he refused to sleep during the day for more than 20 minutes: no time to get anything done. Baby Number 2 used to sleep all afternoon and stayed up until 11 pm. Baby Number 3 woke at 11 pm, 2 am, 4 am, 6 am, for 5 minutes at a time. All three now go to bed on their own."
ANONYMOUS

"I hardly ever went anywhere in the afternoons so she could sleep. She is now 3 and still having an afternoon nap and I still haven't got a life. It worked for me!" BERNADETTE

"Despite all the anti tummy sleeping, this is all my baby would settle with. I kept him on a firm mattress with a fitted cotton sheet, no bumpers, no covers, and checked on him constantly. At night we'd turn him onto his back once he was in a deep sleep."
PURINDER

"In the first six months we adopted the seemingly usual routine of a relaxing bath, large bottle of formula and then 'restfully' pacing up and down his room till he fell asleep, then gently placed him in his cot – and ran like hell to get out before he woke up! It nearly killed us. So much stress, his awful incessant crying – we ended up at a family health clinic to learn controlled crying and establish a sleeping pattern – which thankfully has worked wonders." ALIYAH

more info

SLEEPING BOOKS

If the situation's not urgent, see which one of the books below might fit your style. Some of the titles in "More Info" for the first chapter "In the Beginning" have sections on sleeping. Tracy Hogg's *Secrets of the Baby Whisperer* advocates a gentler, slower form of "controlled crying" tailored to your baby's personality, and calls babies left to cry "Ferberized" (after the author of *Solve Your Child's Sleep Problems*, below). Penelope Leach talks less sneeringly of the pros and cons of "family beds" rather than "co-sleeping". Here's six books: one will suit your approach.

Sleep Tight, Sleep Right: A Practical, Proven Guide to Solving Your Baby's Sleep Problems
by Rosey Cummings, Karen Houghton and Le Ann Williams, Doubleday, 2008.
Written by hands-on staff at an Australian parenting centre. They know how to help parents, usually mums, and overcome crying and sleep problems, among other things (problems often come entwined). A wonderful book, with routines, and charts if you want them (including a terrific one-page sleep chart for newborns to 1-year-olds), simple troubleshooting answers to lots of sleep-related questions and some great settling and calming ideas.

Silent Nights: Overcoming Sleep Problems in Babies and Children
by Brian Symon, Oxford University Press, 2004
Written by a doctor who has made sleep difficulties his speciality. An easy-to-get-into book that identifies problems and possible solutions, starting from earliest breastfeeding and the first 6 weeks through to toddlers and special disruptions such as daylight saving, moving house, relatives who sabotage your routine and first nightmares. At the stricter end of the scale.

Solve Your Child's Sleep Problems
by Dr Richard Ferber, Simon and Schuster, 2002
Dr Ferber is the director of the Centre for Sleep Disorders at the Children's Hospital of Boston in the US. He's against co-sleeping and is known in the US as the "controlled-crying guy". This dense book, with annoyingly small type, also covers night-time

carry-ons, bad dreams, how daytime naps can help night-time sleeping and how to get past night-time feeding.

The Complete Sleep Guide for Contented Babies and Toddlers
by Gina Ford, Vermilion, 2006
More from Britain's routine queen from birth to 3 years old. Case studies and a "how to" of controlled crying. While she never advocates leaving a baby to cry without first assessing its needs, her stern approach may be too difficult for some.

The No-Cry Sleep Solution: Gentle Ways to Help Your Baby Sleep Through the Night
by Elizabeth Pantley, McGraw-Hill Contemporary, 2002
A third way between letting babies cry themselves to sleep and becoming a sleep-deprived martyr. Helps you review and choose sleep solutions, create your own sleep plan, and gives you a few tips for better sleeping yourself. With sleep charts, plans and routines.

Three in a Bed: The Benefits of Sleeping with your Baby
by Deborah Jackson, Bloomsbury, 2003
The standard text of the co-sleeping brigade. All about why, and not much on how. If you decide to "co-sleep" check SIDs guidelines too, at *www.fsid.org.uk*.

SLEEP CLINICS

Some NHS hospitals run sleep clinics, but you might need a health visitor or GP referral. Ring NHS Direct on 0845 4647 to find out if there is one in your area.

SLEEP WEBSITES

Many of the general baby and parenting websites listed in the "More Info" sections for "In the Beginning" and "Your Support Team" also have hints and forums on sleeping issues. Remember that material on co-sleeping is usually written by devotees.

www.askbaby.com
Informal advice on settling the baby, how to cope with sleep deprivation and helping you understand baby sleep patterns. Good summary of various sleep training methods. Also has a comments section on blackout blinds.

www.eyecatcher.tv

Follow the links for Keeping Kids Healthy to order the NHS video/DVD *Sweet Dreams*, used by health visitors to address sleeping issues for babies over 12 months. The Sleep Advice page allows you to access clips from the video.

kidshealth.org

This US website's article on "Co-sleeping and Your Baby" lays out the pros and cons of the co-sleeping debate in a neutral fashion.

SLEEPY MUSIC

Most big music shops have baby-soothing selections.

Baby Sleep

Erato 1997

Soporific classics with stuff by Bach, Tchaikovsky, Satie and the like. No thrash metal, though.

Sleep Easy Baby

EMI Gold 2007

Renowned jazz fusion artist John McLaughlin aimed to write something suitable for inducing sleep in babies that the parents wouldn't want to stamp on. Draws on the canon of traditional lullabies set to folksy acoustic guitars and mellow xylophone sounds, with jazz and world music influences. *zzzzzzzz...*

CRYING

Newborn babies have only a few ways to communicate: the most useful one for them is crying. You might like to regard this as a design fault. If only they could scribble little stick-on notes to let us know exactly what's going on. Babies are used to being in the womb, minding their own business and hanging out at the Umbilical Cord Café, when suddenly they're thrust into a world full of touch, taste, smell, sound and light, with a digestive system that has never had to work this way before. Everything they see, hear, taste, smell and feel is new, every second of the day. No wonder they burst into tears every now and then, especially at the end of the day. The very experience of living is an overload for those first few weeks. The

baby is not crying because you are a bad mother, or an

incompetent dad, or a lousy babysitter.

The baby is crying because the baby is a baby.

THINGS A BABY'S CRY MIGHT MEAN

Don't feel that you should be able to automatically interpret a baby's cry. In the first few weeks and months, a baby's cry can sound the same, yet mean ◉ I'm hungry ◉ I'm too hot ◉ there's a weird feeling in my nappy ◉ I'm all floppy and I used to be snug ◉ that was a scary noise ◉ I'm grizzly and a bit cranky ◉ I'm annoyed ◉ I am bloody furious ◉ is everything okay? ◉ stop waking me and poking me and picking me up ◉ if that's my grandmother, let me out of here ◉ my sister stood on me when you were out of the room ◉ where's that nice smell I'm used to? ◉ I'm tired but I don't know what tired means ◉ I'm tired and I don't know how to go to sleep ◉ I just found out about Britney Spears ◉ there have been too many new feelings and sounds today ◉ ouch! ◉ I'm not used to doing this so I don't like it ◉ I'm scared in the bath because it's floaty but I'm not scrunched up ◉ there's something wrong with me and I can't tell you what it is ◉ my tummy hurts ◉ what the *hell* is THAT? ◉ something squishy is coming out of my bottom ◉ I need a cuddle ◉ I was just checking one of my people was nearby ◉ I'm tired and you keep picking me up instead of letting me go to sleep ◉ pick me up! ◉ I don't know why I'm crying – it's just everything seems so overwhelming sometimes.

Possibly helpful hint
Baby development expert Lise Eliot says a hungry cry is likely to be "rhythmic and repetitive", an angry cry is "loud and prolonged" and a cry of pain is "sudden in

onset, punctuated by breaks of breath holding". Gina Ralston, crying-baby expert says "Most cries sound the same, but the behaviour gets more predictable". You will get to know each other over time.

Crying peaks

"They" say there's a crying peak at about 6 weeks old, and some of these "theys" say there's one at 8 weeks as well. Don't panic if your baby suddenly seems to cry a lot. If you've ruled out a hidden illness, it's quite possibly just a phase, like a mysterious growth spurt that makes them need more milk more often than usual. Being with a baby is about constant little shuffle readjustments.

Babies who cry a lot usually cry even more towards the end of the day, and even some otherwise placid babies do too. This is what's known as "arsenic hour". It can really bring everyone to the end of their tether and often coincides with the partner who works outside the home coming back to scenes of utter despair. I sometimes wonder if it's babies just being fed up with all this new word business late in the day: sensory and neurological overload. I think I'd cry too. Come to think of it, I did cry every day during arsenic hour for the first couple of weeks: big, tired tears – not hysterical, just quiet, exhausted ones.

> *"It's okay to let a baby or child cry for a little bit. If it is the worst that happens to them in their life, then they are very lucky."* KAREN

tHings tHat might stop tHe crying

There are lots of things you can try to stop the crying when it happens.

- ★ Food: is a feed due? Or could the baby be needing extra? (Careful: they might just be over-full, in which case only time and comforting will help! I don't know how you tell the difference either – unfortunately it's trial and error, which takes time.)
- ★ Sleep: is the baby overtired and needing help to go to sleep?
- ★ A nappy change: the baby might have a wet or pooey bot.
- ★ Security: the baby, if under 4 months, might like to be wrapped up snugly to remind them of womb living.

cuddle me!

leave me alone
(no, don't)
(oh, I don't know)

I'm cross

shall I cry?

I'm not tired

feed me!

ouch!

I can't remember
why I'm crying

I couldn't be
more shocked

where's my teddy?

...Sounds like...

I saw a great
big DOG

145

★ **Soothing:** the baby might just need a pat, a cuddle or a dummy.

★ **A carry:** the baby might want to be carried around so that they can hear a heartbeat like the one that ticked away near the womb – a strap-on baby carrier, or older children, can save your arms.

★ **A quiet time:** the baby might be in sensory overload and need to be away from visitors and busy places.

★ **Someone else:** everything may have gone into a vicious circle, with you being tense and the baby being tense – after you've tried for hours, a baby may be quite suddenly comforted by someone else (don't feel too demoralized by this, it happens to us all!).

★ **A big burp:** the baby may have tummy ache and need to have a burp or be comforted until the pain subsides. Hold the baby upright and gently pat or rub their back. Prevent the baby from swallowing air when they feed, especially likely if you're bottlefeeding: hold the bottle so the milk, not air, covers the inside of the teat as the baby sucks. If you're breastfeeding, take note of any foods you've eaten that seem to cause windy problems.

★ **A medical check:** the baby may have a medical problem – have your baby checked out by your local doctor.

★ **A gentle massage with an edible oil:** most people avoid nut oils in case of allergy (look up "baby massage" in the index).

★ **A lullaby:** your voice, no matter how untuneful, is very soothing to your baby. You can even read an adult book aloud, as long as it isn't Stephen King or anything else spooky that makes your voice sound worried.

★ **Quiet music:** CD stores have lullaby compilations.

★ **Time in a pram:** this might even just be being wheeled back and forth, although fresh air is a bonus for both of you.

★ **A warm bath:** babies often enjoy a deep one with a hands-on adult.

★ **Rocking:** this can take the form of a trip in the car, jiggling the cot or a go in a safe and secure bouncer.

★ **A comfy temperature:** a room somewhere between eighteen and twenty degrees Celsius will be fine. This doesn't mean you need to strictly maintain a "perfect" temperature in your place. After all, millions of babies are brought up in the tropics and the Arctic Circle. (Actually I don't know how many babies live in the Arctic Circle. Possibly I mean moose.)

★ **Fewer clothes:** a lot of babies are overdressed. For little babies a general rule is one more layer of clothes than you need yourself as you move about.

★ **A daily routine:** after the first weeks naps at customary times can prevent a baby from being regularly overtired (see the next chapter, "Possible Routines for Babies").

And as the baby gets a little older:

★ distraction, distraction, distraction. Older babies' moods can change in an instant. "Look at those vastly interesting pillowcases flapping on the line!" "Look, wicked old Aunty Beryl's making a hilarious noise!" "What is that funny face Mummy is making?" "Let's look in this book, check out this rattly thing here, play and chat with your older brother/sister/ cousin/passer-by at the bus stop."

It may take a while but, unless your baby is in pain or sick, you can build up some strategies that work for you. It's a matter of trial and error.

Some people reckon babies should be picked up straight away if they cry because otherwise they get distressed and then it's harder to settle them again. Others say leave babies to cry for a minute or two. One thing to keep in mind is to try soothing methods other than picking up every time (singing, rocking, a comforting voice, a rhythmic pat) as your baby may just need to know you're there so they can go to sleep happily. If you pick them up every time, they can get very irritable because they're not getting a chance to sleep or lie about.

Newborn babies need to sleep a lot. Respect this, and don't try to keep them up all day entertaining visitors, no matter what the visitors want. You're the one who'll end up with the wound-up, blubbering flummery bub at the end of the day.

Crying problems and sleeping problems are almost always tightly linked, so have a look at the previous "Sleeping" chapter and don't hesitate to get professional help to set up a sleep routine or learn settling techniques.

BaBieS WHO CRY foR HOURS (OtHeRWiSe KNOWN aS CoLiC)

If nurses and doctors can't find anything wrong with a baby who cries all the time, the diagnosis is usually "colic". What does this mean? That you have a baby who cries all the time. Some people find it comforting to give the problem a name. There's no "cure" for colic, but it's a diagnosis that says it isn't the parents' fault, they simply drew the temporary short straw and got a "colicky" baby.

Generally colic is supposed to be a digestive problem – a pain in the tummy that causes a baby to make a screamy sort of cry – which generally lasts for two to four months depending on which book you read or, more to the point, what sort of baby you have.

Medical suggestions for colic include preparations that are supposed to reduce wind and, as a last resort, sedatives: see your doctor. Off-the-shelf herbal remedies are not a good idea because they are not formulated for babies. If you feel it's hard to know where to start, contact one of the parent services listed in "More Info" at the end of the second chapter, "Your Support Team".

Babies who vomit a lot as well as crying may have a physical problem called reflux (look it up in the index).

"Difficult" Babies

If you have checked out all the possible causes and your baby still cries, keep in mind that you have done everything you can – everything a good parent could do. Your baby may be a "crier", also known as a "difficult" baby. This doesn't mean that your baby is naughty or trying to be difficult. (Happily a "difficult" baby can grow up to be a strong, resilient person who can stand up for themselves.) It just means you'll need some longer term strategies to cope in the next weeks or months – the most important being to rustle up as much help and babysitting as possible to give yourself breaks.

Getting some help

I used to ring up for professional help quite a bit when I felt bamboozled – no doubt I would have been less bamboozled if I could have had more sleep. I'm sure sometimes I sounded completely mad: luckily they're used to it, and nobody ever minded a bit. And there's no such thing as a silly question when you're learning to be a parent. Others have found their

HELP!

mothers' group or playgroup very useful for sharing stories and strategies (and providing babysitting swapsies).

If you can afford it or wangle it, get some child care, either from a professional or a friend or relative, so you know there's respite coming. Even if someone calls in every evening for a while and holds the baby so that you get some things done or go for a walk (try a rota system!), it can be crucial time out. (See the "Coping Strategies for Parents" chapter in *Part 3: Parenting*.)

And if you're absolutely distraught and frightened that you might shake, hit or harm your baby in some other way, see the suggestions for dealing with these feelings (look up "rage" in the index) and get help because this situation will probably happen again.

If you need help now, call one of the specific parent helplines (many run 24 hours a day) listed in "More Info" at the end of the second chapter, "Your Support Team". That's also where you'll find contacts for parent services, which provide counselling, classes in settling and sleeping and residential stays. You can also contact your health visitor or your GP.

WHICH BABIES CRY?

* Babies in stressful homes cry.

* Babies in calm homes cry.

* Babies with good mums cry.

* Babies with good dads cry.

* Lonely babies cry.

* Babies who are never left alone cry.

* Smart babies cry.

* Sick babies cry.

* Healthy babies cry.

* Babies at about 6 weeks cry (for up to an hour and a half).

* Babies who are carried around by their mothers in slings all day in small African communities cry.

* First babies cry.

* Second and subsequent babies cry.

* Safe babies cry.

* Babies who grow up to be delightful children cry.

* Babies of self-assured parents cry.

* Babies of nervous parents cry.

* Babies of child-care experts cry.

"Controlled crying"

"Controlled crying" – the approach of letting babies cry over set periods – is described in the previous chapter, "Sleeping". Only people who care more about theory than real babies suggest using it for babies under 6 months. That doesn't mean you are helpless against the crying before 6 months. Try the strategies already suggested, look at the specialized books given in "More Info" at the end of this chapter, or call one of the parent services.

the Bottom Line about Crying

If a physical problem is ruled out, your baby's temperament is the biggest factor affecting whether they cry a lot. It has nothing to do with your skills or aptitude as a parent. You can learn tricks that may help. Do everything you can, but treat yourself with special kindness. Don't try to do it alone: traditionally babies have been brought up in gigantic extended family situations, with lots of help and a collective approach. Besides, when you're sleep deprived, you sometimes can't see solutions, and that isn't your fault. Above all, take it day by day. This hard time will end.

more info

All the baby-care books in "More Info" at the end of the first chapter, "In the Beginning", address crying. The following books are also very helpful.

Understanding Your Crying Baby: Why Babies Cry, How Parents Feel and What You Can Do About It
by Sheila Kitzinger, Carroll and Brown, 2005
Characteristically caring from the lovely Sheila. Practical hints for mums, and importantly dads, with insightful explanations.

100 Ways to Calm the Crying
by Pinky McKay, Lothian, 2002
Dear Pinky is an Aussie mum and baby fancier who has written a baby-friendly book that looks at the reasons for crying and a range of simple, possible solutions to each kind of crying without having to use the controlled crying approach.

The Fussy Baby Book: Parenting Your High Need Child From Birth to Age Five
by William Sears, MD, and Martha Sears, Harper Thorsons, 2005
The US gurus of attachment parenting weigh in with their kid-friendly approach (look up "attachment parenting" in this book's index for more on the theory). Like Pinky McKay, they don't recommend controlled crying.

Gina Ford's *The Complete Sleep Guide for Contented Babies and Toddlers* (see p.140) also has a how-to of controlled crying for babies over 6 months and toddlers.

Websites   Many of the general baby and parenting websites listed in "More Info" at the end of the "In the Beginning" and "Your Support Team" chapters will have hints and forums on crying.

Helpline
www.cry-sis.org.uk
08451 228669 (9am–10pm)
A shoulder to cry on (excuse the pun) for parents of babies who are crying, sleepless and demanding. The operational hours for the helpline won't give you comfort in the dead of night. Website has extensive checklist for identifying reasons for crying and sleep routines for different ages.

POSSIBLE ROUTINES FOR BABIES

A routine is basically a daily schedule for when to feed, play, sleep, have a shower, clean out the cutlery drawer, that sort of caper. So put down "Eight years from now – clean out cutlery drawer". Having a daily routine when your bub is very new, though, is a bit like your birth plan: the baby might have other ideas.

Babies are not necessarily going to take to a pattern, and even those who do may not like it all the time. Babies going through growth spurts may wake earlier for feeds, and any baby can do unpredictable things such as suddenly change their sleep habits for no obvious reason.

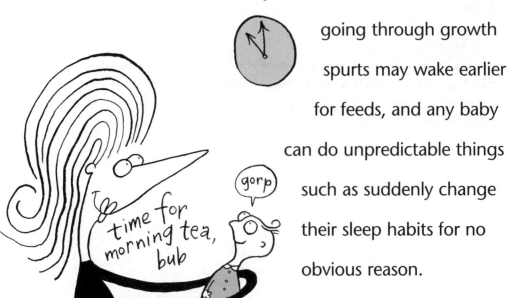

time for morning tea, bub

gorp

After a few weeks you may well be able to work out a bit of a pattern, but you'll have to be ready to abandon it at any point. Little babies can't be fed on a strict schedule that follows the clock or in between precisely timed meetings. Sometimes they will be extra hungry earlier than usual, and sometimes they'll be in a transition period from, say, three big sleeps a day to two big sleeps, and that will take some adjusting.

CuSTomiziNg youR RouTiNe

A routine isn't a set of rules to follow day and night. It's a flexible plan to make things a bit more structured, to make a baby feel secure, to make a little more sense of the day for you and help you grab a bit of time for yourself even if you've never been a fan of routines.

Later on keeping a very strict routine can make it hard for you to go out unless you can organize it so the baby sleeps in the car while you're travelling, in the pram or at someone else's house – some babies are too interested in the world to be able to sleep away from their non-stimulating bedroom, but most will sleep in the soothingly mobile car (although this can create a problem in itself if they automatically wake up every time the car stops). Some people really need to stick to their routine because they know otherwise they'll pay for it with an overtired, grumpy child later that afternoon or even in the night. Others can fiddle around the edges of their routine quite happily. And others would rather eat a placenta than have any routine at all.

Talk to your health visitor about what your bub seems to be up to; together you can work out how to get some structure into the days. "More Info" at the

new baby routine.

end of this chapter lists books you might find helpful (and also see the ones in "More Info" at the end of the "Sleeping" chapter).

aRSeNiC HOUR

Arsenic hour – that delightfully reassuring term for the late afternoon, early evening time when every-one's overtired and cranky and the baby reaches what seems to be a peak of crying – happens, somewhat infuriatingly, anywhere from 4 to 7pm rather than for a strict hour. By anticipating it in your day and experimenting with solutions, you may be able to keep crabbiness to the minimum. Strategies can include getting the baby down for a late afternoon catnap; enlisting help with the baby, a sibling or the cooking; and drinking vast quanti-ties of gin. I beg your pardon, that's not a strategy, it's a typographical error.

feeD, PLay, SLeeP

Many of the sleep clinics and parent help centres talk about the idea of a baby hav-ing a feed, then a play, then a sleep, then a feed, then a play, then a sleep; or, in the case of newborns, a feed, a cuddle and a chat, then a sleep. "Play" for a young baby over 6 weeks old means chatting, being sung to, being taken out for a walk and look-ing at things they can focus on. This is designed to let the baby have a feed, enjoy a social or interesting time and then get enough rest to be able to do it all over again. Importantly it separates the feed and the sleep as many babies get so used to a breast- or bottlefeed being part of their sleep ritual they reach a point where they can't nap or go to sleep without it. There is an exception: unless your baby when older has developed an association with feeding and sleep that you are trying to change, it's fine to give a feed immediately before the big night-time sleep, after about 7pm. The feed is often a deliciously comforting wind-down ritual for both baby and carer.

POSSIBLE NEWBORN ROUTINE

Baby wakes up.
Feed: breast milk or formula.
Play: nappy change; chat, fresh air, cuddle, pre-sleep ritual pat, rock or words.
Wrap and Sleep: as long as the baby wants to. (See page 14 for more detail.)

This feed–play–wrap–sleep block can be repeated six or more times in a 24-hour period.

In the first few weeks the awake part of the feed–play–sleep routine will probably last only an hour or an hour and a quarter, but watch for your baby's tired signs rather than the clock (see "tired signs" in the index). When a baby shows classic tired signs, pop them down to sleep. In the very early weeks they often nod right off wherever and whenever they feel like it, and if a baby takes a laid-back fifty minutes to feed that will eat into their playtime as well.

Many newborn babies tend to want to stay awake for more like two hours in the late afternoon or at the end of the day, contributing to arsenic hour when everyone's fed up to the back teeth. If your baby is showing tired signs at this time, try to get them off to sleep. If they're alert and seem to need the extra time awake, try using a sling to carry them around in or having a relaxing sing, bath or massage routinely at this time to help things stay calm. Difficult if you've dinner to prepare and others such as a toddler to attend to, but perhaps someone else could help.

The feed–play–sleep routine can be repeated as needed into the night, but remember that night-time feeds in dim light need to be followed directly by everyone going back to sleep, instead of playing, to get the baby used to the most excellent idea that there are no playtimes at night.

Remember, sleep all the times your new baby sleeps at night and some of the times during the day too, and be careful that you let them sleep when they want to, instead of keeping them awake to amuse you or your Aunty Norma, who's due to visit at 3.15. Try to keep visitors flexible: make sure they ring before they come so that you can adjust their arrival time with them if need be, or make sure visitors and other kids understand the baby must be allowed to fall asleep and not be disturbed. And watch for those tired signs.

POSSIBLE BABY ROUTINE fROM 3 MONTHS

Continue the feed–play–sleep routine and again watch for your baby's sleepy signs, not the clock. Basically, though, the daytime awake periods will get longer – say, one to two hours – and there will probably be three big sleeps during the day. (Once your baby can roll onto their tummy or wriggle madly you stop wrapping.)

Baby wakes up.
Feed: breakfast (breast milk or formula).
Play.
Sleep.

Feed: morning tea (breast milk or formula).
Play.
Sleep.

Feed: lunch (breast milk or formula).
Play.
Sleep.

Feed: afternoon tea (breast milk or formula).
Play.
Arsenic hour: introduce a restful activity if the baby is cranky or overtired.
Sleep: possibly short or the baby may want to stay awake, but watch for tired signs.

Bath, wind-down.
Feed: dinner (breast milk or formula).
Sleep: about 7pm.
Adult dinner and relaxation or sleep.
Feed: supper (breast milk or formula).
Sleep: through the night (hey, it's a plan!).

Playtime sessions can involve outings, walks, visitors, reading a board book, looking at cars swishing past outside the window, singing, chatting and cuddling. Remember that when a baby wakes for a night-time feed there's no playtime and the light is kept dim.

Put your baby down to sleep at about seven at night, then wake them gently for a non-stimulating, business-only feed about 10.30 or 11pm. This should see you through for a longer period of sleep, until 5, 6, even 7am. If you are not getting a longer night-time sleep of five or six hours by the time your baby is 6 months old, ask your health visitor or call one of the parent services for help with adjusting your routine (see the contact details in "More Info" at the end of the second chapter, "Your Support Team").

POSSIBLe BaBy ROUtiNe fRom 6 moNtHs

The feed–play–sleep routine continues, with the baby moving towards two big sleeps during the day – a big morning and afternoon nap – and probably a catnap at about 4.30 pm. Catnaps usually last twenty or forty minutes.

At 6 months a baby will need four or five milk drinks, and tastes of solids (see the "Learning to Eat" chapter). By 1 year the emphasis is on solids and about 600ml of milk throughout the day or the equivalent in dairy products such as yoghurt and cheese.

Baby wakes up.
Feed: breakfast (breast or formula milk and a taste of solids such as rice cereal or a bit of fruit).
Play.
Possible sleep for a baby closer to 6 months than 1 year.

Feed: morning tea (breast milk or formula and maybe a taste of solids).
Play.
Sleep.
Feed: lunch (breast milk or formula and a taste of solids).
Play.
Sleep.

Feed: afternoon tea (breast milk or formula and maybe a taste of solids).
Play.
Possible catnap if there are tired signs.
Arsenic hour: a restful activity.

Feed: dinner (a taste of solids and a drink of water).
Play (may be longer than usual, but watch for tired signs).
Bath.
Drink: breast milk or formula.
Night-time ritual.
Sleep: about 7pm.

Adult dinner and relaxation.
Possible feed: supper (breast milk or formula) or start phasing it out.
Sleep.

Put your baby down to sleep at 7 or 7.30 at night. After the bub is 6 months old you can experiment with the late evening feed. Drop it and see what happens. If your baby wakes up at 3am starving, then it isn't time to drop that feed yet. But maybe the baby will sleep through until 6 or even 7am. It's not unusual for babies to sleep ten or twelve hours before morning. The solid food introduced at this age helps babies stay full through the night. By about 9 months the late evening feed should be gone and you should be getting a big sleep yourself at night: if you can't quite seem to manage it, ask your health visitor or an adviser at one of the parent services to help you adjust the schedule.

POSSIBLE BABY ROUTINE FROM 9 MONTHS

The same sort of pattern is followed but the late afternoon catnap is usually dropped, leaving just a morning and afternoon sleep; and you can move to getting a longer sleep at night if you haven't already.

Baby wakes up.
Feed: breakfast (solids and breast milk or formula).
Play.

Feed: morning tea (a snack and a drink in a cup).
Play.
Sleep.

Feed: lunch (solids and breast milk or formula).
Play.
Sleep.

Feed: afternoon tea (a snack and a drink in a cup).
Play (watch for tired signs but a very late afternoon sleep may interfere with bed-time).
Arsenic hour: a restful activity.
Bath.

Feed: dinner (food and a drink in a cup).
Night-time ritual.
Drink: breast milk or formula.
Sleep: about 7pm.

Adult dinner and free time for exciting housework.
Sleep: everyone until the morning (fingers crossed).

going from two daytime naps to one

At around a year (maybe earlier, maybe later) your baby may start routinely show-ing no interest or little interest in the second, afternoon sleep, and want to just faff around. This probably means they're ready to go to one sleep a day, which tradition-ally is an afternoon sleep. You'll need a transition period, which will probably last about three weeks, while you slowly winch the morning sleep later until they're hav-ing one daytime nap that eventually starts at midday or 1 or 2pm. As they're making the transition you might find them getting crankier at the end of the day; if so put them to bed an hour or half an hour early. (Splendid news: in most cases this makes absolutely no difference to the morning wake-up time.)

By 18 months most kids are down to one sleep a day, and this can last right through until they start school. Others drop the afternoon sleep somewhere along the way, although it's always useful to pick it up again briefly during those stressful or excit-ing times when they're sick, they're overtired in the first days or weeks of day care or kindergarten or they've been to see Barney the Dinosaur on stage in the morning.

DayLight saving

Spend a few days before each daylight-saving changeover gradually altering your routine so that by the time you get there it's a fifteeen-minute adjustment rather than a whole hour. Or you can start the day an hour later by the clock in summer.

more info

BOOKS WITH BABY ROUTINES

Sleep Tight, Sleep Right by Rosey Cummings, Karen Haughton and Le Ann Williams has charts and explanations of the feed–play–sleep approach, and has routines for babies and toddlers. It answers many common questions about sleep and routine. (See "More Info" at the end of the "Sleeping" chapter for full details and review.)

Tracy Hogg's *Secrets of the Baby Whisperer* has something called the E.A.S.Y. plan – eating, activity, sleeping, you – based on those four principles. She makes suggestions for a kindly routine that is tailored to your baby's inclinations, and also suggests routines for twins. She believed that even small babies like to anticipate and get into a rhythm of life. Gina Ford's *The Contented Little Baby Book* says babies shouldn't be overstimulated at least twenty minutes before a sleep, and that part of playtime can be baby exploring things on their own. ("Hey, what's that thing on the end of my arm? I think I shall have to stick it straight in my mouth!") She's pretty much Mrs Strictypants when it comes to baby routines, but some people and babies will like that idea. (See "More Info" at the end of the first chapter, "In the Beginning", for full details and reviews of both books.)

WASHING THE BUB

Babies were not traditionally washed every day until the scientific cleanliness mania of the 1950s had nutty doctors insisting that mothers wash their tiny tots in alcohol and other antiseptic solutions every day. This, along with soap, contributed to many children developing dry skin and eczema, and also made any existing skin problems worse.

Bathing your baby once every day or two, or even occasionally, is plenty if you're absolutely scrupulous with bot cleaning after nappy changes. It's not like the bub is playing in puddles.

NEWBORNS AND BATHS

Here's my big tip: if your newborn baby doesn't like the bath, just put them on a couple of layers of towel and give them a going over with warm, wet, soapy cotton-wool balls, then rinse them with warm, wet cotton-wool balls or use a very soft flannel, and dry them well by patting them with a towel or let the air dry them if it's a warm day. In other words – avoid stress, no matter what the textbooks might say about bathing.

Newborn babies, used to being curled up in the womb, get all stretched out for a bath so it can be strange for them the first few times. It always helps to explain to your baby what you're up to as you bath them. If your baby still dislikes it, don't continue but reintroduce the bath now and then: most babies eventually love it – at least when they can start splashing about.

BATHING YOUR BABY

Many people use a plastic baby bath but, as long as you can warm the room, a laundry bowl or even a cleared kitchen sink is fine. Baby baths can be so heavy to lift and empty and a pain to fill from kettle and jug, especially as you'll have to put the baby down safely somewhere else if you're dickering about with kettles. Make sure any taps are shooftied out of the way, turned off tight or disabled.

Assemble everything you need on the bench next to the filled baby bath or sink:

★ cotton-wool balls, or flannels you wash after every bottom contact in antibacterial detergent and hot water

★ a soap substitute – however often you wash your baby it's safer to use a non-soap product to avoid dry skin (ask your chemist to recommend one)

★ a soft towel (some fancy ones come with a baby hood)

★ a new nappy, and nappy-rash cream if necessary, plus a clean outfit (cut these out if you carry your bub in the towel to the changing table to be dressed).

The bath water should be a temperature that feels pleasantly warm, but not hot, on your elbow. Don't let the baby get too cold as the water cools: you want to

162

replicate the relaxing amniotic fluid feeling rather than plunge them into a bracing bowl.

Make sure you have one arm under your baby, supporting the neck and head during a bath, and use the other one for washing.

A two-person team bath can be had by one adult sitting in the big bath with the baby bath on the bottom of it. The baby is bathed in the smaller receptacle by Person One, then removed by Person Two, who is also instructed to bring Person One a pineapple daiquiri.

Eyes and ears

If they look mucky, eyes should be washed separately, with a cool sterile saline solution (see "eyes" in the index): don't hold eyes open to wash them.

Don't poke anything smaller than your elbow into a child's ear. This means you can wash any bits you can see (the outside), but *not* inside in case you damage the eardrum or introduce infection.

Willies and girly bits

Babies and toddlers with penises don't need to be washed under their foreskin. Between the ages of 3 and 5 the foreskin will usually become moveable, and you can teach your boy to clean underneath himself, and eventually to understand the importance of doing so for the rest of his life. Until then, don't try to roll back the foreskin. It's tight when he's little because it's there for protection against grit and infection. Just clean the outside of the penis with a cotton ball when he's a bub, and normal soap and a flannel will do in the bath as he gets older. A circumcised penis isn't necessarily

cleaner, and despite rumours is definitely *not* a protection against infections, sexual or otherwise. When he gets a lot older, if you're worried about him getting sexually transmitted diseases, tell your son about condoms.

The folds of a girl's private parts also need to be washed carefully and gently, and this skill passed on to her.

Your health visitor can demonstrate good washing methods for willies and all the nooks and crannies.

safety

Needless to say (but you're not always logical when you're sleep deprived), keep a hand on your baby *at all times* in the bath: this is a hard and fast rule and means you can never leave them or turn away for the mere seconds it can take a baby to drown. And remember, a baby who likes water, or even an inquisitive one, can fall into a bucket or a sink, a pond, a dam, a pool or a puddle. Babies' and toddlers' big heads make it hard for them to right themselves. All water, however shallow, is potentially dangerous to a baby and toddler. Always pull the bath plug or empty a baby bath the second that it's possible: don't wait until later.

Get a non-slip rubber mat for the big bath as soon as your baby is ready to go into it.

washing yourself

In the very early days after the baby's born it's sometimes almost impossible to get time to have your own shower. Take advantage of visitors who can hold the baby or put your bub securely in a pram or a floor basket while you shower. Climbing out of jarmies and getting clean can help you feel refreshed and more in control of your life.

BatH toys

Newborns don't need any bath toys: wait until your baby is reaching for and grabbing things before you introduce a rubber ducky or a floaty plastic anything.

Cheap baby toys that last into toddlerhood and beyond include safe, colourful, soft plastic shell and sea creature shapes; old shampoo bottles that become squirters; sieves; plastic cups and other containers for pouring water into; all manner of plastic dollies and boats; and towelling glove puppets.

Every few weeks you may like to give all the plastic bath toys a good jooshing with a washing-up brush in a bucket of water to which a cup of white vinegar has been added, and then dry them in the sun to make sure there are no germy bits. On the other hand you might figure they get washed every night so get a grip. Regularly squeeze out the old water that splooshes around in the squirty toys because otherwise it gets pretty swampy in there.

BONDING

We hear so much about the wonderful joy

of having a baby that if we don't feel it ourselves

immediately we think there's something wrong with

us, whereas the "slow bond" is just as legitimate an

experience. Some things take practice and experience.

It's okay to have negative or blank feelings: it just seems

particularly awful if they're not balanced by a few good

feelings. This chapter gives you some

options for helping the bonding

process along.

SOME WAYS PEOPLE RESPOND TO THEIR NEW BABY

★ Immediately you see your baby for the first time you feel a rush of protective love and never want to be parted.

★ You look at the baby and wonder what all the fuss is about and feel nothing. Gradually you learn to love your child.

★ As a bloke, when you see your baby being born you realize you want to protect and love them and their mother every way you can.

★ The first time you put your baby to your breast you feel that it's all perfect and natural.

★ The first time you hug your baby to your breast you remember you're a man and feel a bit useless.

★ When the Caesarean drugs or the shock of labour wear off, you slowly begin to marvel at and feel connected to your baby, whether you breastfeed or bottlefeed.

★ As time goes by, you feel more and more loving and confident in your relationship with your baby.

★ After a period of confused and depressing thoughts, you get help from counsellors, a doctor, or a community mental health team or some prescribed drugs perhaps, and you begin to learn how to look after your baby and you begin to care. You understand that this feeling will build, and doesn't come immediately or without effort for everyone.

★ The thought of anyone affronting, let alone hurting, your baby makes you instinctively furious.

With almost every other relationship in life love is earned. And yet we are expected, through miraculous hormones or somehow automatically, to love and bond with our children. This can make us feel terribly guilty if we don't experience great surges of love and bonding straight away, or even in the first weeks.

The process of birth is such a huge thing (and one that we've probably been concentrating all our thinking and learning on for so long) that we may need to stay with our own body recovery for a while and not just snap into the "next episode" immediately. It is very common to feel quite disconnected or helpless when the baby is born, just as it's common to feel a great rush of relief and love. Because as first-time mothers (and fathers) we are often not experienced with babies, we are quite overcome and shocked by how tiny and defenceless our babies look, and this can make us feel frightened to cuddle, frightened of responsibility. And for many of us the birth of a baby (especially the first) can mean giving up and grieving for the permanent or temporary loss of a whole lot of really good things such as independence, cocktails on a whim, an income, and our former kept-to-itself body. All these legitimate thoughts and conditions can give us pause, and get in the way of feeling joy and attachment.

Although the first moment a mother or a father is left alone in a room with a new baby, they may feel complete bewilderment, even fear, this will pass. Even if it doesn't pass by itself, people can get help to move on from feeling empty or frightened to gradually falling in love with their babies and having a happy future together.

getting Help With Bonding

Be patient with yourself and make sure you go to the source of any negative or blank feelings and find a solution. While you're still in hospital, if you feel that you're not equipped to look after your baby, tell the midwives: they'll help you learn the new skills needed. (You don't have to be perfect. You just need to try.) If you feel a bit indifferent and as if you don't know what to do with the baby, it may well be the sheer physical and mental shock of the labour and birth or the dulling effect of Caesarean and recovery drugs.

Tell the midwives if you're feeling ambivalent about the baby. They've seen it all, believe me, and they know you don't need to panic.

If you're home and having these feelings, your first point of contact for help is your health visitor or your GP. Don't worry – that's why they have tissues in their office, they're used to this sort of thing. They'll be able to refer you to a specialist in this problem.

You might also like to talk to other mothers. Your health visitor can help you find a local parents' group.

If you need a voice on the phone straight away there are parent helplines, and lots of parent services, listed in "More Info" at the end of the second chapter, "Your Support Team". And see the next chapter, "Feeling Overwhelmed or Depressed", for the lowdown on general, non-specific "blues" and full-on postnatal depression.

"If your maternal instinct doesn't kick in (mine never did), then read books or seek help from family services." AUDREY

COMMON REACTIONS

* Oh, my GOD. Did it really come out of me?

* I've never felt such a strong love.

* Can I touch him?

* Give her to me!

* They're not expecting me to actually feed that, are they?

* I can't wait to try breastfeeding!

* Don't take my baby out of my sight.

* I really need to sleep: can you look after her for a while?

* I won't know what to do because I'm a bloke.

Common feelings include:

* bewilderment

* pride

* blank exhaustion

* exultation – a high

* fear of Doing the Wrong Thing

* anxiety about the baby's health and safety

* inadequacy at the thought of parenthood

* calm bliss

* a maelstrom of different thoughts and emotions

* shock.

ways to increase bonding

Don't forget to take photos and spend time flaked on the couch just looking at your baby and having as many calm moments as you can. The newborn time feels endless now, but when you look back it really will (cliché alert) seem to have gone in a flash. The only way to get to know baby cries and baby body language is to spend relaxed time together.

★ Sit quietly and inspect your baby from top to toe.

★ Chat to your baby face to face, up close.

★ Name your baby and start using the name a lot, or use lots of special nicknames.

★ Talk or sing to your baby: anything will do.

★ Watch your baby's expressions and try to guess what they mean.

★ Think about what you'd do if someone tried to hurt your baby.

★ Tell your baby you're going to get to know each other over time.

★ Have lots of skin-to-skin contact.

★ Be very still and listen to your baby breathing.

★ Feel your baby's heartbeat.

★ Look at your baby's feet, hands, back of the neck.

★ Hold the baby to your chest when standing or lying down.

★ Gently massage your baby (look up "baby massage" in the index).

★ Watch your baby sleeping. (But not for long – off you go for a nap yourself!)

feeling overwhelmed or Depressed

Parenthood isn't always wonderful: the first weeks will be tiring and stressful. As well as being fascinating – "Look at those darling starfish hands!" – your baby will scream and poo and not explain themselves at all. This is probably your training ground in unconditional love and devotion, and sometimes it's a pain in the arse at best and absolutely maddening and exhausting at worst. The hard aspects can be balanced by the pride and joy of keeping your little one alive and well, and the thrill of getting to know your baby. But for some people the good feelings get pushed to the background or swamped completely, either for a few days or weeks or in tough cases for months: professional help is a must.

a perfectly sane response

To be honest I can't quite work out why anyone *wouldn't* come crashing down after the ultra-stress of birth, the lack of sleep, the realization that this isn't for the weekend but for life, the sore aching girly bits, the carry-on and sometimes early pain of first-time breastfeeding and the anxiety about whether you're doing ANYTHING right. (I wish I'd started using disposable nappies in the hospital – they would have been one less bloody thing to fold properly.) Plus you may be astonished to find that you feel like a worn-out old couch instead of a supermodel.

And that's if everything's going fine. If you are also dealing with outside relationship problems, a sick baby or unhelpful relatives, it can all seem a bit of a disaster. I think parents at this stage can sometimes feel terribly alone, especially sole or single parents and parents whose partners go back to work leaving them – aarrgh, surely some mistake – IN CHARGE. And the house looks terrible a day after getting home from hospital and how are you supposed to eat fresh, healthy food when you can't even get out of your PJs by 5pm and I can't cope, and shut up. Which often leaves partners not knowing what to do to help and be supportive (see the "Dads" chapter in *Part 3: Parenting*).

All this is not helped by the amazingly intense attention that newborn babies need – feeds every two to four hours, nappy changes, comforting – while you're trying to snatch bits of sleep here and there. Honestly I think if you weren't feeling a bit demented at least once a day there'd be something wrong with you.

And you're allowed to have negative feelings about your new role: some of it is hard and tiring and revolting work. That's why sensible societies share the care of a newborn baby, and rich people have full-time nannies. Every other mother (and father) is having the same insecurities – I can guarantee you the first-timers are. And the others are wondering why the things that worked with the first baby aren't working with this one.

All the pictures of mothers and fathers in those baby books are of well-groomed, tidy, rested-looking people reading books and smiling contentedly at chuckling 6-month-old babies, or at least newborn babies who aren't screamingly red as if they've just been lightly parboiled and shouted at.

One of the contradictions I remember feeling through the newborn days was wishing that somebody would turn up and say "There's been a terrible mistake, this isn't your baby and we're going to take them away and have them looked after by more competent folk", while simultaneously knowing that if someone did actually try to take my baby away from me I would kill them with a kebab stick. Or some dental floss.

Sometimes it's hard as hell, and sometimes we're all bad parents who would so fail an audition for one of those margarine ads. I reckon it's time we admitted it to each other and helped each other stumble through, instead of pretending to be superparents who know everything.

"Don't expect to be a perfect mother straight away." A BABY BOOK

"Don't expect to be a perfect mother even if you live to be 856." ME

Somebody get me a helicopter

These days women are more educated than they ever were, and the UK is one of the best places to live if you're a woman (and a mother). There are employment opportunities, civil rights, a national health service: it may not be perfect but it's about as good as it gets for most women in the world. The flip side of this is that many of us are smart, educated women who gave up education or work to have a baby; large numbers of us are used to striding about being independent, spending our own money and demanding that unfairnesses be corrected and equality enforced, and if there's a problem we nail it down and fix it, or get somebody else to fix it. Being a mother, especially in those first weeks, means that no amount of scheduling meetings, ringing up dispatch, rational thought or rope ladder will solve the problems. In most cases we just have to ride it out: we can't walk away or fix it right NOW.

Make important decisions when we haven't had more than three hours' sleep in a row for nine days? Not be able to get dressed all day? Not be able to walk out for the afternoon and have it all solved when we get back? Can't send the crying baby back to the shop for an adjustment? A problem without some sort of immediate solution? We're so not used to that. We'd never start a job and expect that we wouldn't receive any training – yet we expect to somehow be great as parents straight away, even though we haven't trained for the job, or spent weeks and months getting up to speed. Not to mention most new jobs are not 24 hours a day, with no deep sleep for weeks. Call the union!

tHe eaRLy DayS BLUeS

The third or fourth day blues

All those lovely, floaty, hippie pregnancy hormones shut off like a tap just about day three or four after the birth as your prolactin hormone levels gear up for milk delivery. (Progesterone, oestrogen, cortisol and beta-endorphins fall away.) This is often what's called the "baby blues" or the three-day weep.

Recovering from a traumatic birth

Maybe the labour or the Caesarean didn't go the way it was "supposed to". Traumatic births very often result in feelings of sadness, shock or distress that are played out in the open, or suppressed, in the first few weeks of a baby's life. Recovering from a particularly exhausting or surgical birth is a factor often overlooked by people, who simply assume you're fine once the baby comes out. Sometimes many tears need to be shed, and the birth story told or considered over and over, before you feel able to move on.

You need to be patient with yourself about recovering, and you need to understand that having a healthy baby is really all that matters now. It's important to acknowledge the trauma, but also to realize that it wasn't your fault the way the birth turned out. It's the luck of the draw.

Ask your GP to refer you to a specialist counsellor if you need extra help to work through your feelings.

A health problem with the baby

Sometimes babies are born with minor or severe health problems, which can trigger depression. In the intensity of focusing on your child, don't forget to pay attention to the mental health of the rest of the family, including yourself. Don't be afraid of asking for help.

Coping when you first get home

One thing that does seem to help people cope in the early days at home is prioritizing: letting the housework go, not caring too much about your hairdo and just making sure food goes into everyone and sleep is grabbed whenever possible. In the early weeks that's all you can do.

Another thing that helps is getting outside into the fresh air and seeing the sun in the sky: otherwise you live in a twilight world ruled by feeds every few hours, regardless of day or night, experiencing something like self-perpetuating, hideous, endless jet lag.

Support from a partner (if you have one), family or friends is crucial. In the survey done for this book the number of women who ran to their mums and were grateful for them was matched by the number of women whose mums were critical, or had forgotten what it was like to have a baby, or had old-fashioned advice and were offended when it wasn't followed. A lot of people had difficulty with mothers-in-law. And sometimes the child's grandparents can be more of a burden than a help because they are too elderly or out of touch to actually make things easier. It may be that you need to look elsewhere for supportive help.

I realize now that I should have had more visitors to help and chat and normalize things, but I was so tired and felt so inexperienced and down that I didn't want anyone to see me. It's a big mistake to think you have to put on a show of any kind for visitors. If we all pretend, everyone will continue to be shocked by the reality. Believe me, other parents of young children understand.

Although routines can make your life easier at this stage, if part of your routine is Thursday afternoon clean the toilet maybe just go out and have a cup of tea and talk to some adults for a while instead. (And see the "Coping Strategies for Parents"chapter in *Part 3: Parenting*.)

"You're swimming through the day. I don't think I articulated anything. I don't think I showered. I don't think I ate anything unless it came out of a box and fit in my hand. People would say to me 'Let's go out to dinner' and all I could think was 'How cruel.'" TERRI

"I felt like a cross between a milking machine and a washing machine." LESLEY

"Having worked as a private maternity nurse and nanny, I really thought that motherhood would pose no problems for me. How wrong I was. In those first few weeks, with both my children, I had serious doubts as to whether I was really cut out to be a mum. When I finally expressed my concerns I discovered that 99 percent of the mothers I knew had experienced the same physical and emotional problems . . . There I was thinking that there was something wrong with me because it wasn't 'coming naturally'. Turned out I was perfectly normal: it's just that you apparently have to become a mother before you get let in on that particular piece of secret women's business." TRACEY

"When family and friends come over get them to fold a load of washing." ANONYMOUS

"I'm an A-type personality and it was hard not having the control over my life that I used to have." GARDA

"Aaargghh! I ended up in a mother/baby care unit for a week after the first month – thank God for them. Delivered some kind of sanity plus routines that worked for a while." CHERYL

"If you are tempted to look at the stay-home full-time mums of yesteryear and wish for their capabilities, remember that they often had four generations of helpers. Don't compare yourself to a situation that bears no resemblance to your own." MICHAEL

"I wish other mums would stop putting up walls and saying that everything is okay and life is wonderful. Because that is garbage. Having children, a husband and a household is plain hard work. At times enjoyable work, but most of the time just hard work. And part of the time it is frustrating, exhausting, upsetting and stressful. I really didn't know what stress was until I had two kids and a husband." JOANNA

"I was desperate for a baby, and I think I couldn't see past that, and saw the life through rose-coloured glasses. I was quite shocked by how hard it can be and also by how mundane it can be at times." LOUISE

"I think that some people just need to be allowed to feel overwhelmed, I think that we should all be taught that childbirth is a real effort for a lot of women and may not come easily to you." CATHY

"I was so dumb I thought I wasn't allowed to take the baby for a walk after 3 p.m. (I was very taken with a local maternal nurse – she of no children and about 68 years old). The best advice in my experience was to make new friends, even if you never would have liked that type of person. Invite them for morning tea. You will have to get out of your pyjamas and so will she. Go to the local mothers' groups . . . get the baby outside even if he screams for the entire walk. You have achieved something, and it knackers them if they cry for two blocks." SOPHIE

"My baby was nearly 7 weeks premature so I was sent to a class where they taught me calm, sensible ways to look after my baby. Before that I knew absolutely nothing." ANNE

"Sometimes you have to have a good cry and try and remember that the bad days will end." JILLIAN

"What a nightmare those first 6 weeks were. I tried to take everyone's advice, which was contradictory in most cases, and ended up tying myself in knots. Luckily my family ignored my breezy, confident 'I'm fine!'s and were wonderfully supportive." KELLIE

"I found joining a playgroup very useful. It was good to meet other mums going through the same types of things even if their children were a bit older." HEATHER

"My firstborn being a premmie scared me a lot. I hated anyone touching him and breathing near him. I was too scared to put him down. I spent a whole day without eating because I couldn't leave him. It didn't occur to me that I could hold him (in a sling) while I made a sandwich! I think I lost half my brain when my baby was born!" GURINDER

"Accept all help offered whether it be a meal, the ironing or somebody to watch bub for 15 minutes while you ENJOY your shower."
LINDA

"Ignore housework TOTALLY, eat takeaway and frozen foods, ask friends and rellies to do the washing, cook the casserole or have the other kids. Nobody shows up to help these days, we're so busy: you have to ask, and make sure you show your appreciation later when you are on your feet, bake them a cake or buy them a lottery ticket. Don't read too many books by 'experts'."
ANONYMOUS

"Get your husband/partner involved from day one. Teach him the ins and outs or you are setting yourself up to be the only one that settles, feeds, etc. Maintain contact with the outside world and delegate, delegate. Have one day a week that is yours."
FIONA

THINGS THAT MAY HELP HEAD OFF THE BLUES

✱ Understand that the tiredness and stress of a new baby will only get better as time goes by, and that it's okay to be bored, impatient or annoyed by aspects of parenting, as long as you don't take it out on the baby.

✱ Get out into the open air as much as possible – a half-hour walk a day with the pram will reduce stress and make you feel better. It doesn't matter what you look like.

✱ Talk to women who've been through it and come out the other side.

✱ Ask for help – from anywhere you can get it: health visitor, GP, partner, family, friends, postnatal support groups (see "More Info" at the end of this chapter). If you have spare money hire a cleaner and babysitters.

✱ Get away as much as you can: maybe to a movie that takes you into another world.

"I make it a point to have a shower, put on make-up and dress before 9 am. For me it has been important to dress in my trendy gear, not house clothes, even if I am not going anywhere or expecting visitors. It makes me feel good." MARY

"Wear your tracksuit to bed, and then if you don't have time to dress/shower in the morning, you still look like you have!"
ANN

"Bugger the housework." MELANIE

"If you can afford a cleaner, go for it." STEPHANIE AND PAM

"Newborns are so portable. Get out of the house."
MARY

"Ring a helpline if you're worried about anything. Nothing is a stupid question and they have heard them all before. They also don't mind if you cry while you're talking to them because you're sleep deprived or worried. Many times I would ring them when absolutely beside myself and I never found them to be anything other than fantastic and wonderfully supportive." AMANDA

* Understand that you may feel alone in your house but out there there are thousands just like you, about to go into it or going through it, and thousands who have come out the other side.

* Have a long, hard look at what you're expecting of yourself. If a friend came to you with your problems, what would you advise them? Why be harder on yourself?

* Cut off from people who are critical and negative without actually helping very much: you really don't need them, even and especially if they're related to you.

* Go to a mothers' group, parents' group or playgroup, even if your baby is too young to really play.

* Learn yoga or another relaxation technique. Look for a special postnatal class or an instructor who is experienced in postnatal exercise.

> *"In the end it comes down to this: if the baby is fed, clean, warm and loved, then you're doing just right."* EMMA

> *"I didn't get out of my PJs until 3 pm every day."*
> CHRISTINE

> *"Buy an answering machine: your message should be very long and tell the listener everything you might possibly be doing that is stopping you from reaching the phone – hopefully they will either come and help or LEAVE YOU ALONE."*
> ROBYN, MOTHER OF THREE UNDER 3S

ONGOING LOW-LEVEL BLUES

A more specific level of ongoing blues is often felt by women who take a baby home to a family that already has a young child or children. Again a totally rational reaction to such a situation, I would have thought, but one that needs help as depression is – well, dammit, it's depressing, even if it comes and goes. You need help in a situation like this: perhaps coping strategies and the allocation of specific jobs to partners, relatives or friends. Routines might help.

Mild depression usually comes in small doses such as a few days or a week or so at a time. Symptoms include mood swings, crying, crankiness and tiredness. For parent services that can help see "More Info" at the end of the second chapter, "Your Support Team".

RAGE

It's common to feel angry with a baby, particularly a baby who won't stop crying, even when you know how irrational that is – babies can't be "naughty" because they have no idea what they're doing. What's important is that when you feel angry you do something about it that doesn't involve blaming – or harming – the baby.

If your frustration with your baby rises to boiling point and you think you might shake, hit or otherwise harm them:

★ put the baby in a safe place – a cot is best – and walk out of the house (into the garden, if you have one) to calm down

★ or pop the baby in the pram and go and sit in the park – the baby might still cry, but you'll be outside and in public and less likely to do something awful

★ or go straight to your health centre

★ or call one of the parent services or, if it's late, a parent helpline (see "More Info" at the end of the second chapter, "Your Support Team").

A very experienced person in the field of distraught mums tells me a good quickie soother is to stand with your hands palm down in a basin of warm water and breathe slowly.

If you have got to the stage of feeling at the end of your tether you will probably feel that way again, and it may get worse, so it's a good idea to seek some help at this point. I think many, many parents have shouted rather uncontrollably at a baby who "refused" to go to sleep or to stop crying. This can frighten both of you and make everyone cry even more.

PostNatal Depression (PND)

Postnatal depression can turn up straight after the birth or unexpectedly some time in the first couple of years, and often comes on gradually. Even though many people don't talk about it, PND affects thousands of British women each year, and some men too. The depression can be hormonally caused, psychological or even a recurrence of depression from another time. In some cases PND can recur with the birth of each child. This is the black hole from which you can't see a way out: you think it's never going to get better.

PND seems utterly unrelenting to those in it: you don't have any good days, or you have more bad days than good days, and you feel no optimism or enthusiasm for anything. The feelings are intense or constant, and you can't "shake yourself out of it" or "pull yourself together". This, my friend, is completely treatable, and so many mums have been through it: you must tell your partner or someone you're close to and see a professional about your feelings now. If you need it, somewhere near you there's a special residential-care centre where you can go for as long as you need with your baby, get treated, be with other women with the same problem and learn how to get your life back.

Symptoms of PND

These are common symptoms:

- ★ feeling tired
- ★ feeling cranky
- ★ crying
- ★ appetite loss
- ★ black moods
- ★ feeling worthless
- ★ feeling that somehow your "self" has gone missing
- ★ overwhelming despair or pessimism
- ★ feeling numb or blank
- ★ anxiety attack symptoms such as sweating, palpitations, shaking, terror
- ★ insomnia
- ★ feeling bad, guilty, ashamed or inadequate
- ★ thoughts about harming your baby or yourself
- ★ memory blanks
- ★ exhaustion
- ★ feeling uninterested in affection or sex.

Risk factors for general depression

These factors for general depression may or may not contribute to PND:

- ★ having a history of family breakdown or unhappiness
- ★ poverty
- ★ being a victim of some kind of violence or emotional abuse
- ★ a whole bunch of stressful things happening at once (pregnancy or childbirth counts) or one or two big-stress events
- ★ previous depression
- ★ low self-esteem generally.

Added risk factors for PND

These factors are more related to PND than general depression:

★ low self-esteem caused by feeling inadequate as a parent

★ having little or no support with a young baby

★ depression during pregnancy

★ problems with a partner

★ a difficult labour or unexpected or unwanted Caesarean

★ being a sole parent

★ a baby who cries a lot

★ wanting to make things "perfect" or to be "perfect"

★ being a pessimist

★ having a depressed partner.

Some people with PND have experienced none of the above risk factors.

Mistaken identity: postpartum thyroiditis

Sometimes people can be diagnosed with exhaustion or postnatal depression when they really have a condition called postpartum thyroiditis, believed to affect up to one in a hundred new mums. It's an inflammation of the thyroid gland that can have confusing symptoms because hormone levels are depressed, elevated or fluctuating. Symptoms can begin at any time from a couple of months to a year after your baby is born. Symptoms of an underactive thyroid include feeling tired, cold or depressed; a perplexing weight gain; dry, coarse or thinning skin or hair; constipation; and heavy periods. Treatment usually includes daily medication, which boosts the hormone levels, and it can take six months to a year to feel completely well again. Symptoms of an overactive thyroid, a condition that usually sorts itself out without treatment, can include feeling tired, anxious, panicky, hot or cross; a perplexing weight loss; thinning skin or hair; diarrhoea; insomnia; and sweating. A thyroid gland problem is more likely to happen if one occurred after a previous pregnancy. It can be diagnosed with a simple blood test.

"I always thought it only affected mothers who felt no bond with their baby or who had a 'high maintenance' baby. I found out at four and a half months it had nothing to do with any of that. My baby is a happy little fellow generally and I had an instant bond with him . . . I could not fathom how I could go from being a fearless and capable professional to an anxious, fearful, blubbering heap of misery in a matter of months . . . I started spending the entire day watching TV, regardless of what was on. When I yelled at my baby because I couldn't hear the TV, I was certain I was in need of help. I called my health visitor (the nicer one) and she did a PND questionnaire on me. I came up trumps and ... got all the help I needed. It was the best thing I ever did, reaching out to the nurse." MUM

Partners of people with PND

Partners can be terribly stressed and worried about the whole situation, and need to get away sometimes too. Dads can suffer from a form of PND. You can end up in a double depressed situation, which needless to say is really bad for babies and children. For their sake as well as yours you need to get professional help from someone trained specifically in postnatal depression.

Treatment for PND

Treatment may be a combination of any or all of the following:

- ★ counselling – on your own or with your partner (see "More Info" at the end of this chapter)
- ★ group support or therapy
- ★ anti-depressant drugs, which should always be used with other treatments such as getting practical help at home and counselling (drugs usually mean an end to breastfeeding, but this is not necessarily a bad thing)
- ★ hormone-balancing drugs
- ★ discussing and developing a plan for improving your life and routine
- ★ referral to a community mental health unit which would have the full range of psychiatric services and who may be able to arrange home visits
- ★ talking to mums who have been through it and are back on an even keel.

POSTNATAL PSYCHOSIS

This is a mental illness that affects a handful of mothers in every couple of thousand. It comes on in the first month or two after the birth, or even almost immediately, and is characterized by terribly severe depression, hallucinations and other scary business such as wanting to harm the baby or yourself. There is often a known or unknown genetic predisposition, or a family or personal history of bipolar disorder (meaning the wild high and low feelings formerly called manic depression) or schizophrenia.

Some people who develop postnatal psychosis have no history of warning signs at all. Some recover quickly, others need ongoing medication to control the condition. Postnatal psychosis must be treated with drugs to help restore a balanced brain chemistry – this may take some time to get exactly right, and may or may not involve rest and recuperation in hospital until the drugs have kicked in properly. It's very important that the focus is on treating the mental illness. A carer must be found for the baby and breastfeeding will have to stop so the drugs won't affect the baby.

It's possible for mentally ill people to maintain normal and loving lives as mums; but they must have an understanding that they are sick and an insight into their disease that means they keep taking their medication – indefinitely, if necessary. They also need understanding and support from family and friends. Uncontrolled and untreated mental illness can be one of the most lonely and terrifying things for both parent and child. Postnatal psychosis isn't something people can just snap out of by free will. Like other mental illnesses it is made worse by alcohol and all non-treatment drugs. It is very likely that counselling and special explanations will be needed for the child as they grow, to understand ongoing problems and that their parent's illness is not the child's fault. The child will also need an easily accessible, safe haven with friends or relatives.

If you have dark days of depression all the time, serious thoughts about harming yourself or your baby, you are hearing voices or experiencing unusual urges, or you haven't slept for days, get someone to be with you *right now*. Call your doctor or health visitor. Tell them there's a baby involved and you need help straight away. If it's after hours, get someone to be with you *now* and call one of the helplines listed in "More Info" at the end of the second chapter, "Your Support Team", or call 999 if necessary.

If you feel you can wait a day or so, you can make an appointment with your GP to talk about the best way forward, and who to be referred to. You will need to be referred to a specialist psychiatrist so don't be fobbed off with the usual anti-depressant drugs without knowing the exact nature of your illness.

more info

A PERFECTLY SANE RESPONSE

Life After Birth
by Kate Figes, Virago, 2008
Kate Figes has an honest look behind the pretty picture of what many people expect from motherhood: she tackles health and exhaustion; common fears; adjusting to motherhood; the notion of a "good" mother; relationships with the father of the baby; how sex goes out the window for most people; what motherhood can do to your notion of the world, including your sense of self and your circle of friends. An antidote to those pictures of grinning celebrities with new babies saying "I never felt so sexy" and "I love it. I just want to be a mother all day for the rest of my life! (although I do need to pop over to Cannes for my latest premiere)."

> *"Sleeping during the daytime with more than one child is usually out of the question, unless you know that someone else is looking after the baby. Often mothers of one child find that they cannot sleep during the day because they know that at any moment their baby could wake up."* FROM THE "EXHAUSTION" SECTION OF *LIFE AFTER BIRTH*

A Life's Work: On Becoming a Mother
by Rachel Cusk, Faber and Faber, 2008
A beautifully written, by turns funny and exasparated account of the complex and sometimes ambivalent emotions in the early months of first-time motherhood. Cusk's honest description of her journey will strike a chord with anyone who has lain rigid in bed like a soldier on duty, waiting to spring into action for the next night feed.

POSTNATAL DEPRESSION

The helplines and websites listed in "More Info" for the second chapter, "Your Support Team" may also be of benefit. Men can also get help from these sources.

Feelings After Birth: The NCT Book of Postnatal Depression
by Heather Welford, NCT, 2002
Useful little book with clear explanations, treatments, case studies and suggested resources for further help.

www.apni.org

Tel: 020 7386 0868

The Association for Postnatal Illness provides a telephone helpline, information leaflets and a network of volunteer support (telephone and postal) from people who have suffered from "the silent epidemic" of postnatal illness.

British Association for Counselling and Psychotherapy

Tel: 01788 550899

Provides information on all matters related to counselling. Can send you a list of accredited counsellors in your area.

www.depressionalliance.org

Has a publication on postnatal depression which can be viewed online.

www.mama.co.uk

Helpline: 0845 120 3746 (Mon–Fri 7pm–10pm)

Founded by Esther Rantzen, the Meet a Mum Association aims to help mums who are depressed or isolated, or have moved to a new area, find other mums for support. The network is patchy as yet, but the site has some useful information on postnatal depression.

www.mythyroid.com

For information on postpartum thyroiditis, collating all the latest scientific research. It's often misdiagnosed as PND.

ALL KINDS OF DEPRESSION AND MENTAL ILLNESS

www.mind.org.uk

Tel: 0845 766 0163 (Mon–Fri 9.15am–5.15pm)

The National Association for Mental Health is the leading mental health charity in England and Wales only. Counsellors can talk to you about PND, other forms of depression and schizophrenia. They can recommend a support group in your area.

www.samh.org.uk

Tel: 0141 568 7000 (2–4.30pm)

The Scottish sister of MIND. No counselling line but can put you in touch with someone who will help.

Learning to eat

Sorry, I couldn't bring myself to call this chapter "Solids" as

that sounds quite industrial and disgusting – especially

since in the beginning "solids" should

be called "purées" anyway.

Basically it's about when your

baby starts to eat (and throw)

some mushed-up stuff as well

as drinking breast or

formula milk.

When to start

"They" (those shadowy child-nutrition figures in the shadowy Child Nutrition Bunker) used to say you needed to start giving babies mashed-up things at 4 to 6 months; now their latest guidelines suggest 6 months is the best time.

NB if you see a high chair that looks like this, don't buy it!

Many reasons for the change are given (maximizing breastfeeding time, minimizing allergies), but probably the really sensible reason is that this is about the time when babies begin to need more than breast milk or formula can give them. Fundamentally they start to need more iron so that their bodies can make more red blood cells. Also babies at this age start wanting to try real food – sometimes looking at you intently while you're eating or reaching out a chubby fist to try to grab something as the fork goes past.

So beginning on solid food should be when your baby starts looking interested in what other people are eating – it shouldn't be because a book, nurse or relative tells you at 3 or 4 months it is time to start shovelling it in, regardless of what the baby seems to want. When you first start it can seem incredibly stressful and worrying – sometimes because parents think they must force the issue or must feed their baby all sorts of things to keep them healthy. "Piffle!" I hear my inner-Nanna snorting.

Science experiments

While babies are still being mainly fed on breast milk or formula, any beginner's food business is all about experimenting. You don't suddenly start cutting down on milk feeds. In the beginning eating is just part of life's big adventure for your baby, and you get to be there to see amazing facial expressions the first time they try strawberry yoghurt (wooooow!) or something they hate (they make a face like Queen Victoria's). Enjoy those expressions – they're probably the same ones you'd make at a dinner party if you hadn't been taught manners.

In those first weeks of trying mushes don't think of the food as sustenance or keeping your child alive. It doesn't matter if they spit it ALL out, it just means you should put "solids" away until your baby's interested. They're not ready, no matter what the books or charts say. It will just make you all miserable if you push it. Some kids, especially breastfeeders, might hold out longer than 6 months. At this point you're conducting fun experiments in taste – not nutrition.

As long as they're getting lots of breast milk or proper formula milk, you are hereby instructed not to panic about food. Up to 6 months and sometimes beyond babies should still be getting about 600ml of breast or formula milk each day. (I know you can't measure your breast milk if it's coming straight out of your nipples, but if your bub is putting on weight and pooing and weeing as usual the amount will be fine.) If you're worried about quantities, talk to your health visitor (and see "More Info" at the end of this chapter).

Try one new food at a time in case of an allergic reaction – then you'll be able to pick the culprit straight away. And babies will enjoy the unadulterated individual tastes.

The theory goes that the more varied a diet you give your baby and toddler, the more they will experiment with new foods. It's worth a try and makes nutritional sense, but it's not a foolproof way to get adventurous eaters. Another theory, which also makes sense, is that when kids start to walk they get more conservative about trying new foods because evolutionary survival instincts stop them from the equivalent of wandering into the bush and eating an unfamiliar food that's poisonous. Most cheerfully excellent of all, this means you don't have to take rejection of your spoon personally and can't blame the kid or yourself because it's just pointless to expect an instant overriding of in-built tribal survival instincts.

At 6 months a baby should be quite happy buckled into a high chair with their own useful tray for eating off and other fun (for safety details look up "high chair" in the index). Highchairs also have the advantage of being a safe place for a baby while you move around – the baby can amuse themselves with a toy or a finger food such as a rusk.

The following things will mysteriously get food on or in them as your baby spits, flings, squeezes and pats some purée: your hair, the baby's hair, the baby's nostrils, your back pocket, the letterbox, the front of what you're wearing, the back of what you're wearing and the pillowcase in the laundry basket. All I can say is stock up on sponges and tea towels.

some foods to start on

Put the bub in a high chair, or somewhere else wipe-cleanable or hoseable such as the back garden and try a teaspoon or two of one of the following:

★ iron-fortified rice cereal for babies (home-made recipes can be found in baby cookbooks but will be low in iron, or try the supermarket baby aisle): this is usually given first because of the iron and because you mix it up with breast or formula milk so it's not too wildly different a taste for the baby, and it's all runny and easy to swallow

★ cooked, puréed fruit flesh (some raw fruits can be rough on very new digestive systems)

★ mashed ripe, raw banana or avocado (but some bubs hate the "slimy" texture)

★ puréed cooked pumpkin or sweet potato

★ full-fat yoghurts, with live cultures

★ tiny pinches or totally squished-up bits of chicken, fish, beef, lamb or tofu

★ rusks – home-made or from the supermarket baby aisle: good for a teething bub when the baby teeth are breaking through the gums.

Development expert Lise Eliot says "While taste perception is well developed in infancy, the understanding of what is edible is largely learned". Every kid has their own tastes. Some people give a few veggies before they try fruit because they think babies will otherwise just prefer the sweeter fruit. Babies and children do have a natural preference for sweet things, but some babies love sucking on lemons.

Your baby may be more enthusiastic about a taste they haven't liked if you leave it for a couple of weeks and then try again. Or they may need a new

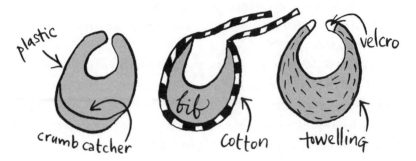

food to be offered up to ten or more times to accept the idea of eating it. And if you don't introduce a food at all during the baby stage, toddlers are likely to be very suspicious of it – unless of course it's a lolly!

NutritioNaL NeeDs

Babies are so individual and such different sizes, have such different appetites, and change so much from month to month and during growth spurts, that it's very hard to say what yours needs in the way of "servings". Basically "listen" to your child and be guided by their interest in food or rejection of it. As long as they aren't offered solids straight after a big breast- or bottlefeed, and as long as they're not sick, they'll probably eat enough to keep them going. And remember, in the first few weeks the "eating" is just experimenting and up to the age of 6 months and sometimes beyond the real nutrition is still coming from the breast or formula milk. Gradually you can build up the amount from a few teaspoons: ask your health visitor what's right for your baby's size, weight and interest in food.

The baby and toddler cookbooks listed in "More Info" at the end of the "Food" chapter in *Part 4: Stuff* have menu plans that can get you started. You could even photocopy a few of those pages at your local library if you check with the librarian about copyright issues. Many of these sources will show you a picture of the Healthy Diet Pyramid, which has all the (unrelentingly badly drawn) things you're not supposed to eat a lot of in the pointy bit up the top (sugar and fat as in chocolates, cakes, kilos of butter) and goes down through the next level (the "eat moderately" gang of proteiny things such as fish, eggs, yoghurt, nuts, meat and cheese), and then to the bottom slice of the pyramid (where you get an open-slather selection of the stuff you can eat the most of – bread, grains, fruit and veggies). I shall spare you a picture of the Healthy Diet Pyramid because I can't draw chicken legs, which somehow always appear on level two.

A specialist child dietician sent me the following list of requirements for babies 1 year old and over (I've rejigged it slightly – she would probably never say "proteiny things"). Don't forget that babies won't eat exactly the same amount at each meal on each day or the same amount each day. Most parents recognize an erratic lurching about rather than a pattern: their child, say, one day munching away, the next not so interested, the next having a huge breakfast then nothing much else, and so on. The cup referred to is the standard metric measuring cup, but the amount suggested doesn't have to be exact, it's just a guide. These are minimum requirements: to have more would be fine!

There's no need, once you get the hang of portion sizes, to weigh and measure food. Life doesn't work like that. Feeding kids isn't a perfectly calibrated science, and besides it will send you screamy la la mad. As long as you have fresh and varied food on offer from the groups listed and your kid is putting on weight, you're doing fine.

Daily needs for babies 1 year old and over

1½ SERVINGS OF CEREAL-TYPE THINGS   A serving is one cup of pasta, rice noodles or porridge; or two slices of bread.

1 SERVING OF FRUIT   A serving is a bit of fruit or bits of different fruit adding up to the size of one apple; or one cup of tinned fruit.

1 SERVING OF VEGGIES   A serving is ½ a cup of cooked veggies; or two large scoops of mashed veggies; or one potato; or one cup of salad veggies.

⅔ OF A SERVING OF PROTEINY THINGS   ⅔ of a serving is one large chop; or ⅓ of a cup of cooked mince; or 60g of any other meat (a thin slice about the size of an adult palm); or 1½ eggs; or ⅓ of a cup of beans (100g).

2½ SERVINGS OF DAIRY STUFF   A serving is one cup of milk or custard; or two slices of cheese; or one small (200g) tub of yoghurt.

Studies consistently show that people pick up more nutrients from fresh food than from vitamin supplements, but if you think your child needs a vitamin boost talk about it with your health visitor or your GP.

Things to be wary of

Current guidelines from child nutritionists (and these do change, so keep up by asking your health visitor about them) say you should delay giving some foods to children.

They suggest holding back on:

★ straight cow's milk (but not formula based on cow's milk) until after age 1 because there is not enough nutritional value in it

★ honey until after age 1 because it may have bacteria in it

★ eggs until after age 1 to avoid early allergy

★ nuts up to age 4 in case of allergic reaction (particularly with peanuts), which is easier to treat in an older child.

There's a section on allergies (and ones on vegetarian and vegan eating) in the "Food" chapter.

more info

First Food and Weaning, National ChildbirthTrust
by Ravinder Lilly, Thorsons, 2002
Small and simple this book may be, but it is excellent for the very early days of weaning
when breast milk or formula is still the priority. Its at-a-glance weaning calenders and
uncomplicated recipes are refreshing after all the razzamatazz of "gourmet baby foods" and
the like on the bookshelves.

Top 100 Baby Purées
by Annabel Karmel, Ebury, 2005
You may not need a cookbook to tell you how to purée a pear (use a hammer) (no don't)
but these recipes help you get inventive. The theory is that if a baby is exposed to a wide
range of tastes, they'll be a "good eater" as they grow up. The book is divided into age
ranges, to help with moving on to the lumpier side of feeding.

BABY DEVELOPMENT (0 to 1)

Babies – and kids – develop skills at different rates. Think of the age ranges given in this chapter as a kind of average. Your baby may roll over very early, but take a little longer than most kids to walk. Honestly there's no need to be worried or ashamed if your kid takes their time: in the vaaaast majority of cases it has no bearing on future development. Of course if you feel your child is consistently slow in several areas, ask for a special check-up with your health visitor or ask your GP if you can be referred to a specialist paediatrician. Some kids miss "stages" altogether: there are plenty of kids who turn up their nose at crawling, one minute doing a funky bum-shuffle or that commando tummy crawling, and the next standing up and wobbling about.

Notes on Development

Much of what seems like straightforward development, such as being able to grasp a toy, helps kids learn other skills as well, such as hand–eye coordination. Every time your baby topples over they are learning what not to do in order to stay upright. So "mistakes" or every day events and movements can be very important for kids learning how to use and enjoy their bodies. Many of their skills are not innate, though; for example, a baby doesn't know how to roll a ball until somebody shows them or they have a ball to experiment with. There are lots of fun and important things you can do to help them develop in their own way.

Your baby could develop at about the pace outlined in the lists that follow – but they're at least fifty percent likely to get to the milestone sooner, or later. This doesn't mean they're "advanced" or "backward". It means they're in the normal range. It's important to think of your baby enjoying the pleasures of experiencing, and not to get hung up on whether they're "excelling". It's impossible not to compare your child's progress with that of others, but all kids are different. How your child develops and which milestones are reached when depend on a complex interaction between their genes, their prior development and their environment: a kid in a sporty family of nine who live on the South Coast will probably be very different from an only child in a family of oboe players who live where it snows most of the year and whose home is full of books. Unless they're the same.

And there's no point in trying to hurry things along: especially when they're babies they need to mature naturally to certain levels before they can acquire more skills. Giving lots of encouragement, praise and cuddles goes for every stage of your child's life and development.

Along with an outline of the various types of activities babies are up to at each age stage, there are sections on things you can do that might be fun and help development. With all these activities the point is for the child to enjoy them and then move on to others when they feel like it.

By the way

★ "Development" in this book is divided into physical, emotional and mental, and communication categories but sometimes there's a crossover, and I just had to choose one category.

★ For premmie babies it's important to adjust the milestones range to the age they'd be if they'd been born on their due date; that is, if your 3-month-old bub was 1 month premature, check out the development range for a 2-month-old baby in the list below. In some cases their abilities may be a little curtailed by the fact they have so much catching up to do. See a paediatrician (a specialist in children's health) about when they'll catch up.

★ Each age given is simply in the middle of a range: it's an average time for a developmental step – it isn't a deadline!

★ Girls often reach milestones, such as talking or wanting to use the loo consistently, before boys.

★ The suggested activities under the headings "What Can You Do?" are fun things to do in a leisurely way together or as a family. It's not a race to teach anything, it's all about experience and exploration. Being home with your baby at this age is the perfect excuse to have dreamy, drifty days. And if you sometimes get bored, make sure you get time off so you can come back refreshed. Sometimes people forget that mothers (or dads) at home looking after kids full-time need their time off too. Part of your child's development is learning to be with other carers, relatives and children. Playgroups (see "More Info" at the end of this chapter) are one way, but you usually have to be there too.

★ See your health visitor or GP. They can refer you to a paediatrician if necessary.

Don't read old, borrowed books about children because they have outdated and often wrong ideas on child development and breezily say things such as babies are toilet trained between the ages of 0 and 4 months, and repeat other complete stuff and nonsense from Dr Arrogant-Pants of about 1958.

> *"Babies want to be enthusiastically enjoyed by other people from the beginning of life. When that happens they feel good about themselves, with a healthy pride and good self-esteem and secure attachment."* FRANCES THOMSON-SALO, CHILD PSYCHOTHERAPIST

Newborns (first 6 weeks)

Physical development

Your newborn:

★ sees faces that are close up (about the distance between a mother's and a baby's face when breastfeeding; they go cross-eyed trying to see anything closer and simply can't see anything further

★ will look towards a light if there isn't an object they can focus on

★ makes movements that are all a bit random and jerky, with sudden kicks and out-of-control arms

★ needs their neck supported as their head's still too big for their body and the neck muscles aren't developed

★ will stay in the position you put them in to sleep

★ sees the world mainly in strong contrasts of light and dark – bold black and white shapes and patterns are good to look at but, let's face it, newborns didn't have these until the last few years when people started selling special mobiles and other marketing ideas – so don't faff about it

★ can smell breast milk and see the dark areola on the breast, and will turn their head and home in

★ loves skin-to-skin-in-the-nuddy contact

★ is just starting to touch, smell, taste, hear – everything, in fact

★ has a curly-up body and curly-up hands; don't try to fight against this – it will not help development and will distress your baby

★ can't hear as well as adults; there's no need to shout, but just speak when you're near them or speak a little louder if you move away – if they startle, it's too loud!

★ tends to need quiet, especially if they're preterm, while their hearing develops to cope with louder sounds.

Newborn reflexes

Reflexes are involuntary movements; the newborn's reflexes are unique to babies and disappear over time.

★ **Stepping:** for about the first 2 months when you hold a baby vertically, and their legs touch the floor or another surface, they'll look as if they're trying to walk.

★ **Rooting** (no sniggering, please): a tickle of a finger, a breast or a nipple on a baby's cheek will make their mouth automatically open for a feed.

★ **Startling** (also known as the Moro reflex): a baby throws out their arms and legs automatically when they are startled or feel lost in space.

★ **Sucking:** for months everything available goes in the mouth because it's the baby's means of checking things out.

★ **Grasping:** a baby curls their fingers around an adult finger, but otherwise keeps them in a fist.

★ **Survival:** a baby should turn their head if their mouth and nose are covered, to get more air.

Emotional and mental development

Your newborn:

★ can't really organize their brain to tell their limbs, or any other part of them, what to do

★ is fresh in the world so is easily startled (imagine if you'd never seen any colours, shapes, people or objects before – frankly I think I'd lose my mind), and needs a soothing environment

★ is learning to trust you and to be soothed by "their people" (family and carers)

★ likes relaxing music (think classical or reggae, not thrash metal) and their mother's and father's (or other carers') voices (especially when pitched higher) and listening to baby talk with exaggerated vowels (babies do love it and people do tend to speak to them like that, but you need to get over it, or at least mix it with normal words and chat, as time goes on or your toddler won't learn to speak anything but baby talk)

★ can recognize the face of their mother, father and other carers if they have a lot of contact, and prefers expressive, but not wildly changing, faces to ones that stay still

★ will have some unconscious and some experimental facial expressions as days and weeks go by, and will learn how to react and how to fit expressions to feelings and mimic the faces they see. This is why an expressionless, depressed face is not something a baby needs to see all the time

★ can recognize their mother's voice and prefers it, although in the very early days they like it muffled as if they were hearing through amniotic fluid (you don't have to talk underwater, it's just interesting to know).

In only a few weeks they can get to know their dad's voice, or another carer's. It's believed that babies who hear their dad's voice in the last few weeks of pregnancy would know it too after birth

★ has a fairly rudimentary system of feelings (as far as we know), which breaks down into hungry, tired, overwhelmed and uncomfortable, and satisfyingly full, alert and cruisy. It takes them a little time to develop more complicated emotions. At this stage your baby doesn't love you, but needs to feel your loving touch and kindness. Your baby knows you, needs you and feels comforted by and interested in you, and will learn to love you along with getting all this brand-new eating, digesting, sleeping, breathing, moving, seeing, hearing and other stuff down

★ dreams – it's now believed that babies probably dream even before they leave the womb. Their dreams will develop as they get older. Some observers think that after a bad day (lots of crossness and tension) babies may have disturbed sleep.

Communication development
Your newborn:

★ communicates by crying. You will often be told this is the only way newborns can communicate, but they can also let you know how they are feeling by being suddenly still and wary, shaping themselves to your body or relaxing with skin-to-skin contact and breastfeeding; or even by staring hard when trying to understand or make a connection with you.

What can you do?
Try lots of baby talk, lots of cuddling, songs and baby massage, which is believed to be calming, especially in the first 3 months, and also helps a baby become aware of their body and feelings of touch and movement (look up "baby massage" in the index). Don't think you have to do anything special to entertain your newborn: sitting still in a chair having a cuddle and a chat for a while before a sleep is good for them and doesn't cost a penny.

When you're talking to your baby, pause for responses: pretend they've answered. This is more entertaining for you, and the baby has time to develop reactions, even facial expressions, that will show you they're trying to keep up and communicate. Bubs can be very good at compensating when they can't hear, so for your own peace of mind make sure you organize a hearing test if one wasn't done in hospital (ask your GP or health visitor to arrange one).

If you have had a grumpy or stressful day, try to start afresh the next hour, after a nap or at least the next day so your baby is reassured.

Staring at a baby a lot of the time or being silent with them is not stimulating enough: they need a lot of chat and interaction (interspersed with quiet times and sleep of course: see the earlier "Possible Routines for Babies" chapter). It doesn't matter if neither of you has a handle on exactly what the other one is thinking: it's important that you both know that an effort is being made. Sort of like different planets in a *Star Trek* episode trying to make contact. (Well, at least you don't have to wear a velour jumpsuit.)

about 6 weeks

Physical development

An awful lot seems to go on at 6 weeks. One day researchers will probably work out why. Some people say it's also a peak time for crying for many babies. Your baby:

* ★ will probably cry real tears because their tear ducts should have started working
* ★ probably smiles at things (before this age "they" say the smiley lips are due to wind, but parents know better, I reckon)
* ★ stares, fixated, at things – maybe a person, maybe an object. Sometimes this is because their eyes aren't yet used to doing what the brain wants them to do, and they just get kind of stuck. If you think this has happened, and it's causing your baby distress, move the whole baby so their gaze is broken from the object
* ★ is less floppy, and can hold their head up independently – there's more head and neck control now
* ★ responds to faces and other things up close, but also notices things further away and more to the side rather than right in front or above.

Emotional and mental development

Your baby:

★ has fleeting "emotions", shown by gurgling happily or crying incon-
solably, although these episodes are over and forgotten practically
immediately. But if the same thing makes the baby cry each time – a particularly loud and bumptious relative, for example – the baby will learn
to cry when that person picks them up and speaks to them in a shouty
voice, and will "remember" the nice smells and feelings of being rescued
by their mum or dad.

Communication development

Your baby:

★ is steadily practising all those newborn ways of communicating with
you.

What can you do?

Give your baby more of those cuddles, chats and songs, but also lots of "tummy
time" to develop their arm, leg and abdominal action: put bub on a rug on the grass
(always in the shade) or the floor. They might get cross at first: it's good to wait until
they can hold their head up a bit so they're not just lying there looking at the rug or
floor! This is also a counterbalance to babies being put to sleep on their backs – one
of the recommendations to help avoid SIDS (for more on this look up "sudden infant
death syndrome" in the index). If your baby doesn't like tummy time, try it on your
chest instead of the floor, giving them the "reward" of seeing your smiling, encouraging face if they lift up their head.

Let your baby uncurl and straighten out at their own pace, but feel free to move
and bend their arms and legs gently if they enjoy it. Put a rattle in their hand and let
them learn what it's for (there may be some preliminary accidental eye-whacking so
make it a lightweight plastic rattle).

about 2 months

Physical development
Your baby:

★ still usually has closed fists most of the time – although they will curl them around a finger or other object, they don't really get it that those hands belong to them

★ is following an object with their eyes more smoothly, with fewer jerks

★ can focus more easily on things to the front and centre, as well as peripherally, now that their initially blurry vision has sharpened

★ waves their arms around trying to get control of them

★ is starting to distinguish colours as well as light and dark.

Emotional and mental development
Your baby:

★ is trying to make sense of so many things at once they can get tired; that's why having lots of sleeps is a good thing

★ is learning emotional responses, taking their cues from you.

Communication development
Your baby:

★ wants to make contact and talk with you

★ smiles more in response

★ makes extended, babbly vowel sounds and has very early, totally incomprehensible chats. Excellent conversations can be had, with each party enjoying themselves immensely. This babbling will get a little more complicated and sophisticated in tone until actual words start to come out (at about 9 to 12 months or just after).

What can you do?
Your baby is learning conversational tone from you so be amazed, serious, thrilled at what they're telling you, and tell them lots of stuff too, even if it's descriptions of mad things happening outside the bus that they can't see. They'll be riveted.

Be lively but not frightening (that'll be when they cry or look freaked out). Sing to them.

Repeat the sounds your baby makes so they can practise the sounds with you.

If you are depressed, get help. A depressed carer, especially one with an impassive face and in a non-interactive state, can have a sad effect on a baby: introduce someone to your baby who can stimulate them and be genuinely enthused, chatty and interested in them. If you get help from a doctor or counsellor, that person can be you.

about 3 months

Physical development

Your baby:

- ★ may have a growth spurt that requires feeds more often for a day or so. Sometimes a baby really does grow during the night
- ★ definitely seems to have worked out their hands are attached to themselves and practises doing stuff with them
- ★ continues to use their mouth to explore the world so puts everything they can in it – this is fine as long as the thing is bigger than a small film canister
- ★ lifts their head to look around while lying on their tummy – maybe with a slight "push-up" action of the arms
- ★ sits when propped up and held
- ★ continues to watch things intently now and again
- ★ grasps something put in their hand.

Emotional and mental development

Your baby:

- ★ can suddenly laugh or giggle
- ★ recognizes familiar people.

Communication development

Your baby:

★ is more sociable

★ smiles at voices, faces and things

★ has funny little noises that more obviously seem to be attempts at making a connection.

What can you do?

Most babies are social and, when feeling secure, love to have new experiences and see new people, places and objects. Keep it simple and don't introduce too many things: learn your baby's tired signs (see "tired signs" in the index) so you'll know when there's been a little too much stimulation and it's time for a nap. Put your baby on the floor a lot, continuing tummy time.

Give your baby shakers and rattles, safe plastic toys in bright colours, soft toys with furry or silky sensuous textures to play with. Dangle things for them to whack and eventually grab.

Keep up the chat and songs and show them simple board books you borrow or buy. Give or pack away your black and white mobiles. Colourful, dangly, musical, revolving mobiles are a hit at this age.

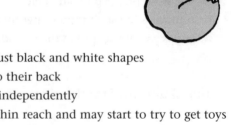

ABOUT 4 TO 5 MONTHS

Physical development

Your baby:

★ is now able to see colours, not just black and white shapes

★ may roll from their tummy onto their back

★ holds up and moves their head independently

★ can grab something dangled within reach and may start to try to get toys that are out of reach

★ is becoming stronger and pushes harder with their legs and arms

★ is feeling things with their hands, but most discoveries still go straight into their mouth for "oral exploration"

★ often drools a lot – some babies need frequent bib changes.

Emotional and mental development

Your baby:

- ★ laughs when you pull funny faces
- ★ likes looking in a mirror
- ★ shows their enjoyment of, for example, music and delight at leaves blowing in the wind; and also shows concern at stressful, shouty situations.

Communication development

Your baby:

- ★ is learning how to interact with people more as time goes on
- ★ is working out how to communicate using their face, body language and babble. Their feelings can be clearly seen in their facial expressions. Until they are much older, maybe nearing school age, young children don't know how to "fake it" – all emotions are pure.

What can you do?

You can help your baby to stand and "walk" by holding their hands if they enjoy it – but "baby walker" contraptions won't help them walk any earlier and are dangerous. Let your baby have a clear view of their own feet, and take their shoes and socks off as much as possible so they can feel things with their toes: this applies to babies of all ages.

Rattles or bells on their wrists and feet can help your baby work out that those bits belong to them and can be manipulated. Try tummy time in front of a mirror so that when they lift their head up they can see their reflection (although they may not yet recognize themselves).

Keep showing your baby simple board books. This will be the start of all sorts of language and understanding development. Kids love stories and pictures even at this age. And don't worry, they all chew the corners.

Play peek-a-boo, make funny noises, blow raspberries on their tum. Play different kinds of music and dance with your bub – but not spooky, scary classical or frenetic hard rock: babies and kids are very sensitive to the mood music creates. Try some boppy songs or some songs especially for babies or kids.

Find time to do some things you like by yourself or with a partner or friends. A trip out of Babyland is a helpful break and you can come back refreshed (see the "Coping Strategies for Parents" chapter in *Part 3: Parenting*).

about 6 months

Physical development

This is another big time in a baby's life (oh, they all are, I know). Your baby:

★ gets their mouth around anything available and is reaching for and grabbing things. They still use their mouth more than their fingers to feel and explore objects

★ can stick their toes in their mouth

★ checks things out solemnly

★ can maybe pass an item from one hand to the other, but usually can't hold things in two hands at once

★ may find peek-a-boo a big hit because they're learning some things that disappear can reappear

★ is starting to enjoy having a real effect on items that can be whacked, thrown, picked up and so on

★ recognizes their own name and perhaps other names ("Here's Mum back")

★ is now, like an adult, hearing high-frequency sounds better than low-frequency ones, but is still not hearing softer noises as well as an adult. By this age a hearing test should have been done by your health visitor or GP if the hearing wasn't tested in hospital. (We were told it would be terribly hi-tech, but a woman just stood behind our baby, first to one side and then the other, and rattled a spoon in a metal cup to see if they turned their head.) Babies found to have partial or total deafness – and their families – need to immediately start to learn sign language and other ways of communicating: the sooner the better (look up "hearing test" in the index)

★ can sit unsupported for a few moments

★ is ready to experiment with solids – otherwise known as purées – and to learn lots of new tastes. The more you give, the more the baby will get used to. Even small babies can enjoy bits of olives, asparagus, rose flavouring and other "exotic" fancies. Most babies will show a preference for naturally sweet foods and a distaste for very bitter tastes, which may be a poison safety instinct. (Unfortunately not all dangerous substances are bitter, and some babies don't mind the taste of anything, so don't rely on this instinct)

★ may have their first teeth starting to come through (see the "Teeth" chapter in *Part 4: Stuff*), just as they get interested in food

★ may put their arms out as if to say "Lift me up".

Emotional and mental development

Your baby:

★ after 6 months will simply be much more engaged with the world around them: this is the time when babies get cast in commercials, dressed for baby fashion catalogues, and become more attractive propositions to some wary friends and relatives who figured newborns were too fragile to hold and not much fun to be around

★ will develop emotionally much more between 6 months and 1 year, and will become aware of more sophisticated feelings (outrage, contentment, astonishment, doubt, amusement, a scoff, cheerfulness, jealousy)

★ finds their mirror image fascinating and it may now be recognized by them as "me"

★ may start getting clingy in the second 6 months of life, which some-times builds to a peak around 18 months. They show a clear preference for the close family circle. A baby (or a toddler) is never happier than when fed and in a group, looking as if they could say smugly "These – these are my people!". A baby can be fixated on one parent, or two, or a carer, or a combo of parents and carer, depending on how "primary care" is divvied up.

Communication development

Your baby:

★ mimics facial expressions and sounds

★ can probably have a funny baby chat with indiscernible words, often seemingly to themselves

★ matches sounds and actions to events – waving is for bye-bye; a ducky goes quack

★ continues to respond to chat from others with facial expressions, body movements and sounds.

What can you do?

Over the next few months your baby will enjoy doing things they seem to have control over: batting at things that make a noise or pop up, or fiddling with objects. Give them lots of interesting food they can hold and feed themselves with: rusks; cheese sticks; a banana, some apple in a stocking or cheesecloth that they can chew and suck without swallowing big pieces; cooked veggies (not hard raw ones, which can be choky).

Songs and nursery rhymes help babies learn tone, rhythm and words. Play together with simple musical instruments – a lot of these, like most things, can be home-made. Try a saucepan and wooden-spoon drum (but don't go mad and DIY a tambourine!).

Flop down on a rug in the shade in the garden or a nearby park and just relax: look at butterflies, blades of grass, talk about the clouds and people going by.

Showing your baby photos of special friends, carers and relatives and talking about them can help to widen their circle when the immediate family are not around for a while.

Encourage and praise independence in your baby, while making them also feel secure. (Yes, sorry, in other words be perfect and do two opposite things at once.)

aBOUt 7 MONtHS

Physical development

Your baby:

- ★ can sit up without being propped
- ★ continues to hone their reaching and grabbing
- ★ will try to see the source of sounds
- ★ tries to move to see something or be nearer something, and will stretch out or angle their head to see better or be part of the action
- ★ still throws up if they cough or cry a lot or something gets caught in their throat or put well into their mouth. This is the gag reflex that babies have from birth, which may last for years: it can be annoying but it's actually a great survival technique
- ★ may be an early starter for crawling or bum-shuffling (some babies miss out on the crawling stage: it's not a problem).

Emotional and mental development

Your baby:

- ★ remembers what certain toys are built to do
- ★ points at things to indicate "I want that"
- ★ plays swapsies with you (you take it – now give it back)
- ★ has worked out how to get your attention.

Communication development

Your baby:

- ★ is becoming more and more social and taking increasing interest in their world and understanding more of conversations and atmospheres
- ★ as always, loves a chat.

What can you do?

Make things available for your baby to grasp and listen to (this applies to all baby ages).

Don't be alarmed if you see your baby adopt strange sleeping positions, even curled up on their tum with bum in the air and head to the side. If your baby can roll onto their tum to sleep they should be able to roll back if they want to: the tum position is more of a worry for younger babies who can't move themselves. This new mobility is a sign of your needing to worry less – not more!

Make baby sounds such as "bub bub bub" for your baby to copy, and listen to their attempts to communicate, responding as if in conversation. Repeat the names for things and put them in sentences, so that "hat" is associated with that thing that goes on the head, and "drink" is the wet yummy stuff referred to in "What would you like to drink? Milk? Rightyho." Repetition is the key to building a vocabulary of understood words. Explain to the baby what's going on around them. Read simple storybooks to them and explain the pictures. Babies this age love animated conversation: play with facial expressions and body language. Let them watch you dance, and "dance" them in your arms.

Over the next month or so, introduce paper and big crayons and pencils, things with wheels such as large plastic trucks, and building blocks (knocking down might come before building up so get in there and help).

Roll a ball to your baby and encourage them to roll it back. Keep giving them toys they can have an influence on – especially those they love where something pops out or makes a noise when they press a lever. Also introduce them to shape-sorting post-it toys or other toys that provide putting in and taking out opportunities; and to a sturdy cart or toy to push along.

Give them careful swings and slides at the park, where they can also watch kids playing.

About 8 months

Physical development

Your baby:

- ★ may start to crawl from now on
- ★ can look for and find a toy you hid
- ★ likes to fill things up and empty them – any game of now you see it, now you don't
- ★ can sit alone but might fall over once in a while
- ★ should turn their head to locate the source of a noise, but the turning may be slow.

Emotional and mental development

Your baby:

- ★ may start to develop separation anxiety and attachment to certain people and things, although they also start to understand that if you go you come back
- ★ can discern your mood by your tone and body language.

Communication development

Your baby:

- ★ is developing more control over the babble and their "words" sound more like real conversation

★ in the next month or so will develop greater powers of concentration and learning from what they've seen. This means if they've always had milk in a green cup they may be dubious about a yellow one.

What can you do?

Gently broaden your child's circle of carers. Help your baby with the idea of something going away and coming back – hide a toy under a tea towel and let them reveal it.

Continue to build up that group of toys that they can have an effect on: blocks to build up and knock down and banging and shaking things such as musical instruments. Toys that can be pushed, pulled or go on wheels will help your baby learn to get mobile themselves. Lift the flap or other hiding and revealing books, games and toys are also perfect for this age.

Walks with lots of pointing out of things and chats with neighbours and shopkeepers can be fun: remember what's mundane to you may be perfectly thrilling to a baby. (Which is why you can be infected with the delight, but need to have the odd morning and afternoon off so you can do adult things! You can only go ga-ga over a dandelion so many times when you're a grown-up.)

9 MONTHS TO 1 YEAR

Physical development

Your baby:

★ is crawling or shuffling

★ is climbing over or going around things (but they usually prefer to go right through them if possible!)

★ can pull themselves up to a standing position, look confused and fall down on their bot

★ can "walk" when an adult holds their hands, may be able to totter from, say, a piece of furniture to a nearby knee and back or may walk alone

★ drops things for you to pick up

★ can pass things from hand to hand

★ loves to throw things

★ claps hands

★ can wave bye-bye

★ wants to use a spoon or a fork, hold a cup, clutch food

★ can pick small things up; by about 1 year they've mastered the true "pincer movement", using their thumb and first finger

★ starts to phase out putting everything in their mouth (but this will continue as part of the repertoire until 2 years old or so).

Emotional and mental development

Your baby:

★ will show more of their "personality" and quirks will become recognizable – even if you don't realize this until later, when your child is older and you look back

★ becomes an alert observer

★ even though they can't see an object, they know it still exists ("object permanence" – a friend of mine says this never works with her ex-boyfriends)

★ knows where things "belong" on a shelf and which way up they should be

★ is grasping simple concepts and explanations

★ enjoys familiar songs and rhymes or sets of words

★ may become more clingy as they gear up for crawling and walking – evolution's way of keeping babies safely close to home instead of pootling off into the wilds

★ might show a preference for a fluffy toy (some kids never have favourites, or they rotate them).

Communication development

Your baby:

★ can follow simple instructions and sentences ("Find Nanna", "Can you give me the book, please")

★ can respond to their name or familiar words, and more and more loves babbling words

★ recognizes familiar voices and copies sounds and words

★ is making sounds that are definitely more like words, some with several syllables

★ may, at about 9 months, start practising sounds that start with a consonant and end in a vowel, such as "dada" and "fa", building up new words as the months go by.

What can you do?

Allow a crawler to crawl as much as they like, but make sure you babyproof their environment first. Help them to "dance", whether standing, sitting or lying down. As with any new skill, the more they have the opportunity to do something, the better they get at it, so they can move on to the next step. Provide an opportunity for them to do their stuff but don't prod a baby to do something or "teach" them to crawl or walk. It doesn't happen that way.

Hand your baby things to hold in their shopping-trolley seat, and help them to reach for some things on the shelves.

You can respond to their "Barbufdubbadubpaddca" with "Oh well, yes, I shouldn't be at all surprised". It helps to teach the art of conversation and is a more amusing way for you to pass the time.

1 yeaR

Physical development

Your baby:

★ stands up from a sitting start

★ may be toddling

★ is learning to drink from a cup

★ can put things into a bag or box and take them out again

★ will try to fit the noise to the item, such as an animal or a car.

Emotional and mental development

Your baby:

- ★ is very fascinated by and enjoys other kids but is not into sharing toys with them
- ★ may be clingy
- ★ enjoys interacting with you – passing objects and looks.

standing

Communication development

Your baby:

- ★ understands many more words
- ★ is building on their vocabulary every day, but at this stage uses far fewer words than they actually understand.

What can you do?

Help your baby to do things for themselves: pass them objects to hold and experiment with. Continue to roll balls to them and have some soft ones they're allowed to throw. (See the "Being Active" chapter in *Part 4: Stuff*.)

Make jokes by using funny voices or doing odd things such as putting a shoe on your head. Enjoy favourite songs and books together, and introduce new ones. Keep playing disappear and reappear games with toys and your face.

Use new words and practise familiar ones. Give them room to reply or react in conversation.

You might like to take your 1-year-old to a playgroup: they'll probably enjoy the play and watching other children, and it's also a chance for you to see kids at different stages of development, regardless of precise age.

The "Toddler Development (1 to 3)" chapter in *Part 2: Toddlers* carries on from here. (And see also "More Info" opposite for books on baby development.)

more info

Your Baby and Child by Penelope Leach has great sections on development for each age group, broken into physical, speech, playing and mental development. She recommends ways of speaking to a baby and toddler, and play activities and toys for each stage. If you're not used to babies, the book gives you a good idea of what they're up to. (For full details and review see "More Info" at the end of the first chapter, "In the Beginning".)

BOOKS

From Birth to Five Years: Children's Developmental Progress
by Mary Sheridan, Routledge, 2007
The standard guide for child assessment, so rather "text-booky", but with lots of easy "bullet-points". Describes the stages of development for this age group including movements, vision, hearing and speech,social behaviour and play.

Why Love Matters: How Affection Shapes a Baby's Brain
by Sue Gerhardt, Brunner-Routledge, 2004
Far from the cuddly self-help book that the title suggests, this is a technically detailed and scholarly analysis on how parenting style actually affects how a baby's brain develops. Relying heavily on attachment theory and the importance of showing affection it's the result of the author's own observations and subsequent practice as a psychotherapist.

WEBSITES

Many of the general parenting websites listed in "More Info" for the first and second chapters of this book list the milestones of baby development, and have tips and variations on old ideas for play with babies.

www.bbc.co.uk
Search "traditional children's songs" from the main page for a burst of sing-along nostalgia.

www.parentcenter.com

Note the US spelling: search "Activities" on the home page for the stuff to do with kids sorted by age and situation. (Is it raining?)

PLAYGROUPS

Mother-and-baby playgroups (as opposed to playgroups where an older child can be left) are weekly informal, drop-in groups in local halls, often run by the parents themselves (there might be a small charge to cover costs). You get to chat with other mums over tea and a biscuit, while your bub gets a change of scene and some different toys to play with. You may have to try a few before you find one you like – the better ones sometimes have waiting lists. Your local authority will have a list of registered playgroups in your area, or look at the community boards in your library or doctor's surgery, or ask your health visitor for a recommendation. Locality-orientated websites or newspapers may also be a good source.

toys and games for babies

Toys and play are fun for babies, and they're also an essential part of their development and learning process. You'll see from this suggested list – based on info from parents who responded to the survey undertaken for this book – that I've edited out most of the merchandising or brand-name favourites. I figure they don't need the advertising. Lots of the suggestions are low-budget options. All kids will have different favourites: some kids never get turned on by dollies, others never really like cars.

Keep a small swag of toys – say, enough to fit in a laundry basket – in the cupboard and rotate them every few days or weeks so that your baby always has a fresh lot of things to be interested in. (Obviously real favourites such as special comfort or sleepytime toys can't be whisked away.) A huge selection of toys leads to a jaded baby.

Always check the safety and age-appropriate labels on new toys (see "toys" in the index). Make sure toys that are safe for one age group don't get used by younger babies. Look out for damaged or elderly toys, with bits coming off. Anything that fits into a plastic film canister can be a choking hazard for kids up to about the age of 3.

> Didn't Incy-Wincy spider get BORED?

ideas from parents

Use your common sense for safe versions of all these suggestions. (See also "More Info" at the end of this chapter.)

Good toys for babies (0 to 1 year)
◎ Dangly toys to hang on the pram or above the baby to swat at – if they make noises so much the better ◎ small things that are easily grabbed, such as cars or blocks ◎ floor mats with interesting patterns, for tummy play ◎ "touch and feel" books ◎ balls too big to swallow, easy to grasp with two hands and not too hard

or full ◎ rice in a tightly sealed plastic jar to rattle ◎ a teething rattle or teething ring that plays music ◎ crackly packaging for grasping (but be careful: it will be eaten if possible) ◎ a baby photo album with photos of family and friends for you to look at and "talk" about together ◎ a safety standard bouncing harness ◎ little toys with wheels, which they can pull or push, or a small trolley or doll's pram to push along if they're toddling already ◎ stacking cups ◎ a ball with a bell inside ◎ a low toy shelf rather than a box so that they can see things better and learn to take them off and then, you hope, put them back ◎ plastic chains or rings ◎ soft toys with long ears or tails for sucking ◎ plastic ware and cooking utensils ◎ net bags used for oranges, filled with scrunched-up paper ◎ tightly sealed plastic bottles filled with coloured water or rattly dried beans ◎ broken or toy phones (battery removed from old mobiles) for pretend calls and button pushing ◎ a soft drink can holder for holding, biting, pretending to drink, rolling or putting things into (but not soft enough to bite off bits – that is, not polystyrene) ◎ a packet of crisps (unopened) to pulverize ◎ blocks ◎ board books ◎ an activity play centre ◎ teddies and fluffy toys (some babies and kids never really get into fluffy things, although they're often given heaps) ◎ a yoghurt container, with a plastic block in it ◎ books that have little flaps to open and look under ◎ a musical mobile ◎ unbreakable plastic spoons ◎ a xylophone ◎ a hammering game (pegs or balls are pushed or whacked through holes with a hammer) ◎ cloth books ◎ a cloth dolly with a rattle inside ◎ a battery-operated piano-style keyboard ◎ a cardboard box to be sat in, to put things into, and to be pulled along in down the corridor at warp speed ◎ cardboard tubes (not toilet ones, sturdier cling-wrap ones) ◎ an inflatable ball ◎ sticky tape half-stuck on something for the baby to pull off and put on (but don't let them eat it) ◎ a babyproofed cupboard for unpacking and packing contents ◎ the saucepan cupboard ◎ foam jigsaw bases with numbers or letters that pop in and out ◎ a napkin or tea towel for playing peek-a-boo with ◎ a tissue box with bits of ribbon, material and different-textured things to put in and take out ◎ large plastic animals ◎ a small squirting animal ◎ a set of key rings with lots of keys ◎

ball with a bell in it

Knitted thingo

221

different-sized plastic doovers

pegs either by themselves or pegged onto something ◎ a baby-sized plastic watering can for bathtime ◎ balloons (but make sure the baby doesn't eat bits when one pops or deflates – get it straight into the bin) ◎ empty plastic yoghurt containers to experiment with (babies love to stick their hands in, roll them, put other things in and rattle, and tip things out of) ◎ a stuffed caterpillar ◎ a toy wagon ◎ a safe mirror ◎ a large rubber bath plug ◎ a tambourine and anything else musical ◎ a broken calculator, phone or anything with buttons to press ◎ a sturdy plastic potato masher ◎ old paperbacks or magazines with pictures of kids and animals ◎ a clothes basket and pegs ◎ a squeaky duck ◎ finger puppets (big ones can be scary) ◎ stacking rings.

=tight lid=

Good games for babies

Child-care workers (and maybe some relatives) will know lots of baby games and rhymes: ask them to teach you some for your baby's age. Most large bookshops have compilations of nursery rhymes. ◎ Peek-a-boo ◎ hide something and make it reappear ◎ the baby throws and you catch (they won't be able to catch yet) ◎ rhyming games or songs ◎ "What noise does a duck, cat, truck (or whatever) make?" ◎ Pat-a-cake ◎ blow bubbles for them to look at and try to catch ◎ flap a cot sheet or coloured fabric gently above the baby, cover them with it and remove immediately ◎ Round and Round the Garden.

beads in a bottle

moRe iNfo

365 Activities You and Your Baby Will Love: An Idea a Day for Baby's First Year!
by Roni C Leiderman and Wendy Masi, Bonnier Books, 2007
Simple and imaginative games and ideas for play from the Gymboree empire.

www.landofnurseryrhymes.co.uk
Lists over 1000 nursery rhymes and their melodies.

www.preschoolrainbow.org
A US pre-school teacher's site with ideas for finger play, action poems, nursery rhymes and songs, grouped into themes, such as animals or numbers.

www.elc.co.uk
The "Play" area of this major toy store website has lots of age-appropriate ideas for play that won't cost you anything (and are not tied in with their products), such as pretending to go on a motorbike ride with the baby on your lap, or making a "postbox" for the bub out of an old shoe box. Hints on creating a "balanced diet" of active, imaginative and creative play.

2

TODDLERS

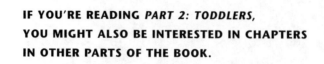

IF YOU'RE READING *PART 2: TODDLERS,*
YOU MIGHT ALSO BE INTERESTED IN CHAPTERS
IN OTHER PARTS OF THE BOOK.

PART 3: PARENTING

Parenting philosophy
Unpaid work and paid work
Dads
Coping strategies for parents
A you-shaped family
Teaching kids how to behave
Child care

PART 4: STUFF

Equipment
Home safety
Clothes
Teeth
Food
Health
Being active
Immunization
Insidey activities
Birthday parties and presents

EXTRA RESOURCES

WHO'S THE CENTRE OF THE UNIVERSE?

The toddler years are roughly those from 1 to 3, depending of course on when your cherub first takes to their tootsies. It's all so sudden – the baby months seemed to stretch on forever when you were in them, but now they're over. No more just plonking bub somewhere and expecting them to stay put when you turn your back for a moment.

Your little baby isn't such a bubba any more. They still have their baby face, but they're growing into their own little person and trying to balance how much they need

you with how much they want to feel independent and in control. Wanting to be a "big kid" – to use the toilet, for example, or be able to do up buttons for themselves – may cause great frustration until their capabilities catch up with their desires and ambitions. (Maybe that's why some politicians look so pouty and petulant.)

wHat's a toDDLeR?

Although "toddler" refers to a new physical stage, it is also a time for lots of mental and emotional action. Toddlers are growing into little people who, depending on their personality traits, will observe the world keenly, adore a chat, explore objects and places and make and take a joke, although be careful with that one. Kids under 5 are not able to fully understand sarcasm, it's just confusing or hurtful. But they may love some elementary contradictions or slapstick: your putting an umbrella in the fridge, spilling a cup of water into the bath or pretending to eat their wellie.

When kids get mobile, a new lot of safety issues come into play. Reorganize your house along toddler-safe lines (see the "Home Safety" chapter in *Part 4: Stuff*) and be extra careful about pools, ponds, baths, buckets, puddles and other watery dangers at your place and elsewhere. Kids are programmed to be curious so it's safer to remove anything dangerous rather than expect them never to touch it.

Your new (eventually) all-talking, all-walking kid will soak up as many experiences as they can from social interaction, books, art and music. They'll probably have firm ideas about what they want to eat, do and perhaps even wear, and be more interested in playing with other kids their own age than they were. Toddlers are also building on their communication skills and will communicate with you not just through words, but through behaviour and body language. You may find that varying the way you explain things – by using facial expressions, drawing a picture, acting out the physical effects of a feeling, allowing the child to thoroughly examine something new with their fingers, even if it's gloopy or disgusting (jelly, not dog poo) – will help you work out which ways your child most enjoys learning and communicating. Their curiosity is insatiable and their capacity for mimicking and copying almost endless.

When you've heard "Why?" for the 678th time, you may have to be creative. Surf the Internet with them. Take them to the library. Keep a promise to go on an excursion that will help explain something, such as to the zoo or the museum. Get your child to ring up Nanna or Grandad and ask them if they know. It's good to answer a query with "What do *you* think?" and then be positive about the answer – "Yes, that could happen". And if you're really stumped, I suggest you feign unconsciousness. Or perhaps I mean incompetence.

Your toddler's personality is developing and they're experimenting with how to get what they want. This can turn into an ongoing fight between a little person and a big person over who gets total control of which bits of life; or into continual push-me, pull-you negotiation. You'll need to show them (sadly by example mostly) how to react to frustrating situations. For instance, I like to lie on the floor, kick my legs and swear in a shouty way.

Giving your toddler as much control and as many choices as possible when the outcome doesn't matter ("Do you want pineapple or mango?", "You be the boss: shall we go to the beach or the park?") will allow you to get away with other negatives and absolutes ("You can't touch that because it will burn your hand and hurt a lot", "We are tidying the room now, but after that you can choose whether to go to the park or the shop"). If you give in to tantrums, the toddler learns that they're a good way to get what they want.

Hints on how to avoid these and other potential battlegrounds (move to another country) can be found in the "Teaching Kids How to Behave" chapter in *Part 3: Parenting*. And, nope, it's never too late to change your expectations and your kid's behaviour as long as you explain the change, help them to make the transition and then consistently stick to your approach. (I know it's easy for *me* to say!)

Now that your toddler is mobile and exploring the world, you'll need to dress both boys and girls for normal days in ways that allow them to get dirty, fall down and climb things at the adventure playground, and although everyone likes to spruce up for a party, a long skirt or bowtie is not conducive to play. Prepare to face the reality of what happens to the clothes and bodies of normal, healthy kids. Kids get dirty. They need to get dirty so they can learn stuff about themselves and the world around them.

Despite the fact that girls and boys often (although not always) show different traits, you may want to ask yourself how much is genetic and how much is suggested by the reactions and expectations of grown-ups and by the opportunities that are given to them. Are the boys always first to the construction toys at playgroup so the

GOOD THINGS ABOUT TODDLERS

* Toddlers are growing out of their baby face and into their own face, and personality.

* Toddlers want to learn to do things for themselves.

* A toddler's laugh is a wonderful sound.

* Toddlers listen to you carefully, even if they don't "get" it all.

* Toddlers' attention spans vary, but can be surprisingly long.

* Toddlers can entertain themselves for short periods.

* Toddlers think housework is fun (hee, hee, hee).

* Toddlers are fun to watch when they're determined (to get a sock on, for example).

* Toddlers force you to slow down to their pace (yes, I know this can be infuriating, but it's probably good for you).

* Toddlers can kiss and cuddle you – for a possibly short period between not being big enough to and not wanting to any more.

* Toddlers are amazed by things you have come to take for granted.

* Toddlers' emotions are all out there in pure form – sheer joy and terrible misery – so you usually know how they feel.

girls do playdough? Are the boys allowed to have a cry if they hurt themselves or told to be a "brave little man"? (Look up "gender" in the index.)

Make allowances for children as individuals: if someone isn't keen to play a contact sport because they're scared of getting hurt, that should be accepted – it doesn't matter whether they're a boy or a girl. Everyone deserves some leeway, patience and understanding.

Always ask for professional medical advice if you think development in a certain area has stalled. It probably hasn't as there's a very wide range of kids' capabilities at any age – in almost all cases everyone "evens up" eventually.

These are the bridging years between baby and nursery school child, a time when you can make firm friends with your kid; get to know them really well; help them experiment; rejoice that they have a longer attention span and can amuse themselves

✱ Toddlers are so adorable when they're asleep (or quiet and not bouncing off the walls).

✱ Toddlers often bond with their attentive family, friends and carers but warm to others slowly. This is wise and safe behaviour, and not to be criticized as being "too shy".

✱ Toddlers say unexpected things that make you see the world from a new angle.

✱ Toddlers get excited and show it, without trying to act cool.

✱ Toddlers' fatty-nappied bums are Teletubbie-cute.

✱ Toddlers have reached the last years when you can kiss their bottom without it being annoying or weird.

✱ Toddlers are easier to pick up and carry than when they get older.

✱ Toddlers usually still have an afternoon sleep so you can too.

✱ Toddlers love books and the idea of stories.

✱ Toddlers pretend to read.

✱ Toddlers love songs.

✱ Toddlers start to imagine and pretend.

✱ Toddlers so intensely care about what they're doing that they remind you that little things can be as important as the "big" stuff in life.

✱ Toddlers don't want to borrow the car yet. (Actually they probably do.)

for – oh – whole minutes on end; and perhaps launch them a little way into the world even though they, and you, know they can run back to you for comfort any time.

For many people this is also the stage when they have a new baby so they have to attend to their special needs as well as those of the toddler, who might wonder why they're no longer the centre of the universe (see the "A You-shaped Family" chapter in *Part 3: Parenting*).

Not to mention parents wondering why *they're* no longer the centre of the universe . . .

> **"Some fairy dust will be lost after washing."** LABEL ON TODDLER UNDERPANTS

more info

TODDLER-CARE BOOKS

As well as the toddler-care books that follow, see the child-care books, by Penelope Leach and Miriam Stoppard, reviewed in "More Info" at the end of the first chapter, "In the Beginning", in *Part 1: Babies*. Gina Ford and Tracy Hogg also both have books that carry on their philosophy to the toddler years.

The Mighty Toddler: The Essential Guide to the Toddler Years
by Robin Barker, M. Evans, 2002
A book approximately the size of the average toddler, with dense, serious, detailed info on just about anything anyone would worry about. Ms Barker has kindlier versions of Time Out and "controlled crying" than many toddler "experts".

What to Expect the Toddler Years
by Arlene Eisenberg, Heidi Murkoff and Sandee Hathaway, Simon and Schuster, 2006
It has the same huge Q and A format as their *What to Expect in the First Year*, and everything from getting shoes fitted to immensely detailed food lists and step-family issues. Very American.

Your Toddler Month by Month
by Dr Tanya Byron, DK, 2008
Child psychologist and TV reality show star Dr Tanya (*Little Angels, House of Tiny Tearaways*) provides a kind, child-centred approach to understanding your toddler's needs and finding a parenting style that fits. Useful info all the way up to school age on tantrums, toilet training, routines, play ideas and how the toddler brain works (they can't think and analyse like we do, so "reasoning" with a toddler is sheer folly).

www.raisingkids.co.uk
Informative and easy-to-use site on a wide range of toddler issues: health, sleeping, parenting skills, out and about, child care and preparing for a second baby.

TODDLERS AND EATING

Some days your toddler will not be interested in much food, the next they'll be starving. Don't get too worried about lists of servings or measuring and weighing foods. Toddlers like to "graze" – have little snacks here and there. It's too long between three meals a day for them to last.

DAILY NEEDS

Basically keep the food choices as varied as possible. Every day offer full-fat dairy food, meat, veggies, fruit, and cereals or bread. The "Learning to Eat" chapter in *Part 1: Babies* has the food requirements for babies of 1 year and over. Here and there you can throw in the chance of different foods such as parsnip, coconut, watermelon or something new in season. Your job is just that: to offer it. If your kid doesn't eat it, offer maybe one alternative but don't jump through hoops to provide fourteen other options. (See the "Food" chapter in *Part 4: Stuff* for info on cooking for babies, toddlers and the family, general nutrition and books with things such as weekly meal plans, if that's the sort of person you are.)

Don't stress about what your child should be eating – you can get lists issued by children's hospitals and nutritionists, although they're mostly for kids over 4 years old, and the suggestions can change from professional to professional and in the time between your having one baby and the next (see "More Info" at the end of this chapter. Experienced child-feeders say it's better, and far more relaxing, to think of your child's food intake over a week rather than over a day, so that you're not obsessing about covering every food group each day. Then if one day they eat nothing but yoghurt, the next nothing but pasta etc it's not so much of a problem, as long as they've had enough protein, veg etc over the entire week. The trick is to keep offering from a wide range of food, not just stick to to their "favourites".

When in doubt, talk about your child's eating pattern with your mother-and-baby health visitor and have a reassuring weigh and measure so you know your kid is thriving. Gaining weight slows right down after the first year. Babies by about 5 months have usually doubled their birth weight and by 1 year have normally tripled it, but after that they only gain 2 kilos or so in the next year.

Be extremely cautious about people who recommend exclusion diets for children such as wheat-free, dairy-free or low-fat programmes. These diets can be *very* dangerous and are, in a HUGE majority of cases, unnecessary. They can exclude a range of essential vitamins and minerals for brain and physical development so do at least please check them with a qualified dietician. (Look up "vegetarian kids" and "vegan kids" in the index.)

"Junk" or "fast" food is fine once a week, but is virtually useless for giving kids the nutrients they need. It would be faster and easier to stay home and open a can of soup, make a sandwich and hand over an apple. It's a good idea to get kids used to seedy wholemeal bread at this age or they'll only ever want white bread, which usually has about as much fibre as a piece of Fuzzy Felt – and probably half the vitamins. (Also look up "drinks" in the index.)

The main thing is to cover the basic food groups and to keep offering as many different foods as you can. Not always cheese sticks; sometimes yoghurt with fruit in it. Not always chops; sometimes stir-fry. Not always Mum; borrow Madonna's personal chef. That sort of thing.

yum

tHiNgs to tRy if youR KiD WON'T eat

First consider the possibility of a physical problem such as a sore throat, mouth ulcers or an illness coming on. Or your child might just be having a day when they don't feel like eating as much as usual, and it will even up the next day.

SOME TODDLER EATING TIPS

✱ Eat together as a family, then you don't have to cook for two sessions of dinner (or even three if you have other kids). Also the "How was your day? What's new?" aspect of the family meal is great for developing children's conversational skills and a comforting family vibe.

✱ Give toddlers morning and afternoon tea. Toddlers need to have little snacks here and there.

✱ When your kid seems to be getting too big for the high chair, say at 2, let them use a plastic booster seat, which sits on top of a normal chair; cushions are not stable enough (see "booster seat" in the index).

✱ Let your kid start using a toddler's cutlery set – although just a spoon is still the easiest implement, especially when they're tired. Sets are available at supermarkets, chemists and baby shops.

✱ Listen to your toddler: don't be strict about a food "routine" if they're getting genuinely hungry at different times. Remember if overall they're eating a wide variety of foods (stop laughing), they should be getting all they need.

Understand also that fussy eating is really evolution at work. The theory is that toddlers are hard-wired to refuse food until they're really familiar with it – when they've been served it up to ten times, for example. This instinct is designed to kick in when babies start walking and prevents them from wandering away from the tribe and eating unfamiliar, poisonous berries. And doesn't explain why they still won't eat spinach after 456 offerings.

✱ Many kids simply feel already "full" – of juice or milk – before a meal. Cut out commercial juice, which is often just sugary water with a dash of vitamin C extract, and once they're weaned from breast or formula milk only give three cups of cow's milk a day after meals, not before.

✱ Explain that the bread in their tummy is having a party and the carrots want to come. And the courgette is all dressed up, with its cheese hat on, ready to go too. Give them a choice of a few foods they can invite or not invite. In other words you choose what to offer and they choose which of those foods to eat. This makes toddlers feel as if they're making decisions.

tummy ache!

- ★ Shout and pull at your hair and lie on the floor and hold your breath and drum your heels on the floor. No, sorry. Maybe do some exercise with them to try to work up their appetite, and try to interest them in food again at the next meal. Or the next day.

- ★ Offer smaller helpings: it might be that you're expecting a toddler to eat a larger serving of food than is actually needed – toddlers don't grow as fast as babies. Many people experienced with toddlers say parents give servings up to four times larger than necessary.

- ★ Don't take it personally. If painstakingly prepared food is chucked around or ignored, skip the painstaking stage. Offer something simple, even raw, instead. That's what fresh fruit and veg – and now and then things that come in packets – are for.

- ★ Make a game of eating little bits of different colours – a green mange tout, a piece of orange carrot, a grey mushroom, a white potato cube, a red cherry tomato. Bonus: this usually makes better nutritional sense than eating three scoops of the same thing.

- ★ Get over it. Your kid's not a prize-winning eater. Keep offering stuff on the plate and don't fuss about it or push the issue. When they're hungry, they'll eat. They can survive and thrive on such teeny amounts as to raise the eyebrows on the statue of Venus de Milo. Or even the arms.

"Kids tend to be grazers. They eat a little bit, regularly." SHELLEY

"We realized that she wanted to be independent and feed herself. She was quite happy when given a spoon of her own." JENNY

"Give it to the dog." CHRISTOPHER

"Put hundreds and thousands on vegetables." SALLY

"At 1 he pushed food away. If I held the bowl down so that he could see what he was eating, and how I put it on the spoon, he was happy." WENDY

"Friends ask how I get my kids to eat wholemeal bread and I just say they didn't know there was anything else." FIONA

"Let someone else feed them." LILIAN

"Send them to creche. We have many children who won't eat at home, but put them at a lunch table with five or six others and suddenly the attitude becomes 'I'm doing what she's doing!' or 'I'd better try this or miss out!'." KAREN

"Don't worry. They won't starve." HEAPS OF PARENTS

"Make a smorgasbord plate of six or seven different things (we call it 'Sixes and Sevens') and say the game is they have to have at least one bite of everything (or two . . .). Help them count. Or try giving sticks of carrot, opened pea pods or half mushrooms as an entrée while they're distracted with a book, game or video, then serve just meat and potatoes at the table." ME

MORE INFO

A BOOK ABOUT EATING

Optimum Nutrition for your Child: How to Boost Your Child's Health, Behaviour and IQ
by Patrick Holford and Deborah Colson, Piatkus, 2008
Heaps of interesting info about vitamins and minerals you've heard of and some you haven't – and which bits of the body or development they're good for. Specific advice is given on using diet changes to tackle the symptoms of allergies, sleep problems and hyper-activity. Not to be relied on as a sole treatment for your child's health problems – and take the "IQ boost" claims with a grain of (iodine-boosted) salt.

toddlers and sleeping

The toddler years are often the time when a battle of wills sets in between parents and a determined child who doesn't want to go to bed, screams, uses delaying tactics and simply refuses to cooperate. It's a battle of wills that parents need to take control of without crushing the spirit of their child, which becomes even more difficult when a kid can get out of bed and open the bedroom door. Not to mention stand on the bed and shout until they throw up (you may want to invest in a hazardous-waste-protection jumpsuit and matching helmet).

Daytime Naps

Gradually the morning and afternoon sleeps become one, early afternoon sleep. The "Possible Routines for Babies" chapter in *Part 1: Babies* has the lowdown on this. Most toddlers need an afternoon nap when they're 1 – and most phase it out before they're 3, or 4, or 5 (some time before secondary school anyway). Some won't have a nap and are always falling-about tired before bed; some always have a nap; and some have an afternoon nap occasionally. You'll have to be guided by your child: if they're horribly ratty in the last two hours or so before bedtime at 7pm, they may still need to be persuaded to have an hour or so of sleep in the afternoon (look up "afternoon nap" in the index).

At this age you can explain to them how a nap means they get two sleepytime stories, or it makes them strong and gives them energy to play or to get ready for that party at the weekend. Keep the room dark and have a familiar bedtime ritual.

Even if your toddler doesn't actually sleep, it's almost always a good idea for them to have a quiet time in bed because it gives everyone a break. And you never know your luck – if you take the pressure off, the nap might happen anyway.

Night-time Sleeps

Some parents let their kids stay up until they maraud around the house, even to ten or eleven at night. Others insist on a bedtime of 7pm, with stories until 7.30. You may find that a fairly early bedtime is best because toddlers need to get ten to twelve hours' sleep a day and sleep-ins may not suit your mornings. And a toddler who always wakes at 7am almost certainly won't get enough sleep if they're going to bed at 10pm.

Introducing controlled crying or controlled comforting

This approach is explained in the "Sleeping" chapter in *Part 1: Babies* (look up "controlled crying" in the index). The principle is the same for establishing a bedtime and ensuring your toddler doesn't want to play in the middle of the night. It isn't too late in the toddler years to set a bedtime and stick to it. The problem is that, as well as yelling, a toddler is now physically able to get up and try to get out of the bedroom. Calm consistency from a sole parent, two parents or carers is the only way to achieve a regular bedtime.

The difficulty with controlled comforting is that it makes some children go berserk and scream maniacally until they throw up over everything. But there is no doubt that the slow, patient version, with firm consistency, no cracking and no going back to bad habits, can sometimes have a problem fixed in literally a couple of days, depending on the personality of your toddler. But patience is very hard to maintain evening after evening so it's good if someone else can help you to be utterly consistent about what's expected. To make sure the toddler always feels reassured, and to withstand the barrage of hot, tragic tears, it often takes at least two adults – one sobbing in the corridor and stopping the other from going in to the toddler for another 5.6 seconds, and then swapping roles the next evening.

Toddlers who can escape from their cot must be gently put back each time, otherwise they learn that tantrums and escapology will be rewarded. What about toddlers who can reach the door knob and then barge out of the bedroom? Remove the door knob and have a hook fastener on the outside, but reassure them that you will come in if they need you. (You will have to abandon or modify these ideas depending on your kid's personality.)

Night-time ritual

A night-time ritual will always help a kid understand it's time to go to sleep. This can include your toddler:

- ★ fetching a non-spillable drink and putting it next to the bed
- ★ going to the toilet
- ★ putting toothpaste on their toothbrush
- ★ getting into jarmies
- ★ putting Mr Whiskers (or similar) in the bed
- ★ turning on the night-light (continue to make it a very diffuse light that isn't near their head or eye line)
- ★ singing a song with you
- ★ hearing a story
- ★ saying a special or traditional goodnight rhyme or well-known story with you.

STALLING AT BEDTIME Head off any toddler stalling strategies by planning ahead and have counter-strategies that build up over a few days. Wants a drink? Make sure one's already placed next to the cot or bed. Needs the loo? "You went just before you got into bed. You can go on the potty next to your bed."

BaD DReams

Toddlers will need to have dreams explained to them: they're things you see in your sleep, but they're not real. Sometimes you have a good dream, and sometimes a bad dream. If you have a bad dream, you can wake up and the dream is gone.

Some parents like to resettle their toddler in their cot or bed after a bad dream. Others bring the child into their own bed. And some hop into the kid's bed until they are "dismissed". But if you sleep with your kid you might create a habit and a new problem for yourself.

In cases where a bad dream is recurring or prompted by a traumatic event or ongoing stress, talk to your GP about seeing a child psychologist. It's important to understand that a toddler in a stressful family situation will have disturbed sleep and nightmares that can only really be "treated" by an improved home life.

Monsters and night fears

If your toddler says "I'm frightened", talk about why and deal with those specific fears. Being in a dim or dark room on your own can be a very frightening experience for little kids, although some will use it as a stalling tactic.

Make sure there isn't a pile of toys casting a scary shadow on the wall or an open wardrobe that looks as if it might have monsters in it. Try to distract your toddler with a funny goodnight song, one verse or bits of which they have to make up.

Some props can help you get rid of monsters: a torch, a garden sprayer with lavender water, labelled "Monster Spray", to frighten monsters away with; or a dolly that is put on guard to tell monsters not to come near. You will need to work out something psychological that suits your child's personality.

You might like to tell them "Tomorrow we can ring up Aunty Gail, who knows where monsters go, and she can explain there's none in this country". That sort of thing. One mother I know sat her little boy down while she dialled the "Monster

Department" on the phone and told them in no uncertain terms her son insisted they not send any more monsters. The trick is to find something that makes your child feel empowered.

from cot to bed

night-drink, night-book, night-light, night-night

Traditionally a kid goes into a bed when they've worked out how to climb up and fall out of their cot. (You can postpone this if you have an adjustable cot by putting the mattress at a lower level, once your baby can stand up.) Most kids go into their own bed at about 2 to 2 and a half years old.

To prevent falls you can buy a bed guard for a single bed at baby equipment or bed shops, or you can put the mattress on the floor for a while.

Give your toddler plenty of warning about the change. Talk about getting a new bed being a fun, grown-up thing to do. Saying that there's a little baby somewhere who needs the cot is usually very persuasive when swapping it for a "big girl's" or "big boy's" bed. But try not to do it at the same time that a new baby arrives at your home.

"My daughter is 22 months old and ever since about 3 months old she has had Barry, a small soft toy with a bell (unfortunately), that she goes to bed with. When it's time for her to go to bed or naptime we get her to call Barry and we wander around the house until we find him (surprise!). This works 90 per cent of the time: lately we've had Barry and Elmo waiting for her in bed: she can't wait to get there generally. All of this happened by accident." KELLIE

more info

TODDLERS AND SLEEPING

Most of the books given as "More Info" at the end of the "Sleeping" chapter in *Part 1: Babies* also cover toddler sleeping. *The Mighty Toddler* by Robin Barker has a chapter on sleep that includes a section called "The Basic Principles of Teaching-to-sleep", which is her version of controlled crying, plus tips on other side issues and common problems, from night frights to early morning waking ("More Info" at the end of the "Who's the Centre of the Universe?" chapter has full details and review).

www.pediatrics.about.com
US site with a whole host of articles on childhood sleep issues, including dropping daytime naps, what night terrors are and how to deal with them, and how much sleep is normal. Most baby and parenting sites have sections on sleeping issues and slumber strategies. (See p. 140).

Possible Routines for Toddlers

Oh, toddlers do LOVE a routine! You might like to copy good child-care centres, which have built-in times for morning tea, lunch, an after-lunch sleep or quiet time and afternoon tea, and spaces throughout the day of not more than an hour long dedicated to learning about something, outside play, music, cleaning up and art projects. You can add cooking; running and jumping in the park; going to the park or for a walk, with stroller time if they get tired; going to the shops or the post office and chatting to everyone on the way; doing housework; having a time for the self (yours and your toddler's); feeding the pets; and bath, stories, bed.

I sometimes wonder if the love toddlers have for a routine and familiar things isn't almost perfectly balanced by the fact that for all their life so far they've been learning

new words, new actions and new concepts and analysing their world every day. The things we see as commonplace are discoveries for them as they understand more and more. This means a new song or phrase will tickle and delight them, but you'd better not try to move their bed to face another direction without consultation and preparatory chats. You may not want a routine of course – in which case go read another chapter!

getting a routine going

Base your routine around your individual lifestyle while you can: when morning nursery starts, you probably won't be able to put a toddler to bed at 10pm: kids this age need ten to twelve hours sleep a night and most kids tend to wake up at 6.30 to 7.30am, especially if light comes into their room. Below are suggested routines to use as a base, to cut up and rearrange – or to ignore entirely.

By age 1 your child may have dropped one of their daytime sleeps or be on the way to doing this, as outlined in the "Possible Routines for Babies" chapter in *Part 1: Babies*.

possible toddler routine from 1 year

7am   Breakfast, chat.

8   Play and usual morning activities.

9   Possible morning sleep.

10   Play.

11   Morning tea or lunch.

12   Play.

1pm   Possible afternoon sleep.

2   Afternoon tea.

2.30   Play, visit or adventure, including some physical activity.

4.30   Possible twenty- to forty-minute catnap if two daytime sleeps have dropped to one.

5.30   Dinner.

6   Bath.

6.30   Stories or quiet time.

7   Lights out.

POSSIBLE TODDLER ROUTINE FROM 18 MONTHS

7am   Breakfast, chat.
8   Play and usual morning activities.
10   Morning tea.
11   Play.
12   Lunch.
1 or 2pm   Afternoon sleep.
3   Afternoon tea.
3.30   Play, visit or adventure, including physical activity.
5.30   Dinner.
6   Bath.
6.30   Stories or quiet time.
7   Lights out.

Kids approaching 3 years old may be dropping a daytime sleep altogether (look up "afternoon nap" in the index).

DAYLIGHT SAVING

Some parents keep to "real" time so the day always starts at 7am, which reads as 8 in summer. Or you can take a week or two before daylight saving starts (or ends) to change the bedtime by a quarter of an hour every few days.

using the toilet

Children don't even know they're weeing until about halfway through their second year. Because we're so used to what's happening.

I'm not going to call using the loo "toilet training" because there's no point in training when the trainee couldn't give a toss, and before the kid is physically ready to identify the warning signs of an imminent wee or poo. It hardly ever comes together reliably before the age of 2. I remember thinking what if the neighbourhood kids learned to use the loo before mine? Would that mean I had a slow learner (and after proudly producing such a gifted vomiter)? In the end I think it dawned on me that I was worried about bottoms that weren't even under my jurisdiction. So – no big deal.

fascinating

wanting to graduate to the loo

Don't listen to grandparents and other parents about when kids should be fully "toilet trained". In the olden days (like when you were a kid, maybe, even) children were more often in smellier, much wetter and more uncomfortable cloth nappies and couldn't wait to get out of them. These days disposables are so much easier for kids and parents that the in-nappies period is bound to go on slightly, especially in colder areas where children can't run about, bum out, in the garden for much of the year. And so much of what grandparents and parents reckoned was toilet training was actually them chasing after a kid with a potty and whacking it under at the first sign of any action.

There is absolutely NO POINT in trying to teach your child to use the toilet each time they need to do a wee or a poo if they're not interested. They just humour you for a while and then it turns into a nagfest or a carnival of wet bots. Actual interest is when they ask you questions about it and want to see what's going on when people go to the loo. Any work put in earlier than this will probably end up being a colossal waste of time.

Basically by the time they're interested, they'll be able to tell when they're going to wee or poo and be physically able to use the potty or loo: it just takes practice to get it all together.

when are toddlers ready to learn about the loo?

Signs include being interested in reading a book with you about using the toilet; being interested in hearing about where poo and wee come from and go to after you flush, and what the flush is; asking about other aspects of the toilet and wee and poo, and watching older or other kids and family members going to the toilet; talking about, and looking forward to, no more nappies, and about being a "big boy" or "big girl"; and being interested in undies generally or a special pair in particular. (See "More Info" at the end of this chapter for books for kids.)

Sometimes interest wanes, or a kid regresses temporarily because a new baby in nappies is getting so much attention. Don't fall for the old-fashioned assumption that teaching them about the toilet has to be a frustrating battle to get the idea into their head. Every now and then try to spark some interest – a story about where wee goes; "Look at what Mummy's doing"; "Here, sit on this toilet seat"; "Wow, won't it be good when you can wear undies!". Wait until your kid is really interested and wants to do it, then help them – much less stressful for everyone and also much more successful.

Most of the books I've consulted say kids are ready between the ages of 1 and 3, and the average age is before 2 years old. Out in the real world I've NEVER heard of a kid having sustained interest before about 18 months and hardly anyone before 2, and the average seems to be somewhere between 2 and 3, with plenty saving it for 3 or 4.

There's a common perception that boys generally start and finish learning to use the loo later than girls. There's no way of knowing whether this applies to your little individual so, hey, forget about it: it's really not useful info. Some kids get it all over with very quickly; others foof along in fits and starts until some time after their third birthday.

It's usually easier for a toddler to know when they're going to poo than wee. Wee doesn't herald itself so obviously to a child and can come too quickly in times of excitement or great interest in something else. Nap and then night-time control take the longest to get the hang of: almost invariably after age 3. It's very, very common for kids to be in night-time pull-ups at age 4, or using a potty next to the bed. It's a long trip down the hall to the loo at this age.

How long does it take?

Learning to go to the toilet regularly can take only weeks, or even a few days if your kid is really interested. Otherwise months and months. Be prepared for potty and toilet using to go backwards at unexpected times or to take a sudden leap forward.

How to explain the gig

It's always useful to explain to your child that their body takes all the food and drinks they have and uses these to make them grow and be strong, and the stuff the body doesn't need comes out as wee and poo; and that wee and poo are a bit stinky (though not a big deal, heavens no) so we need to flush them down the toilet (but *kids* can't ever be flushed away – and toys shouldn't be!). Having a poo often makes us feel more comfy and as if we have more energy.

It's also a good idea to explain what happens to wee and poo after we're finished with it: that they drop down into the water in the toilet, and then we push the button and the water goes whoosh, whoosh, and then the wee and poo disappear down all these pipes, go into other big pipes and finally into a big smelly pond in the ground a long way away, and eventually are spewed into our seaside spots by governments that need to be slapped around. Well, maybe not that last bit, it's a little complex. But sometimes explaining the whole process demystifies the experience for kids, otherwise it's quite abstract.

LOO PHOBIAS If kids are scared about what's in the loo (sharks, monsters, the Unknown), explain where all the poo and wee goes, and that it's like the plughole in the bath: stuff goes down, but nothing comes up.

WHat you migHt NeeD

You might like to use:
- ★ a plastic potty in the bathroom – and one next to the bed might be a solution if your child finds it hard to get to the toilet in time in the middle of the night when they reach that stage
- ★ a smaller-sized toilet seat to fit on yours
- ★ a stool or a step for access to the big loo
- ★ "training wipes" – flushable wipes that a kid can use to take care of more poo than toilet paper would
- ★ pull-on half-nappy, half-undies things (see below)
- ★ a night-time nappy for a while (a toddler before using the toilet will have needed three or four nappies a day)
- ★ a properly fitted waterproof mattress cover – this has waterproof plastic underneath with cotton on the top so they're not nasty, sweaty and uncomfy to lie on. One on the bed and one for emergencies is a good call.

251

★ a "care mat" – a bit like a giant flat nappy placed under the top sheet, which will absorb most leakages and can be thrown away afterwards.

Pull-on half-nappy, half-undies things

These are a kind of final nappy – one that pulls on and off like a pair of undies. If you find one full of poo, lay the kid down and tear down the papery side bits, then take it off like a nappy (and put the poo in the toilet). They are often used as transitional pants when a child is learning to use the potty or toilet, and when a kid is using the potty or toilet except at night.

Some parents want their kids to go straight from nappies to the potty or toilet – and it's true that many kids are likely to poo or wee in a pull-on nappy because it's convenient, although a big poo isn't any more pleasant in a pull-on than a nappy.

Potty or loo?

Some kids start on the potty and graduate to the loo. Some parents like to start with the potty because a kid doesn't need help to get on; others take their kid straight to the loo because they figure they want to start as they mean to go on.

Potties are cleaned by tipping the contents into the loo, wiping them out with toilet paper and then dousing them with disinfectant – if necessary, clean with a loo brush before the disinfectant. (It's much easier to deal with wee in the potty than poo, so if you can manage it have your child poo in the toilet.)

some "toilet-training" ideas

★ Let your kid watch you on the toilet and have a look in the bowl afterwards to see what happens when you flush.

★ Keep talking to your child about why you're asking certain things of them. This will encourage them to explain to you why they're doing what they're doing or why they're afraid.

★ Some books suggest that kids should be put on the potty or toilet at regular times such as after each meal and first thing in the morning. (If I were a kid, I would find this far too prescriptive.) Others suggest trying to teach the child to get to know how it feels when they "need to go" and to tell a parent, who can take them to the loo.

★ Some people encourage reading or playing on the loo, others think this distracts from the business at hand.

★ Many parents suggest you wait until summer once your kid is interested, then let them run around the garden a lot with no pants on – they'll be more aware of weeing and pooing and any accidents will be easier to clean up.

★ Put a non-flushable floating target in the bowl for boys to aim their weeing willies at: corks and ping-pong balls are popular.

★ Some people swear by teaching boys to wee sitting down; others say the key is getting a bigger boy or man to teach them. A boy starting on a potty will have to graduate to stand-up weeing later.

★ Teach girls how to wipe their front bot with folded toilet paper, from the front towards the back, so poo is not wiped forward as this can cause infections.

★ Show kids how to wash their hands with soap and dry them on a clean towel.

★ A sticker or star chart can be set up to show everyone the marvellous progress, and sharp, barking cries of admiration made frequently. (Okay, that was a joke. I don't want any complaint letters about children frightened by woofing noises.)

★ But avoid over-the-top, extravagant praise – buying full-page ad space in a newspaper to announce the first unassisted poo is likely to lead to a child developing weird ideas about the glamour and importance of waste management issues.

253

★ Try a smaller toilet seat that sits on the regular one if your toddler is worried about falling in or needs more comfort.

★ Use incentives: divinely pretty undies, or ones with pictures of their favourite character, are often a great bribe for the kid who can use the loo.

★ Don't make a fuss or go on about the disgustingness of poo and wee: this can cause psychological problems. And I think we can do without references to "Mr Poo Poo coming out", thank you very much.

★ Always treat an "accident" matter of factly, with a "Never mind, it's just a wee (ha!) accident".

★ Don't put a kid in overalls or tights that are hard for them to get out of quickly themselves.

★ Give your toddler lots of water, fruit and veggies to help a hard poo or constipation problem. Giving fibre without extra water often only makes constipation worse.

★ Let a bathroom tap trickle in a wee-like way if your child is having trouble being able to wee; or sing a little rhyme or line that relaxes them such as "Wee, wee, wee, all the way in the loo".

★ Apologize for being grumpy if you find yourself getting angry or exasperated with "yet another" wet or pooey accident, or have a laugh with your kid about your grumpiness. If it's too late, make sure you're consistently nice about the next few.

★ Wanting to be like the older kids is often a big motivation. Child-care centres can be a great help, as can older siblings, cousins or close pals. (Most nurseries won't accept children until they're out of nappies, but won't make a fuss about the occasional "accident".)

★ An older toddler can be mortified by accidents – don't add to the embarrassment, and remember "Never mind". Just help them to clean up in private if you're out, and hide the evidence in a placcy bag in your toddler bag or handbag.

★ If your toddler seems always wet, rather than sometimes dry and sometimes wet, check out with your GP whether it means they have a urinary tract infection or any other physical leaky problem.

★ At night have a dim light all the way to and inside the loo, a rug on the floor if it's cold and the smaller-bot seat and stool in place, or the potty near the bed.

★ Always get the kid to go to the loo before you leave home, child care, a friend's house or the shopping centre. Little people have bladders that are also very little and they need as many opportunities to go as possible. (This is especially true when you're using public transport because it's always a longer trip than by car. You can carry a pull-up to slip on your toddler just for emergencies.)

★ If you're going to be weeing outside on a day-trip have them wear something on their lower half that can easily be pulled completely off and then put back on. Tights or shoes wet with wee after a squatting accident are no fun.

★ Always carry extra undies, trousers, wipes and at least two plastic bags for accidents (one bag is for throwaways, another is for the dirty clothes).

★ Always stay with your child in a public loo, and if there's no unisex parents' toilet use the handicapped one as long as nobody disabled is waiting – the extra room is often a boon, and it can be much nicer for a bloke who wants to avoid taking his little girl into the men's.

★ When you're out, help your child to balance on a grown-up seat.

Regression

A kid who's been using the potty or toilet for weeks or months and then suddenly isn't any more probably has some kind of common physical reason such as an infection, or a psychological problem caused by ongoing stress or a traumatic event (although it may not have seemed traumatic to you), so see your GP.

A kid who forgets to go to the loo a lot is probably just not interested enough yet.

Night-time accidents

Few children never wet the bed. (If it's an ongoing problem into the preschool years, look up "bedwetting" in the index.)

twins and the loo

Most people in the kid business recommend waiting until all the twins (or triplets) are ready and moving on together – but if one toddler is determined to go ahead and it's not worrying the other, one at a time may be less work for you (although some say going through the process twice is worse). Just be careful that the praise given to one doesn't seem like something the other is missing out on because they're not good enough. Perhaps there might be something else to praise them for. Before you start, speak to as many parents of twins or triplets in similar situations as you can – but remember, you've got yourself a bunch of individuals in your family (there's more on them in the "Multiples" chapter in *Part 4: Stuff*).

"One Monday morning he said wearing undies was cool and by the end of the week he was completely trained much to my relief." [Loo using at 3 years 5 months.] ANGELA

"All my kids initially trained themselves ('How clever am I!'), then decided to regress to nappies ('That game's not fun any more') before they were properly trained." [Loo using at 2 years 6 months.] MELISSA

"She did pretty well at 22 months until her brother arrived! Then she would demand a nappy like him. She used toileting as a way of controlling me and would demand to go to the toilet when I started feeding him or would just wee in front of me if she didn't get what she wanted. She managed eventually. I had him out of night nappies (2) before her (4). Every child is different." SARAH

"Children are scared of the flushing water and scared of 'What if I fall in'." CHRIS

"Don't put a nappy on at night. While we had a nappy he wet. After I left off the nappy, I only had one or two accidents." JUDI

"We bought Thomas the Tank Engine undies and had very few accidents after that. The James undies took the brunt of it."
SURITA

"They do it when they're ready and not before."
JEANETTE

"I bribed him with a lolly for a poo and by God it worked!" [Loo using at 3 years 6 months.] TRACY

"It felt like it was never going to happen for us. He or she will let you know when they are ready. Try pants during the day and regularly ask them if they need to go. They will eventually get used to this and go themselves. Still working on nights!" BIANCA

"At nearly 3 he is not interested in toilet training. I have tried special pants, stickers, stamps, cuddles, praise and even chockie bribery but nothing works. This has been the hardest of everything." REBECCA,

"Our son finally admitted he was scared of the toilet. My friend Debbie said she'd arrange for the Poo Fairy to come . . . Debbie and her three daughters all dressed in bright colours, tutus, fairy wands (homemade cardboard and stick) and fairy suitcase . . . my son said, 'You're Aunty Debbie', and she said, 'Not today', as she strode purposefully to the bathroom. She spent 10 long minutes in there with my son, anointing the toilet with stick-on stars and plastering the bathroom with fairy dust (very hard to get rid of). Without any other discussion, on the third day [after] he ascended the throne and hasn't looked back since. It would never have worked on my second son: the secret is acknowledging their fears and devising a scheme that will suit your own child." LESLEY

"He had a couple of times when he wet the floor and got very upset. I had a talk to him and said that if he was going to get so upset when he had an accident it might be better if we left it for a while and tried again when he was a bit older. He was very appreciative of this. When he did make the transition to the toilet (3 years 3 months) it was only a matter of a few weeks before we risked no night nappy and were off and running. Yay! No more spending £10 a week on nappies! It was well worth letting him do it under his own steam." DIANNE

"Explain the body parts (kid friendly) and how things work and practise. Even after accidents we are just practising, and we are doing so well. In my opinion no potty if we are telling kids they're old enough to go to the toilet. That way they know the routine: wipe, flush and wash hands. It makes them really feel like a big person." CATHY, NANNY

"On hearing she wasn't toilet trained, my otherwise gorgeous nanna said, 'Oh, I'm so surprised. She's such a bright little thing!' Arrgh! Wise and experienced mums all say the same thing – if they aren't ready it will be months of agony. If they are ready, they'll do it themselves in a few days." KATE

"We made the stepping stool together, he painted it and decorated it with his mum and within 2 days had it sussed." [Loo using at 2 years 6 months.] JOHN

MORE INFO

LOO BUSINESS

What to Expect When You Use the Potty
by Heidi Murkoff, Harper Festival, 2004
From the endless US What to Expect franchise. Weirdly the author actually imagines you might decide to teach your child to call poo a "stool". I ask you. (The only stools I'm interested in at this point are bar stools.) But the book does create interest in what poo is and where it goes.

The Story of the Little Mole Who Knew It Was None of His Business
by Werner Holzwarth, Anova, 2007
A "plop-up" (oh, puhleese!) picture story about a mole who was pooped on and goes in search of the animal culprit. Not a "how to", but a depiction of different poos. (Grandparents and the easily grossed-out may have palpitations.)

Everybody Poos
by Taro Gomi, Frances Lincoln, 2005
A picture book with animals and people. Who, I think you'll find, all poo.

I Want My Potty
by Tony Ross, Kane/Miller, 2007
Part of the Little Princess series of toddler experiences. Simple enough for even the youngest to understand.

TODDLER DEVELOPMENT (1 to 3)

By about 1 year your "baby" should have a repertoire of several emotions and will be influenced by your reactions to situations (drop glass on floor, say filthy word). They should be able to wave goodbye and associate other simple movements with situations (the word "Goal!" is accompanied by hands in the air).

If your kid is in child care, ask the professional workers, who are trained in this area, to let you know when they've checked your child's development for their age range. Professional child carers are often very reassuring because they see kids of all ages come along splendidly in their own time.

If you're concerned about the rate of development, see your health visitor or GP. Some babies go straight from bum-shuffle to walking, without crawling; some walk months earlier than others – it usually evens up in the end.

1 year to 18 months

Physical development
Your toddler:

★ can see things in the distance and tries to get them
★ is shuffling, crawling, bum-dragging, just walking or walking alone, perhaps moving with a tentative, stiff-legged totter, with feet wide apart for extra balance
★ may be climbing onto ladders, chairs, boxes, tables, uncles
★ can let go of something with controlled movement

★ starts to stack things inside or on top of each other

★ uses a spoon with greater dexterity

★ is learning to get simple clothes off and to help to get them on

★ starts to drink from a cup, a straw or a pop-top bottle.

Emotional and mental development

Your toddler:

★ is bonded to one or two consistent carers at home and may want one or either parent primarily, depending on how the child care is divided

★ may develop separation anxiety when they start walking or improve rapidly at walking. This can happen with other new developments too

★ is developing their memory – many girls are a little better at some aspects of remembering at this stage than boys, although this mostly evens out by about age 3 (women still do better than men on some short-term memory tests). A toddler may remember how to do a task or action they saw up to four months ago, and observe and copy actions seen on the telly – but you can't rely on them to remember things you want them to remember

★ often says "NO!" to test their control over things – and perhaps because they hear no a lot

★ is showing great interest in books

★ is starting to ask or look for things that are not in sight, such as a drink

★ is affectionate with familiar pals, but can be wary of new folk and strangers (sounds like an adult)

★ gets excited about something that is coming up, such as unwrapping a present

★ if frustrated might hit, kick, scratch, claw or bite to show their frustration, even if they've never seen anyone else do these things.

Communication development

Your toddler probably:

★ begins talking, has a vocabulary of a few words (see if you can get "please" and "thank you" in as early as possible) and may even put two or more words together. Girls often progress more quickly than boys

★ will start to pick up more and more words every day at some point near 18 months old, give or take a few months

★ listens to and understands the gist of conversations and the particular meaning of words without having the skills to join in verbally.

What can you do?

Pull-along or push-along toys are good fun. Encourage outdoor play with balls, sand, and supervised water, climbing, swings and slides: it helps them to develop physical skills and to exercise – and tires 'em out so they have a good sleep. All play involving objects with wheels, such as prams and ride-on toys, or water needs constant vigilance and age-appropriate expectations.

Even "doing the dishes" in the sink is water play (always supervise the play, then pull the plug afterwards). Let them "help" you with chores: give them a feather duster, a sponge for rudimentary wiping work, a wooden spoon and bowl for stirring something safe while you're cooking. And they'll enjoy picking things out of the clothes basket to be hung up by you and passing you the pegs.

Teach your child early on to put their head back for washing off shampoo. Toddlers usually hate water on their face and eyes, which may be a survival instinct: this can be something to gradually work on in the bath or pool or at the beach.

As the kid gets more mobile and can reach to tabletop level and climb up bookcases, do another safety check of the house and places you regularly visit (see the "Home Safety" chapter in *Part 4: Stuff*). Find places where they can explore freely instead of being always restrained. Better to hide your heirloom vases for four years than have them smashed or a frustrated toddler who can't go anywhere near one corner of the living room.

Read your child simple stories and together look at picture books with images they can point to and name or flaps they can lift.

Play different kinds of music. Sing and dance together. Make up songs with familiar names and words in them. (See "More Info" at the end of this chapter for good books on having fun together.)

Don't put a kid in front of confusing or violent TV programmes or stuff that isn't specifically made for their age group, including the news, which is distressing and disturbing for children this age, who cannot process the information (this will be the case for many years to come). Have DVDs handy rather than just turning on the telly.

Talk to your child and give them space to talk back. Explain what you are going to do before you do it and why. Kids pick up an incredible amount just by listening and repeating. Their brains are making millions of connections, including the right uses and placement of words. This applies to all ages.

Don't "correct" a misuse of a word, but instead use it correctly yourself in a reply. "I putted my hat." "Yes, you put on your hat: that's great!" instead of "Don't say 'putted': that's wrong". If your kid isn't talking much, try not to anticipate their needs too efficiently so that they are encouraged to ask for what they're after, or offer them a choice and wait for the response.

Use simple terms to explain things, but now and then add some words that help them build a bigger vocabulary – kids of this age can understand words such as "bizarre", "fragile" and "ridiculous" in context – and it will stop you going mad from using only "cat sat on mat" type vocabulary.

Kids pick up on tone at least as much as words and they won't understand irony for years to come: everything is taken literally. This means you can't do one thing while saying another, or say "Well, that's marvellous, isn't it?" when you mean "Ooh, I think we'd better clean this up".

Explain that kicking, biting, punching and gouging are not good ways to solve a problem – reward other ways of behaving with attention and praise, and remove a child from interesting action if they behave violently. Say "Use your words" to encourage verbal expression of crossness. You can also begin now to say "It's not okay to push" or "We don't hit". Kids reinforce their learning by saying things back to you for confirmation such as "We don't bite, do we?".

Try to give choices so your toddler has to say yes to something and feels in control. Instead of saying "Put on your coat", say "Do you want your blue jacket or your yellow coat?". And try to let them do some things for themselves.

18 moNTHs to 2 yeaRs

Physical development
Your toddler:

- ★ is working on that stiff-legged walking style, getting more proficient and experimenting with going faster
- ★ runs straight-legged
- ★ can see things in the distance – their eyes are working at full capacity now
- ★ understands what the purpose of things is – a bowl is stirred, a page is turned, a shoe goes on a foot

★ can throw a ball, although catching is more problematic – they hold out their arms but aren't able to anticipate the arc of the ball and move to where it will fall

★ climbs stairs and other things – usually more up than down but can go down (usually on their bottom, rather than backwards, if they get practice on stairs in their home)

★ is still testing a lot of things in their mouth, although not doing it all the time

★ can take off their hat and other clothes but is still not so good at putting them on.

Emotional and mental development

Your toddler:

★ has quite clear feelings of wanting to cuddle or wanting to be free and doing things by themselves

★ as well as recognizing themselves in the mirror, experiments with moving their head and making faces. Kids often try out emotions before a mirror (including crying) as if to say when I feel like *this* I look like *that*

★ is terribly, terribly BUSY

★ can amuse themselves for short periods at the same activity if an adult is comfortingly nearby

★ will try to help with housework chores and grasps fundamentally what's required even though they couldn't get a job as a cleaner

★ is affectionate

★ is quick to feel frustration and possibly has tantrums

★ as when younger, can be upset by a vibe evoked by bright or flashing lights, loud, scary music or a tone such as sarcasm

★ probably can understand simple directions and what's usually required for regular events, such as how to behave at dinner or at Uncle Roscoe's house (not allowed in the garden with the dogs without an adult), but can't be relied on to always remember the directions or instructions

★ may remember or describe dreams more than in the past, and nightmares may happen

★ may develop fear of things such as dogs, people in animal suits, water, being at the top of the stairs or anything that it makes sense to be scared of, as a survival tactic

★ shows sympathy for other children who are distressed

★ wants to explore and touch everything

★ cannot anticipate dangers or consequences but can learn from very specific events ("the last time I touched that oven thing it hurt so I'm not going to touch it again – this heater looks jolly interesting, though . . . Ouch!")

★ can express jealousy and selfishness (which can also be interpreted as a survival technique).

Communication development

Your toddler:

★ is developing more words and language skills, such as using very simple sentences, as well as full-on "nonsense" chat. This is normal and healthy (also amusing)

★ is copying sounds, actions and reactions from adults. This is often the age when you realize your reaction to dropping something is to say "Oh, buckety fuck" because your toddler says it in the post office to stunned silence

★ is learning lots of names for things

★ makes the right sounds when an animal is named

★ learns bits of songs

★ will tell you or show you if something is in the "wrong" place

★ will show you how they are feeling and respond to the obvious feelings of someone else

★ likes a five-minute warning before a new activity ("Very soon we'll need to put the blocks away and go to the shop", "Let's put on our shoes because we're about to go down to the washing line to look for fairies").

What can you do?

Play chasey with your toddler. Kick a ball together. Play throwing and catching games with the emphasis on them throwing and you catching. Toddlers (and nursery-age children) find it easier to catch something that's not hard and unyielding, and not too small (tennis ball) or heavy (basketball). Try light, smaller-sized beach balls, not too tightly blown up, and, even better, adult-palm-sized beanbags.

Beg, borrow or buy a ride-on "bike" without pedals for them to zoom around on.

You can start to teach your kid at this age actions that they'll get better at steadily as time goes on: washing and drying their hands; stringing large beads; sorting colours and shapes (this will be just an idea at first, but they'll get there); identifying everyone, including themselves, in family photos; playing in sand; stopping at the kerb and other road safety actions; playing in safe water in the bath or outside (unless there's a drought); singing bits of songs; matching words to situations and feelings.

Help your toddler learn to dance on their own feet, although you may need to hold hands. Develop some favourite songs and make tapes or CDs for them (avoid the radio if possible because of distressing news breaks, stupid ads and bad boy bands). Make music together with saucepans and rattly things.

Read to them, look at picture books together and encourage independent looking at books. Make up and tell stories: toddlers often love to contribute, frequently trying to exactly copy your stories but eventually coming up with independent details.

As with a younger toddler, use lots of different words when you speak to your child; don't "dumb it down". A child of 2 can understand what "amazing", "completely loopy" and "schemozzle" mean, and using lots of words gives them a wider range of reactions and explanations. They also have fun saying them. You have to converse with kids for them to understand the language; you can't just sit them in front of a radio or TV and expect them to soak in what they hear like a sponge. They need to ask questions and use words in different contexts to see which ones fit.

Try not to say no all the time; instead try out some variations and distractions: "Hey, I've got a great idea! Why don't we do a jigsaw puzzle instead!"; "You know what, if you hold your cup with two hands instead of one you don't spill the drink inside"; "Instead of throwing Granny's mangy scarf in the bin, why don't we hang it up in the hallway where we can't see it?"; "Well, it's not an ice-cream day, but you can choose whether you want scrummy strawberry yoghurt or a banana milkshake!". This expands their vocabulary and preserves their self-esteem; it cunningly gives them the illusion that they have more choice and are more in control than you because they get to choose stuff.

One child psychotherapist says about the fears or phobias children may have from now on: "I'd try a mix of talking and reassurance and being very low-key about it. I think lots of children have these fears (and they probably served us well in evolution when we lived in natural habitats). Help the child deal with their own anxieties (rather than dealing with them FOR them). If they persist in a marked way and cause the child distress and giving some strategies doesn't help, I'd consider getting professional help." Strategies to overcome night-time fears are suggested in the earlier "Toddlers and Sleeping" chapter.

Try to be patient as toddlers veer from rude independence to wrapping themselves around your neck when you drop them off at their beloved grandad's for a couple of hours.

2 to 3 years

Physical development

Your toddler:

- ★ can jump up and down when asked
- ★ can stand on one leg
- ★ runs around confidently
- ★ may be showing signs of right- or left-handed-ness
- ★ can work out how to get the lid off some things and open some doors
- ★ is starting to get good control of a pencil or crayon and makes marks on paper that represent some-thing, even if these are not recognizable to you
- ★ has all the fine motor abilities in place – little things can be picked up and put down deftly and pages turned neatly
- ★ can build a tall tower from several blocks
- ★ can feed themselves and use appropriately non-pointy or sharp toddler cutlery. As with all things this is not automatic but comes with practice. If a 3-year-old hardly ever sees a knife (or a chopstick), or isn't gently reminded how to use it, they won't suddenly be good at it
- ★ goes down stairs usually by getting two feet on each stair and then pro-gressing, but is now going up one foot per stair (and probably needs to be reminded to use the stair rail or wall for support)
- ★ may become very aware of nappies and want their dirty ones changed, but may not yet be making the leap to being interested in using a potty or the toilet
- ★ has a basically adult sense of taste, but still with a reflex against bitter tastes
- ★ can learn to ride a trike with pedals.

Emotional and mental development

Your toddler:

- ★ has a more developed sense of who "I" is

★ is starting to understand more of your conversation and more simple concepts and feelings – "I'm cold", "over there", "falling down" – rather than just the names of things

★ understands more than they can show. They are learning emotions and the way people interact as well as facts

★ doesn't seem to recognize characteristics such as different skin or different-shaped eyes much at all, but may ask for explanations if they hear others referring to these details

★ can understand simple explanations such as "Some people are always grumpy" or "Some people are not kind to everyone, and we just try to ignore them"

★ may have tantrums as a response to frustrating situations

★ will work out the best ways to manipulate a situation to get what they want and use it (a tantrum will stay in the repertoire if rewarded)

★ remembers rhymes and information that are interesting to them

★ understands more about the world – boats go on the water; the postie leaves letters

★ likes to help and doesn't see routine things as boring – housework continues to be fun

★ wants to be more independent and to get their own way

★ imitates sounds, actions and reactions, with some of their own personal variations.

Communication development

Your toddler:

★ understands more words from listening to them in context

★ will often repeat words several times or stutter as their brain races ahead and their vocabulary expands so quickly. The stuttering usually stops within a year or so

★ wants to participate in conversations, singalongs and group activities, and asks questions about the right terms and actions

★ chats away, building daily on their vocabulary if given the opportunity, and works towards constructing more complex, complete sentences such as "Please go down there".

What can you do?

Obviously there's a big gap between 2 and 3 years old: don't see the suggestions as stuff your kid must be able to do by the stated age, but as something they may already be doing by that age – or may pick up in the next six months to a year.

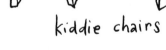

kiddie chairs

Stick close to them, although this is never foolproof, because they want to investigate things all the time. (What's behind here? What happens if I throw this? What will it look like to take all this out of a jar and feel it on my hands?)

By the age of 3 your child might find a trike with pedals fun. And you can help them practise their "ball skills" – have fun with balls.

When reading together, ask your kid to point out and explain things in familiar books or to guess what's happening in new ones.

If your child – and you – aren't getting at least some fresh air and exercise every day, think about how to change this so they're not at risk of becoming bored or getting above a healthy weight.

Give them more music, more art, more nature rambles, more water play, more books, more jokes. Enjoy and share the small things in life that are fun for you to rediscover and all new for your kid: animal-shaped clouds, a big red truck, the way a duck waddles. (See "More Info" at the end of this chapter for good books on all this.)

A kid this age might enjoy 15 minutes of a sports event like footy, but rarely all of it: try to see things from their point of view. Time is much slower for little people.

Rotate batches of toys so your kid sees them with new eyes. Give them crayons that have intense colours – better to buy one good set with strong colours or oil pastels, and look after them a little more carefully, than sets with pale, wimpy colours.

Understand that kids this age prefer to play next to each other rather than with each other (one with a truck, one with a spade, for example). Sharing toys can be a bit of a challenging concept.

Make TV, DVDs and computer games occasional, not daily, activities. Kids need to interract with others to learn the listening and verbal skills essential to the first year of school. Organize play times with other kids by using child care or swapsie arrangements with other parents: your child develops social skills and you get some time to yourself here and there.

Do lots of praising: if something isn't "right", praise something that is, or the effort, and try again later. Almost always, unless there's a safety issue, the experience and the fun are what's important.

Everything you do and say will be repeated or acted out, so if you blow up every time something goes wrong you're teaching tantrums, and if you punch the wall whenever you're angry they will too. If you hit them, they will hit their siblings, the dog, their toys or you. As always, they will be guided by your example as much, if not more so, than your words.

more info

Many titles in this area are aimed at nurturing your child's intelligence, but rather than worry about this I'd say just concentrate on having some fun.

Your Child at Play: One to Two Years: Exploring, Learning, Making Friends and Pretending
by Marilyn Segal, Newmarket Press, 2007
Treat it as a resource for finding out what you and your baby might have fun doing together.

365 Activities You and Your Toddler Will Love
by Roni C Leiderman and Wendy Masi, Bonnier Books, 2007
All the activities cost nothing, using things that you would have round the house: a doll's hospital from shoe boxes, an animal island using the sofa. Strong on imagination.

www.childliteracy.com
This site outlines some skills that littlies can enjoy developing before they learn to read, including understanding which way books go (front to back), and playing with rhymes and words. Includes hints for reading to your children.

www.toddlertoddler.com
Over 250 suggestions for craft activities, simple exercises and home-made games, with some useful printouts.

www.webtots.co.uk
Fun, brightly coloured site with games, music and songs, and art for toddlers.

toys and games for toddlers

The list that follows of fun toys and games for the 1- to 3-year-olds was compiled from suggestions by people who responded to the survey undertaken for this book. As in the earlier "Toys and Games for Babies" chapter, I've selected them with a bias towards cheap fun, and kept away from brand names and merchandising toys, many of which are also lots of fun.

For further ideas about games for kids ask child-care workers and older people, and keep a lookout in charity shops for books about kids' activities, "parlour games" and indoor play. See what ideas you can get from books and activity days at your local library, which may have a toy-lending section too.

mum's
PLay-
DougH

ideas from parents

◎ Cars, trucks, trains ◎ large click-together blocks ◎ a plastic picnic set ◎ baby dolls and a baby doll's stroller ◎ playing pretend games (such as mummy mouse and baby mouse) ◎ drawing and painting using non-toxic, washable poster paints ◎ pasting using bits of fabric, paper, pictures torn from magazines, cut-up streamers ◎ plastic tools and a construction hat ◎ books ◎ musical instruments, particularly bells and a recorder ◎ printing with large potato stamps and paint ◎ stickers ◎ any dress-up clothes, for either sex ◎ a box of Band-Aids, which can get emptied and filled, emptied and filled, over and over ◎ coloured wooden blocks ◎ high-heeled shoes ◎ a tricycle ◎ a tea party set ◎ playing pretend to fix things ◎ kid-sized kitchen utensils to pretend to cook with ◎ a wipe-clean magnetic drawing slate ◎ a tent or cubby with blankets ◎ biscuit cutters, rolling pin and playdough (if using home-made add food colouring and see the "Playdough" box opposite for a note on safety) ◎ a small train set ◎ ladybird beetles in various incarnations ◎ pretending to be dinosaurs ◎ plastic frogs ◎ bangles ◎ wooden or plastic farmyard animals ◎ balls ◎ CDs and tapes ◎ "sewing" enormous buttons onto a piece of cardboard with holes punched in it, or threading beads with a shoelace ◎ bubble blowing (but an adult needs to work with the child on this one) ◎ party whistles (the ones that roll and unroll when you blow them) ◎ coins and a money box ◎ letters and a posting box ◎ alphabet and number posters ◎ early jigsaw puzzles ◎ old purses and handbags ◎ coloured chalk on the footpath ◎ toy phones ◎ cardboard boxes ◎ pretending to have a tea party or playing "cooking stuff" ◎ playing "shop" with or without fake money and a cash register ◎ sanded offcuts of wood to stack or arrange ◎ soccer and footy ◎ a toy hammer to hammer golf tees into styrofoam ◎ a spinning top.

PLAYDOUGH

Home-made playdough recipes usually have a large amount of salt in them. A high concentration of salt can damage a child's internal organs. Kids, especially babies and toddlers, should be supervised so they don't eat a lot of home-made playdough. The commercial stuff should be a major brand and labelled non-toxic: it shouldn't contain salt.

NO MORE BABY FACE

Well, it's not as if 3-year-olds are ready for school – but they're almost certainly steady on their feet, probably at the very least starting to learn to use the toilet, and can be most indignant at being associated with babies and toddlers. And seemingly in a flash they really will be off to school, usually at the age of 4.

preschoolers

Your baby is now very much enjoying being their own person and physically changing from their toddler shape into a kid shape (leaving behind the Teletubbie-nappy-bot is a good start). Physically and mentally they're making great leaps and bounds, and are ready to test themselves alone and with others in playgroups at nursery.

GOOD THINGS ABOUT 3-YEAR-OLDS

* Now all those stain-removal ads make sense.

* 3-year-olds enjoy being "grown up" and helping with things.

* 3-year-olds tend to think you and their carers are brilliant.

* 3-year-olds speak the unadulterated truth.

* 3-year-olds have more stamina for outings.

* 3-year-olds can learn the rules of simple games.

* 3-year-olds want to understand about jokes (like the prime minister).

* 3-year-olds are open to suggestions (unlike the prime minister).

* 3-year-olds can be very determined to succeed and improve.

* 3-year-olds, with help, can understand the "nothing has to be perfect" vibe so they don't feel crushed by "failures".

* 3-year-olds are getting better at catching and throwing a ball, making some throwing games less of a complete shambles.

* 3-year-olds have great big enthusiasms.

* 3-year-olds are fun to watch when they're concentrating and learning.

* 3-year-olds are more and more developing their own personality, whether it's shy, analytical, boisterous, all three – or something else.

* 3-year-olds love the idea of having friends.

* 3-year-olds can be introduced to more of the world and they love it.

* 3-year-olds preschoolers can go to the toilet by themselves.

* 3-year-olds can get themselves a drink.

* 3-year-olds can eavesdrop on your conversation and then repeat what you said in front of the wrong person, leading

goodbye to toddler days

Nursery-age children can understand much more complicated concepts and situations than before, and continue to explore and to ask questions about how things work and why, and who and what and when (not to mention "Huh?"). Despite the fact that 3-year-to social and family mayhem. Okay, maybe that's not such a good thing.

✱ 3-year-olds can be good judges of character: they can often sum up for themselves when someone isn't sincere or seems scary.

✱ 3-year-olds are often shy at first and then warm up: this is logical behaviour. After all, we don't walk into a party and bellow "Hello, everyone! I'm ME and WHO ARE YOU?" – not unless we've had a few voddies anyway.

✱ 3-year-olds can invent or follow quite elaborate stories.

✱ 3-year-olds are great inventors of theories and left-field solutions.

✱ 3-year-olds are pleased by simple things.

✱ 3-year-olds can dress themselves.

✱ 3-year-olds will keep asking questions until they feel finally satisfied with the answer, which trains you to be more precise ("No, there are no bears near here", "No, there are no bears anywhere near here. They live a long way away", "No, bears cannot drive cars to come here", "No, there is very little chance of a bear coming through the post. They're too big", "No, no bears will ever come here, not even for a visit. Not ever. Bears are not allowed to come here, and all the bears have read the memo").

✱ 3-year-olds want to be more independent, but they still need you very much as their kindly haven: which means that, even if they're rationed, you still get cuddles.

✱ 3-year-olds have a longer attention span.

✱ You can have lovely conversations in quiet times such as after lights out and before the last kiss goodnight.

olds can be friendly companions, and enjoy being more grown-up, they're still the littlest of kids, needing to feel safe and that they always have a haven.

This is the time when kids build on their physical and mental skills, and the foundations for healthy self-esteem and confidence are laid down. They need to know they're wonderful and that it doesn't matter if they make mistakes or don't get things "right" all the time. And that there may be a number of correct answers to the same question. It's a time when they watch you very closely to see what being a person is about.

They will constantly try to push the boundaries of behaviour, wriggle out of cuddles and dash here and there – only to come running to you when they need love and reassurance. This is also often the time when your child first moves away from you, even temporarily – while still seeing you as the centre of their world. So don't feel too sad that they're going off to nursery and eventually school – enjoy the fact that they still see you as clever, comforting and the font of all knowledge. In a few short years they'll find you hideously embarrassing and roll their eyes a lot.

Your nursery child may come home with new ideas and words you didn't even know they had, stories of new experiences or having heard about a terrible event close to home or elsewhere in the world. Talking about these, rather than getting upset or angry, will encourage your child to know they can be open and don't need to hide things from you.

Everyone bangs on about the terrible twos, but nobody seems to warn you beforehand that "discipline" issues go right through the preschool years because your little kid is still testing to see who's in control of what and needing to under-stand the balance between rights and responsibilities (see the "Teaching Kids How to Behave" chapter in *Part 3: Parenting*). They'll imperiously shout orders from another room and treat you as a slave if you let them.

And they'll also expect you to solve every problem for them. Even though it may be quicker just to do this most of the time, a child will really love it when you ask them what *they* think – and say "Yes, maybe" instead of "No, that will never work", and help them through discussions with grown-ups and other kids. Even more than when they were a toddler, you can help them arrive at answers to their own questions through "research", by talking to an "expert" such as an engineer friend, getting a book from the library or seeing what happens when they're allowed to fill a cup to overflowing in the sink.

It's also time to rejoice that occasionally they'll listen to reason, at least in the morning before they get exhausted. Or if they're not in the midst of that seemingly endless period of colds and gastro caused by the inevitable gap between stepping up contact with other kids and building immunity against most low-level illnesses. Or you haven't caught them at a low ebb when they need something to eat or drink. (Oh, let's face it, sometimes they're unbearable for no apparent reason.)

Some kids can't wait to grow up, others want to stay 4 forever, before they launch into the world of school and beyond. These, then, are the days when you'll always be there when they graze a knee, know exactly what they had for lunch and what they've been told about how people make babies. Your kid still needs you, but is quite happy to inform you sternly, "I'm not your baby any more. I'm a big kid now."

3
PARENTING

IF YOU'RE READING *PART 3: PARENTING,*
YOU'RE PROBABLY INTERESTED IN . . .
EVERYTHING ELSE IN THE BOOK!

PARENTING PHILOSOPHY

Some people follow a general philosophy or even strict rules about parenting. Others religiously follow an advice guru, or combine a few theories, or muddle through without having a set of ready-made values and guidelines (motto: "Whatever's working!"). If it's not working, don't blame yourself – try another theory. No approach is "one-way fits all". You're the recognized authority on your own child, even if, like everyone else, you need help from time to time.

choosing an approach

A bunch of "parenting philosophies" are collected in this chapter so that you can see if anything takes your fancy. Some of the ideas listed here represent a fundamental personal decision behind parental decision-making ("I was smacked when I was little, and I want to avoid doing that to my kids"); others are based on research or a background in caring for other people's children.

You'll already have some sort of a philosophy based on your own experiences and expectations, even if you don't have a name for it. Some people rely very much on family advice or memories of how somebody did things in their family. This person can be a mum, mum-in-law, godparent, aunty, granddad, sister or friend. The good thing about this is that a solution is almost always on tap – "I'll just ring Aunty Jean" or "I remember Great Uncle Desmond used to . . ." The downsides include that the solution might not work for your kid, or might be hopelessly out of date: "Yes, just pop some leeches on him, dear, that'll deal with the diphtheria", or the fact that Aunty Jean is bonkers.

The parenting theories outlined here are all different – so they can't all be exactly right for everyone. Some ideas from some approaches will work for some children. That's about the most scientific it gets, I reckon. You might find a method works well for your first child and just makes the second child look at you as if you've got to be kidding. Most people giving informal advice will just tell you to do what they did; and their way may not suit you or your family. Rather than being "ruled" by a particular theory, it's good to be flexible enough to change if it isn't working – and to ask for help. There's no shame in saying "Jeez, I never expected to be up against this problem. I think I need a new solution." That's parenting.

Through the short history of parenting theory, plenty of books, especially the older and stricter ones, are by men who have never spent day after day looking after their own children, let alone anyone else's. These days, people who look after other people's children are often the ones with the wide experience – and time – to write their manifesto or develop it into a TV series. Different approaches come in and out of fashion depending on whether somebody has a current TV series, or if there's enough people to argue about it, or it's extreme enough to get lots of publicity.

At the way outer edges of all parenting theories you'll find a weird strictness and inflexibility, always putting the theory first – even if it's not working or is making everybody miserable. But most approaches probably have some ideas you might find useful. You may want to "cherry-pick" ideas from two or more authors or theories, rather than having a "bible" to guide you on everything.

See the "More Info" section at the end of this section for all the books and websites for the parenting philosophies listed below.

Extra books based on various approaches, are listed in "More Info" sections throughout this book, including these chapters: "In the Beginning", "Crying", "Dads" and "Teaching Kids How to Behave". Many of the books should be in your local library so you can give them a test run. (Rather than buying or borrowing an old copy, always get the very latest version of any book, to make sure you're not reading any outdated health or other important info.)

> *"My philosophy is common sense with a bit of luck."* KIM

> *"[My philosophy is] anything my mother DIDN'T do."* A MUM

CHiLD-CeNTReD PHiLOSOPHieS

Many parents who themselves grew up in strict or cold families want to create a more loving and harmonious environment. Others want to continue their own tradition. They lean towards the philosophies of less rules, more involvement with their children, and a closer and more affectionate relationship.

Parents try to understand and tolerate the actions and ways of children, rather than imposing strict rules on behaviour. The upside of this of course is a happier, more humane family, and a contribution to a better world by raising kind children.

But at the extreme end, if they've been taught they're wonderful and have no need to care for the feelings of others, this can result in children who know no boundaries, no manners, and eventually have no real friends.

Such children learn they can control their world and their parents, don't follow any rules (even the simplest of manners such as saying "hello" or "please") and their behaviour alienates others. Such children may have parents who never prevent them from being unkind or even violent against other children.

Attachment parenting
This philosophy, most strongly associated with the US author partnership of Dr William Sears and his wife, nurse Martha, is based on parental closeness with the baby

and child. The basics include breastfeeding, sleeping with your baby and carrying them in a sling most of the time. Having one consistent carer rather than several is emphasized. (In almost all examples it seems to be the mum who does most of the attaching.)

Discipline is non-physical and separations are minimized. Parents are encouraged to respond immediately to their child's wants. Attachment parenting advocates do not believe in leaving a baby or a child to cry, even for very short times.

At its best it's a warm and loving approach. At its most useless it's applied to create a world where nobody's needs matter except baby's, an overtired baby is picked up instead of being helped to a desperately needed sleep, the kid turns into a smug dictator and any problem with the child is blamed on the mother for not being attached enough.

"We know of wonderful mothers who do not [breastfeed] at night, but they are willing to get up and respond to their baby in the night, no matter how many times that might be." ATTACHMENT PARENTING WEBSITE

"One day he'll be 16 and answer 'Is there anything to eat?' when I say hello to him. I need all the cuddly baby memories I can get!" EMMA

Happy children

Most people say they just want their child to be happy. (This doesn't mean insisting that the kids look constantly thrilled and grin like freaked-out chimps all day.) The trick is to give children lots of reassurance, build their self-esteem and confidence, and help them be resilient in face of troubles. The assumption is that good behaviour will follow.

At its extreme, this can be taken to mean that kids must always be happy rather than being generally happy. Kids need to feel secure about being able to express their natural and inevitable feelings and reactions, including disappointment, anger and sadness.

"If children know they are loved, then they are able to cope with most things life throws at them, so I always try to make home a happy and safe place and encourage them to confide in me without fear of reprisal. Communication lines must always be kept open." JUDI

"I love being a mother. I've been quite ill the past two years and now I appreciate so much more. I love every day and have fun every day. I get down and get dirty with the boys and laugh and carry on and just have fun. I wouldn't swap this time for all the world." KARYN

Kids first

Penelope Leach, is a child psychologist whose bestselling book, *Your Baby and Child*, has lots of followers because she puts the child's needs first. Many people swear by her "bible". Other people go a shade of furious mauve when they hear her name. It's good to know that Ms Leach is always on your child's side, and it's great to get her inside info on what babies and toddlers will enjoy and how to interact with them, as it gives you a big head start on developing your own instincts and getting to know your child, as well as being ready for each new development stage. But typical quotes such as this one can really annoy parents: "If you take [the baby] around with you wherever you go, you can go almost anywhere you might want to go as a treat". Yes, Penelope, except a bar, a cinema, a theatre, a club, a dance party, many schools, restaurants that ban babies, a row boat, a gym or anywhere at all on a whim or overnight or during the baby's "sacred" sleep time. Not to mention Sub-Saharan Africa. (See "More Info" at the end of the "In the Beginning" chapter in *Part 1: Babies* for full details and review of Ms Leach's handbook.)

"Penelope Leach seemed to make the most sense to me.." ELENA

CHILD-taming approaches

At the other end of the child-care spectrum come philosophies which emphasize parental control. These parents argue that their methods result in an ordered and consistent parenting style, which results in a happy child and good behaviour. The idea of routines and rules can seem particularly attractive in the early, chaotic months, and for parents who need to get other kids to school or themselves to work.

Downsides can include parents not realizing that in the first weeks, many babies are simply unable to fit into a routine, especially a feeding one. And at the very extreme end, the result can be an inflexible and punishing atmosphere in a home ruled by the fear of a controlling or dominating parent.

Rules and routines

Many well-known child-care experts base their philosophies on achieving a calm and ordered home life and good behaviour through establishing a clearly defined set of rules and routines. (You'll recall the Routine Queens Gina Ford and Tracy Hogg from *Part One: Babies*.) The other big names in the area are Dr Christopher Green, who made famous the term "toddler taming" and gives parents permission to "discipline", and "Supernanny".

"Supernanny" Jo Frost's books and TV series have targeted parents who seem to have lost control of their children and are miserable about their family life. Ms Frost helps parents come up with an agreed set of rules, and offers a variety of discipline techniques (getting the kid involved in the task, the naughty step, one-strike-and-you're-out). Her guiding principles – things like consistency, praise, boundaries, and warnings – rest on a bedrock of keeping your cool and being realistic about what your child is capable of at certain ages.

The upside of rules and routines is that everyone knows where they are and what's expected of them, and it can lay a blanket of blessed peace over a family that's been in chaos. It's good for kids to know what consequences will follow if they do the wrong thing. These approaches can be misapplied if the consequences are too severe (scary smacking, sarcasm, shaming or out-of-control screaming), or the expectations are unfair (it's natural for toddlers to spill things accidentally, or to get dirty).

> *"There is no such thing as an 'average' baby, nor is there such a thing as an 'average routine' that will work for everyone."*
> **KATHLEEN AUERBACH, US BREASTFEEDING SPECIALIST**

> *"I don't agree with everything Green says but at least he sees the funny side."* KATH

> *"I stopped reading Green when I got to the part about tying your kid's door shut with a rope during Time Out. You've got to be kidding."* MARGARET

Strict religious groups

Some people look to a religious book such as the Bible or the Koran to frame their household values and rules. Others who follow religions more usually called "cults" tend to have rules imposed by a "leader" or "prophet". Those who follow the fundamentals of these religions place a religious leader or doctrine above the father, who is clearly above the mother in a chain of command. Most emphasize strict rules of behaviour. Some

Christian and Muslim groups prescribe the clothing for girl children as young as 4 or 5, which can include banning trousers and making wearing a headscarf compulsory, usually to indicate submission to religion, modesty, or chastity.

The good thing about a strict religious upbringing is that everyone knows what the rules are. The worst thing is that in extreme cases the rules can be impossibly harsh and isolating, with the tiniest of transgressions punished the same way as large ones. Rejection or severe punishment by the family or group is often the price kids pay for independent thought or questioning. Children who are brought up to be passive (waiting for instruction) can be at great risk in the real world.

Singular approaches

Other philosophies abound. Here are a few of the more notable which don't really represent either "friendly" or "taming" approaches.

The "natural" approach

While it often seems a reaction against the conformity of commercialism and the harsh rules of a rigid religion or society, there can be just as many rigid "rules" with this approach, which may have been called "hippy" in times past. These may cover what is acceptable to wear (only organic natural fibres), eat (various restricted diets including organic-only, or veganism) and play with (plastic is a no-no, merchandising is frightful). Generally these things will be embraced: breastfeeding, cloth nappies, recycling, herbal remedies, wide (or no) boundaries for behaviour. And these things are often rejected: disposable accoutrements and chemicals of any description, packaged food, TV of any kind, 1950s-style repressive discipline, the bouffant.

At its most useful the approach offers the central and attractive idea of treading lightly on the earth and encouraging the child's free spirit. At its least useful it involves turning away from the real world to home schooling and other isolationist activities, just like some strict religions in which children can find it hard to fit in to the wider world because of the restrictive rules on what they're allowed to eat, do or play with.

Maximizing potential, accelerated learning or hothousing

Some parents like to maximize their child's development by finding out which stages are coming up next and scheduling activities and lessons to stimulate and encourage their child in that direction. This can include trying to teach babies to read(!), and toddlers and other under-5s having maths, music and language classes. Some parents want to give their child an advantage by having them learn or accomplish things before most kids their age do. Some people believe their toddlers are "gifted" and need to be "challenged" or "nurtured" more than others.

According to many child-development experts, accelerated learning can lead to kids being bored at school, take the fun out of learning and result in no advantage in the long term. In other words children will be "ahead" when they're 4, but possibly stressed out and feeling no pleasure from "success", and when they're 6 will probably only be where they would have been anyway. Others argue that if the kids are having fun and learning stuff they wouldn't otherwise have, it can only be a good thing, or they argue that all kids should be able to benefit from accelerated learning techniques – when they get to school.

Many of the parents who believe in this way of teaching children are persuaded by advertising that their kids need special advantages and are unaware of the research that shows children learn all the time, in great leaps and bounds, just from doing things that are fun, including chatting to themselves, pottering about, a bit of a sing along and making a cake. The upside of "maximizing potential" is that knowing what development stage your child is at can help you introduce new games and fun activities, and allow them to explore their full potential. The downside is that putting on pressure or trying to "build a genius" will almost always result in stress and disappointment.

Parents against "over-parenting"

This is a bit of a mixed bag, but the basic ideas can include: you don't need a guidebook to look after kids; parents should stop worrying so much about whether they are doing the right thing and whether their child is in danger; parents need to learn to trust their own judgement; and parents need to back off from pressuring their kids with lots of expectations, classes and planned activities. This line can help an anxious parent relax, but ultimately parents themselves have to assess their own children's capacities and risks. And all parents need help sometimes. (See "More Info" at the end of this chapter for a book on this approach.)

"I'm the expert on my kids." WENDY

Helicopter parents

This is the rather scornful name given by others to parents who always seem to "hover" (like a 'copter) over their children; parents who accompany their child around a children's party, play every game with them, supervise every activity by standing over and watching everything their children do, and give up every aspect of their own career and hobbies to be their child's constant companion. Helicopter parents say they're "involved", others say they're stifling.

"I just fly by the seat of me pants." ALISON

"If Mum's happy, then everyone's happy, that's my motto." NICOLE

Nursery or school-based systems

Many UK nursery and primary schools follow a learning and cultural philosophy. These include Reggio Emilia, Steiner and Montessori. Parents will have to make their own assessment of whether any of them are appropriate for their child. Montessori and Steiner have aspects some parents consider religious or outdated – others still swear by them.

talking about your philosophy

Be careful when you speak to other parents that your chosen methods are not presented as the only way. One person's common sense is another's feral fascist load of waffle. (But probably best not to actually say THAT.)

"When I have low self-esteem regarding any aspect of raising my child, I think of people who have raised children successfully even when they were in much more difficult situations than me – young parents, single parents, people with disabilities." BROOKE

"Shrug off the guilt and enjoy the kid." FILIZ

more info

ATTACHMENT PARENTING

The Attachment Parenting Book: A Commonsense Guide to Understanding and Nurturing Your Child
by William Sears, MD, and Martha Sears, Little, Brown, US, 2009

The US go-to gurus give their take on bringing up baby close to you, with an emphasis on breastfeeding. Features their take on a kind and inclusive approach to discipline. The Sears' *Baby Book* reviewed in "More Info" of the chapter "In The Beginning", in *Part 1: Babies* has a chapter on attachment parenting. *The Good Behaviour Book: How to Have a Better-behaved Child from Birth to Age Ten*, also by the Sears, is reviewed in "More Info" at the end of the "Teaching Kids How to Behave" chapter.

www.pinky-mychild.com
Australian Pinky McKay has a child-centred and relaxed approach to dealing with babies and toddlers.

www.attachmentparenting.org
US-based website for Attachment Parenting International. Outlines the eight central tenets of ABI philosophy.

HAPPY KIDS

Raising Happy Children: What Every Child Needs Their Parents to Know – From 0 to 11 Years
by Jan Parker and Jane Stimpson, Mobius, 2004

Really useful info and suggestions are delivered in short, relevant bits. The book starts with how to bond with your baby, shows how to talk with your young child so they keep talking to you, and how to talk about fears and bad things without either dismissing or being overwhelmed by them. It also gives great practical advice on encouraging good behaviour, how not to smack, tantrums, sibling rivalry, bullies, grief, blended families and lots more.

The Complete Secrets of Happy Children: A Guide for Parents
by Stephen Biddulph and Shaaron Biddulph, Thorsons, 2003

Mr "Raising Boys" Biddulph teams up with his wife to tackle child-rearing in general, from babies and toddlers to older children and teenagers. Strong on "soft love" (touch, praise) and "firm love" (discipline through teaching and being involved, rather than punishment).

KIDS FIRST

See "More Info" at the end of the "In the Beginning" chapter in *Part 1: Babies* for full details and review of *Your Baby and Child* by Penelope Leach.

RULES AND ROUTINES

Supernanny: How to Get the Best From Your Children
by Jo Frost, Hodder and Stoughton, 2006

Jo Frost's before-and-after "personas" are rolled into one on the cover of her book; the stern, law-maker looking over her specs, who's also sometimes a lady with her hair down and a teddy bear in her handbag. In this well-designed book, top ten rules are applied to a range of challenges, such as fussy eating and dressing, learning to use the loo and have a bedtime, and battles of will. She's not an advocate of smacking, but says "not smacking" isn't enough of an approach to get your kids to change their behaviour, and suggests alternatives which can include temporary banishment of a toy, or the child themselves. As well as rules, she's big on a calm atmosphere, and taking the time to know and have fun with your kids. Tracy Hogg and Gina Ford both have toddler versions of their routine philosophy for babies (baby versions reviewed back in *Part 1: Babies*.)

New Toddler Taming A Parent's Guide to the First Four Years
by Christopher Green, Vermilion, 2006

Dr Green's jaunty prescriptions for gaining control. I can't recommend it, especially on "discipline" issues: he advocates smacking in controlled and prescribed circumstances. To be fair, it's popular with many parents.

THE "NATURAL" APPROACH

www.thegreenparent.co.uk
A site supporting UK's *Green Parent* magazine with articles, forums and blogs on environmental parenting.

www.earthmamasweb.com (Australia) and **www.mothering.com** (US) are other sites with an earth-centred parenting philosophy.

MAXIMISING POTENTIAL, ACCELERATED LEARNING OR HOTHOUSING

www.acceleratedlearning.co.uk
Info about emotional and other intelligence, accelerated learning, play and children's brains; a site by Nicola Call, the author of books on accelerated learning for primary school-aged kids.

www.babyeinstein.com
A commercial site with CDs, DVDs and other products claiming to boost intelligence. Einstein himself didn't speak until he was 4 so do try to relax.

PARENTS AGAINST "OVER-PARENTING"

Paranoid Parenting: Why Ignoring the Experts May Be Best For Your Child
by Frank Furedi, Continuum 2008
The author says we all need to lighten up and stop trying to be the perfect parent who communicates in exactly the right way with their children all the time – sometimes we need to just get the shopping done instead.

NURSERY OR SCHOOL-BASED SYSTEMS

www.ltscotland.org.uk
From the home page of the government's curriculum body, Learning and Teaching Scotland, choose Early Years then Reggio Emilia to see a local version of this creative learning approach. Bringing teachers, parents and children together, it has continually developed and is now used in preschool education worldwide, since being introduced by parents in the Reggio Emilia area of Italy after World War II.

www.montessori-uk.org
This site explains Maria Montessori's methods and philosophy, based on child-led learning methods developed in the early 1900s, while **montessorieducation.co.uk** gives details of participating nurseries and schools in the UK.

www.steinerwaldorf.org
Information and lists of Steiner schools in the UK, based on the teachings of Rudolf Steiner in the late 1800s.

UNPaiD WORK AND PaiD WORK

Some parents give up work outside the home, others work part-time or full-time. Some parents share both roles. And everyone is as busy as an ant at a picnic.

This chapter isn't a blueprint for restructuring your life. It covers your options and what to consider in making a decision about who works where. These choices are so individual that no one should ever presume to tell you which way to jump, or when or if you'll be ready to go "back" to work.

I'm going to miss you, darling!

PAY PACKET

Staying at Home

As well as dealing with all the brand newness of being a parent, you might be coming to terms with another huge transition: the change from paid work "out there"to home work that's unpaid and undervalued. What mother has not made a huge effort to get on a frock and out to a barbecue only to be asked "What do you do?". Her choice is simple. If she doesn't want to be snubbed under the washing line she should say "I'm a space shuttle pilot who strips in her spare time", not "I'm a mother at home".

In a world where our work is supposed to define us, "I'm a stay-at-home mum" causes polite snorey noises in most new acquaintances. Even worse is having made all that effort, made it into Adultland, only to be stuck with another parent in the corner shouting about green poo over the Coldplay.

Although most of the people who make this transition are women, an increasing number of blokes are "staying at home" while their partner becomes the only breadwinner. And another big lot of parents are juggling, often with both parents doing part-time jobs, or one full-time, one part-time, and some child care thrown in. There's also a rapidly growing number of parents sharing custody, and sole parents (most of whom are women).

Unfortunately many parents find it hard to see what it's like for somebody doing it differently. This is especially potent for mothers because it feeds old-fashioned notions of what a "good" or "bad" mother is. Mothers who stay at home are often contemptuous of mothers who work, but secretly envious of their independence, money and better dressed, seemingly more glamorous lives. Mothers who have another job often have to rush around breathlessly, feeling that they've failed as both paid worker and parent, and they envy what is seen as the calmer, one-job life of staying at home (as if that's easy). The truth is, both situations have upsides and downsides.

Even those who seem to have the most in common probably don't. Consider the at-home mum with a wealthy partner, or even an independent income, who has her own car, a cleaner, unlimited babysitting, lots of splendid holidays and a hairdresser who gives them a blowdry most days at 3 o'clock sharp. This person has very little in common with a stay-at-home mum who has to do all her washing and drying at a laundrette, who has to get a bus to the supermarket with the stroller, who has no help from relatives, and who will lose almost all her government benefits if she moves in with a bloke. There is a world of difference between women who know they

THE UPSIDE OF HOME WORK

* "Kids are only little for a short time. I want to be there."

* "I have given myself up to being at home for the time being so I don't need to worry about work, child care or conflicts between work and home."

* "Watching and helping a baby develop into a child can be a wonderful and absorbing experience."

* "I've waited so long to have a baby, I want to immerse myself in the experience."

* "This is far more important than the job I had before."

* "My partner is earning more money than I could at the moment, and later it will be my turn again."

* "Apart from the housework, there's a lot of stuff to be organized and fixed around the house and garden that I've been meaning to do for years and can get done now."

* "It has forced me to slow down and see the world through the eyes of a child."

* "I decide what we do every day."

* "I know what my child is eating and what they are learning. I know them better than anybody."

* "I'm learning how to live on a budget."

* "I've made new friends among the parents at playgroup."

are making considerable financial and other sacrifices to stay at home and women who never expected to do anything else or have made a much more unambiguously pleasant "choice".

Being the Home CEO

Please don't read a book called *Sidetracked Home Executives: From Pigpen to Paradise* – it is full of awful stories from two American wives who wanted to be more organized, partly because they weren't getting their husband's breakfast or making enough effort to be pretty for him. (I've said it before: if a man can't make his own breakfast, you're better off living in separate postcode areas.) The women solve this problem by running their lives with the aid of a series of little white cards on which are filed chores and – yes, lordy – compliments they get on their housekeeping skills. Here is a quote from one of their husbands: "I thought that if you loved me then I wouldn't

THE DOWNSIDE OF HOME WORK

* "I miss earning my own money."

* "I used to be respected and listened to; now people ignore me or their eyes glaze over because I'm 'just a mother.'"

* "I used to be respected and listened to; now people say I'm doing something interesting and they wish they could do it too, but I can tell they are scornful of my decision to be 'just a father.'"

* "Because I'm the person at home I do almost all the housework and it's boring."

* "I know the money is supposed to be 'ours', but it's hard to see it that way sometimes."

* "I feel trapped."

* "Sometimes I feel like a cross between a cow and Cinderella."

* "I feel bored and boring."

* "I miss the work I used to do."

* "I miss the social side of work."

* "Inevitably I have lost friends."

* "I only get to talk to kids or people who want to talk about kids."

* "I feel like my work is moving on without me, I'm missing the progress in the industry and it will be harder to get back in."

* "I want to go back to work part-time (or full-time) but child care around here is too expensive, booked out or not to a standard I'd like (or the older kids finish school at 3.30)."

have to go to work hungry and wearing wrinkled clothes. I figured if you really cared, you'd try harder to look as pretty as you were when I married you." You will be surprised to learn that this husband had the use of his own limbs, and that his wife did not explain that being the homemaker meant that she was to look after the home and the children, but not necessarily the breakfast needs of a grown man – and that doing a grown man's ironing and washing is not a responsibility but an act of generosity and kindness.

This is not to say that homemaking can't be a satisfying job – but it's hard to make it wholly satisfying otherwise I think you'd find very rich, powerful men would do it. There is an element of drudgery and sacrifice that has to be acknowledged, although you need to guard against going into that mad martyrdom where you want everyone to be grateful for your every polish (of course too far the other way and you'll feel like a doormat). Housework can have immediately satisfying results – the room does look neat and tidy – but those results are so easily and quickly turned into chaos that it's important not to lose yourself in the role.

Many books have lists (and lists of lists) to help you declutter the house (almost all books supposedly about home management are actually about decluttering), clean the house, spring-clean the house, throw a party, book a holiday. But you can make up your own. (See "More Info" at the end of this chapter for some useful books on housekeeping and DIY.)

Basically to get really organized you are going to have to get a handle on:

★ household cleaning and maintenance
★ whose money is whose and why
★ household finances
★ living within a budget
★ balancing everyone else's needs and wants with your own
★ making sure you're the home organizer and not a slave.

More importantly, in a household with two parents or two adults, the above list will need to always be open for discussion. It's a lot easier if everyone knows what their responsibilities and rights are and that these can be adjusted. To really understand each other partners need to know what the other person is doing with their day and how it makes them feel. Otherwise you're not in the same boat together. You're in separate canoes, missing a paddle and wondering how bad this metaphor can get.

One very stark example of how things can end up is the issue of family holidays. The home partner usually researches and books the holiday (and is therefore "responsible" for its success or otherwise); packs; washes, cleans and cooks throughout the holiday; packs to come home; deals with everything that arose while the family was away; and gets everyone ready for school or work again. So who really had the holiday? (Of course even this may sound a wee bit like gorgeous luxury to a single parent.)

Don't forget to find out if you're eligible for any government grants or assistance.

Don't be everyone's assistant

The world expects stay-at-home parents and people who work from home to always be available for them. It will be assumed you have time to burn. You will be approached for committees, car pools, helping other people's children learn to read and looking after other kids. Of course you may enjoy doing these things, but other people shouldn't assume it's your duty to do them. Sometimes people will even ask you to run errands for them.

Blokes at home

Blokes who are unpaid, home-based parents may find the housekeeping and handy-work books in "More Info" at the end of this chapter helpful (and also the next chapter, "Dads").

WHY PARENTS DON'T automatically go "BACK" to WORK

There are a great many people who assume that at-home parents will go "back" to work when their kids start school. Anyone who's ever been asked why they haven't should photocopy the "What Do You Do All Day?" list coming up in a minute and silently hand the person a copy.

Parents of preschoolers often don't return to their previous full-time paid work because many nurseries are part-time or morning or afternoon only, and at best finish by about 3pm. And many parents of primary school kids don't either because school ends at 3.30 or earlier. Some first terms for Reception involve mornings only or fewer than five days a week. Some kids aren't suited to after care, especially in the early years when they're tired at the end of the nursery or school day. Most jobs don't give you the school holidays off.

"What do you do all day?"

Well, someone has to ◎ shop ◎ remove clothes stains ◎ wash the clothes ◎ dry the clothes ◎ fold the clothes ◎ iron the clothes ◎ distribute the clothes to drawers and cupboards ◎ do the financial planning ◎ do the toilet ◎ do the floors ◎ plan a week's-worth of menus ◎ drive people in different directions and pick them up on time ◎ do the dusting ◎ wait for tradespeople ◎ get put on hold for 45 minutes at the bank ◎ organize the bill paying ◎ be the family liaison person who arranges events and care rotas ◎ cook the meals ◎ do the dishes ◎ make the lunches ◎ help with homework ◎ play with the kids ◎ talk to them about their lives ◎ make the costumes ◎ talk to teachers about their kids' development, problems and important breakthroughs ◎ plan everything ◎ clean the fridge ◎ bake for the fete ◎ fund-raise ◎ hassle the government about stuff it's doing wrong ◎ run the tuckshop ◎ be a Parent Governor of the school ◎ help with reading ◎ run community projects ◎ help the elderly neighbours ◎ look after ageing parents ◎ be there when a kid is sick ◎ be there

---

SOME TERMS OTHER THAN HOUSEWIFE/HOUSEHUSBAND

You might like to call yourself:

* homemaker

* stay-at-home mum/dad

* home executive

* chief executive officer of (your address here)

* full-time mother/father/parent

* part-time nanny, driver, cleaner, teacher, medical triage officer, retail consultant, stylist, home decorator, chef, events coordinator, project manager, company director, entertainment facilitator, arbitration expert, and so on.

---

on Sports Day ◉ help with the school concert ◉ be one of the people whose house kids go to until their parents come home from work ◉ do the spring-cleaning.

I could go on but my editor said sixteen pages would be too much to photocopy.

Juggling Paid Work and Unpaid Work

Most parents are involved in part-time or full-time paid work, especially as their kids grow older. Well, unless they're independently wealthy and simply swan about their hobby trout farm or something. Many parents choose to work from home if they can.

If you work for a business, find out what policies your employer has on flexible and family-friendly work practices and hours. Ask your union about entitlements in this area. Your local employment office will have information and training opportunities for people wanting to re-enter the workforce.

Whether you do paid work full-time or part-time outside or from your home, much or all of the housework will probably be done by you too if you're a woman, statistically speaking. Have a look at the earlier "Staying Home" section because some of it will be relevant. To help yourself get organized see "More Info" coming up next.

The world of constant juggling and adjustment, of feeling guilty about home and guilty about work, is familiar to lots of us. Only you can judge whether you've bitten off more than you can chew, or whether spitting some out will make you feel better. Or if some element of mad scramble will be normal from now on.

THE UPSIDE OF PAID WORK

* It's, well, paid.

* It makes a nice contrast with the vacuuming.

* Looking after a baby or small children can be boring: having time away means you can go back to them refreshed.

* You're a better, more patient parent because you don't have to do it 24 hours a day.

* You don't feel so isolated from the world.

* You keep up with what's going on in your industry or somewhere in the outside world at least.

* Loving your job.

* There's only so much you can talk about with a toddler.

* For many people, it's a relief to get back to work.

* You usually have to change out of your dressing-gown.

* If you're lucky, you can get part-time or flexible hours to maximize parent time.

THE DOWNSIDE OF PAID WORK

* Either you're feeling guilty about not being a good enough parent or you feel insecure about whether you're giving enough to work.

* Women especially who feel guilty about needing flexible work hours often do a lot more work than they're paid for.

* Kids don't run to a schedule.

* Kids don't want to be with anyone else when they're sick.

* Kids need "quantity time" with parents, not just "quality time" (short bursts of contact here and there). Make sure you can hang out together for an hour or two a day at least.

* Co-workers and bosses often don't understand what's needed when it comes to your family (like having to take off suddenly, or what it's like trying to concentrate after three nights of constantly broken sleep).

* There are not as many opportunities for food fights.

* It's much harder to balance life and get things done if you don't have a partner or somebody who shares custody with you. Or a housekeeper and a valet.

more info

HOUSEKEEPING AND DIY

Home Comforts: The Art and Science of Keeping House

by Cheryl Mendelson, Phoenix 2002

Even if you don't do everything (or anything!) this fabulous book recommends, it's all here – from how to read laundry-care labels and the best way to hang out the washing to preserving family records and how long you can keep things in the fridge or freezer. A huge book that's great for anyone who has to run or share the running of a household or is moving out of home, and anyone who has argued about whether to wash the glasses or the plates first.

Reader's Digest DIY Manual (with CD-ROM)

Reader's Digest, 2007

No, I'm not saying this is a great time to renovate! But you're probably going to have more time than money in the short term at least, and not be able to splash out on tradespeople. (But please – no electrical work or other stunts by yourself.) This book covers virtually everything: all the common household and garden jobs, plus a ready reckoner for estimating material quantities such as how many rolls of wallpaper you need.

STAYING AT HOME

I don't like most of the books for stay-at-home parents that are available (mainly from the US) because they seem to assume things such as you want to home school the kids or you want dieting tips (!), or their main aim seems to be criticizing parents who work outside the home, part- or full-time, rather than giving practical help or reassuring info for people who choose to be full-time parents.

Websites

Many of the general parenting websites listed in "More Info" at the end of the second chapter have discussion boards and articles relevant for the stay-at-home parent. Other specific sites are geared towards offering "earn money at home" schemes, rather than ideas of what to do with your children.

www.fulltimemothers.org

This site is against what it sees as the relentless drive to get all mothers out to work and children into child care. It aims to increase the status of stay-at-home carers (yes, fathers too) and argues for changes in the tax and benefit systems to allow parents a real choice about staying at home (such as using tax credits to pay yourself). Supportive of working parents, and campaigns for the development of employment policies that meet the demands of being a "fully engaged mother". Interesting archive of relevant news stories.

WOMEN'S LIVES

Wifework: What Marriage Really Means for Women
by Susan Maushart, Bloomsbury 2003

Ms Maushart looks at the inequalities within many marriages and what can be done about them. This book could make you feel very cross about how much housework your partner isn't doing if you weren't a bit grumpy already. She tries to work out why women feel they have to do all the organizing while the blokes get to play. She says because of the kids it's worth finding a way to make marriage succeed and be fairer.

The Price of Motherhood: Why the Most Important Job in the World Is Still the Least Valued
by Ann Crittenden, Holt Rinehart and Winston, 2002

Feminist reporter turned feminist mum at home Ann Crittenden asks why conservatives always bang on about being family friendly, but in fact full-time mothers are still not respected by society and politicians. She talks about the career sacrifices that are made, mostly by mothers, and the way mothers are perceived by others. She argues that if they "had more resources and more respect, everyone – including children – would be better off". And she explores why people say "motherhood is the most important job in the world" and then ignore any mothers in the room or refer to "mothers who don't work". An American book so the legal and some of the social aspects it discusses are not relevant to the UK.

The Bitch in the House: 26 Women Tell the Truth About Sex, Solitude, Work, Motherhood and Marriage
edited by Cathi Hanauer, Penguin, 2003

This lively bestselling collection covers many things close to women's hearts: being cross about why men don't see the work that women do; the difference between being a girlfriend, a wife and a mother; being sweet in the office and a gorgon at home; struggling to balance work and home; the theory of wanting a child versus the reality; having to look after your children and your parents; what motherhood can force you to give up and the emotional riches it bestows. The 26 speak about their different lives and make many honest observations that women are often scared to say out loud.

Perfect Madness: Motherhood in the Age of Anxiety
by Judith Warner, Vermilion, 2006

Lively and funny analysis of the control freakery of modern motherhood: no nights out, no sex, no sleep – and manic cake-baking at midnight. Penetrating and plain spoken.

www.timesonline.typepad.com/alphamummy

Blog on the UK newspaper site for mums who work, used to work, or want to go back to work one day (as if looking after children isn't work enough). Well-written, newsy articles and plenty of comments from readers.

Piffle

The Amazon.com bookselling website lists *The Surrendered Wife: A Practical Guide to Finding Intimacy, Passion, and Peace with Your Man*, by Laura Doyle, along with other useful titles such as *Liberated Through Submission* by P. B. Wilson, *The Proper Care and Feeding of Husbands* by Dr Laura Schlessinger, *Men Are from Mars, Women Are from Venus* by what's-'is-name, and the gobsmackingly titled *You Can Be the Wife of a Happy Husband* by Darien B. Cooper. It's a book about how you should get yourself a husband and then do everything he tells you to do and never contradict him. Tremendously reassuring and useful if you are lost in the wilderness and you have a copy of this book, a jerrycan of petrol and a box of matches. Toast a marshmallow for me.

JUGGLING PAID WORK AND UNPAID WORK

Working Parents: How to Work, Raise Great Kids and Have a Life
by Michael Grose, Random House, 2002

Looks at child care; guilt; when your child is sick; working from home; family disapproval; being organized; employer attitudes; the questions you get asked; preschool and school-age kids. He says working families need "hang around" time, focused time and family rituals.

How Not to be a Perfect Mother
by Libby Purves, Thorsons, 2004

An invaluable tongue-in-cheek survival guide to the early years with children: how to cut corners and bend rules that never really mattered. Hilarious accounts of the toddler years, fraught outings, nannies and careers.

How to be a Great Working Mum: The Happy Baby Plan
by Tracey Godridge and Martine Gallie, Foulsham, 2008

Ignore the annoying cover with blissful businesswoman carrying a baby bag; presumably not trying to remember whether she put knickers on this morning. Lots on organizing your time, finding support, and negotiating with a partner. From pregnancy to the teen years, in point form.

I Don't Know How She Does It
by Allison Pearson, Vintage, 2003

Although a fiction book, many will recognize themselves in hard-pressed Kate Reddy, a working mum who strives to keep all the balls in the air. Based on journalist Pearson's *Daily Telegraph* columns, this novel is funny and many will envy the conclusion.

The 24-Hour Family: A Parent's Guide to Work-Life Balance
by Polly Ghazi, The Women's Press, 2003

Practical self-help manual with helpful sections on knowing your rights, negotiating with your employer and advice on work–life options, and how that might change from the toddler to teenage years.

www.ivillage.co.uk
Useful section on work–life balance, flexible working and family-friendly employers.

www.motheratwork.co.uk
Webzine with a guide to your employment rights, a "High Street" for online shopping, and a list of companies who have demonstrated their commitment to a good work–life balance.

www.mumandworking.co.uk
Some useful advice and links if you are setting up your own business.

www.netmums.com
Has posted the results of their own survey of 4000 mums entitled "The Great Work Debate", which makes interesting reading.

DaDS

Yes, well, no more sex for you, and if you try to do anything for the kid we'll roll our eyes and laugh at you and make snide comments about your hopelessness for the task, just to make us feel more competent as mothers. That's the worst-case scenario. Unless the baby keeps vomiting down your neck. No, really, it's all going to be marvellous. Parenthood *is* marvellous – and boring and complicated and hard and hilarious and silly and guesswork and exhausting, and makes you proud and

furious and bewildered and tired and more full of love than you thought possible.

This whole book is for dads as well as mums, but here's the men-only section.

good ways for men to be a real partner

One minute there's a floaty pregnant woman demanding that the baby come out, and the next minute she's an exhausted wreck saying she can't cope, her bosoms don't work, she'll never be able to be a good mother and boo hoo hoo. Not much to be done, chaps, except pitch in and be true to the word "partner", emotionally and around the house. It can be tricky, especially in the early days with all the raging hormones and exhaustion and bosoms akimbo but off limits.

Then you go back to work (we'll get to stay-at-home dads in a mo) and have a crying baby thrust at you every night after her long, hard day.

This is your chance to be a real hero. Listen, sympathize, don't try to solve everything immediately, do everything you can to reassure your partner that she'll work out the breastfeeding, and talk about being in it together and riding it through. This would be a good time to dip into any spare money for a weekly cleaner, even for just the first eight weeks. Get your relatives and friends to donate food and do shopping.

Women can feel trapped in a new role they can't get out of – "housewife", "milking machine" or "walking zombie". Without making it a competition, sympathize and say you feel trapped into being the main or only breadwinner for the next twenty years (or whatever your individual situation is).

Many dads love to have their kids for hours on end – they hang out for the prospect. And many understand that parenthood is a joint venture. Having a supportive partner in these early days can make all the difference for women between mild blues and thinking they're going mad. Mothers, especially those who are at home full-time, may need regular nights, mornings or afternoons off at the weekend.

"It can be very overwhelming for dads too. We kept in close touch with family and friends, and the local health visitor for reassurance that we were doing the right thing. Sharing the home duties helps too." SCOTT

"I pay someone to come on Sunday mornings and hubby and I go out for brunch (think of the cost as 'marriage insurance'). We tried going out to dinner but were falling asleep at the table by 9 pm." KATE

While recognizing common differences between men and women, there's no reason why men can't become as competent or even more competent at being a parent, if you don't count the bosoms business. Mums don't have a monopoly on baby knowledge.

tHiNgs meN ofteN NeeD to KNoW

You probably have just as many parenting instincts as your partner. You'll both be learning new things all the time for the next few years. Talking honestly with other dads will show you that feeling scared or inadequate is not unique or strange.

The more you do things, the better you'll be at them. This includes nappy changing, bathing, getting clothes on and off a wriggler and talking to your baby.

Anticipation is needed – try to think ahead about things that might happen and how to deal with them. You'll be better prepared. Don't wait until you're out of baby formula to buy the next lot, for example. Have baby paracetamol in the cupboard. Get the kid a coat and hat before the first really cold days of winter. If you go to the supermarket for milk, get bananas and toilet paper too.

Stuff doesn't just "happen". It often happens because your partner has made it happen. Think about what wouldn't be done if she suddenly wasn't there. Not many dads do the planning stuff. Many or most dads wouldn't know how to make an appointment at their kid's hairdresser, find somewhere to take them for swimming lessons, tell a doctor their kid's habits and routine or organize a birthday party, complete with invitations. But there are a lot more dads now who know how to do this stuff, and do this stuff, than ever before, and it would be helpful if you knew how – partly because sometimes you'll need to, and partly because it will get you many Brownie points and days off for golf or whatever it is you mysterious creatures do.

Write lists for yourself if that's a good way for you to get things right. Have notes about what needs to be in the baby bag at all times, and a list of essentials that have to be bought weekly or regularly at the supermarket.

Sometimes we women don't know you're afraid of the anger we turn on you if you get something "wrong": please don't stop doing things. So you dressed the baby in a stripy top and floral trousers that don't match. Who cares? If your partner is horrified by this, find a couple of failsafe versions – that is, have on hand a few tops and pants that are the same colour.

Women can often do six things at a time while planning another four in their head. Men often think and do only one thing at a time. Either develop the womanly ability or explain that you'll get the six things done but it may take a bit longer.

"My number one piece of advice for a new mother would be to ask the midwife in hospital to help your husband give the baby its first bath. After that, never suggest in any way that you are more competent or any better in any way at caring for the baby. If he is parenting from day one he will get good at it, and it's very sweet to see a daddy confidently nursing a little bub!" JUNINE

Don't get squeezed out

If you're a stay-at-home dad for the day, week or year, you have to do housework as well as look after the kid(s). In this arena I think you need to do the housework properly, even the bits you don't "see": think "dirty" – the loo needs to be done at least weekly, even if it doesn't seem as bad as the footy club ones.

If you don't know what needs doing, ask for a list, and for the tasks to be explained if necessary, as well as the standard of cleanliness needed for hygiene or family harmony purposes. This can help avoid the "What pile of dog poo under the carpet bigger than a bread bin?" syndrome where some chaps seem to be legally blind in the presence of things many women think are obvious problems. (Of course it's entirely possible that the sex roles may be reversed in this argument. I've just never heard of it.)

Don't take any crap, though, about small stuff such as the washed cutlery should be propped up to drain, not laid flat. Have a meeting on the separation of tasks and negotiate the standard to which they should be done.

Some men and women are happy to divide things sharply – women at home get to make all the decisions at home, men "out" at work get to do all that stuff. But if you want to be involved with your baby and kids, don't be shut out by any insecurity or arrogance that manifests itself as a woman saying she always knows best and you're incompetent because you're the man (even though you still have to take the garbage and the spiders out). If she thinks you're incompetent, ask her to teach you.

It's never just about housework. If, for instance, a woman feels that her central role is being a mother she might be devastated if her child runs to Daddy for comfort as well as Mummy. You'll probably need to talk about this.

Sometimes problems arise from a complicated psychological situation in which the woman thinks she's no longer good for anything else and needs to make you feel less competent on the home turf so she feels more competent. (In most families it's the woman who stays home with a young baby, and it's the woman who takes the biggest hits to her career or the other life opportunities she had before motherhood.) It would be most splendid for everyone to work through the situation tactfully and supportively (says Mrs Authoresspants of Perfectville).

Very often the "mum always knows best" thing comes from generations of social conditioning and has developed because sometimes it has been the only control women have had in their lives. The best way for your partner to get over needing to be the Home CEO is for her to feel you're useful and reliable enough to take charge while she's out capering around somewhere.

Sometimes it drives women crazy when their partner asks them what to buy at the supermarket or how to wash something. We have to remember that you men want to do it right, that you don't want us to be mad at you for doing it wrong, and that if you weren't doing it we would have to get off our arses and do it ourselves.

If you want to know more about how to do the housework properly or how to decipher those strange cleaning symbols on clothes labels, check out *Home Comforts*, a how-to book reviewed in "More Info" at the end of the previous chapter, "Unpaid Work and Paid Work".

"We need to know not only that women can do what men can do, but also that men can do what women can do." GLORIA STEINEM, QUOTED BY CATHY YOUNG IN "MATERNAL CHAUVINISM IS A DAD'S GREATEST OBSTACLE TO PARENTAL PARITY", ON WWW.SALON.COM

BLOKeS aND BaBieS

Most importantly you need to bond with the baby too, and this can take a while. The best way is to get to know your baby by spending time together, changing nappies, having quiet chats (you can crap on about anything to a baby – they just like to hear you and see your face).

Don't let your partner, family members, in-laws, friends or people in the street make you feel bad that you are learning how to look after a baby. If you do the wrong thing, that's just a step towards doing it the right way – or your way, which doesn't have to be how everyone else does it, as long as it is safe.

Looking after babies is too important and difficult and rewarding to leave it up to the women alone.

"We find out what women have known for decades. You can't truly be a star at work if you're truly serious about being there for your kids as often as they need you. There will always be some hot-shot who's willing to give up more to get where you could go if not for what you need to do at home." STAY-AT-HOME WRITER–DAD, JONATHON KRONSTADT, IN "THE NEW DAD" ON WWW.SALON.COM

BLOKeS aND SeX

Many blokes are astonished to find out how much parenthood gets in the way of a sex life. Keep talking about how you'd like things to change. Here are some reasons your partner may be uninterested in sex.

- ★ Her body has not been truly her "own" for a long time. Especially if she's breastfeeding, she may feel the pressure of too many demands.
- ★ She's tired all the time.
- ★ Her libido (sex drive) isn't what it used to be.
- ★ She doesn't want to get pregnant again.
- ★ She feels unattractive because of weight gain or loss, bosom changes or stretch marks.

THE SPECIAL USES OF BLOKES

(Obviously the talents listed aren't exclusively male, but this whole section generalizes about things so shut up.)

* Blokes can let mums know they're not in parenting alone, even if they're separated.

* Blokes can be secretly smug because a baby usually says "Dadda" before "Mumma".

* Blokes are especially good at understanding the boisterousness of little boys.

* Many blokes can perform the incredibly useful task of getting their girls interested in ball skills and sport.

* Blokes can provide a fresh approach to settling kids – and at least provide a new target for them while Mum takes a breather.

* Blokes don't have to be the strong disciplinarians, just present a united, agreed-upon front with mums.

* Blokes can show kids that they enjoy being with them, which builds self-esteem.

* Blokes can show boys it's okay to cry and do things like dress up.

* Blokes can show girls how to climb, hammer and do other traditional "bloke things".

* Blokes can be affectionate and available. So many modern men who had tough upbringings and cold relationships with their own fathers are bravely going a new way, determined to be loving and cuddly with boys and girls, and setting up a healthier and more rewarding future.

* A bloke who is careful and kind to a child's mother is showing how to behave. Kids learn by example more than words.

What you can do

* Keep talking about it.
* Make her *feel* attractive as well as telling her. (Show it by your actions.)
* Get help with housework.

★ Wear three condoms at once or do something else sensible about contraception – then everyone can relax.
★ Be patient.
★ Ask her what she wants.

DADS WHO NEED HELP WITH DEPRESSION OR FAMILY RELATIONSHIPS

Dads, like mums, can suffer parenting or postnatal depression. Even if it's your partner who is depressed, you may still need help too. There are special support groups for blokes to talk about their postnatal depression, dealing with their partner's problem or family relationships (see "More Info" below). Many of the websites listed at the end of this chapter have forums or links to other organizations that deal with depression in fathers, and research has been done by the UK's thinktank The Fatherhood Institute in this area too (see "More Info").

"The answer to the question about housework makes my husband seem like a sexist layabout, but the reality is he's out of the house for 10 to 12 hours a day. Five days a week. He would dearly love to spend more time with our son, but by the time he gets home he's often asleep. Also I'm more than happy to do most of the housework as I'm the one at home. Before we had a baby we had a cleaner, so neither of us had to come home from work and clean the house, but we can't afford that luxury now. No matter what your views are on sexual politics, equality, etc., it's pretty hard not to start living a 1950s lifestyle if the parent at home is the woman and the 'working' parent is the bloke. And our son and I agree: he's a top Dad!" KATE

more info

STUFF FOR DADS

For hands-on how-to, see also *A Dad's Guide To Baby Care* by Colin Cooper and *The New Father: A Dad's Guide to the First Year* by Armin Brott, reviewed on p.18

Best Things Fathers Do: Ideas and Advice from Real World Dads
by Will Glennon, Conari Press, 2008
Celebrates fatherhood and aims to give dads the tools (dads do so love tools) to build close bonds with their children. If you can cope with the slightly New Age tone, this book has many lovely thoughts and ideas.

Dad Rules: What I Learned From My Girls
by Andrew Clover, Fig Tree, 2008
Based on his observational columns in *The Sunday Times*, Mr Clover brings some realism, some surrealism and a story of trying to hog the gas in the delivery room.

Full-time Father: How to Succeed as a Stay-at-Home Dad
by Richard Hallows, White Ladder Press, 2004
A guy who's had this increasingly popular job looks at common worries about what

---

MEN: AN INFURIATING CHECKLIST

* Bring in vast wage.

* Work flexible, part-time hours.

* Be fabulously artistic and amusingly unpredictable but also totally reliable.

* Be competent at all kid stuff but never usurp or contradict mother superiority.

* Make woman feel attractive and sexy.

* Be endlessly supportive.

* Talk.

* Shut up.

* Talk again.

* No, not about that.

* Oh, for heaven's SAKE.

---

others will think and future career prospects, as well as practical advice on how to structure your day and tiptoe through the financial and housework issues.

How to be a Great Dad
by Ian Bruce, Foulsham, 2005

Based on the reassuring fact that it's okay not to instinctively know what to do, this book helps build the skills of learning how to do the practical things, understanding the minds of babies and kids, how to approach discipline, and how to have fun together.

The Father's Book, Being a Good Dad in the Twenty-first Century
by David Cohen, Wiley, 2008

His psychology background informs his parenting and discipline strategies. Although there is some newborn info (how to touch and play with your child in the first few hours), its information is more useful for older children.

Fatherhood: The Truth
by Marcus Berkmann, Vermilion UK, 2008

A sports columnist commentates on being a dad through pregnancy, and includes essential advice on matters such as "what if your baby is ugly?" and, well, there's no getting around them, breasts. The fainthearted may want to skip the chapter called "Piss, Shit and Vomit" but as they'll be dealing with the real thing, maybe it's time to man up.

www.dad.info
Accessible site, with lots of guidance on how to navigate your child's emotional development, dealing with postnatal depression (yours and hers), life skills to teach your kids and debunking the biggest myths about dads.

Homedad.org.uk
Forum for stay-at-home dads and involved fathers generally.

www.dadsanddaughters.org
A US site about just what it says, with lots of hints and articles.

www.fathers.com
A store of articles and links on a US website. It covers many different topics and ways of being a dad.

BOOKS ABOUT DADS FOR KIDS

What Dads Can't Do

by Douglas Wood, Simon and Schuster, US, 2000

A gorgeous story about companionship between a small crocodiley creature and a dad crocodiley creature. Dads and kids will get different frissons, and share some, from this book.

My Dad

by Anthony Browne, Corgi Children's Books, UK, 2001

A greatly inventive kids' writer and illustrator looks at all sorts of dads and their best points.

SUPPORT SERVICES FOR DADS

Helplines and parent services are listed in "More Info" at the end of the second chapter, "Your Support Team". See also "More Info" for "Feeling Overwhelmed and Depressed" for general help with depression, or call NHS Direct on 0845 4647.

Dads-uk.co.uk

Newsy support site for fathers, including help for divorced or separating dads and supporting fathers' rights.

www.fnf.org.uk

Tel: 020 7613 5060 (Mon–Fri 9.30am–4.30pm)

Helpline: 08707 607496 (Mon–Fri 6–10pm)

"Families Need Fathers" is a social care and campaigning organization which supports fathers wanting to keep contact with their kids after separation.

www.fatherhoodinstitute.org

Website of the UK's fatherhood thinktank, with lots of worthy articles, publications and information about policy.

coping strategies for parents

The following coping strategies are general ideas, and not all of them will work when your baby is very little. Keep some for later: only a fool would suggest you need a new hobby in the first few weeks or months! Everyone needs something different: one woman's exciting owl-shaped macramé project is another's sure road to screamy madness.

ideas for Less stress

★ Sleep, meditate, or lie down and listen to soft music or read when the offspring is napping. Set yourself a bedtime and stick to it, even if the dishes still aren't done: there'll always be something to keep you up until 1am, even if it is Jerry Springer.

★ Ask each visitor to fold ten things from the washing basket, wipe down a surface or make a cup of tea. Don't wait on them.

★ Make sure you eat well and don't skip meals. Never skip breakfast or have something silly like half a grapefruit.

★ Once a week you can try to cook big batches of things to freeze for the days ahead. Cut up raw veggies and put them in ziplock bags or plastic containers with tight-fitting lids. These can be kept in the fridge and the contents thrown in the steamer or microwave when needed each night.

★ Getting outside, moderate exercise and chasing some sunshine (with UV protection) are factors that turn up all the time in studies and surveys about beating depression. If it's winter, invest in a raincoat for everyone and get out amongst it.

★ Try exercising together as a family at a time when everyone is at home. Have the meal ready to heat up when you get back and go for a relaxing, debriefing walk. Or go with a friend.

★ Set very small goals and build up over months: today my special project is to shower, read a chapter of a book, go out for a drink with a pal without baby vomit on the back of my top, get away for a whole weekend, become prime minister. Once-a-week activities such as a martial arts class, a craft group or a walking club are also good to aim for – they're often more realistic than a daily routine early on. Once-a-month activities can include a reading group, a gardening club, filling in the details in the baby book – whatever takes your fancy.

★ Kid-free time is important for every full-time or part-time carer of kids. If your partner won't pull their weight, explain that you need them to do their share or you'll lose your mind and get carted off and then they'll be stuck with the lot.

★ Set yourself a regular session of your own time to do a class or hobby or to go out and kick your heels up: your partner or other babysitter will

317

always know that's the time they're needed. It could be a Friday night or a Monday morning.

★ If you don't have a relative or friend who can babysit for you, find another parent who can swap babysitting duties with you. You have permission to sleep, read a stupid magazine or a smart book, or go to a movie – don't do the housework or any other work.

★ Pick a hobby that has a meditative aspect, a team sport, a craft with a creative or intricate component – anything where you have to think about nothing but what you're doing for a while. Give your mind a holiday from humdrum stuff or worries.

★ Be careful of solitary, home-based crafts and pursuits that can increase your isolation. You might love them or you might be better off finding a hobby that involves making friends or staying in touch with old ones. Have some friends you talk to about children stuff and some other friends who aren't interested so you talk about different things.

★ If going out to dinner or a movie with your partner is too hard or you're always too tired, try a Sunday brunch.

★ See a film at a "parents and babies" screening once a week. Many city and many suburban and country cinemas have daytime sessions for parents or other carers that they can take their babies to and nobody cares if a baby cries. This is harder if you have toddlers as well. And please be careful about choosing the movie; babies can be very sensitive to foreboding or loud music, unpleasant arguments and shouting, or your reactions to stressful emotions. *The Godfather Part III* is probably not a good idea. It's just more social to go out with other parents than to crouch in front of a video on your own.

★ Use the local paper, free child magazines and your local council to find out what services and baby- or child-friendly free entertainment are available to you.

★ Formal or informal weekend events with other people who have kids will at least give you some time to sit down while someone else takes a turn pushing the swings.

★ A parent who is at work all day can set aside special times for the baby or kids, including a wake-up welcome-to-the-day ritual (you and the kid fetch the paper you won't have time to read, go outside and check the weather), and an evening routine that involves perhaps some quiet play or a bath or story before bed.

★ Plan what to do with any spare time at home: do you love to read, just lie on the couch with a tub of ice cream and the TV guide or learn to rumba? Try to get into another room, into the shed or to the corner café away from the kids so you're out of sight, out of mind.

taking stock

If you feel like having a child is ruining your life, unruin it. What are you resenting? What is it you'd love to be doing? What do you miss most? Work out what it is and a way to do it again. (If it's being a submariner, it may have to wait. Is there something else you could try, at least on Saturday mornings and Thursday nights?)

Ask other people what they do to help themselves cope better or cheer themselves up (and see "More Info" below). And if you're having a really hard time and some stupid book (ahem) suggests all these perky, impossible ideas that make you want to throw up, why not burn it in the backyard in a 44-gallon drum?

more info

The parenting websites listed in "More Info" for the first and second chapters of this book have supportive suggestions for keeping stress at bay and where to get fresh ideas on parenting.

And Baby Makes Three: The Six-Step Plan for Preserving Marital Intimacy and Rekindling Romance after Baby Arrives
by John M Gottman and Julie Schwartz Gottman, Three Rivers Press, 2008
US relationships experts (who refer to "mom" throughout) give their take on how to stop being so cranky you can't communicate, how to be friends as well as lovers. If you're still awake after reading the title, maybe you can put some of the advice into practice.

The Secret of Happy Parents: How to Stay in Love as a Couple and True to Yourself
by Stephen Biddulph and Shaaron Biddulph, Thorsons, 2004
Yes, I know it's the Steve-and Shaaron show again, but why should your kids get all the
benefit of their wisdom? Entertaining and highly readable advice on maintaining your life
as a couple after children.

**The 7-Day Parent Coach: Halve the Stress, Double Your Energy and Become a
Great Parent**
by Lorraine Thomas, Vermilion, 2005
Build up baby steps everyday to one giant step at the end of the week to have the
relationship you really want with your child. I'm not convinced that the whole thing
will be solved in this time-frame, but breaking the week down into the most stressful bits
– morning rush, evening "arsenic hour", taming tantrums (yours) – is bound to help those
of us so caught up in the everydayness of life that we can't see the wood for the trees.

a you-SHaPeD FaMiLy

Families, like netball players, come in all different shapes
and sizes. Here are some thoughts on big and little families,
preparing an older kid for an alien invasion – a new baby
in the family – the differences between girls and boys and
approaches that can help when sisters and brothers fight.

family size

People who say things such as "She has no self-control" when a woman's eighth baby comes along, or "It's cruel to have only one child", are only showing their own ignorance. They have no idea why others do what they do: a person may have always wanted a big family, or there could be medical reasons why another child isn't possible. It doesn't matter. They should just shut right up.

There are many more families with only one child than ever before and far fewer with, say, twelve or more (hoorah for contraception). There are many different family set-ups now. Parents of "only children" are usually pretty conscious of giving their child opportunities to make friends and have special companions, including cousins. Only children will make their own friends and family groupings as they get older, just as we often have our kids call our close friends "Aunty" or "Uncle" even when there's no familial relationship – cousins in the next generation may have to be in inverted commas too. (See also "More Info" at the end of this chapter.)

Most of the websites I could find about big families were based on specific religious denominations, including some of those bizarre home-schooling cults in the US. Other hints and books I came across were just generally about parenting, not about dealing with a big bunch. You're probably better off searching in other categories on the Internet such as organization and storage; and recipes for large families or gatherings. I do know some people colour-code their kids' stuff by asking each kid their favourite colour and then buying their clothes and other items in that colour. My guess is the kids would have to agree to make it work and keep agreeing for years (and what about the hand-me-downs?). I'm sure your best bet is to ask some mums (perhaps from an earlier generation) about dealing with a heap of kids.

Birth order

Many people believe the position of children in the family determines their personality. I think this belief is too restrictive and only slightly more based on observation than horoscopes. But what would I know? I'm Sagittarius so I'm just jovial and tactless. (See "More Info" at the end of the chapter for resources on this subject.)

MATCH THE KID WITH THE PARENT!
draw a line to match them up

A. SHOCKING OLD CYNIC

1 CRUISY BABY

B. CALM, SKINNY POET

2 ALERT, SPORTY GIRL

C. EXCITABLE BANK CLERK

3 ECCENTRIC, CHUBBY CAR-OBSESSED TODDLER

A THAT'S RIGHT: IT COULD BE ANY OF THEM!

MINDING YOUR OWN BUSINESS

Don't say "I see you're having another baby" or ask "How pregnant are you?" before the person in question tells you they are pregnant. They may not be pregnant at all, and you and they will be hideously mortified.

Don't ask people "when they're going to have children" or "Are you going to have another one?". If they want you to know, they'll tell you.

Don't ask "Were you on IVF?". Likewise all variations on "Who's the father?".

Don't ask "Do you work?", "When are you going back to work?" or "What do you do at home all day?".

PRePaRiNg a SMaLL KiD FoR a NeW BaBy

Wait until the pregnancy is well advanced before you begin to prepare your child for a new arrival. Apart from the issue of making sure it's a viable pregnancy, time stretches out endlessly for kids and they'll find seven or eight months too long to wait.

★ Tell the child quietly and happily when only the immediate family is present, not when you tell anyone – or everyone – else and there's lots of carry-on and no time for reflection and questions.

★ Explain it in a way that helps them understand the baby will belong to them as well as you, using terms such as "your brother or sister" and "our baby". They'll need you to tell them a number of times.

★ Don't forget to explain that the baby will be coming to live with you – not just for a short visit.

★ Tell them that the baby will be bringing them a special present and follow through on the day of the birth with something whizzbang: the kid's idea of whizzbang, not yours – you might be thinking a scale model of a Tunisian royal palace while they're just desperate for a balloon.

★ Talk about what it will be like to have a baby around – how they cry quite a bit, need lots of attention and sometimes drive everyone mad. And that all babies are like that and that's how they were. Talk about how you love a baby even when they're difficult and noisy.

★ Talk about how the baby won't be able to play games at first because it will be so little and will often want to sleep instead.

★ Describe what the baby might look like.

★ Talk to your older kid about when they were born and look at photos.

★ Get anything you need from your older kid for the baby, such as a car seat, months before the baby arrives if possible, and give them new "big kid" stuff so they don't associate the baby with things being taken away.

★ Give the kid important jobs such as helping you to buy things the baby will need or to get the nursery ready.

★ Explain that Mum will go into hospital so the midwives will help the baby to be born, and that Mum isn't sick.

★ Explain to your child that Mum wants to give birth in private, and that a person your kid knows will take care of them during the birth. Plan and tell them about some special activities, such as a trip to the zoo, that they will be involved in while Mum is away or in her room at home. Have a trial run or lots of discussion about what it might be like to find Nanna there in the morning and Mum and Dad gone to get the baby.

★ If you want a kid (over 7) at the birth, they will have to be very carefully briefed and have a grown-up minder assigned to them to explain what's happening or to go for a walk with them during any scary bits.

★ Get your older kid to draw pictures of where the baby is now, and what it will be like when the baby comes home, and discuss the drawings with them.

After the baby arrives

★ Teach your older kid to hold the baby gently on their knees, with an adult sitting next to them. Never leave an older child alone with the baby – toddlers may treat the baby as a doll because they're not old enough to understand yet.

★ Show the older kid how to gently stroke the baby and put their finger into the curled-up fist.

★ Be aware that your older kid may be only responding to ineluctable survival instincts that give a very good impression of being what we modern folk call "jealousy".

★ Make special times to be alone with your older kid and for them to have special times with other people without the baby.

★ Don't insist your older kid helps with the baby, but reward helpful behaviour, and make it fun to help by, say, passing things to Mum.

★ Expect some possible regression – the older kid wanting to revert to nappies or thumb sucking. It's temporary.

★ Try very hard to keep your older kid to their routine: if it needs to change, run the new one in before the baby arrives so the association isn't made.

★ Remind your older kid that the baby needing so much care is a temporary situation: the baby will grow bigger quite soon.

★ Give toddlers special activities to do while you're breastfeeding – spraying water on a wooden floor and then wiping it with a towel, sorting red buttons into one jar and blue into another, or anything that will occupy them.

★ A toddler can have a dolly to breastfeed or bottlefeed while Mum does the real baby.

★ If you can't pick up your older kid because you have had a Caesarean, get them to sit, stand or kneel next to you on the couch or lie beside you on the bed for cuddles and one-on-one chats.

See also "More Info" at the end of this chapter for books about the arrival of a new baby that you might like to read to your older child.

if sisters and brothers fight

All sisters and brothers (and small friends) have disagreements, but some seem to have them all the time. Here are some approaches that might help.

★ Try to work out the reason for the fighting and how to avoid it.

★ Ask friends and relatives for hints.

★ Give your kids separate activities.

★ Try to unite them against a common enemy (not you! – maybe a puzzle that's tricky).

★ Get each of them to play with their own friends for a while.

★ Talk to each kid separately and get them to nominate the good points about each other.

★ Reward them for playing well together.

★ Take away disputed objects, but make sure one kid isn't always being disadvantaged.

★ Ask them for solutions in more rational moments, not in the heat of battle.

★ If the fighting is really making family life unpleasant, ask your GP for a referral to a family psychologist: better to get independent help now than to live with this for fifteen or twenty years!

★ Protect kids from rough play, especially smaller and younger ones.

★ Don't saddle older kids with responsibilities that can cause resentment. A child under 12 can't be expected to look after another child and be fully responsible, for however short a time. Try instead to foster a sense that the older kid is protective, smart and a helpful role model for their little sibling, and you're proud of them for that.

★ Make sure the older kid knows they can still have negative emotions, want a cuddle and be Mum and Dad's little one too.

★ Give kids their own, individual rights and responsibilities. Discuss what these might be and make the decisions together.

★ Give yourself time to think about how you may be showing favouritism, even without realizing. I know a house where there are many photos of the first three children and virtually none of the fourth, who, even in adulthood, finds it deeply hurtful. Explain your methods so it's harder for kids to accuse you of favouritism.

★ Try to be thrilled with the achievements of all your kids, even if you've seen those milestones reached before and an older kid was better at them.

★ Maybe you can prove the "experts" wrong and not expect the best only from your first, not neglect your middle child and not baby your youngest.

gender blender

Some parents are surprised to find that a 3-year-old boy in a sensitive household thunders around and plays swords at every available opportunity and reacts to seeing a toy by shaking it, whirling it about and shouting "Raaaarghhh!!!!". Others wonder why a girl who's been quite interested in trucks decides, at 4, that she will never wear anything else but a "twirly dress with a pretty tiara". Many of us know a boy who liked make-up and wrapping himself in spangly fabric when he was 5 and is now an enormous, straight footy player. We know girls who never wanted to wear a dress when they were little and still don't. In all the debate and research about nature versus nurture, and girls being quicker to learn most things, especially language and communication skills, and boys needing more space and tolerance of testosteroney behaviour, we mustn't lose sight of the most important thing: all kids are individuals.

Each kid needs to be supported in whatever they're experimenting with. Each kid deserves a chance to play with both dolls and cars, to build up and knock down, to attend a tea party and wear a pirate hat to attack the tree in the garden. Each kid deserves to be able to develop their skills and enjoy their favourite activities without being labelled, ridiculed or pushed around. And praise shouldn't be rationed and given only for activities shared or approved of by parents or siblings. Kids need to be allowed to have "phases", private loves and pursuits, and to enjoy things their parents think are dead boring or even odd.

Parents can ask themselves the following questions.

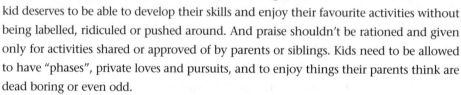

★ "When the boys take over the building-block corner at playgroup, why can't the girls have another building-block corner for themselves?"

★ "Would I let a girl run around the house screaming like that?"

★ "Did I really just tell my weeping boy to be a 'little man'?"

★ "How can a girl climb on the adventure playground in a long dress and those silly shoes?"

★ "I've worn only trousers since 1989, but if my little girl wants to wear a pink frock every day why should I stop her?"

★ "I don't mind my boys tumbling about, but should I draw the line at them pretending to have guns that kill each other?"

★ "How can I communicate with my son, and listen to him, in ways that don't include words?"

★ "So I've got a sensitive boy or a tomboy girl – why should that be seen as a problem?"

Ultimately the response to all the palaver about gender is to be as clear-eyed as possible about the pressures that might be put on your kid by you or anyone else around them to change their natural inclinations. Are they being offered an opportunity to enjoy something or being pushed into a shape someone else wants them to be? The only way to get close to the answer is to know your child as well as you can, to accept them for whatever and whoever they are, and to respect what they choose to do when they've been offered a range of possibilities without judgement or criticism. (Unless they're biting the heads off frogs, in which case get them an agent.)

more info

Extra Resources at the end of the book has sections on "Single, Sole and Shared-custody Parents", "Gay Families" and "Teenage Mums".

ONLY CHILDREN

Parenting an Only Child: The Joys and Challenges of Raising Your One and Only
by Susan Newman, Broadway Books, 2001
Good for batting down old stereotypes and asking yourself the right questions if you have settled on a one-child family, or are deciding whether to "go again". Addresses all the common worries like "They'll have no one to play with on holiday" and "They'll be spoilt and self-centred", with loads of advice on how not to over-indulge your child and learning to "let go".

What's So Bad About Being An Only Child
by Cari Best, Farrar Straus Giroux, 2007
A picture book for small children about an only child who wants to have brothers and sisters. Beware their solution seems to be masses of pets, rather than friends.

www.onlychild.com
The site of US online magazine *Only Child*. Offers subscriptions and an advice service.

BIRTH ORDER

The Birth Order Book: Why You Are the Way You Are
by Kevin Leman, Fleming H Revell, 2004

I think too much pigeon-holing goes on when people assume first-borns are achievers, second kids are more passive, and so on. But it's a popular theory that birth order affects personality so here's one of the major texts in the area, written by Mr Leman, an unlikely combination of US psychologist, prolific parenting author, Christian humourist, and founder of a birth-order online dating service (yes, really).

GENDER BLENDER

Girls Will Be Girls: Raising Confident and Courageous Daughters
by JoAnn Deak and Teresa Butler, Hyperion, 2003

Dr Deak is a social psychologist and a mother of daughters who explains the early social pressures on girls (expected to be sugar and spice rather than play with puppy dogs' tails) and takes you right through all the biological and emotional aspects of the teen years. Good reminders of how our actions and the words we use as parents can have an impact in ways we don't realize, or want. A great section on dads and daughters.

Raising Boys: Why Boys Are Different – and How to Help Them Become Happy and Well-balanced Men
by Steve Biddulph, Thorsons, 2003

Fast becoming the classic text of its kind, it debunks the myth that children are born "gender neutral" and analyses the three stages of boyhood in a simple, jargon-free way. Helps mums especially get a grip on how boys think, and ways to help parents let boys be boys, but also be confident, kind and thinking boys.

BOOKS FOR KIDS ABOUT PREPARING FOR A NEW BABY

Truelove
by Babette Cole, Red Fox, 2002

Truelove the dog feels left out when the new baby arrives – but what a happy ending. A picture book with naughty cartoons and a modern approach.

Za-za's Baby Brother
by Lucy Cousins, Walker Books, 2005

From the creator of the Maisy books. A zebra gets a new sibling.

My Little Brother
by Debi Gliori, Walker Books, 2004
The New Baby
by Anne Civardi, Usbourne, 2005
Pretty standard straightforward stories for kids about a new baby arriving.

IF SISTERS AND BROTHERS FIGHT

Siblings Without Rivalry: How to Help Your Children Live together so That You Can Live Too
by Adele Faber and Elaine Mazlish, Piccadilly Press, 1999
Beyond Sibling Rivalry: How to Help Your Children Become Co-operative, Caring and Compassionate
Peter Goldenthal, Owl, 2000
Insightful and practical suggestions on increasing family harmony and avoiding tribal factions under the one roof.

Rosie's Babies
by Martin Waddell and Penny Dale, Walker Books, UK, 1999
Picture book for little one about the arrival of a new baby.

teacHing kiDs HoW to BeHave

Everyone gets into a tizz about "discipline". It combines all the elements of having children that are difficult: being grumpy when you're tired, not being in full control of your life, reacting in immature ways to situations – and that's just the parents.

A baby has been learning how to interact by observing for months. Somewhere along the line

the parents start using the word no and the baby understands. The baby begins to learn about boundaries, and some time after – usually about the same age as they walk – they start trying to rule their world, and conflict can take over. Aarrgh! Not to mention Aieeee!

WHat DiscipLiNe is

Unfortunately when people talk about discipline they often think it just means punishment. The point of discipline is not to punish a child, but to teach them to behave with kindness and consideration, and understand the rules. That's why this chapter is called "Teaching Kids How to Behave". Discipline sounds a little bit like what Tory cabinet ministers get up to in expensive London dungeons with bored ladies called Mistress Nannypants.

Try to think of yourself as the coach rather than as the punisher. It's impossible for a child to have the mental capacity to put themselves in *your* shoes, but you can, in every situation, try to imagine you are a child attempting to work out the right way to behave. And you know that nobody's perfect. You may as well set up an atmosphere in which, if you lose your temper or your child does, you can apologize and all's forgiven.

Here are some approaches you might find helpful.

- ★ Think of your child as your ally or apprentice, not the enemy.
- ★ Show your child the right way to behave.
- ★ Help your child learn when a behaviour is wrong and why.
- ★ Recognize that your child may at first not understand or care why they're supposed to behave in a certain way, but establish a pattern of explaining why they must, even briefly, so it doesn't seem like a "no questions asked" army camp.

★ Give your child choices of things that don't matter so much – a bit of apple or a bit of pear – but not whether or not they can bash the telly with a cricket bat.

★ Establish a small core of simple ground rules that are consistently observed, such as bedtime is seven o'clock, no hitting and you don't get what you ask for if you use a whingey voice – so the child isn't over-whelmed by trying to remember 56 rules.

★ Be clear that the aim is for your child to understand what are the right things to do, not that it's to humiliate them or make them feel inad-equate or guilty when they do a wrong thing.

Above all set reasonable boundaries early on – these can start when your child is 1 or 2 and build through their preschool years.

WHY is tHE KiD "BEHaViNG BaDLY"?

It's always useful to know why a child is "behaving badly". Reasons (and their solu-tions) can include the following.

★ **They're starting to get sick.** But they don't have the understanding to know what they're feeling or the words to explain. Check for an ear infection, temperature or other common causes of "bad behaviour" that really mean they're not well.

★ **They're tired.** Give them more fluids, introduce a nap or an earlier or stricter bedtime.

★ **They're hungry.** Produce a snack with protein and carbohydrates rather than a sugar base.

★ **They don't know what's expected.** Give short, clear explanations or instructions.

★ **They're grumpy about something.** Try a mood changer such as a nap, a bath or a massage, or keep in the cupboard a standby activity that always cheers them, such as balloons or bubble-blowing solution (and see also the "Bad-Mood Changers" section later in this chapter).

★ **The kid is having a non-specific bad mood.** Explain that people do have bad moods or not feel very cheerful sometimes, but that doesn't

BOUNDARIES FOR KIDS: SOME IDEAS

✱ We must be kind and gentle with people and animals.

✱ Kids must be in bed at bedtime (with perhaps half an hour to read or play in bed).

✱ We don't scream in this house.

✱ We use our words to fix a problem, not hitting or pushing.

✱ If we do the wrong thing or make a mistake, we say sorry.

✱ Parents are the bosses, but they let you choose some things.

✱ We need to say please and thank you.

✱ We need to say hello to people when we meet or they visit.

✱ We don't throw balls in the house.

✱ We don't throw our food or say it's yucky.

✱ We have to try a new food, but if we don't like it we don't have to eat it.

✱ When we get a drink or a piece of fruit, we ask if anyone else would like some.

✱ Kids don't go on the road without holding an adult's hand.

And

✱ Allowances will be made for a kid who is tired or otherwise having a hard time.

mean they can be rude – or put the budgie in the toilet. Suggest a choice of activities to snap out of it.

★ **They're bored with or understimulated by the general company or routine.** They may need a change of scenery or a new activity. Perhaps get them into a playgroup or child care, or have a relative or friend babysit for a while.

★ **They're testing the boundaries.** Be consistent with the rules and the consequences of breaking them.

BOUNDARIES FOR PARENTS: SOME IDEAS

✱ Parents should speak to children with respect.

✱ Parents will decide not to hit.

✱ Parents need to say please and thank you.

✱ Parents will be consistent with rules and not confuse kids by varying their reactions to the same bad behaviour (and will explain why if they do).

✱ If parents do the wrong thing or make a mistake, they say sorry.

✱ Parents will try not to yell.

✱ Parents will apologize if they have a tantrum or are rude.

✱ Parents are allowed to go into their room for quiet time.

✱ Parents must arrange time away or to be on their own to balance all the time they spend with kids.

✱ Parents will try not to throw their food or say it's yucky.

And

✱ Allowances will be made for a parent who is tired or otherwise having a hard time.

★ **They want a show.** It's kind of interesting when Mum goes off like a firecracker. Stay calm, be consistent.

★ **They can't grasp the consequences of their actions.** Explain cause and effect – don't expect them to work this out by themselves or to necessarily remember after the first time.

★ **They don't seem to feel compassion or empathy.** This doesn't come naturally to all kids: explain that certain things will hurt feelings or cause pain to other kids, adults, babies or animals. Don't try to explain too hard that a dolly doesn't feel hurt but a baby will – try to get the child to be kind to the dolly too because they can't really understand the difference. Kindness, like patience, is mainly taught by example.

★ **They don't know how else to react to a situation.** Explain how you can say "Oh, bother", like Pooh bear, or try again; that it doesn't matter if the tower falls down – you can build another one.

★ **Past annoying behaviour has been rewarded.** A child without much language who can bang rudely on the door and shout "DOOR!!!!" and have it opened has worked out the magic formula. It's better for them to learn that the door isn't opened until a polite request is received at a lower decibel. Of course you have to know they're capable of this. When

babies are very little, a pat on the door and the word "Dodo!" can be met with "Yes, I'd love to open the door for you!" because you're interpreting their efforts to communicate.

★ **They want everything to go their way.** Acknowledge this and say you wish everyone could do whatever they wanted, but it doesn't always work like that. Don't be sucked into end- less explanations of why not!

★ **Their usual routine has been disrupted.** Try to do something that gets you both back into at least one of your routines or a comfort zone.

★ **They know that a threat isn't always carried through.** Don't use threats you can't, won't or shouldn't make good on.

★ **There is an underlying problem.** A trauma, a problem causing stress in the home or a worry, possibly even an overheard one, is causing your child to change their behaviour. Deal with the family stress, getting pro- fessional help if needed: start with your GP.

★ **The explanations, concepts and expectations you're giving are not age appropriate.** Find out what your kid is capable of at different ages. Try to think about a subject from their point of view. If they look confused they are confused. Answer questions about why a certain behaviour isn't right and explain what's expected as well as what isn't acceptable.

★ **Things escalate too quickly.** The kid seems to go off like a rocket. Have you been accidentally setting an example of freaking out at the smallest things and making molehills into mountains and mountains into volca- noes? Do you say "OH, MY GOD!" at the slightest thing? Wind it back and watch the kid do the same.

★ **They ignore nagging.** Reminding your kid 78 times a day to say thank you isn't as effective as holding onto a requested object until thank you is said, even if you have to remind them of the words.

★ **The kid is desperate for attention.** Even negative attention will show that you're interested in them. Give them lots of attention when they're not naughty.

★ **There's a vicious circle.** Everyone's tired and angry with each other. Your child feels humiliated or furious, you feel guilty or disappointed for hitting or shouting. Remind yourself that every new day is a fresh start as a parent and every hour can be too.

★ **You're both in a rut of reacting to each other in negative ways.** Try a mood breaker. You might even say "Right, let's pretend to get up and start again. We'll even pretend to have breakfast." Kids over, say, 2 and a half sometimes love that sort of make-believe. Never tell yourself you've painted yourself into a corner so you have to keep hitting, shouting or accepting bad behaviour. Even old dogs can learn new tricks – they just need a brilliant incentive. And having a calm relationship with your kid is a great incentive.

★ **The kid keeps forgetting the rules.** Write a list of the simple rules and routines such as bath, dinner, teeth cleaning, bedtime. This can be made into a chart with illustrations so the kid – even a non-reader – will get to know what's expected. Put the list down low on the fridge or noticeboard and perhaps award stickers or stars for completed tasks. Sometimes, even if your child won't take your word for it, they'll "listen to the chart", especially if they took part in compiling and decorating it.

You need fresh ideas

Sometimes the kid is "behaving badly" because you're caught in a generational vicious circle. You find yourself saying the things your parents said, which you hated, and hitting your children because that's what your parents did. It's the last thing you ever wanted, but it seems to be your instinct when you're stressed or angry – and who isn't, at least sometimes?

See "More Info" at the end of this chapter for help with learning new strategies to avoid repeating upsetting and useless patterns.

trying for patience, kindness and consistency

It's not just crying babies who can make parents feel rage. Toddlers can be maddeningly rude, shouty or difficult. But teaching kids how to behave requires patience, kindness and consistency. And sometimes they're in short supply (I myself had a tantrum only this morning) – which is why the following always help.

★ Have a consistent, agreed-on set of rules that all parents and carers (including grandparents) know and follow: for example, the only TV allowed is the BBC between 3.30 and 4.30pm; one lolly each a day and it's before 5pm. If this isn't possible, make sure that older kids (getting on for 5 or more) at least understand there are different rules at Grandma's from at home, and behaviour tolerated there won't be indulged at home.

★ Have a consistent approach to bad behaviour. (One parent should not be the lone "disciplinarian" if there are two parents available.)

★ Get as much help as you can.

★ Get away and do other things as much as you can to fortify yourself.

★ If you find your anger and resentment rising, give yourself time out. Put the kids in front of a video, go to another room and lie there, scream into a pillow, do relaxation techniques, read a chapter of a book – anything to get your frustration level down and reduce your fly-off-the-handleability. (It is so a word, shut up.)

★ Imagine your kid was your best friend and behaved the same way: your first reaction would not be to shout or say something rude.

★ Imagine you're in public or actually go somewhere public to react.

★ Take every opportunity to rest and enjoy your own pursuits – a happier person is usually a kinder, more patient person.

PaReNTs WHO DON'T WaNT To HiT

I think not hitting a child is a fundamental break we can make with the past. It isn't about fashion, it's about progress and finding new ways. Kids used to bounce around in a car without seatbelts a generation ago and most of them survived: it doesn't mean kids without seatbelts is a good idea. I know people say "I got hit as a kid and I'm fine" – in fact I heard a homeless drunk say it in the park across the road just the other week – but I think it's a statement that needs further looking into. And anyone who has hit their children can learn new ways of dealing with their anger.

There are lots of people who were hit who wish they weren't; there are lots of people who know right from wrong who were never hit; and there are lots of people who were hit who can't tell you what the hitting taught them that another method couldn't have. Lots of us broke our arms when we were little or got badly sunburned. We're over it now, but it might have been better if it hadn't happened.

Arguments against hitting include:

★ it doesn't alter many kids' behaviour – instead it teaches them that if someone is bigger, stronger or believes they are right, hitting is okay

★ it often results in them hitting other children, siblings and animals when frustrated

★ it punishes rather than teaches

★ it makes kids wary of any of their own actions and words in case they're wrong or frowned upon and will result in physical pain

★ it can escalate to abuse

★ it might have long-term effects because children are vulnerable to being emotionally and physically damaged.

Many parents feel that hitting didn't fix the behavioural problem. Many parents recognize they hit not because the child was naughtier than usual but because the parent was at the end of their tether. Determined not to repeat their own past, they promise not to hit any more and then later find themselves doing it again, causing terrible feelings of guilt on their part and betrayal on the part of the child.

It seems to me that the urge to hit is very hard to break – firstly because it's a natural reaction we are born with to try to protect ourselves or get what we want (but we need to learn more sophisticated ways of behaving as we grow up otherwise we'd all be in the slammer), and secondly because most parents in the generations before us thought nothing of spanking and smacking their children or threatening to, just as they also thought nothing of kids being driven around without seatbelts. It's easy to say "I don't want to hit", but it takes some effort to learn new coping skills and new ways of disciplining.

It's only recently that alternatives to smacking have become widely known. I know some parents say they have found a quick, smart swat to the bum has stopped their children behaving badly. And sometimes that's the important thing at that moment. But even if your child is doing something very dangerous, say, sticking a toasting fork in a power point, it may be better to knock them out of the way or, if you have time, grab them quickly and remove them from harm's way rather than punish them. Perhaps the best outcome is to make the power point safe with a snap-over cover, keep the toasting fork out of reach and explain why it's dangerous as soon as the child can understand.

The worst thing about smacking (apart from the fact it's a large person deliberately hurting a small one) is that at best it teaches the child "Don't do that because you will get a smack that hurts, shocks or humiliates you". Instead kids can learn to stop doing something because "it hurts someone's feelings so they feel sad and don't want to play with you", "it's dangerous and could hurt you", "it makes a mess that you'll need to clean up", "it will break your toy and you won't be able to play with it any more" or "it will kill the plants and then the flowers won't grow". In this way kids learn more, eventually make more connections and develop a deeper understanding of what might be wrong, hurtful or dangerous, and why.

Some parents say their hitting has no effect on behaviour or causes hysteria, shame on both sides and great guilt for the parent, who didn't want things to go this far. One depressing comment from a mum in the survey undertaken for this book was "I hit him up to twelve times a day and it doesn't make any difference. I'm sure he'll catch on soon." Another wrote "Sometimes you feel like a broken record and you feel like you're smacking them all day but they will eventually learn." If it isn't working, you need to try something else. This chapter is for any parent who needs help with discipline that isn't working or who wants to find alternatives to smacking.

So many of the people who responded to the survey undertaken for this book said they didn't like smacking – most often a slap on the hand or a swat to the bottom – but they still did it. One letter that made me sad said it had to "sting". Some of these parents said that a smack was effective; most did not. That's why I've put a lot of suggestions for alternatives to smacking in this chapter: not because people who smack are terrible (I'm sure the vast majority of parents have smacked at least once), but because so many parents want not to smack any more.

I think it's much harder to always be calm and consistent if you're a sole or single parent and don't have help in disciplining; if your partner wants to hit and you don't (or vice versa); or if you've got yourself into a rut where you keep "disciplining" but the kid's behaviour isn't changing. You may need more support and babysitting help to let you have a break; couple counselling to work out a united front with the kid; or to start afresh with some new rules and methods you can be consistent with. (See "More Info" at the end of this chapter and "Relationships" in Extra Resources at the end of the book.)

It is illegal in some places to hit a child with an object such as a kitchen implement or anything else. This is because objects can cause worse injuries than a hand, and some objects are heavy or dangerous. It is pretty much universally agreed that hitting a child repeatedly, hitting a child with a closed fist, "belting" or beating a child, or hitting a child on the face or genitals is child abuse. Others consider any striking, including slapping and spanking, to be abuse.

If you are at the end of your tether and feel you might hurt your child, see the family crisis contacts in "More Info" at the end of this chapter or ring one of the helplines listed in "More Info" in "Your Support Team", the second chapter of *Part 1: Babies*.

Smacking and religion

Although this will come as a surprise to many fundamentalist Christians, the phrase "Spare the rod and spoil the child" (in other words, if you don't use an instrument to hit your child, they will be spoiled) is not in the Bible and never has been. Most of the biblical approval for hitting children comes in Proverbs: Prov. 22:15, "Foolishness is bound in the heart of a child; but the rod of correction shall drive it far from him"; Prov. 23:13, "Withhold not correction from the child: for if thou beatest him with the rod, he shall not die"; Prov. 23:14, "Thou shalt beat him with the rod, and shalt deliver his soul from hell". (Incidentally the Bible also says it is okay to sell a daughter into slavery under certain circumstances, but this is now illegal in the UK.)

The majority of Christians of course do not interpret the biblical invocations as being about physical punishment, but rather about non-violent discipline.

"I always like to remind parents that the shepherds used the rod, for the most part, to guide their sheep, not whack them over the head."
DR KEVIN LEMAN, CHRISTIAN WEBSITE SPANKING ADVISER

"I believe in the Christian principle – spare the rod and spoil the child." SARAH

SWEARING

One of the problems with punishment is that a child doesn't always know the behaviour is considered wrong. They learn so much by copying that if they see someone (it may not even be their parent) hurt their finger and say "Shit", they think that when you hurt yourself you're supposed to say "Shit". Kids usually don't start this stuff until they're 3 or 4 and expanding their vocabularies quickly. It's good that they're a bit older when they start repeating words because they can also understand a chat about "naughty words" or "swearwords". I reckon "dirty" and "potty mouth" are phrases best left out of it. Kids need to know that dirty just means getting dirt on themselves and not to confuse their own poo, or going to the toilet, with something wrong or naughty.

- ★ Don't swear yourself. (Bloody hard, I know.)
- ★ Understand that kids don't know why words are "wrong", and before 5 is too young to explain great hulking swathes of sex and religion to them.
- ★ Explain that some people are offended by some words and that's why we don't use them. (We can talk about baby Jesus, but not say "Jesus" if we're cross because it hurts some people's feelings.)
- ★ Get a range of acceptable alternatives and practise them. Try something that amuses you – perhaps "lordy pants", "crikey" or "my giddy aunt".
- ★ If a kid has worked out that a word is shocking and repeats it for effect, get everyone to ignore it and pay attention to better behaviour.

Washing their mouth out with soap is not a successful way to stop a child swearing: it makes a huge deal out of swearing, it can be dangerous to your child's health, and it's unfair when the child learns a new swearword and tries it out, not knowing it's a "bad" word. Think of all the new words they learn all the time. I mean, it's not as if you can hand them a list of words they're not allowed to say and ask them to memorize it.

WHiNGeiNG

Not really naughtiness or defiance, whingeing (mostly referred to in the guidebooks on kids as "whining") is a case of a kid thinking it's the best way to get what they want or to express many emotions. Some parents do anything to give the kid what they want because they find a whingeing tone so irritating

The consensus on this one is you should ignore whingeing tones and that sort of carry-on and explain that you will respond to a question asked in a "nice voice" or a "normal voice". This way a whingeing tone is never rewarded so it doesn't become the lever of choice. (Same thing goes for tantrums.) You'll have to follow up by really listening to the non-whingery. Kids may have to also be told that "pleeeeeeeeaaaase" does not work, and that asking 67 times won't either. You must stick to this or you will be doomed to Endless Whingeing Hell. Distraction is often the answer to whinge-ing so think about learning to tap dance.

taNtRums

Tantrums, or hissy fits, can start before 2, last well past 3 years old and get worse in phases (especially with actors): tantrums are mainly a toddler's reaction to not get-ting their own way and part of their natural development towards independence. Having a tantrum is basically an immature reaction to a problem, which many adults themselves haven't yet grown out of. It's the best way a kid knows to express themselves about this thing that makes them feel so cross: you need to help them learn other means.

★ Tantrums should be ignored whenever possible.

★ A tantrum thrower who gets what they want learns that tantrums work.

★ Reward the non-tantrum thrower and behaviour.

★ Try to avoid tantrum recipes: tired kid, bright supermarket with lots of temptations, having to get in the car and be somewhere IMMEDIATELY, a toddler not being given any choices at all – that sort of thing.

★ To ignore a tantie you may need some strategies: walk away; count to ten; do a meditation exercise; sing your favourite song to yourself, even if it's got a funny phrase in it such as "Climb Every Mountain!"; pop out the back for a moment. Use the Time Out technique described in the next section.

★ The post-tantrum thrower may be in need of a cuddle because they've freaked themselves out.

★ If the tantrum whips you into a frenzy or fury, try to remove yourself for five minutes, otherwise you'll end up losing control and smacking, or behaving in a very tantrum-like way yourself, which doesn't get across the message that tantrums are not acceptable.

> *"There are few actors who like seeing the audience walk out mid-performance and even the most thick-skinned toddler will tend to get the message."*
> **CHRISTOPHER GREEN,** *TODDLER TAMING*

time out

Different kid experts have different versions of Time Out. Parents who use Time Out differ about whether it is a cooling-off period or a punishment, but it's universally agreed by experts that it isn't meant to be used as a punishment. Unfortunately the approach has been passed on by word of mouth among parents and morphed so that in some homes it has become a punishment along the lines of "Go into the boring utility room for five minutes".

Time Out was devised as a way to quickly and decisively show a kid that their behaviour isn't acceptable and won't be rewarded; to give the kid time to reflect on what they did and what the result was; and to give the parents time to cool off. One thing that helps reinforce this with kids who've hurt another child is that the other child gets lots of attention while they have Time Out. That wasn't what they wanted to happen at all!

A version of Time Out
The following version of Time Out is a cool-down period for everyone, not a punishment.

1 The kid does something totally defiant or unacceptable that they know is defiant or unacceptable. (That is, you don't give Time Out to a kid who accidentally spilled a drink. You give it to the kid who, after you say "If you keep your eyes looking at the milk, you can be careful not to spill it", looks you straight in the eye and deliberately pours their milk on the carpet or chucks a screamy, kicking tantrum.)

2 The kid is told that their behaviour is not acceptable, in a firm, not shouty way, and that it's now Time Out for them because of this behaviour: "Go into your room for Time Out, please, and come back when you're ready to say sorry and behave properly again." The carer needs to be calm and very boring – and not turn on a fascinating display of their own.

3 The kid is escorted, herded or carried firmly if necessary, or stalks off to the bedroom. (Some parents use a utility room because they think it's more of a punishment since there are no toys there – but kids are so socialized they know that going to their room on their own is not a reward.) Quietly playing with toys is fine.

4 The length of Time Out is always kept pretty short. Suggestions vary, but include thirty seconds for kids less than 2 years old, with one minute per year of age after that; or until they are ready to say they're sorry or they'll be "better behaved".

5 *The Mighty Toddler* author, Robin Barker, cleverly says that after Time Out there needs to be a different activity from the one that caused the problem.

6 Sometimes Time Out needs to be followed shortly afterwards by a nap because tiredness is the actual cause of the behaviour.

> Popular Time Out locations:
> ★ the child's bedroom
> ★ the (safety-overhauled) utility room
> ★ a special seat in the living room
> ★ on the stairs (safely)
> ★ the back doorstep (in good weather).

DiscipLiNe iDeas witH a HiDDeN DOwNsiDe

Although they may "work" to stop a child's behaviour and so may seem successful to parents as methods of discipline, the following approaches can have more psychological impact than we realize.

It's very important not to crush the spirit of a child by making them feel they are a bad or terribly disappointing person. Humiliation can lead to real depression and sadness in a child. Make sure you get across that it's the behaviour you want changed, not the person. It's better to say "My feelings were hurt when you said that. Let's think of a nicer thing you could say" than "I'm so disappointed in you. Get out of my sight."

Coldness or indifference in a parent is a much harsher punishment to a child than an adult may think. An icy stare or similar cold-shoulder treatments can create inner panic and fear and an unspoken, desolate sadness because they feel that they are not loved.

Saying "You're very, very bad" can make a child feel crushed and can have lasting effects on their self-esteem and confidence. Use something like "Let's try that again in a different way". If you separate being disappointed in them as a person from being disappointed in their behaviour, they know that changing the behaviour is a plus. But if you say you're disappointed in them as a person, all they can do is feel inadequate.

Shutting yourself in the loo or locking the kid outside the house can create a sense of panic in a child, especially if they have a temperament that makes this punishment very frightening.

ways to encourage and reward good behaviour

"Yes"

Try to give kids lots of things to choose from and say yes as much as you can instead of saying no all the time. Put a positive spin on things: say "Hey, come over here and splash in the sink with this squirty thing" instead of "Stop putting lipstick on the cat".

"Sorry"

I think that everyone in the family should be able to say a sincere sorry and have it accepted – but not if it's a stalling tactic before they do the same thing again, or a spat-out or shouted "SORRY!" in very unsorry tones. Parents as well as kids should be able to be genuinely sorry and say so. This helps kids to understand the concept of pain to others, and hurt feelings,

> **SOLIDARITY**
>
> If you see a kid throwing a tantrum in a public place and their parent ignoring them, ignore them too and smile in a conspiratorial way with the parent before you move off without comment. Don't assume the adult is a terrible parent. You might be in the same supermarket aisle in their situation next week.

and gives them one way of helping make the situation better. If apologies are just as sincerely accepted, this should cut down on grudges, sulking, seething and revenge strikes.

Praise

Say:

- ★ "I'm so proud of you for saying/doing that."
- ★ "That was fantastic!"
- ★ "You tried so hard, it was wonderful."
- ★ "I love it when you do that."
- ★ "You are so good at that."
- ★ "You have lovely manners."
- ★ "What a great boy/girl."
- ★ "I really like doing this with you."
- ★ "Those colours are fabulous."
- ★ "What a splendid job."
- ★ "Daddy/Mummy/Nanna will be so happy to know you did that. Shall we tell them straight away?"
- ★ "Good on you."
- ★ "Yer blood's worth bottling." (Well, maybe not.)

Body language – encouraging nods and smiles, eye contact, thumbs up, applause, handshakes – or stickers on a chart or on the hand can be good non-verbal things to add to what you've said.

> *"Go easy on yourself. Everyone yells sometimes, everyone gets tired and not everyone can react calmly when their child shows them how well jam toast fits in the CD player."* FIONA

"When attempting to get numerous children, parcels and the dreaded car keys in the bag, I tell my boys to stand with two hands on the car. If both hands are on the car, there's only so far they can step away from it. Also there is the psychological reward of looking at your kids lined up like gangsters." DIANNE

"I scream and shout and rant and rave and nobody listens. But when I'm calm, I get down to their little height and get them to look at me by speaking softly and telling them that 'You really scared Mummy when you opened the front door and ran up the road following the recycling lorry.' My 4-year-old son listened to me and hasn't done it again." SOPHIE

"When it's 5 in the morning and you haven't tasted your coffee yet and your 3-year-old is having a tantrum because you cut the toast the way he liked it yesterday, it's difficult to be consistent in your discipline. I aim not to yell too much, provide consequences of actions and just get through the day!" SARAH

"If my kids are alive at the end of the day, I've done my job." COMEDIAN ROSEANNE BARR

"What works for one child will not necessarily work for another. Consistency, fairness, continuity and perseverance. My son is no angel and even angels wear you down in the end . . . Treat them how you would expect to be treated yourself. Don't back down, once you've made a decision stick to it or they've got you sussed" KIRSTEIN

"Always praise when they're good." DEBBY

"Boring, long-winded lectures." PAMELA

"[When they're well behaved] they get a star sticker on a chart on the fridge. When they've collected a predetermined number of stars, a special treat is allowed: a sweet, a date with Mum or Dad, an extra bedtime story – this really works wonders. We have four children trying to earn as many stars as possible." TIFFANY

"We have two rules for our 19-month-old son. Don't touch the power points and don't touch the bin." EMMA

"No performance will go on without an audience . . . [And] if they have hurt another child, they should help hold the flannel or ice pack to understand the consequences. Yelling makes them yell back." WENDY

"She sits in the hallway with her back to the living room for 30 seconds – then my good girl returns. She would go hysterical if I closed the door of her room on her so this works well for both of us." JOANNE

"Give a clear choice: stop hitting your brother with the [toy] hammer or we will have to put it away." MARY

"Missing out on TV works every time. There is a no-hitting rule in our home." JENNY

"Time Out and bribery!" RUTH

"Mostly discipline is what you do to encourage good behaviour." WILLIAM AND MARTHA SEARS, *THE DISCIPLINE BOOK*

"Removal of the object they are fighting over is always useful." KAREN

"We always explain why we do things: he might not understand it yet, though. I think it's really important to discipline the behaviour, not the child, if that makes sense. Let them know it's the behaviour you find unacceptable, not the child." VANESSA

"If any of my boys threw a tantrum, it was often when we were in a shop and they wanted something and I said no. My advice is to walk away and pretend they aren't yours." DALE

"My husband barks orders and commands, which are promptly ignored." ALISON

"There's nothing worse than arguing with a 2-year-old when you're 30." HELEN

"As he got more logical he was entitled to tell us in the mornings he was a bit grumpy and then we would not expect too much of him." SUSAN

"We have two Time Outs – one for them to go to their room and come out when they're ready to apologise; the other Time Out is when I'm so angry with them I need time to cool down: they are told to stay in their room until Mummy comes to talk to them. I've used changing rooms, baby rooms, even a lift for Time Out – we rode up and down until my 3-year-old had screamed herself hoarse." MAREE

"Do not argue with a child. A 4-year-old wants ten pieces of cake, but you know one piece is enough, so one piece it is." TRISHA

"The happy chair. When a child does the wrong thing we give a warning; if it happens again we ask them in a calm voice to go and sit in the happy chair and think about their actions. We use a stove timer: 2 minutes for the 2-year-old, 10 minutes for the 8-year-old. After that we usually get a cuddle and a 'sorry'. Sometimes the children will take themselves there. When we're out, any chair can become the happy chair." GAYE

"Between her and the dog I say 'no' a lot: so my daughter knows not to dig up the garden and the dog knows not to throw food." NICKY

"I do as he demands." GREER

"I do explain how I expect something to be done, and that they need to listen carefully and maintain eye contact. I make sure kids know the rules and can repeat them back to me. Usually there's a warning and then there's thinking time in a corner, the utility room or near a wall. It's not punishment, but time to think about what they've done, how they can do it next time or what not to do, and to apologize if necessary. It's very important to explain it's about what the child has done, not them personally, but the behaviour we are fixing. I don't like using words like 'naughty'." CATHY

"It's important to distinguish between 'I want my own way' tantrums (which can be ignored) and more general meltdowns where everything gets on top of them and it spirals out of their control. With a meltdown there's usually an underlying problem like hunger, tiredness, boredom or anxiety, and I just HAVE to stop whatever I'm doing to deal with that. The trick is to address the problem without rewarding the behaviour." KATE

BaD-mooD cHangeRs

These ideas have been suggested by parents who responded to the survey undertaken for this book – they're worth a try for a kid who's woken up on the wrong side of the bed (or cot), to avert a tantrum or to stop a bad situation getting worse:

★ a bath – even a kid reluctant at first usually winds down with toys, splashes and home-made squirters in the bath (although some kids hate baths, in which case skip it)

★ safe water play of any sort – splash in the sink or bath and on hot days let them play with the hose

★ food – often kids who are grumpy haven't had enough carbohydrates (try rice with veggie bits, mashed spuds, even a sandwich, but not sugar)

★ water – a dehydrated child is a tired child

★ magic glitter gel – glitter mixed in sorbolene to wipe on themselves

★ take them outside – even rugged up and waterproofed

★ a favourite video or book

★ special toys put away for just this purpose

★ a favourite music CD

★ be funny or ask silly questions (underpants on head, shoes on ears, "Shall I eat this chair?")

★ create some favourite pictures and sounds to run on the computer

★ have a cuddle and talk about what may be wrong

★ promise a special made-up story at bedtime – and make sure you deliver

★ sit or lie down for a quiet time, with or without a cuddle

★ go out and look for birds, butterflies, orange cars

★ a roll-around wrestle

★ allow the kid to let off steam by going into the garden or the park to yell and run around in a circle or all the way to the swings

★ a weird rendition of a favourite song such as "Twinkle, Twinkle Little Star" sung opera-style

★ "Appeal to their sympathies . . . once out at the shops I grabbed them and dashed for the public toilets. I was about to have an accident and they had to be quick! They forgot all about what they were making a fuss about because they had to save Mum from eternal public embarrass-ment!"

★ play with their dog

★ feed the ducks

★ hold them close and sing

★ put on some music, pick up your kid and dance

★ a massage

★ water the garden and pull out the weeds Mum points to

★ allow them to rip something into pieces (give them the newspaper) – older babies and young toddlers love this

★ dress-ups – even the parents

★ housework – the kid feels needed, useful and accomplished. Give them a feather duster, a sponge or a dustpan and brush, or let them splash around in the sink "washing the dishes" (supply a towel for mopping up)

★ go to see what's happening at the neighbours' or the shops

★ pretend to go to sleep on the floor

★ ask what you can do to make them happy

★ put most toys away and rotate them – too many are overwhelming. The new ones can appear, not as a reward for a tantrum, but when you sense boredom that could end up as a tantrum

★ respect their mood – you're not nice all the time so why should they be?

★ see if they want to play on their own for a while, knowing that you're close by if they need you – you may have been "in their face" too much

★ bring out the playdough

★ grab the maracas and sing "I Go to Rio"

★ carry handbag-sized pencils, pads and other activities and games to head off trouble when you're out

★ an occasional surprise chocolate frog

★ sing a song with actions together ("Incy-Wincy Spider", "Here We Go Round the Mulberry Bush") – there's so much to concentrate on they'll forget the grumbles

★ cook something easy together such as muffins

★ a swing

★ suggest they play quietly in their room until they're in a better mood – not as a punishment, but as a way for them to have a play and eventually decide to snap out of it

★ talk to Grandad on the phone

★ a tickle (although if a child is tired this could make them demented – always respect the rule that you stop tickling when a child asks you to)

★ water pistols in the bath

★ separate two kids if they are fighting and give them different activities for a while

★ talk in funny voices and accents, walk like a pompous person or look frightened, as in exaggerated charades – kids are fascinated by emotions and body language because they're trying to learn them all the time

★ go for a drive and talk about what you can see

★ hide under the washing in the washing basket

★ make a den with blankets and chairs and throw in a cushion and a favourite toy

★ make the Crumpet of Joy or award the Magical Sticker of Smiley Boys – use your imagination

★ check if they might be in a bad mood because you are – if you are, think what would make you feel better and suggest it (sex with a stranger in Trinidad is probably best left off the agenda at this point)

★ swap roles – you be the kid and they the parent – and see what words they give you and how they behave as you (it's a real insight)

★ make a puppet out of a toy and have it chat away with your child – kids over 2 and a half will happily chat to a toy with a silly voice even if you're sitting right next to it with your lips moving and your hand up its bum

★ a cold shower – I don't think it would work in the Outer Hebrides

★ make faces

★ blow bubbles

★ talk to them about how different emotions make us feel and what we can do about them – how everyone is sometimes angry, cross, confused, tired – and draw faces with your child of the different feelings. (Here's a tip: most of the time you only have to change the eyebrows!)

> *"My husband is really good at breaking a tantrum. He goes into the room and without looking at the child, starts to play with a toy. Eventually the child starts to watch and register that they're not receiving any attention, and slowly they start to join in. My husband never mentions the tantrum and just keeps playing. Things go back to normal and we can all move on."* TRISH

maNN·eRS

Some people don't bother teaching their children manners, but that's a short cut to having a child who is disliked. There's a difference between using the right words – please, thank you, thanks for having me, and hello – and common courtesy, which means learning to wait your turn to speak, not pushing people out of the way to get where you want to go and consideration for others.

Common courtesy is mainly taught by example and creates an environment in which everyone in the family says stuff such as "Would you mind if I borrowed your glitter glue?", "Would anyone else like a guava mocktail while I'm in the kitchen?" and "Sorry, I didn't mean to whack you with a piece of lettuce". Children will learn that courtesy is a part of life (at least in your house – they may get a rude shock elsewhere).

It's obvious that a lot of parents don't think manners are important. I wish children could see that. At the very least, knowing how to use manners is a huge social advantage and an excellent manipulation tool – much better than whingeing. People adore a child with good manners and will give them lots of attention and unsolicited presents in shops and elsewhere just because they're so thrilled to meet one. A child will have an easier time of it if they learn that "lovely manners" will get them further in life than being a surly grasper (unless they go into business or politics).

Don't make a big fuss of bad manners, but reward the good.

The pleases and thank-yous are pretty much a matter of automatic speech – children usually learn to say them before they really understand that they are forms of politeness. The quickest way to reinforce these is not to hand over the goods until please has been said. The common, grating parental prompts include "What's the magic word?", "What do you say?" and "I can't hear you". Swore I'd never say them. Say them all. Hopeless.

Kids learning to actually share is a different matter and needs to be reinforced with talk of people "each having a turn": kids see that as fairer than the concept of "sharing" – both claiming ownership at the one time. Talk to your child about who owns what so they understand that they don't own everything in the world. (You don't need a full-scale explanation of the global economy, just a notion of your blocks, Mum's shoes, Aunty Fatima's car, Caitlin's hairclips.) Help your child understand that their toys will always come back to them: after all, you wouldn't let just anyone walk off with your TV. If there are some very special toys they don't want to share, agree to put them out of bounds to guests and hidden away during visits.

General manners

General manners include:

- ★ saying please and thank you
- ★ saying hello when introduced to someone or seeing an acquaintance and goodbye when leaving them (shy kids shouldn't be forced to do anything else in the way of conversation)
- ★ acknowledging guests but staying seated – young children shouldn't have to stand when adults enter the room because it is outdated, control freaky, apt to be misunderstood and impossible for them to remember at an early age (also it goes against common sense as it's likely to result in drink or paint spills that are really not the kid's fault)
- ★ being kind and courteous to people and animals
- ★ not teasing
- ★ good sporting behaviour – watch some sport together and explain who's doing the wrong thing (tantie-throwing or thuggish footy players) and who's doing the right thing (players congratulating each other: hmm, you may have to demonstrate this yourself)
- ★ no screaming, especially in public places (that shrieky squeal of excitement can be misinterpreted by strangers as distress and is anyway very annoying and disruptive for others).

Interruptions

To avoid interruptions during conversations, on the phone or otherwise, try the following.

★ Give your kid something to do while you're talking.

★ If it's not a business call give them a turn, having asked the caller if they'd mind – this should not be longer than one quick exchange per call or it's too tedious for the caller unless they know them really well.

★ Tell your kid how long you need to be on the phone. For older toddlers set a timer for five minutes and for nursery-age children ten or fifteen if it's an important call, and make sure you finish when you said you would. Give lots of rewarding praise for their long wait.

★ Put on a video if you simply have to talk for half an hour in a work kerfuffle or family crisis.

★ Remember time is a lot slower for kids than adults – "in a minute" means something different to them.

★ Reward them for waiting their turn with a thank-you, great praise, a sticker or a big cuddle.

Always assume your child can hear and understand your conversation even if they seem absorbed in something else.

Table manners

Children can grow up at home without learning any table manners because their family doesn't eat together at a table or has lots of takeaways, eaten with the fingers or just a spoon. As kids get older – between 3 and 5 – they become good at feeding themselves and can start to learn a few table manners. Here are some basics.

★ Teach your kid how to set the table.

★ Take them to a café or restaurant and talk about how the table is set or where we place the cutlery.

★ Tell them that napkins (aka serviettes) – you can refer to these hilariously as adult lap bibs – go on the lap.

★ Let them practise putting forks on the left, knives and spoons on the right.

★ Show your kid how to use a knife and fork together (or chopsticks).

★ Explain how it's considered good manners to eat with the mouth closed; not to make loud chewing noises; not to spit food out; not to put too much in the mouth at one time; and that smearing banana on the waiter's hair is not on (especially if the waiter is you).

★ Show your child how to put their knife and fork together on the plate as a sign that they are finished, and remind them to ask to be excused from the table.

★ Kids who can manage it should proudly be responsible for taking their own plates to the worktop near the sink.

more iNfo

IF YOU FEEL OUT OF CONTROL

The National Society for the Prevention of Cruelty to Children (NSPCC)
www.nspcc.org.uk
Helpline: 0808 800 5000
The NSPCC is there to help parents who feel under strain, or who need advice on how to cope. The helpline runs 24 hours, and you can call anonymously. The society's website has lots of info on how to avoid losing control, and helpful ways to impose discipline.

HELP WITH GETTING KIDS TO BEHAVE

There are many programmes and books to help you learn new ideas on parenting if a theory you've been trying doesn't seem to be working in your family. Or they may just help you to fine tune or add to your bag of tricks. Most theories are based on understanding a little bit of child psychology, allowing your kids to play, how to speak in ways that are respectful and they understand, and letting them know what's expected and what will happen if the rules and conventions aren't followed. Most will offer ideas for a pretty straightforward family situation, as well as some pointers for extreme behaviour. If you need more info than you get in a book, parenting classes can provide practical help and support: a health visitor or GP can recommend one in your area.

How to Behave So Your Children Will Too!

by Sal Severe, Vermilion, 2004

As if we needed reminding that parents aren't themselves perfect, this book gets you to examine how your actions influence your child's behaviour, and has devised strategies to help you manage your own reactions, with consistency as a key element. Along with lots of practical suggestions for effectively managing Time Out, and advice on how to use punishments that teach (and without punishing yourself), it guides you in how to be a positive role model for your children.

How to Talk So Kids Will Listen and Listen So Kids Will Talk

by Adele Faber and Elaine Mazlish, Piccadilly Press, 2001

Down to earth book that aims to take the stress out of the relationship with your child, with plenty of hints on how to tune into their feelings and use positive language to get the result you want without arguments and bad feeling.

Parent Effectiveness Training: The Proven Programme for Raising Responsible Children

by Thomas Gordon, Three Rivers Press, 2008

A US communication programme which teaches parents a positive way to speak with and listen to children based on the principles of Active Listening and I-messages (now a part of many parent training programmes). So when a child says "There was a monster in the cupboard", instead of saying "No, there wasn't" you say "There was a monster in the cupboard? Tell me about it." An I-message is used to put emphasis on the effect, not the wickedness, of the action: "I was hurt when you hit me" rather than "Don't hit, it's naughty." The downside is that it can be extremely boring for adults to talk parrot-fashion, and that a child will sometimes want you to suggest a solution, not just mirror their feelings back to them. As yet the network of instructors in the UK is still small, predictably with more coverage in the South. However, in areas where it is currently difficult to undertake the usual weekly course, you can use the Home Study Programme, with study guide and DVD, and an instructor can then act as a consultant either in person or by phone.The website **gordontraining.com** has free downloadable articles.

The Incredible Years: A Trouble-shooting Guide for Parents of Children Aged 2-8 Years

by Carolyn Webster-Stratton, Incredible Years, 2005

Designed by a US clinical psychologist, this programme is divided into twelve steps to promote children's social, emotional and academic competence. Initially designed to deal with serious behavioural issues (its approach has been modelled by the US Office of Juvenile Justice and Delinquency Prevention), the principles of active listening, clear boundary setting and the like also work well in the average family setting. The website incredibleyears.com outlines the overall approach in more detail and gives information on the different styles of programme for the relevant age group. Use the site to find a programme in the UK.

The Parent/Child Game: The Proven Key to a Happier Family
by Sue Jenner, Bloomsbury, 1999

Based on her work as a clinical psychologist at one of the country's leading hospitals for mental health, the Maudsley in London, this book is also backed up by Jenner's experience as a mother and grandmother and has a gentle, loving feel. The emphasis is on building a positive relationship with your child through play, before moving on to address behavioural issues.

The Good Behaviour Book: How to Have a Better-Behaved Child from Birth to Age Ten
by William Sears, MD, and Martha Sears, Harper Thorsons, 2005

A child-centred guide to creating a home where kids feel safe: for the early months this is based on the principles of attachment parenting, and later on recognizing the developmental stages of children and helping them become independent people who look to you for guidance, reassurance and boundaries. It helps to identify the times and situations when bad behaviour happens and how to avoid those "recipes". It presents many options for kids with different temperaments and varying needs, including kids with attention deficit disorder, hyperactivity and severe timidity, but spanking is not one of them. The Sears's Time Out is a break so that the unacceptable behaviour stops, the child reflects on their action and the parent is able to calm down and avoid hitting or screaming. A lovely, useful book.

> *"Your discipline doesn't always have to make sense to the child. Sometimes all that is necessary is giving your child the message 'because this is what I want you to do': children expect us to be adults. That knowledge frees them to be children."*
> **WILLIAM AND MARTHA SEARS**

www.triplep.net
The website of the Positive Parent Programme which can locate a practitioner in your area. Triple P is a ten-step parent education programme developed by Professor Matthew

Sanders at the University of Queensland, Australia, and now used in many other countries. Extremely practical, it outlines the things kids do that drive parents nuts and takes you through clearly defined steps in response, to prevent you accidentally rewarding misbehaviour. Strategies include reward charts and Time Out, and there's advice on how to set rules and establish a good bedtime routine. At other levels the programme can be used to address specific behavioural problems and prevent or stop the abuse of kids at various ages.

"Research shows that children who live in families where there is a lot of conflict and stress between the marriage partners have more emotional and behavioural problems than those raised in stable one-parent families. Serious marital problems should not be ignored. Conflict over parenting causes inconsistency, which in turn makes many behaviour problems worse." PROFESSOR MATTHEW SANDERS

BOOKS ON OTHER "DISCIPLINE" APPROACHES

1 2 3 Magic: Effective Discipline for Children 2–12
by Thomas Phelan, PhD, Child Management, 2003

While I think the strategy of saying "I'm going to count to three, and if I get to three it's Time Out for you" may work with some kids, it won't work with all of them. (Someone I know goes into a real panic, shouting "Don't count! Don't count!" because counting distracts her from thinking through the situation.) Also, although the book claims the strategy works for very young children, it seems geared to primary school kids and even teenagers. The thing I really don't like about this version of the 1-2-3 method is that Phelan says "Think of yourself as a wild animal trainer": that is, there is no emphasis on why some behaviour is unacceptable or on sitting down and explaining to kids why things need to be done a certain way. Even if a kid can't fully grasp your logic yet, they'll understand that you're being kind and patient and you respect them enough to try to help them learn. It also makes life so much more pleasant to explain something rather than just order people about.

In *New Toddler Taming* Christopher Green sets out clear, easy-to-follow steps for his version of Time Out, controlled crying and all his other recommendations (for full details see "More Info" at the end of the "Parenting Philosophy" chapter). As I've said in "Parenting Philosophy", Dr Green is a mainstream paediatrician who presents some reassuring conventional wisdom that's strong on generally accepted common sense and realities. I part company with Dr Green when he advocates smacking if it is "used correctly": I don't believe it "aborts escalation" as he claims (for some kids it's such an escalator it may as well have metal steps and a moving rubber railing), but I'm sure his views are shared by lots of parents.

PICTURE BOOKS FOR SMALL KIDS ABOUT MANNERS

How Kind!
by Mary Murphy, Walker Books, 2003
All the barnyard animals do each other favours.

Miss Spider's Tea Party
by David Kirk, Hodder Headline, Scholastic, 2007
A book about inviting people, being scared or shy, and a vision of a splendid, happy tea party with a beautifully set table.

Dora's Book of Manners
by Nickelodeon, Simon and Schuster Children's Books, 2006
With help from Dora the Explorer, Grumpy Old Troll learns to say "Please", "Thank you" and "I'm sorry", so that everyone can be friends again. Now, now, parents, try not to throw up, you grumpy old trolls.

CHiLD CaRe

Only you can decide how many days of child care, if any, are okay for your kid and how much you can afford. Only you can decide whether being with your child 24 hours a day, seven days a week, is good for you or them – or is going to turn you into a shrieky-mad harpy. Only you can decide whether your child needs or wants to be with other kids their age. Only you can decide whether particular grandparents are energetic, willing and capable enough to provide a stimulating environment for a baby, a toddler or a preschooler all day or for several days in a row. Only you can decide who wants or needs to be at work, juggle part-time or full-time rosters, and all the rest of it.

paid less than some guy who runs B P

I think I just pooed

waiting Lists

The first thing to say about child care is get from your local council the details of centres within reach and put your baby's name on the waiting lists NOW, even if they're 2
months old and you don't expect to want part-time care until they're 2 years old. No,
I'm not kidding. Waiting lists for child-care centres can be several years long. Put your
child's name down at a couple of different ones and take a good look at them when
you're ready. If you move to another area, first thing you do before you sit down: put
your child's name down in the new area. If their name comes up before you're ready
you can always defer and stay at the head of the queue.

So many parents are finding themselves without the child care or nursery they
want and need because they didn't look ahead a few years. It's going that way that
people thinking of having sex should probably call a child-care centre first, just in
case. (And while you're at it, put your name down for preschool or a nursery school
too – your local council will have a list – because you won't want to miss out.)

so-called studies

Okay, I want you to prepare yourself. Train yourself now to chuck out any newspaper, turn off any radio, throw a boot at any TV examining the "child-care debate".
Whatever decision you make about how to look after your child and have your child
looked after, there will be people who disapprove and periodic "studies" reported
that say you're turning your child into either an aggressive, attention-seeking prima
donna or an anti-social throwback. Whatever kind of child care you use, you can
find a study to "prove" it's making your child a more well-adjusted genius – and
another that says your choice of child care is guaranteed to make your child stupid
and confused for LIFE. It doesn't matter whether you have your child at home with
you every day, you work full-time and have a nanny, you use part-time crèche or full-
time child-care centre or your parents look after the kid sometimes. It's important
to realize that mothers can do no right and everything that can go wrong will be
blamed on you, even if you have a husband with mutton-chop whiskers who makes
all the decisions. Or some of your "decisions" didn't involve choices at all (there
aren't many child-care centres in remoter parts of the UK).

Of all the studies conducted by people in various countries on different kinds of child care, not one makes an assessment of what's best for an individual child: and in particular not one of them is about your child. They're usually studies of fewer than three hundred kids – I've seen some reports with screaming headlines about how bad (or good) child care is based on a study in Finland of fewer than fifteen kids!

Take a front-page newspaper report not long ago (please), under the headline "Child Care Can Be Harmful: Study". Yes, the study of 212 Australian kids from twelve different schools, by a university researcher, "found that children who are in child care for four to five days do not adjust to their first year of school as well as other children". The study says three days a week in child care is okay, but that kids who go to kindergarten (which basically is a form of child care and can add up to four or five days a week) "demonstrate higher levels of social skills and academic competence than those who don't". You may or may not be astonished to know that not a single child was spoken to as part of the survey. Their parents answered a questionnaire, and teachers rated the children on "social skills and academic compe- tence": there were as many definitions as there were teachers asked. What a waste of time and money. *No* conclusions can be drawn from such a survey.

Ultimately all this regular kerfuffly study releasing isn't helping us make up our minds about what's best for our own kids. That's going to take listening to our own conscience and knowing our own children and, frankly, experimenting until we get the balance right. Sit down and think and talk about what you'd like, and then see if you can make it happen. Stay flexible. The only way to work out what kind of child care is good for your kid is to work it out yourself, according to their needs, the needs of your family and what kind of good-quality child care is available, and by watching your child's progress and communicating honestly and openly with the carers you've thoroughly checked out. If you have access to a child-care centre that is staffed by lov- ing and cheerful, well-trained people, with a sensible ratio of staff to children, and your child is happy to go, the activities are varied and age appropriate and the other kids are mostly well adjusted and untroubled, you're already ahead of the game.

Commentators and debates

When people respond to media reports of child-care studies, there's always a flurry of faffing: radio phone-in stuff, columns in the newspapers and something on *Panorama*. What usually happens is that people line up according to what they've done with their own kids. The media get some mums who've stayed at home the whole time and say no child care is good, they get some mums who work full-time and say there's nothing bad about child care, and they make it look like the equivalent of a mothers' playground scrap. And the rest of the time they don't run enough stories on the quality or prohibitive expense of child care, or why blokes are hardly ever asked how they can work full- or part-time when their kids are little, or how decisions about child care can't be made on the basis of statistics.

Here's the big scandal of child care: governments that bang on about family values and children being important don't fund child-care centres properly. There is almost always a crisis in child care because governments rarely put their money where their mouth is, private operators want to make a profit, and professional child-care workers leave their jobs because the pay is pathetic, given their responsibilities, level of training and accomplishments – not to mention the fact that we put our children's lives in their hands.

We should stop judging and blaming parents who choose different ways from ours. I know parents who work full-time, parents who work part-time and parents who have never worked outside the home. I know full-time at-home dads and dads who work part-time so they can spend more time with their kids. Everyone I know who is a parent who also works outside the home has taken hits to their career because they need to be available to their family, and they feel too busy, and too guilty, most or part of the time. Everyone I know who has stayed at home wishes they could have their own money and misses grown-up stuff. But all of them are doing the best they can with the options they have and the choices they've made. The last thing we should be doing is fighting among ourselves.

CHiLD-caRe teRMS

There are loads of terms for child care: preschool, nursery, kindergarten, crèche, play-school, playgroup and so on. "Nursery" has two quite different meanings in the UK, one referring to all-day child-care centres which take children from approximately three months (sometimes six weeks) to five years, and the other to half- or full-day "educational" sessions at a state school or private set-up for three-year-olds and up until the child starts school. Sometimes a playgroup means a drop-in mother-and-baby group where you have to stay with your child, sometimes a place where you can register your child for a number of sessions of all-day care. For places where your child can be looked after all day (with meals included) I shall use the term "child-care centre"; a set-up which is really meant as a precursor to school I call "nursery" (see more on this later in the chapter). You'll need to check when you approach them just which sort of institution they are.

Costs will also vary, although the government is now committed to a policy of a free nursery place for every three- and four-year-old (which can often be used as a credit with a private nursery or child-care centre). It is in the process of streamlining the provision and funding of child care under a ten-year plan, "Every Child Matters". Check with the relevant authorities to see if you are entitled to any other benefits. (See "More Info" at end of this chapter for more details on policy and entitlements.)

Sadly people in remote or rural areas will have fewer options and may have to get a tad ingenious about kid-swapping clubs ("I'll have yours on Wednesday and you take mine on Thursday"). Complain to your local member of parliament if you don't think there is enough care available in your area and the waiting lists are gargantuan. And don't forget to tell them you won't vote for them unless they fix it.

informal family arrangements

Many people use informal or formal arrangements with grandparents, either to give themselves a break here and there or so they can go to work. This can be great, but only if you have the right kind of grandparents. Looking after kids this young can also be an unfair strain on grandparents as they get older.

Some grandparents also have their own jobs or busy lives and don't offer more than an hour or two every few weeks, if anything at all. Others will have a child for an afternoon, but don't seem to have room in their life for overnight visits. Some kids go to their grandparents' house for days on end. There are grandparents who show little interest in babysitting grandchildren or few skills at all: this can change as the child gets to 4 or older and can use the toilet and becomes more engaging and conversational. Grandparents often like the idea of being grandparents, but confine seeing the kids to short visits, sending postcards and little presents between times or turning up on birthdays or Christmas. Further complications include grandparents who have remarried someone with their own family commitments and grandparents who have short-term companions or ones you don't know well.

Sometimes grandparents want to look after the grandchildren but have forgotten how, or are unable to see important safety or nutritional points such as that a baby needs to be in a proper car restraint or a bag of lollies just before going home to bed is not exactly an Einsteiny manoeuvre. It is impossible for some to properly stimulate the development of a toddler or older child for an extended time.

You'll just need to feel your way in making a decision, but a good indicator is whether a grandparent regularly offers to help and actually follows through. Another good indicator is a grandparent who seems stimulated by the encounters, rather than simply exhausted, and shows they want to really get to know their grandchildren.

Lots of people also have regular or irregular swapsies with siblings – or friends – to give themselves a break. You'll need to make sure they know how to take care of *your* child.

CHILDMINDERS

Local councils inspect and license certain people to look after other people's kids in their own home. This can range from one morning a week to all afternoons or full-time, long-day care. Go through your council to find your local accredited carers. Usually a carer can only have a maximum of, say, six kids, including their own, at any time. Children of differing ages often attend so a child is in a "family" situation, and the smaller group can suit some kids better. It also has the advantage of being more flexible, and in a home environment rather than an institutional-type set-up. The downsides can include varying quality of care (although of course this can apply to family or child-care centres too), relying on one person as the carer, who doesn't have other staff back up in case of sickness, and the chance that the policy on things like TV watching or visits from the carer's friends or relatives may not thrill you. The care will probably be charged by the hour and is less expensive than child-care centre rates.

CHILD-CARE CENTRES

A formal child-care centre has professionally trained staff and complies with a huge range of government regulations related to everything from the kind of fencing and equipment needed to staff ratios and what to do with the pooey nap-

GOOD POINTS ABOUT CHILD-CARE CENTRES

✱ Staff are usually dedicated beyond the call of duty and certainly the pay packet.

✱ Child care helps parents have a more balanced life.

✱ It helps full-time stay-at-home mums or dads have an essential break now and then, or once a week.

✱ It can allow a parent to be a better parent because they have breaks.

✱ It helps parents stay out of poverty as it allows them to take paid work.

✱ It comes closer to the sharing kind of child care in a tribal environment than does the isolation of one person at home with a child.

✱ Toddlers tend to adore the child-centred routine.

✱ Trained staff know lots of songs, games and tricks for the right age group, and tend to have the energy to make giraffes from egg cartons.

✱ Staff can focus on the children as they don't have to perform other tasks during the day such as the washing and shopping.

✱ Kids get the opportunity to socialize with other kids of various ages – especially important in these days of smaller and one-child families.

✱ Many centres put on more staff than are required by regulations.

✱ Some centres are community run and the profits are directed back into facilities for children.

✱ Programmes for optimum development have been prepared by professionals.

✱ A structured, kindly social environment can help children overcome shyness, aggression and other social problems.

✱ Child care is a much better environment for a child than a home where they are not wanted or are resented.

✱ Good child care is good for kids.

pies. Some will be registered with the Office for Standards in Education, Children's Services and Skills (Ofsted) in England (see "More Info" for regional equivalents) and subject to regular inspections to ensure the quality of their care. Do visit all the centres in your area. One person's popular and groovy centre is another person's nightmare.

Some child-care centres are community run, others are profitable companies. They may be purpose-built or in a modified building and have large rooms, an out-

BAD POINTS ABOUT CHILD-CARE CENTRES

✱ Long hours in a child-care centre, such as 8am to 6pm, five days a week, are generally regarded as not the best situation for a small child. A kid may, however, be better off there than in many home environments.

✱ UK staff-to-children ratios are relatively good, but they can be better, and they should be standardized nationally.

✱ Good child-care workers leave because the pay is so outrageously crappy.

✱ It's a high-pressure job and some workers are better at it than others. You may not live near a centre that can afford to be picky.

✱ Many centres are run for profit and governments don't put enough money into child care.

✱ A parent can come to rely on child care and get locked into a work schedule, and then it's harder for them to adjust when their child needs a break or fewer hours, or is ill or needs them.

✱ Child-care centres can have small grounds, and of course outings are problematical. A child at the same centre for years, or doing very long hours, can be understimulated by the never-changing environment.

✱ Not enough men are attracted to the profession, and men who are child-care workers can be regarded with unfair suspicion ("Why would they want to do that?").

✱ The child care available to you may not match the personality and needs of your kid.

✱ Bad child care is bad for kids.

door play area and lots of organized activities. Most also have a full- or part-time cook on site to provide meals. (Ask if the cook is considered part of the staff-to-child ratio: obviously it's better if they're not.)

Some centres have "family groupings" – rooms are occupied by children of different ages to simulate a family with different-aged children – but most take advantage of the fact that children at similiar stages of development want to be together and group activities can be tailored to their needs. Centres have to have special programmes for each age. Many centres have a system where kids are with their own peers for some of the day and with all ages at free playtime in the afternoon, for example.

Some child-care centres will take babies from 6 weeks old; others may start at age 1. Some allow half-day attendance; most don't. Kids can be booked in from, say, 9 to 4, or longer or shorter hours, depending on the policy of the centre. You may be charged for a whole day even if you only want care from 10 to 4 as you'll be keeping out someone who wants the longer day. Fees are sometimes calculated by the hour. Check with the centre whether you're eligible for government help with them. (See also "More Info" at the end of this chapter.)

a NaNNY

This is probably the most expensive form of child care because you're paying one person's wage, without any subsidies, and you need to organize tax for them and their national insurance. For more details on your obligations contact your local Inland Revenue office or see the website listed in "More Info" at the end of this chapter.

Some people share a nanny to look after a couple of kids, perhaps swapping between homes. Very few people can afford the money or space to have a live-in nanny.

The bonding and one-on-one care of a nanny is a huge bonus; the flip side is that the child can be very sad to be parted from them if the nanny wants to move on or you run out of money.

Nannies don't have to be registered in the same way as childminders, but they can become "approved" by joining Ofsted's Voluntary Childcare Register in England (see "More Info" for regional equivalents). Hiring a nanny through a specialist agency means it's easier to check their references, training and work history. If a problem arises, you can take advice from the agency if you wish.

People who are employing a nanny through an agency as well as those who are employing them privately should observe the nanny with children, ask exhaustive ques-

THE NaNNY INTERVIEW

QUESTIONS TO ASK ABOUT A CHILD-CARE CENTRE

Before you decide, visit the centre more than once, if you like, and ask a carer and yourself these questions.

* What are the available hours, and which weeks are holidays?

* Who oversees the centre: the local council, a parent committee, a private for-profit company?

* Is the centre affiliated with a religious group or based on a particular philosophy?

* Can I get involved in the management?

* Is the centre accredited by the Ofsted and for how many years has it been?

* May I inspect the premises? (Check that it looks clean but not weirdly clean.)

* Will my child be with kids of the same age and gender?

* Is the centre's Early Year's Programme really an up-to-date, challenging curriculum geared to learning development, or tarted-up child care?

* Is there lots of space inside and outside?

* What's the vibe?

* Are there any kids off on their own, looking sad?

* Are the carers covered in cuddly kids or does the place seem a bit stand-offish?

* Are the kids outside wearing hats and sunscreen?

* What happens when a child cries?

* Do the staff speak respectfully to the children?

* Do the carers get down on the children's level or bring them up to theirs or do they always supervise from adult height?

* Are the kids absorbed in something and busy?

* Do the children look interested and happy?

* Do the staff seem to get on well together as adults?

* Is there a method to the madness or does it look like chaos and seat-of-the-pants stuff?

* Is it always like this? (Allow for reality – imagine if someone came to your place at a bad time.)

tions and personally check all references and educational qualifications such as nanny or child-care ones. (Less effusive references can be coded criticisms.) Most people prefer a nanny with child-care qualifications and a current first-aid certificate.

* Sit in the corner for a while, come back at different times, talk to the staff: is there a clear coordinator or director of the centre, who is around to answer your queries and advise and support the staff?

* Who should I speak to if I have any worries?

* Is there someone always at the premises who has current first-aid qualifications?

* Who works or lives on site? Can I see or meet 'em all?

* What happens when a child is sick or needs emergency care?

* What do I have to bring? (Change of clothes, bottles, nappies, fruit?)

* What sort of meals do they serve? Are they cheap and nasty or is the centre too obsessed about organic?

* Do the kids watch TV or DVDs and for how much of the day?

* Do the books, toys and activities look interesting or like merchandising hand-me-downs?

* Is a wide range of toys available or are there strict rules such as no plastic toys and does the answer fit your philosophy?

* What activities and programmes are available, and how do they encourage creativity, fun and development?

* Can my child call me (if they're old enough) at any time?

* In the early days, if my child is overwhelmed or shy, is there a quiet-time space for them?

* What is the staff-to-child ratio in the room where my child will be?

* What discipline measures are used?

* What is the policy on bullying?

* Can I hang around a lot, when dropping off and picking up, to familiarize myself with the centre and make my child feel secure?

After your child has been going to the centre for a while, ask these questions:

* Is my child adjusting to being left?
* What does my child like doing?
* Who are their special friends?
* Is my child fine after I leave?

* Is there a day, morning or afternoon when the mix of kids creates a nasty or a difficult dynamic for my child?

When you interview a nanny, make sure your baby or child is with you. Watch how the nanny interacts with them. It's a good sign if she (or he) is more interested in the child than in you: you want someone who sees the child as the first priority.

You need to sort out upfront, before the nanny starts, whether you expect them to do any housework or cooking aside from kid food. You should also make your expectations clear; for example, friends and other nannies can visit, but no taking the baby to the pub for a shandy.

If your instinct tells you it isn't working out, or the nanny seems to have a problem that will impinge on your life, don't hesitate to move on – the sooner the better, before bonding happens.

a babysitter

Before you leave your house in the care of a babysitter make sure all doors can be opened easily from the inside or that keys are always kept on the inside lock: it's important not to deadlock people inside the house. Give the babysitter a spare key in case they have to leave the house with the kids for any reason.

A noticeboard or a folder with plastic sleeves inside to keep essential info in is a good idea. You can even attach the folder to a nail on the wall or pin it on a noticeboard close enough to the phone for a number to be read while dialling. You might like to make some photocopies of the "Info for Carers" sheet coming up soon to use when you have a babysitter.

It may seem heavy but in "Extra House Information" on the info sheet you might want to record, for example, that "There are bars on all windows. All rooms have smoke alarms. In case of fire, drop to the floor to avoid smoke and get the kids and yourself out the front or back door, whichever is nearest. Nothing else matters." And in the "Special Instructions" part, something like "Ari is allergic to peanuts".

A note about teenage babysitters
Sometimes it's convenient to have a neighbourhood teenager or an older sibling take care of young ones. These babysitters should always have access to adult help, nearby or on the phone, as even the most responsible teenager is still a teenager. It's not their fault, but teenagers do not have the brain capacity to understand every cause and effect, and they are usually inexperienced and inadequately briefed on what to do in a variety of emergencies.

QUESTIONS FOR A CARER, NANNY OR BABYSITTER

* What's your family situation?

* What are your child-care and first-aid qualifications?

* How do you feel about me working from home or popping in at any time?

* Why do you like children? (This often flushes out those who don't, and is subtly different from "What do you like about looking after children?".)

* What are your strengths?

* Why did you leave your last three jobs?

* What are some of the things you do with a kid this age?

* Do you have a philosophy or approach to child care?

* What are your feelings on setting boundaries and discipline?

* What are the bad things about the job?

* What are the worst kind of parents to work for?

* The baby has been crying for an hour and nothing seems to work. What do you do?

* The baby vomits a feed, feels very hot, falls asleep and you can't wake them up. You can't contact the parents. What do you do? (Right answer: call an ambulance.)

* I ask you to do something a certain way and you think it's the wrong way. What do you do?

* How much notice do you want to give for holidays? And how much notice should we give for our holidays without you?

* Can my toddler phone me to come home or to come and get them, or for a chat at any time? (Often kids feel more secure knowing they can bail out when they want to, and relax into enjoying the day.)

Occasional-care centres

Most commonly called crèches in the UK, these centres provide child care for an occasional, limited period of time. They are often attached to shopping centres, leisure centres or colleges, and are particularly useful for parents who are usually at home with their children, but need a brief break or to get to an appointment without kids. Centres have to register as full-time nurseries if they offer more than two hours

iNfo foR caReRs

Kids' names and ages: _____

_____

Parents' full names: _____

_____

phone: _____ mobile: _____

Our home address and phone number: _____

_____

We'll be at (address): _____

_____

phone: _____ mobile: _____

Emergency numbers – police/fire/ambulance: 999

NHS Direct (for non-emergency health worries/telephone support): 0845 4647

Neighbour's name, house number and phone number: _____

_____

Back-up relative or special friend's name and phone number: _____

_____

Kids' doctor's name and phone number: _____

_____

After-hours doctor-visit service: _____

Our children's painkiller is kept: _____

First-aid box is kept: _____

Torch is kept: _____

Nappies or pull-ons are kept: _____

Towels are kept: _____

Bin bags are kept: _____

Cleaning stuff is kept: _____

Toilet rolls are kept: _____

Extra house information: _____

_____

Kids' bedtime: _____

Usual bedtime ritual (including whether nappy necessary): _____

_____

_____

_____

Any other needs: _____

_____

_____

_____

Special instructions: _____

_____

_____

_____

_____

© The Rough Guide to Babies and Toddlers

of child care a day and be staffed by trained, qualified workers. They usually take bookings on the day you need them (subject to demand) and the fee is by the hour or per session, and they may have a minimum age limit. The children in a crèche are unlikely to be regularly cared for together and the age range may be much wider than is normally the case. For these reasons your child might find it more difficult to be left there without you, although if you use one place regularly this should diminish over time.

NURSERY

Every 3- and 4-year-old in the UK is entitled to a free nursery place for up to 12.5 hours per week, 38 weeks a year. This can mean mornings or afternoons only, three-days-a-week arrangements or every day from 9am to 3pm, to a variation of these. Nurseries are often state run and affiliated with or attached to a primary school for ease of transition. They can also be private set-ups, and in either case will follow the government's Early Years curriculum to make the most of children's development at this age and help to prepare kids for school. If they are registered with Ofsted or its regional equivalents (see above) they will be subject to regular inspections and you can ask to see the report or view it online (see "More Info" for contact details). Many nurseries also offer before- and after-school child care. Your local council will have a list of nurseries in your area – you may need to register your child with several at least two years ahead.

It's now generally accepted that kids who've done a year or two at nursery will be better prepared for a transition to school – but, as always, trust your own instincts as to what is right for your child.

SETTLING INTO CHILD CARE

If possible, especially in the first days and weeks, spend as much time as you can helping your child to settle and bond with the carer or carers or the nanny. It can be a delicate situation leaving a child you know will be happy two seconds after you leave, but meanwhile is weeping piteously and clinging to you for dear life. Some kids initially need to be "eased into the day", yet will end up hardly giving you a backward glance as they race to an activity ready for them on the kid-sized tables at child care or to hold Granny's hand and wave you off to work.

Never sneak away; always let your child know you are going and what time you'll come back (even if they don't quite "get" times). Check later with the centre or carer to make sure any tears on your departure cleared up after you left, and that your child isn't showing signs of continuing separation anxiety or sadness throughout the day. Feel free to check up on their progress during the day even if they weren't upset when you left: you can tell your kid you rang when they were happily playing in the sandpit and they'll feel secure and become aware of the bridge between home and the child-care centre, or between you at work and them at home. Depending on their age, your kid can understand they're allowed to call you at any time.

Make sure the carer or carers know they can talk to you openly about your child's feelings, demeanour and development.

guilt about child care

Guilt about using child care is minimized if you can stay home with the child when they're sick or when they don't want to go: this can be very hard when you have other job commitments. (The juggling has begun!) The other way to minimize guilt is to try to look very dispassionately at your set-up and honestly assess whether your kid is happy and thriving after a few weeks of care. Don't make your decision based on other people's theories, what your mother thinks, a survey in Finland or indeed the experiences of anyone else's children.

The real key to dealing with guilt is to make sure your child is having a happy, stimulated, social childhood, whatever child-care options or combination you choose. To do that, you have to spend enough time with your child to know them very well.

"It's Thursday afternoon and my son, Edward, is in child care so his mother can go to work. At least that's how most people would view our household arrangements. Edward is also in child care so that I, his father, can go to work. But few would consider that. Or that it might have been my decision to leave Edward in care, or that I decided to go to work rather than staying home with him. Nobody would bother to analyse my motives and my morality. Nobody would think I was selfish or a bad parent – because I am a father. But it's completely different when you're a working mother." ANGUS HOLLAND, *REAL DADS*

Permission to relax

If your kid is in child care or with a babysitter, relative or friend for a few hours – and it's not one of those times when you have to be at work or have to do housework, shopping or part-time paid work – you are allowed to read a magazine, watch a DVD or go to sleep. In fact this should often be compulsory. For sole parents and at-home parents who don't get weekends or any nights off, a bit of child care is a godsend.

Sometimes the parent who is the full-time carer has a little wobbly on the first few days their child is in care: for some it's the first time they haven't had to be responsible and on 24-hour watch. Some women have told me they sleep all day long or even hit the bottle or other drugs, legal and otherwise, for the first day or so, straightening up by the time they need to pick up the kid. While this is understandable and in some ways tempting, if you do it for more than a day or two you'll need some professional help (start with your GP). Sleeping or other relaxing pursuits such as eating and having a bubble bath don't quite give you the same wipe-out, but oblivion isn't going to work when they ring and say your kid's been vomiting and needs to come home. Besides, wanting oblivion on a regular basis is usually a symptom of something that's going to have to be tackled.

more info

www.cafamily.org.uk
Helpline: 0808 808 3555
Contact a Family is a voluntary organization offering information and support for families with disabled children, where you may be able to discuss your child-care needs with other parents in your area.

www.childcarelink.gov.uk
Helpline: 0800 234 6346
Launched as part of the National Childcare Strategy which aims to help people back into the workplace by removing the child-care barrier. Provides details of your local Children's Information Services (CIS), which can give face-to-face or phone advice on all aspects on child care in England and Wales. It also lists the child-care providers in your area.
For information in Scotland, contact **carecommission.com** or **scottishchildcare.gov.uk**.

www.direct.gov.org
A range of information for working parents, including links to local nanny agencies.

www.hmrc.gov.uk
Tax Credit Helpline: 0845 300 3900
Inland Revenue website for information about the Childcare Element of the Working Tax Credit, which can be used to help fund your child care, and your obligations regarding a nanny's tax and National Insurance.

www.ncma.org.uk
Helpline: 0800 169 4486
The National Childminding Association is a charity and professional organization which supports quality child care. Has lists of approved childminders and nannies in your area.

www.ofsted.gov.uk

English inspectorate of children's services. View their reports online and check on their voluntary register for other approved child-care providers. For Wales the Care and Social Services Inspectorate website is **csiw.wales.gov.uk** and for Scotland, Her Majesty's Inspectorate of Education website is **www.hmie.gov.uk**.

www.parentscentre.gov.uk

One-stop shop for information on maternity and paternity rights, choosing child care and a guide to the Early Years curriculum for parents to help support their child's learning.

www.surestart.gov.uk

Sure Start is the government's ten-year plan to create a joined-up system of health, family support, child care and education for children. Website has excellent downloadable booklet on *Looking for Child Care*, listings of child-care options in your area, ways to find out if you qualify for benefits, and lots of useful links.

www.workingfamilies.org.uk
0800 013 0313

Information on employment rights, flexible working and child care with lots of downloadable factsheets from the website.

HOW TO BE PERFECT

Being absolutely perfect at all times is utterly essential.

Here's how.

a Day in the Life of the Perfect mother

★ Get up before everyone else, wearing a peignoir (I don't know what it is either but I think it's see-through and has feathery bits) and prepare a nutritious cooked breakfast, with precisely balanced portions containing the five food groups, essential fatty acids, minerals and vitamins – for everyone.

- ★ Practise yoga for one hour.
- ★ Learn how to spell Pilates.
- ★ Exercise strenuously for another hour.
- ★ Shampoo and style hair of all household guinea pigs.
- ★ Shampoo, dye and style own hair, with something cheap from the supermarket, so it looks like it was done in a salon.
- ★ Cleanse, moisturize, tone. Neck cream, eye cream, elbow cream, foot cream, earlobe cream.
- ★ Foundation, powder, lipstick, mascara. Curl eyelashes, exercise pelvic-floor muscles, brush eyebrows, pluck nostril hair.
- ★ Brush teeth.
- ★ Floss.
- ★ Wake adorable children. Read them the original *Alice in Wonderland* and engage them in absorbing, quiet activities that develop their brain while providing wholesome, low-key fun.
- ★ Dress children in comfortable imported Italian separates.
- ★ Wake husband up (get husband if haven't got one) with firecracker sex, during which he is struck by uncanny resemblance of self to a young Michelle Pfeiffer, and save time by discussing the family financial situation during the afterglow.
- ★ Do hair and make-up again.
- ★ Dress quickly and deftly in very inexpensive clothes, designed and sewn by self, that look like designer-wear.
- ★ Reheat and serve breakfast.
- ★ Using a bar of antiseptic soap or a hard-bristled brush dipped in Pine-O-Cleen, scrub the poo off yesterday's nappies or the gastro vomit from the crevice down back of couch.
- ★ Breastfeed a couple of children: yours if necessary.
- ★ Search organic vegetable garden for caterpillars and kill them by hand.
- ★ Air the home thoroughly and hang four loads of washing out, well spaced on lines, in a stiff, warm breeze.
- ★ Make some Christmas presents out of raffia, driftwood and dried cannellini beans.
- ★ Give self manicure, including false nails.
- ★ Put youngest offspring down for the morning nap, making sure they all go to sleep instantly, at the same time of day, for precisely an hour and a half.

★ Weed, mulch, harvest, converse with plants.

★ Mosaic the garage wall as an artistic role model for next generation.

★ Do dishes.

★ Buy or make presents for all husband's relatives, write and send cards, and keep up with all gossip and concerns of older generation.

★ Iron sheets, towels and any lingerie bought this week.

★ Spend several hours' quality time with the children involving new activities, age appropriate for each child, that exercise all aspects of their physical, mental and emotional development, and making each feel they have full attention of self.

★ Drive children to three or four different schools, child-care centres, relatives and sporting fixtures.

★ Shop for items needed by different members of the family.

★ Attend Pilates class.

★ Surf Net.

★ Flirt with passing fireman.

★ Go to immensely fulfilling and undemanding part-time job that allows unlimited time off without warning for children's illnesses and other needs, and pays as much as the average full-time (male) wage.

★ Power nap.

★ Shop locally for cheap, fresh, in-season, biodynamic foods, as foods are not in peak condition by the end of the week if only shop once, and will be own fault so must shop every day.

★ Read half of improving novel.

★ Listen to radio and read three daily newspapers to be well informed.

★ Discuss matters of state and global importance with friends who don't have children so as to keep in touch with the Other World.

★ Adjust push-up bra.

★ Exfoliate feet.

★ Clean up sick.

★ Morning tea: nutritious, quick to prepare but not at all fattening, such as a polystyrene cup of raffia, driftwood and dried cannellini beans.

★ Browse homewear shops and buy throw-up-proof throws.

★ Update first-aid and foreign-language skills.

★ Wax legs.

★ Wax earlobes.

★ Inject poisons into forehead to pretend life hasn't caused facial lines.

★ Have a philosophical discussion with a 3-year-old about what's fair and what's not, and win on logic.

★ You Time: why not try a round of golf or learn a new skill such as electrical engineering?

★ Practise tinkling girlish laugh.

★ Test drive a new, attractive car that's practical for the whole family.

★ Lunch at small bistro; half carafe of wine.

★ Pick up brochures from travel agent.

★ Tuckshop duty.

★ Reading duty.

★ Purchase something for self: jewellery or perfume; or perhaps one-bedroom flat in Chelsea.

★ Pick up children – on time – from various schools, child-care centres, relatives and sporting fixtures.

★ Rearrange children, including extras, and deliver them to new set of locations.

★ Go out for drink with promisingly useful work colleague.

★ Pick up children in car and have meaningful dialogue with each individually, paying particular attention to bonding, nuances of unspoken feelings, opportunities for a learning experience (for you and for them), their own special ways of listening and learning, with eye to making important decisions that will determine their entire future.

★ Use a spatula, some home-grown produce and some free-range cruelty-free sturgeon from your own slaughterhouse to fashion a nutritious and delicious meal that husband and children both enjoy, to later be served, according to the needs of family members, at half-hour intervals from 5 until 7.30pm.

★ Go out to see a new Hollywood film.

★ Bathe children, paying special attention to individual needs, water restrictions and sibling fights involving pre-sharpened metal implements and sustained high-pitched shrieking.

★ Feed, water and question guinea pigs.

★ Greet husband, on his return from work, dressed in cling wrap and a strategically placed quince.

★ Play mind-expanding games or listen to radio with children in their freshly pressed pyjamas as you do not have television but only home cinema system used for educational purposes.

★ Teach children to read.

★ And write.

★ Supervise homework.

★ Give husband hand relief in utility room.

★ Give children dinner.

★ Eat own dinner – a small sprauncelet of filleted reef fish with a julienne of fresh, seasonal vegetables and a coulis of curly endive.

★ Discuss the Congo situation, with particular reference to Bavarian history.

★ Get felt-tip pen stains off bathroom ceiling with white vinegar and cream of tartar.

★ Do cryptic crossword.

★ Feed and water livestock.

★ Service CD player.

★ Put children to bed, each with different story.

★ Attend night classes in rowing.

★ Clean out school bags, catch up on handwritten, postal correspondence.

★ Wax bikini line and attach raffia merkin.

★ Unpack and wash lunch boxes.

★ Moisturize neck.

★ Remember Bavaria no longer a country. Pore over atlas.

★ Sew name tags into each piece of clothing owned by offspring, including hats, socks, velvet capes and matching wands.

★ Accept phone calls from internationally recognized experts on child psychology.

★ Make set of queen-sized sheets with unbleached calico.

★ Check supplies of sun cream, Marmite, clean towels, underpants, lunch boxes, children, garden implements, vases, soap and hot-glue guns. Make shopping list for tomorrow.

★ Pay bills, balance chequebook, pay credit card on time and compile tax records in three-ring binder.

★ Invite extended family to Christmas dinner.

★ Listen to relaxation tape.

★ Scrub grouting.

★ Go to bed.

★ Get up, make school lunches for tomorrow.

★ Go back to bed, stare at ceiling, ask unanswerable questions.

★ Close eyes.
★ Listen to a child somewhere audibly vomiting.
★ Pleasure self with dustpan and brush.

a Day in the Life of the perfect father

★ Listen, I'll get right onto this list once I've emptied the compost bin.

4

stuff

Names and Paperwork

Some people have the first names all ready for a boy or a girl: some even know the gender and the name before the baby is born. Others um and er over names for weeks – even months – after the baby's born. I couldn't find any research on this at all, just billions of books and websites full of lists of baby names; nothing to help people who seem unable to close their eyes and jump with a name.

Should I call you Morty-bob or Siiiiimon?

Erp

And once you've decided on a name, who do you need to tell, what lists should your baby be on and what other paperwork has to be done?

CHOOSiNg a fiRSt Name

Some cultures give their newborn babies a cute name or "milk name", which may be a diminutive of the formal name or a nickname: Carmelita instead of Carmel; Bird instead of George. In this way the formal name is in waiting. Some names – such as Reginald or Lucretia – don't suit babies. But Reggie or Lulu might, until they need the other one.

Don't let family members or a bureaucratic official stampede you into naming your baby in the first week or two just so they can write something down on their form. Say firmly "No, *don't* put down 'Ferdie'. We'll let you know when we have decided."

Part of the problem may be that you're waiting for the kid to "look like" a certain name. This is no good: it actually works the other way round. You give the baby a name and they start looking like it.

You may have some psychological trouble putting a name to the amazing thing that's happened in your life, represented by this little person. Explain to yourself you're not describing the whole head-spinning trip, just giving the kid a name. If you're still having trouble naming your baby after a few months, it's probably a good idea to have a chat with a counsellor – not because you're crazy, but because at this stage of everyone's parenting life and lack of sleep, an independent eye on the situation is often a good idea. Your GP can recommend a psychologist. And don't be embarrassed. (I'm not suggesting you ask the GP to name the baby, but to help with the feelings you may be having that have led you to being unable to name the baby, possibly because you're struggling with identifying what's happened to your life, as well.)

If as a couple you can't agree, think about it for a while, then find three names you can each live with and do the hat thing. Promise that you'll go with the order they come out of the hat. If you pull Luke first, then Luke it is. You do have to be a responsible parent at this point and part of your job is to name the child. There is no wrong answer. Any decent name will become your child's own, and you'll love your kid and their name: eventually they're indistinguishable.

You can still use nicknames. Other kids in the future will bestow their own nicknames: you can't control what your child is called forever. ("Well, her name is Penelope. Nobody will be able to call her Penny.")

Don't saddle your kid with a name that usually belongs to the other gender: Kim goes both ways, but Fifi and Butch really don't. Leave the kid to make up their own cross-gender names in the future if they want to.

Stick with the name and keep using it – everyone will grow to accept it. All names seem okay, then weird, then okay again. Everyone has second thoughts and wonders if the name they have given is right. If you feel sure you've actually used the wrong name rather than just being unsure about it, change it – but only change once. You can't keep messing around.

Your child may change their name when they grow up. I know one boy who was bored with his name, changed it at 3 to Huckle and took that into adulthood. Others have changed their New Age names to mainstream ones or vice versa. Most young kids, sometimes at about 4 years old, either insist that you use their formal name, not a diminutive or a nickname, or make up an imaginative one for themselves.

family Names

Most babies are given the family name of their father, stemming from the days when a wife and children were seen to be owned by the man. Some are given the family name of their mother. Some get a double-barrelled name, and some have their mother or father's family name as a middle name to avoid the hyphen. Some mothers use their first family name professionally and use their husband's or partner's name for anything to do with the child's world, such as school. Personally I only ever use my partner's name if I am trying to hide my involvement in an off-shore diamond heist or otherwise behaving suspiciously, and my daughter has her dad's last name because, let's face it, who wants to have your mother's name when she's written books with chapters on stuff like "Bosoms" and "Bottoms"?

Registering a Name

Births in England, Wales and Northern Ireland must be registered within 42 days (21 days in Scotland). This can often be done at the hospital, but if this has not been possible then you can do so at any register office, although in practice it will be your nearest one – your local authority will be able to tell you which that is. Many offices operate an appointment system, sometimes with several weeks' delay, so it would be good to get onto this soon after the baby's birth. If you are married either parent can register; if not, then the mother at least must attend. If the (unmarried) father is unable to go with the mother but wants his paternity to be acknowledged then he must fill in a statutory declaration form (see "More Info" at the end of this chapter) or he will not be deemed to have parental responsibility (although he will still have to help pay for the child's upbringing).

If you don't register a child's names, all sorts of benefits may be denied them because they officially don't exist. A child can be registered without a first name, then that name added later. A child who is months old before they are registered will usually have their details double-checked with the hospital where they were born or with the attending doctor at a home birth. Each child, whether a twin, a triplet or whatever, must have their own form. After giving the registrar all the information required you will be asked to check carefully and sign, before being given (free of charge) a "short" certificate with details of the baby's name, sex and date and district of birth. Full birth certificates containing all the information on the register, and further copies of the short certificates, will be available to buy – and you can also order copies at any time in the future.

All sorts of ludicrous details that are none of the state's business may be required on the registration form, including the age, marital status and occupation of the parents (mothers in the past almost always had their occupation put down on their marriage certificate as "spinster" and on the birth certificate, ever so respectfully, as "none"). The number of previous children by the present partner, or any former partner, will also be asked for.

A very boring bureaucrat insisted to me on the phone that mothers who knew the father of their child must put his name on the certificate: this is partly so government agencies can try to chase him for support money. If you don't want the father's name on the certificate because you don't know who it is, or because you know he will never want to be involved with you or your child, you may have to officially say he is unknown, but don't let them actually write "unknown" on the certificate as this can be hurtful to your child in later life. Make sure it says something neutral such as "not stated" or is left blank.

Unfortunately some bureaucrats can be very inflexible about things such as this: don't let yourself be bullied. You may need to have the advice of a solicitor who specializes in family law before you fill in the birth certificate and decide what to put down. Many people believe it is always a child's right to know who their father is: this is a separate issue from whether the father's name should be on the birth certificate.

OTHER PAPERWORK

Wills

You, or you and the baby's other parent if there is one handy, should agree on who is to have care of your child should anything happen to all available parents and put this down in a legal will or your wishes may not be followed. Consult your family lawyer, or contact Legal Aid or a community legal service (see the *Yellow Pages* or online).

Health and Money

A NHS medical card is issued when you first register your child with a GP (in some cases this may happen automatically if you have been under GP care for your

---

PUTTING YOUR CHILD'S NAME "DOWN"

Putting their name down used to be essential only for people whose kiddliwinks were trotting off to the sort of private school that has a waiting list as long as the list of prefects who went on to join the Conservative Party. These days – AND I'M ONLY GOING TO WARN YOU ONCE, MY FRIENDS (well, okay, the warning's also in the "Child Care" chapter) – you need to put your child's name down for child care, nursery and, in some cases, school WHEN THEY ARE BORN. I know some of you think this is mad and you'll ignore it. Just don't have a tantrum in three years' time when the kid has missed out on a place.

---

pregnancy). It will have a unique number on it which will remain theirs for life and will enable them to access all the NHS services.

Most people bringing up a child qualify for Child Benefit, a weekly tax-free sum that is not affected by income or savings. You should receive a claim form from the hospital at the time of giving birth, or you can print off a form from the HM Revenue and Customs website (see "More Info" at the end of this chapter). You will need to supply the child's birth certificate, and the amount is usually paid directly into a bank or savings account every four weeks.

All new babies are now entitled to a Child Trust Fund, a savings and investment account which belongs to the child and cannot be touched until they turn 18. You will receive a voucher of some hundreds of pounds with which to open an account on their behalf, and the government will add another similar sum when the kid turns 7. You can choose from different types of accounts and pay into it yourself at any time up to a given maximum per year. The theory is that the child will have some money behind them when they start their adult life, and get into good habits about saving. Or blow it all on tattoos and whisky.

MORE INFO

www.childtrustfund.gov.uk
Details of the Child Trust Fund scheme, what sort of accounts there are and what yours might be worth.

www.direct.gov.uk
Child Benefit Helpline: 0871 434 0458
To find out the current amount of child benefit, whether you qualify and how to claim.

www.gro.gov.uk
Explains how to register the child's birth in England and Wales.
For Scotland, visit **www.gro-scotland.gov.uk**; for Northern Ireland, **www.groni.gov.uk**.

www.hmrc.gov.uk
The website of Her Majesty's Revenue and Customs, where you can print out a Child Benefit claim form.

equipment

You're going to need some stuff.

A LOT OF STUFF.

PRAM

shopping

safety standards

If you're buying new babies' or children's equipment, make sure that each item has a current certified safety standard label, which means it complies with British, European or adopted European and international standards. The label will have a number that corresponds to the requirements for that item; for example cots are currently covered by BS EN 716, car seats by ECE R44-03. The British Standards Institution (BSI) is the only organization that can grant a licence for the Kitemark, a world-recognized symbol of safety. In terms of car seats at the time of writing there is currently no BSI designation for car seats, which are currently covered by United

Nations/European labels though this is likely to change in the near future with new legislation in the offing. Keep an eye out.

It's usually best to shop at a section of a department store or a shop that sells different brands of baby gear so that you can compare prices. Do your homework if you plan to buy second-hand stuff – you may be buying things that are unsafe, illegal or superseded. And if you're acquiring something second-hand, get hold of and scrupulously follow the manufacturer's directions about construction and use. If there's no paperwork, contact the manufacturer and ask whether the gear conforms to the current safety standard and, if you can, purchase a manual. Remember, standards are regularly amended.

For some bizarre reason not all the safety standards are enforced by law (although cots and car seats are, for example). Buyer beware!

SAFETY

Don't assume everything available in the UK for children is safe. The Consumers' Association often finds safety hazards when testing kids' equipment. For consumer reports and reviews of specific equipment and for lots of essential info on what's cheap, certified safe and useful, become a member of the Consumers' Association and consult their consumer magazine, *Which?*, or you can visit their website (see "More Info" at the end of this chapter).

See also the "Home Safety" chapter for info on general home safety (it's the next one).

Big stuff

Buy, beg, borrow or hunt down the following.

* ★ A large-capacity clothes washing machine: if it's a front loader move it onto a very strong bench so you're not lifting heavy things from ground level. Bending down to a front loader is a pain – go for a top loader if you're buying new.
* ★ A tumble dryer: unless you live somewhere sunny and can get through a rainy season without one.

★ A car that has or can have an anchor point installed for baby and child restraints. As I said in my book on pregnancy, *The Rough Guide to Pregnancy and Birth*, don't buy an SUV or four-wheel-drive car (this doesn't apply to all-wheel-drive sedans). Four-wheel drives are over-represented in accidents where children are hit in their own driveways – and a child hit by a four-wheel drive is statistically very much more likely to die. (For the same reason, have any bullbar removed.) Proximity alarms, lenses and video-checking systems are not a guarantee of safety and can promote false confidence, according to car accident authorities. Blind spots occur in all vehicles, especially low to the ground. Estate cars can be fitted with a cargo barrier so dogs and other heavy stuff don't fly in from the back in an accident, causing mayhem.

CHILDREN AND CAR AIRBAGS

Children under the age of 12 or less than 135cm in height must not sit in the front seat of a car because the automatic deployment of an airbag can kill a child by breaking their neck. An airbag hitting an adult or a taller child in the chest will not have the same effect.

Basic Baby Equipment

Here's what you need.

★ A new infant carrier (car seat) suitable for the baby's weight. Babies up to about 10kg (usually about 9 months old) need to be rear-facing in a Group 0 or 0+ carrier, which will have an internal harness to secure the baby. The whole thing can then be strapped in the car with a normal adult three-point seat belt, but if your car has Isofix (the standard system for all new cars) you just plug the carrier into the mounting points in the car. Don't buy a second-hand one. If one is given to you, make sure it's no more than a few years old, it's never been in an accident, all straps are in original condition and there's no Velcro involved (experts say the Velcro lasts for one baby's use only). Some baby seats are built to face backwards until the baby weighs about 12 kilos, after which it faces forwards until the kid's about 18 kilos. Then you're into toddler-seat territory (see below). Some adjustable baby and toddler booster seats will take you from 8 to 26 kilos (about 6 months old to 7 years).

★ A bed of some sort: you may want to skip the moses basket or crib stage and go straight to a cot. Some cots can have their side panels of bars removed to become "cot beds", a useful toddler-stage bed, although not so handy if you need the cot again for a new baby.

★ A baby bag: any big bag with a zip or fastenable top will do (see "The Baby Bag" section later in this chapter).

★ A changing table, mat or an area that's set up with everything you need to change a nappy (look up "changing table" in the index for more info).

★ A pram (some convert to a stroller): your pram will need a wet-weather cover and a sunshade or an umbrella or, if you live in Yorkshire, both on the same day. Your pram or stroller should suit your lifestyle. If you walk to the shops a lot or out in the country, get a sturdy pram with fixed wheels and a large metal shopping basket underneath. If you live in an upstairs, walk-up flat, you'll need something that folds into a light, convenient package that can be hauled upstairs. Swivelly wheels on a pram or stroller can be invaluable for manoeuvring round small spaces or crowded shops.

★ A stroller: babies can't sit up in strollers until they have good sitty-up control, usually at about 6 months (strollers sold for kids older than 3 months should be able to be set virtually flat, like a pram, then re-set to a sit-up position after they reach 6 months or so). Some strollers have a small drinks tray that goes in front of the toddler. The expensive strollers are usually more comfortable for long walks or shopping. Strollers need to have a five-point safety harness so a toddler doesn't make a bold bid for freedom when you're halfway across at the lights. Jogging strollers can be harder to get in and out of a car and may not fit easily or at all on public transport: some brands have been rated unsafe, but jogging strollers can be fantastically good for long walks or different terrains.

★ Bike gear: having a baby on a bike in a safety-standard approved seat, even with the regulation helmet on as well, is not necessarily safe. Think about what would happen if the bike was hit by a car or the rider lost control. Similar concerns also exist for bikes towing a baby carriage: even if the trailer has a flag on a flexible stick, it's much lower than anything drivers expect to see associated with a bike. Babies in these should wear a helmet and are still vulnerable to serious injury in such an unprotected and not very visible device. Riding in places where there are no cars is certainly a big head start for bicycle safety when it comes to babies and toddlers.

★ A high chair: you'll need a high chair with wide-apart, stable legs; a lockable tray so the bub can't whack it up and down on their fingers; and a harness that goes around the waist and over the shoulders, with a strap between the legs that goes up to the waist strap. If you always strap your baby in, as you do in the car, they'll assume that's the go and not fuss (fingers crossed). Always put the kid in the high chair yourself: don't let them climb in themselves. Don't leave the room when your baby is in the high chair. Kids are known to do sudden acrobatics you never thought possible – without a safety net. And they push against a table or another chair with their feet, which can tip their high chair over – usually backwards. (See "More Info" at the end of this chapter for safety research by *Which?*.)

★ A booster seat, which sits on an ordinary chair: toddlers graduate to these when they're good at climbing up and down. They are available at chain stores and baby shops and are usually made of hard, moulded plastic in a hideous beige; some come with anchoring straps so they can be attached to the chair. Some have a deeper seat on their other side for when the kid gets taller. Booster seats without straps are notorious for being involved in children's falls because they can move around and be halfway off an adult chair as a toddler starts to climb on or off, so if you buy one you'll need to supervise its use.

For other items you'll need see the info on baby clothes and first-aid kits in the "Clothes" and "Health" chapters a bit further on, and look up "nappies" in the index.

Equipment beyond the basics

You might want some of these.

★ A portable or folding cot for guests or travelling: these really do need to be absolutely bang up to the safety standard and the instructions for their special assembly and use strictly followed.

★ A baby monitor: these are one-way walkie-talkies so you can be at the other end of the house or outside in the garden (take your keys) and still hear if the baby cries. Most baby monitors have two channels – so if there's more than one or two babies with monitors in your street you may be tuning

wah
wah
erp!

baby monitor

into the wrong baby. We listened to Number 38's baby monitor for two days straight before we realized our baby appeared to be chatting to a builder about plans for the dining room.

★ Bouncy things: many safety experts say these are dodgy for babies and too much of a risk. A bouncy chair should always be used with a restraint. It should be placed on a safe surface where it can't travel over the edge of the stairs, and never near a heater or a fire. It should be abandoned as soon as the baby can roll. Babies love to be reminded of womb-like feelings so enjoy baby bouncers, or bouncing swings, and hammocks of any description, but choose carefully and take notice of the manufacturer's age and weight recommendations.

★ Those tenty things you can put up at the beach for a little shade: remember they can get hot inside – a bit of wet clothing or hat action can help. Most baby shops sell them.

★ A strap-on baby carrier: get one with the best back support you can – not just a scarfy thing that ties around you.

What not to get

These are downright dangerous or potentially dangerous.

★ Bumpers: these soft, padded sidey-bits that tie onto cots stop the free flow of fresh air and babies can also get their heads wedged underneath.

HEATING THE BED

For many reasons, including the danger of spilled drinks, wee or the blanket being left on or turned on when it shouldn't be, an electric blanket is not suitable for babies or kids under 5.

A young baby cannot move away from a heat source when they need to, and a hot-water bottle can cause overheating or even slight burns. A hot-water bottle for a toddler should be avoided or filled with warm – never hot – water. It's best to regulate bed heat with blankets (but not puffy bedding such as a duvet for babies). (See SIDs information p.40 for safe bedding info.)

★ A baby walker: I can't understand why they're still sold – every safety mob between here and Neptune says they don't help kids learn to walk properly and cause a lot of accidents.

★ Bunk beds: these are not suitable for children younger than, say, 7. They're a common cause of broken limbs from falls. It's no good telling the kids not to go up the ladder or horse around. That's what kids do.

Basic Toddler Equipment

The following items are essentials.

★ Stair gates: you can get expandable safety standard barriers from baby shops. Have them fitted by someone good at it.

★ A forward-facing Group 1 or 2 car seat for use in the rear of the car from about 10kg up to 4 years. There will be an internal harness for the child, and it can remain in the car, secured by an adult seat belt or the Isofix system (see "Basic Baby Equipment" above).

★ A stroller (see "Basic Baby Equipment" above): a cheapie may be all you need.

★ A toddler bag: stash in it the stuff listed in "The Toddler Bag" section later in the chapter.

★ Socks with raised plastic bumps on the bottom: these will stop your toddler slipping over indoors.

★ A sturdy step stool so your kid can reach the toilet and hand basin.

Carting it all around

If you use a car, you'll want to keep a stash of useful kid stuff in it. If you're out and about there'll be a great deal of stuff you'll need with you.

The baby bag

You don't have to have a wildly flash, celebrity-endorsed designer bag. You need one that stuff can't fall out of – so it needs to zip up somehow. Men: you may want a small backpack or courier-style bag so it's not too girly. Women: you may want to get a handbag with a long strap that you can wear across your body so your hands are free. The time for a clutch purse or a lone wallet may be gone for several years to come unless you fancy the look of gaffer tape. Backpacks are also excellent because they leave your hands free. Keys can be attached somewhere to the bag with a clip so you never lose 'em.

"I buy a poacher's waistcoat with plenty of pockets for bottles and rice cakes and tiny boxes of raisins. I do not look like a poacher . . . I look like the Unabomber. But I can't get away with a handbag." IAN SANSOM, THE TRUTH ABOUT BABIES

Things to keep stocked in the baby bag:
* ★ nappies
* ★ baby wipes
* ★ plastic bags tied in a knot for safety
* ★ a waterproof roll-out changing pad, plus soft cloth nappies or a muslin for laying over it or to use instead of it
* ★ sachets of formula milk powder if you're bottlefeeding (see the "Bottles" chapter in *Part 1: Babies* for the full info)
* ★ a spare shawl or a muslin
* ★ a bib or two or three or four . . .
* ★ a change or two of clothes
* ★ baby toys or rattles.

Things to put in at the last minute:
* ★ medicines, with childproof caps, and inhaler if necessary
* ★ sterilized bottles of sterilized water if you're bottlefeeding
* ★ sunscreen lotion and a sunhat
* ★ a jumper and a warm hat
* ★ snacks

★ a bottle of water for you (and one for the baby, depending on their age)

★ a dummy or other comfort item.

The toddler bag

It's always good to have a bag on an outing. Things you could include in it:

★ pull-ups if the toddler is just starting to use the toilet or finding a toilet could be impossible, or nappies if your toddler's still using them

★ baby wipes

★ plastic bags tied in a knot for safety

★ a change of clothes

★ toddler toys or games

★ portable CD or cassette player, with safe, kid-friendly earphones (from, say, age 2 and a half) – a luxury item

★ a paperback picture book.

Things to put in at the last minute:

★ medicines, with childproof caps, and inhaler if necessary

★ sunscreen lotion and a sunhat

★ a jumper and a warm hat

★ snacks

★ a bottle of water for you and the toddler

★ a comfort item.

MORE INFO

www.which.co.uk

Website of the Consumer's Association, an independent campaigning organization on behalf of the consumer. Has tested many baby and children's products, but you may need to become a subscriber to access the full range of reports, and to receive their magazine, *Which?*.

www.bsigroup.com

The website of the British Standards Institution, which ensures minimum product standards and administers the Kitemark scheme. You'll need patience to winkle out the relevant details for baby and child products and equipment.

www.pricerunner.co.uk
www.kelkoo.co.uk

Two of the many price comparison websites, where you can check the best price for baby equipment.

Home safety

As I said in my book on pregnancy, *The Rough Guide to Pregnancy and Birth*, the only way to childproof a house is to never let a kid into it, but you can try to make it safer. The more mobile a baby gets, the more dangerous the house becomes. There's a wide age range for milestones: your baby could be an early roller, your toddler could be an early climber.

HELMUT

The most common causes of death and injury in little kids (oh, this isn't at all cheerful) are falls; poisonings; car and pedestrian accidents, often in their own driveways; drowning, even in nappy buckets; choking; suffocation; burns; and electrical accidents. The good news is you worry less once you've made everything as safe as you can. (As safe as, well, houses.)

Basic Home Safety

The checklist that follows will give you an idea of where to start, although the hints are probably more useful for city folk (not much point only being worried about a puddle when you also have lakes, rivers and ponds at the back of your garden). You might also like to check out the "Safety Standards" section in the previous "Equipment" chapter for info on UK safety requirements and the "First Aid" section in the later "Health" chapter.

- ★ There should be a working smoke alarm or several. Change the batteries, if yours isn't electric, each time you switch to or from daylight saving time.
- ★ Make sure your fuse box is fitted with a safety switch that will automatically turn off the power if someone is getting an electric shock.
- ★ Use power-point covers (from a hardware store or the safety section of other shops).
- ★ It's expensive but "they" say all kitchens should have an extinguisher that covers every kind of fire and which you know how to use.
- ★ Get a tamper-proof poisons cabinet and first-aid kit, and reorganize cupboards so that the following are on higher ground, safely out of reach: poisons, cleaning agents, medicines, alcohol, cigarettes, matches, lighters, batteries, pesticides, plastic bags, mothballs and camphor, soaps and shampoos, cosmetics, essential oils, and sharp things such as needles and scissors.
- ★ Store dishwasher pellets and powders high up in a safe cupboard, with other strong caustic products such as bleaches and cleaning solutions that can burn a baby or kid's throat and stomach. Only put detergents in just before you turn on the dishwasher and make sure a baby or kid can't get at the dishwasher.
- ★ Anything that will fit into a film canister is a choking hazard for kids up to an average-sized 3-year-old.
- ★ Set your hot-water thermostat at fifty degrees Celsius. At this temperature a child would have to hold, say, a hand under the water for one and a half to two minutes to cause a serious burn. At 65 degrees burning will take just over a second.
- ★ Tie knots in all plastic bags and lock and get rid of old fridges, trunks and other suffocation hazards.

★ Put safety locks (from hardware shops and the safety sections in other stores) on all drawers and cupboards with anything sharp, heavy or pointy in them. (This probably leaves you with only saucepans and old Tupperware accessible.)

★ Anchor all TV sets to the wall or floor. Toppling front-heavy sets have injured many kids.

★ Plate-glass and other windows can be replaced with "safety glass", which breaks into non-cutting pebbles, or covered with an invisible film that will hold shards together. Look in the *Yellow Pages* for a glazier.

★ A child can drown in a centimetre or two of water. If you have a pond in your back garden make sure it is either fenced off or covered by a rigid metal grille just below the water's surface. A swimming pool needs to be similarly fenced with a lockable gate. All other sources of water, including ponds, paddling pools, water butts, water features, toilets and recurrent puddles, need to be considered – kids can drown in a couple of centimetres of water. Your baby might walk before 12 months and crawl way before that. And children virtually never cry out and often don't make a splash when they fall in or get into trouble. All it takes to drown is a couple of minutes, and parents of toddlers know how many times they suddenly realize their child isn't where they thought they were. (Don't have a false sense of security about any young kid who has had swimming lessons: they are just as likely as the other kids to sink to the bottom because they do not have a water survival instinct and often forget to swim. No child or adult is drown-proof, no matter what their experience and capabilities.)

★ Check that your garden fence and gate are secure, and that any chemicals, such as weed killer or fertilizer, and garden tools and electrical equipment are locked away after use. Never let young children near barbecues or a bonfire and remember that they stay hot long after you've finished with them. Many common garden (and house) plants are poisonous or can cause sickness, so teach your child never to put any plants or seeds in their mouth. (See "More Info" at the end of this chapter.)

★ All play should be supervised: children's hospitals see many casualties each year caused by trampolines and other common childhood garden play equipment, especially those involving wheels.

★ Make it as hard as possible for a non-scheduled wander to roads, rivers and other neighbourhood hazards. Often older children and adults leave doors and gates open no matter how many times they're reminded.

THE FREEZING GAME

It's a great idea to play a fun, special game with your kid as soon as they're old enough to "stop" or "freeze". Sometimes give rewards, and spring the game on them every now and again. You can say "STOP!" in all sorts of safe situations – such as randomly in the park and before driveways when you're on a pavement (you can never rely on them to remember to always stop here).

This way, when your child is running somewhere dangerous, such as into the path of a car, you can say "STOP!" and they will automatically stop – perhaps just long enough for you to get to them or for the car to miss them. Otherwise if it's out of the blue and they're frightened, they might run across a driveway into danger. And sometimes you really need them to be still in cases of danger, whether it's animal related, traffic, or close to a cliff edge.

You might also like to read the "Kitchen Safety" section in the later "Food" chapter; see the index. Your local health centre or GP's surgery should have standard-issue safety pamphlets.

DoiNg a "safety sweep" tHroUgH tHe HoUse

Pretend you're an inquisitive baby or toddler. Get on the floor and look around the room: is there anything irresistibly dangly, such as a tablecloth or an iron or a kettle cord that looks like it needs pulling? A slippery rug that could be skated on (not to mention Ming vases and other valuables that could be knocked over)? A sharp coffee-table corner at eye level? Something high up that looks tempting that a chair could be pushed near? (Pianos and sofas make great ladders. So do ladders.)

Are there dry-cleaning bags hanging over clothes in the wardrobe? Plastic bags or sharp things in kitchen drawers? Bottles and sprays of spirits or cleaning products that are temptingly accessible? A dodgy fire guard that could be squeezed around? A hair dryer near a sink filled with water? A maniac in the wood shed?

TOYS

All toys sold here should meet a safety standard and be age appropriate. Most are labelled with an international safety standard (ISO) that is acceptable to the UK. (The local standards are less used on toys.) A few toys slip through without being inspected for safety standards compliance and some that initially meet a standard are sold and then recalled as a problem is found because of injuries to children. Keep in mind also that some toys safe for older children can be dangerous for smaller children.

aNimaLS

I do not refer here to unmentionable exes, but the pet variety. Many animals and children do not mix. There are more and more diseases being passed on by "exotic" animals to humans, and even some traditional pets, including caged birds, can spread disease too. The list of unsuitable pets for health, safety or conservation reasons is quite long and includes poisonous snakes or other creatures; anything with large jaws and a genetic history of guarding or attacking (that is, many breeds of dogs); crossbred dogs; native or other wild animals; animals that are easily harmed, even by a well-intentioned small person. Also elephants. And Crazy Ants.

All children should be taught not to approach or pat animals that they are not familiar with, whether or not a person says sweetly "Oh, he never bites" or "She's harmless".

It is not within the intellectual powers of a child under 5 to take responsibility for the feeding, grooming and other care of animals, although they can help with these things under supervision. Before buying a pet for the family, research the species or breed at the library or on the Internet (and see "More Info" at the end of this chapter).

Dogs

This is shocking, but thousands of Britons, mostly children under the age of 5, are bitten by dogs each year: many are disfigured or disabled, and a very small number are killed. Most dog bites happen in private homes. The common biters are German shepherds, rottweilers, dobermans and bull terriers but any dog, even small dogs and

WHAT TO TEACH CHILDREN ABOUT DOGS

If you have a toddler, start with the simplest info listed below and add more info as needed or as the child gets older.

✱ Never go near a dog you don't know.

✱ Never touch or go near a dog that is eating or sleeping.

✱ If an adult is with you and says it's okay, approach a dog with the back of your hand held down flat for it to sniff.

✱ Don't bend down and put your face in front of the dog's face.

✱ Pat a dog gently and calmly.

✱ You don't have to pat a dog because someone tells you to: it's okay to be scared and to stay away.

✱ Don't talk loudly or in a high-pitched or excited voice, or wriggle about when you're patting a dog.

✱ The warning signs of a bite or an attack include raised hackles, growling, lips drawn back and ears down.

✱ Stand still if a dog approaches and don't look it in the eye or go down to its level.

✱ Move away from dogs that are fighting: never try to stop them.

✱ Never touch dog (or any other animal) poo: it's yucky and has germs in it.

✱ Always wash your hands after patting a dog.

lifelong docile dogs, can and do bite or attack. Labradors and golden retrievers always feature high on the lists of dogs who have savaged or bitten a child – not because they are bred to be vicious or cranky, but because the very opposite is true. People assume these dogs (and many other family favourites) are safe and leave them alone with children.

Older babies and toddlers can get into a tussle with a dog over food (either animal or human food) or accidentally or deliberately torment an animal by poking or intimidating them. No dog is a rational being that makes decisions. A dog has inbred responses to certain situations: even if later they "know" they shouldn't have bitten, they will bite in some situations. Even one bite can severely disfigure or damage a child.

Putting a face near a dog is considered a challenge by most dogs. And a child's face is very much at the height of the face of many dogs, especially when the child does things such as hugging them. The majority of bites to kids under 5 are to the

face, with hands and arms the next most likely parts. Because children are smaller than adults, the bite or injury is usually more serious and needs hospitalization more often. Another point to remember is the bigger the jaws, the more damage that can be done before a dog is pulled away, even if there has been only one bite. Have a look at the head of your baby or child and the jaws of your pet or another dog and draw your own conclusions.

Sometimes people say their child is so used to being with dogs that the kid thinks they are one, but the pack mentality of dogs makes this situation very, very dangerous. When the kid arrives in the family after the dog, the dog usually considers the child lower in the pack hierarchy. This is a recipe for disaster, especially if the child is in the habit of wandering around with food, gets between the dog and its food or tries to take something from the dog such as a stick or a bone. Trainable animals such as dogs must be taught to recognize all members of the family as superior animals in the pack. If possible have the child first and get the dog as a puppy when your child is old enough to be a "top dog". A puppy can be "socialized" to accept small children and other dogs. But regardless of training or temperament, dogs – and cats, and all other animals – should never be left alone with a child or baby.

Some dogs off leads will attack a child who is running or on a bicycle, or for no apparent reason. Some dogs, even accidentally, can knock down or badly frighten a child. If you take your child to areas where dogs are off the lead, you are relying on every dog being firmly under the voice control of their owners.

Cats

Although they don't have the size or the power of dogs, cats can also be harmful to babies and small children. A bite or warning nip can be painful, as can a scratch from sharp claws, particularly on the face. Cat poo is a known cause of toxoplasmosis, which can cause damage to a foetus when it infects a pregnant woman. Pregnant women, or women who might be pregnant, should be gloved and meticulous when disposing of cat litter, should garden with gloves on and keep other people's cats away from their garden.

Children too should not come in contact with cat poo because even though the cat may be healthy it can carry diseases and parasites. As with dogs, kids need to be told they must wash their hands after they've touched a cat because cats have germs and lick their bottoms. Cat fur (and the hair of some other animals) can cause an allergic reaction.

more info

BASIC HOME SAFETY

www.capt.org.uk
Tel: 020 7608 3828
The website of the Child Accident Prevention Trust has safety advice by age group and all the relevant safety considerations for in the home, such as what to do about burns and scalds, poisons, fire and electrical hazards. Road and garden safety issues are also covered. They have a range of downloadable leaflets, including one which lists poisonous or sickness-inducing plants.

First Aid Fast for Babies and Children
Dorling Kindersley, 2006
Produced by the British Red Cross, this is a handy first port of call for basic first aid through to life-saving procedures. Clear illustrations and colour-coded for when you're in a hurry.

www.saferpets.co.uk
This non-profit site recommends safer dog breeds for homes with kids, and includes handy hints on pet care and training (both kids and animals).

CLOTHES

Really expensive imported kids' clothes that cost more than yours are a waste of time and money as children grow out of them so quickly. Many of them are ludicrously impractical and more for the sort of person who likes to dress a child as a little adult, which is always kind of creepy. They are often made of child-unfriendly fabrics such as leather and require dry-cleaning, hand washing or an on-call staff of cashmere-laundering valets. Some catalogues for children's clothes look more like very dubious kiddie-porn, what with their lipstick and bikini tops for people who won't have breasts for another twelve years. I don't know why I'm mentioning this, it's just that it gives me the whim-whams.

saving money on clothes

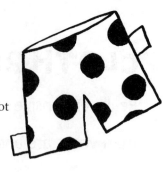

Generally most of the expensive sturdy brands of clothes (not the frou-frou brands) are better made and longer lasting, although price is no guarantee. Some designers now are making clothes with let-downable hems and arms so they last longer.

Sensible gear such as vests, undies, T-shirts and long-sleeved tops are best bought at cheap department stores, especially sales. Boys' departments are often cheaper for no good reason except that a plain vest is cheaper than one with a fairy on it. You can buy a girl the cheaper boys' trousers since at this age they don't know the difference. Discount outlets and charity shops are great sources but do keep an eye out for shoddy clothes – "cheap" means expensive if they fall apart in the second wash.

You can shop at sales if you plan ahead and buy clothes out of season and squirrel away bargains for use in a year or so, although you need to predict what size your child will be next summer or winter. I bought a dress for a 9-year-old on sale for my daughter when she was 6 months old but I think I was technically demented at the time from lack of sleep – in fact I can't think what I was doing out of the house.

It's always useful to hook up with someone with kids a little older than yours so you can get their hand-me-downs, and to find someone to hand yours on to, unless you're saving them for another baby. Once kids get to the toddler and nursery stage they're a lot harder on clothes than babies are and don't grow out of them so quickly so there'll probably be fewer inherited or handed on, or they'll look a little shabbier than the baby hand-me-downs.

Parenting magazines, especially freebies, often have ads for clothes-swapping shops and sales outlets for kids' stuff. Websites such as eBay can yield interesting bargains.

Being able to sew really comes in handy for children's clothes. Fabric shops always have details of nearby sewing classes.

for a baby

Try to grab baby clothes from charity shops, NCT sales, school and church jumble sales. You need lots of each item because, although babies don't run around getting

dirty, they can have quite surprisingly explosive poos and vomits and you can't always be at the washing machine. Don't dress babies in unnatural fabrics: a polyester–cotton blend and polar fleece are as unnatural as you want to go. Nylon is definitely a no-no: partly for comfort and "breathability" reasons – nylon can be hot and itchy – but also because children's clothes must be as fire-resistant as possible. Make sure all baby clothes are machine washable and, unless you live in perpetual sunshine, will go in the dryer. Clothes with stretch and a soft feel are best, which is why "broken in" second-hand clothes are great – it's such a strange new world outside the womb that most babies are extremely disgruntled by being changed.

furry hat

Babies need six to ten vests. Some come in wool, but this can irritate a baby's skin and lead to overheating even in cold areas as babies are usually inside in nasty weather. You'll need cotton for the summer.

Sunhat

Tiny babies could have three or four cotton nighties so it's easier to change their nappies without fuss. After a couple of weeks to a month those little all-in-one suits are good, but make sure they're always a bit bigger than your baby as babies grow quickly.

Expensive flouncy outfits should be left to the relatives and friends to buy: they're such a hassle for babies at this age, who throw up on them anyway.

You'll need three to ten bibs, depending on how dribbly your baby is – once babies start to teethe they seem to dribble a lot. Towelling bibs are good; plastic-backed ones can become a bit humid underneath. Tea towels, muslins and cloth nappies make excellent substitutes (and are good for wiping up spills as well).

Winter babies will need warm clothes and a warm polar fleece or woolly hat, extra layers and bootees. In summer they will definitely need a sunhat (and baby sunscreen lotion) wherever they live. Get a sunhat that really does shade the face and neck. Babies sometimes become fascinated by a hat on their head. If everyone else in the group wears one, and the baby is given something else interesting to distract them, hat-staying-on may be more achievable. Ideally go for hats such as soft cotton ones without nylon-sewn labels so they're not itchy or uncomfortable.

CLOTHES SIZES

Clothes for babies are usually labelled in sizes of 3- or 6- month leaps, say "0–3 months" or "12–18 months" up to the age of 2. Don't buy clothes labelled "Newborn" 'cos they'll have grown out of them in a blink of an eye. Clothes for premmie babies are labelled as "Tiny Baby" or "Early Baby" or by the weight. For all-in-ones there is often an indication of length so that you can be sure there's enough kicking space for your baby's growing legs and feet. After that, kids' clothing is marked in yearly stages up to age 14. And some European clothes have sizes such as "116". Ask for help or move to Milan, darling.

Brands vary a lot with their sizes: some are generous and some are not. A kid aged 2 may be into a "Age 3" regardless of whether the kid is small, average or big for their age.

You can store sales and charity shop bargains in bags or boxes marked "Age 2", "Age 3" and so on.

for a toddler

Clothes get dirty now that the kid is on the move so you'll need lots of tough outfits. They should be easy to get out of for using the loo and so that the child can start to dress themselves. Long skirts or dresses on a girl will restrict their ability to learn physical skills such as climbing ladders or running.

It's nearly always good to buy the next size up so your kid's clothes will be comfy and not too tight, and they can wear them a bit longer. Shoes should be fitted at a children's shoe shop or department store. Kids don't need a proper pair until they're walking steadily outside, and even then they should go barefooted often for their development.

You'll work out the rest as you go along.

Dummies and Thumbs

Man, those little creatures like to suck. It calms them and they make cute noises like Maggie Simpson. But enough about businessmen with cigars.

Some people are very stern about dummies (and some of the sternest end up using them). Some want to use a dummy but the baby spits it out every time. Others never feel the need. Some parents prefer their kids to suck their thumb and then realize that there can be serious teeth misalignment, resulting in eating or speech problems. Other people say Praise Be the Dummy and the Thumb for Yea, Verily, a parent gets a better night's sleep. Dummies and thumbs (or fingers) are certainly not newfangled ideas: both have been used for generations.

Dummies (or "soothers")

Good points about dummies
- ★ Most babies love them.
- ★ They will temporarily soothe an upset baby unless they're hungry or have a shockingly irritating nappy.
- ★ They can help solve a sleep problem.

The trouble with dummies
- ★ Using them in the first month or so can confuse a baby learning to suck from the nipple in the right way.
- ★ They cost money.
- ★ They deteriorate.
- ★ They get lost.
- ★ You usually need a few to rotate.
- ★ If a baby can't replace their own dummy, they'll cry until you come and do it about 94 times in the night. (This is a very good moment to give it up: one or two nights of fussing and it's over, otherwise it's weeks of getting up those 94 times to pop the dummy in again.)
- ★ Dummies are addictive.
- ★ When the kid has a cold and they want to suck on their dummy, they can't breathe.
- ★ They can "buck" and misalign teeth, especially the longer they're used.
- ★ If used a lot, they deprive a baby of time to learn to feel with their mouth, speak and sing.
- ★ They need to be sterilized.

Using dummies
Don't use dummies:
- ★ to shut a child up instead of trying to find out what's wrong
- ★ unless they're going to sleep
- ★ if the child always spits it out.

Dummies need to be:

★ latex-free (in case of allergies) and for the right age – see your pharmacist

★ sterilized regularly (after your kid gets bigger and you see what else goes into their mouth you probably won't be quite as rigorous with sterilizing – but, still, sticking it in your own mouth is amazingly NOT, technically, sterilizing)

★ checked regularly for nicks, cuts, tears and any other damage – throw out any damaged ones

★ rotated – always have a few spares and one or two in the baby or toddler bag or your handbag in a clean container with a lid.

Getting rid of the dummy

Here's some advice from parents who responded to the survey undertaken for this book. You'll need to match a suggestion to the personality and sensitivity of your kid or gently experiment.

★ Either give the dummy up when the baby is young enough to not be able to put it in themselves, or wait until the child can participate in the decision to stop, so it's not traumatic.

★ Don't try to do it when a new baby comes along and needs a dummy.

★ Leave it out for Santa, the Easter Bunny or the Dummy Fairy to take. Something appropriate will be left in its place – a present maybe.

★ Give it up on an important birthday: explain that the Birthday Dummy Fairy will come.

★ Post it to a newer little baby who needs a dummy.

★ Don't tell the child it's wrong to like the dummy, just that older kids don't have dummies and they should let you know when they're old enough not to have one. Older siblings, cousins or friends can help by saying they don't use one now, but they mustn't ridicule the littlie: get them to just set a non-critical, matter-of-fact example, maybe even saying they missed theirs for a few minutes on the first night they didn't have it, but then they forgot about it.

★ Say "You're a big girl now" or "You're such a big boy", and have a discussion about getting older, then ask them if they're ready to give the dummy up themselves. (Some children will just announce that in that case they most certainly are not big, thank you.)

★ A ceremonial throwing in the bin is good – but you must be firm and not go backwards by admitting you can buy new ones at the chemist.

★ Pretend you've left the dummy at home, at the holiday place or at a friend's, or that it's lost. Be very sympathetic but positive about not having a dummy any more.

★ Safety-pin the dummy to a teddy or dolly who needs it more than they do that night and the next, and then teddy or dolly can lose their dummy.

★ Cut the dummy using down strictly to only sleeptimes in the cot, then to only night-time, and then go cold turkey.

★ Introduce another aspect to the sleep ritual (such as a special sleep toy) before you take the dummy away.

★ Let the child choose when to swap their dummy for a new toy they really want: then it's their decision.

★ Get up early together and give the dummy to the refuse collectors: you can watch them go away in the big truck and then have a special breakfast to celebrate getting older.

★ Cut down to one or two dummies, then "accidentally" drop the last one in the toilet.

★ Plant the dummy in the garden to see if a dummy tree grows.

★ Pierce the dummy – a large hole means it won't be satisfying any more (but make sure bits can't break off and become a choking hazard).

I have to say a lot of kids will see through any ruses. For the sort of child who's likely to say "Well, why don't we buy one with my credit card on the Internet?", the direct bribery approach is best.

This was the worst suggestion I've EVER heard: "The Dummy Monster took it away". It almost made *me* cry.

Many parents said to let the child go until they decide – which they sometimes do to save embarrassment on sleep-overs.

Raggies, Blankies and Other comfort items

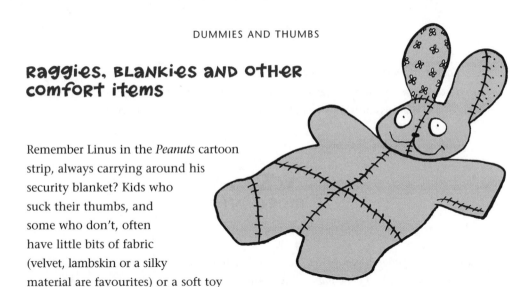

Remember Linus in the *Peanuts* cartoon strip, always carrying around his security blanket? Kids who suck their thumbs, and some who don't, often have little bits of fabric (velvet, lambskin or a silky material are favourites) or a soft toy to stroke while they're sucking – part of the comfort ritual. It's always a good idea to rotate a few pieces so they don't get too filthy and there's one on the go while another's in the wash. And keep a spare in the baby bag in case one is flung out the window of the car.

It's usually tough for everyone to give up a comfort object and a dummy or thumb sucking at the same time. You will probably need to have a programme of cutting down, then eliminating, the comfort object, following some of the suggestions for getting rid of a dummy, before you can start tackling the thumb sucking. (I know a grown woman who still sucks her thumb and rubs a piece of fabric – but not when she's on a first date.)

Thumb sucking

Thumb (or, less commonly, finger) sucking is certainly cheaper than buying dummies, but you can't throw away a thumb and know the habit has stopped, and it's more likely to cause buck or misaligned teeth. This situation is obviously more serious when permanent teeth come in (at 6 or 7 years of age). Most parents use a gradual, conscious cutting down and rewards system for stopping the thumb sucking. Daytime stopping is largely a matter of keeping the hands busy and night-time will need some new comfort rituals or objects.

Apart from gently taking the thumb out if it creeps in when the kid's asleep, many people suggest something bitter tasting on it to break the habit before adult teeth come in, with an extra-special reward given when the habit stops. This is a bit too much like a punishment rather than an encouragement and support: it's probably best to give it a miss and skip straight to help, reassurance and a bribe.

more info

Many of the general parenting websites listed in "In the Beginning" and "Your Support Team" in *Part One: Babies* have hints and tips on how to eliminate dummies and thumb or finger sucking. And if you really want to get freaked out go to **thumb-suckingadults.com** for pictures and lots more. Actually, don't.

Little Thumb
by Wanda Dionne, Pelican, 2001
Kids' book of rhyming reasons why a thumb really shouldn't go into your mouth.

teeth

Some kids are even born with weeny teeth, but the majority have their first couple start to come through between about the age of 6 and 10 months. They usually get the teeth at the front first, often at the bottom, and then the rest are "filled in" over the

following months. These first ones are sometimes called "milk teeth". There is a diagram in your child's "red book" for dating the appearance of teeth, and you can ask your dentist if you want to know the usual order, and what a lateral incisor is.

aargh

bib

Generally a kid has enough teeth for a good chew by the time they're 1 year to 18 months old, and all their teeth by the time they're 2 and a half to 3: the full mouth is about twenty teeth. (Eventually, with the second, or permanent, teeth, the kid will probably have thirty-two.)

WHat aRe tHe symptoms of teetHiNg?

Sometimes a baby rubs their gum, cries or is cranky from the pain of the teeth coming through. The following symptoms are not recognized as teething related by baby experts but are often attributed to it by parents: drooling, red cheeks, a runny nose, fever, nappy rash, sleep disturbance. The gum will often look red, then you'll see a bit of white poking through and suddenly there's a whole tooth. Each tooth that comes through may cause the baby to be cross and feel pain or they may hardly notice.

What can you do?

Explain soothingly to your baby what's happening: even if they can't grasp everything they will feel reassured. Give them lots of cuddles and perhaps rub their gum gently with your finger. Giving babies frozen things or ice to bite on can be too harsh and freeze the tissues in the mouth. Mostly kids want to chew on something, whether it's really cold or not, which is why rusks (like tiny, hard breadsticks) are popular: check that any you buy are sugar and salt free. Give them teething rings from the chemist that can be refrigerated (but don't freeze them). Sucking on a dummy also often helps the pain. This can be a good time to start your baby learning to sip from a spouty cup because babies find biting on the spout, like biting on a rusk, gives them some relief.

Teething gel, which is supposed to numb the gum, is not recommended by a lot of doctors because it gets sucked off quickly. You can give a baby painkiller if the pain seems really bad.

Prepare to have the usual sleep routine messed up as your baby deals with the new feelings of pain and soreness. They can find it hard to resettle themselves on the nights when a tooth is about to appear.

Looking after teeth

The main thing is not to give any sweetened drinks or undiluted fruit juice (it's very acidic so dilute it 1:1 with water), or to let babies or older kids suck on bottles of milk or juice for ages, particularly at night. All these things almost guarantee decay and, in the worst-case scenario, the unhappy prospect of a general anaesthetic and the pulling out of lots of milk teeth before kids get their permanent ones. It's best to give a bottle of milk before bed, then clean their teeth. Any daytime drag-around drinks or night-time sips should be water. Breastfed babies can also have their teeth wiped or brushed after the last feed of the day. Avoid sweetened medicines, but if you have one prescribed with sugar give it before teeth-cleaning time. Make dessert and treats a "sometimes" thing, not an everyday or always-after-dinner thing.

Some kids genetically have "strong teeth" or ones that are shaped better to avoid decay, but they will still need to take care of them; others may have to work harder to get the same protection with cleaning. When the teeth arrive, take the kid to the dentist once or twice a year.

Cleaning teeth

Kids are supposed to have their teeth brushed twice a day – it's most convenient after brekkie and after dinner. Very sugary or acidic drinks, including fresh unsweetened citrus fruit slices and juices, as well as sugary foods, can create an acidic environment in the mouth that makes tooth enamel very vulnerable to wear and tear. So, keep these to a minimum and wait an hour after they've been eating or drinking them before brushing your kids' teeth. For the very early baby days dentists recommend using a soft cloth – but if your baby has a strong gag reflex you'll have to be careful. See if your chemist can find you a tiny brush. There are baby and toddler toothbrushes and toddler toothpastes.

bad, BAD toothbrush

Ask your dentist or chemist what's appropriate for your kid in the way of fluoride: it will vary depending on the fluoride they're already getting from the water supply.

At first you can do the teeth cleaning, making sure you get to every surface. When your child is a toddler, and if you can afford it, introduce a battery-operated toothbrush – the kid can do more themselves and get more surfaces done properly before you give a final once-over. Babies and kids should only have a tiny amount of toothpaste for each cleaning. It's usually described as no more than the size of a pea (your guess is as good as mine as peas vary in size – the ones under my mattress do anyway): ask your dentist. Put a mirror where the kid can see it – it will guarantee more time spent cleaning the teeth. Kids aren't able to clean their own teeth thoroughly until they're about 10.

going to the dentist

Explain why we need to visit the dentist (because they help us look after our teeth, not so we can enjoy the blindingly painful razzle-dazzle of root canal work). Practise at home or at child care, especially opening the mouth and letting someone look inside, being on a big chair that goes up and down (pretend or visit someone with one of those TV-watching recliners the size of an aircraft carrier and shine a light in). Take your kid with you a couple of times when you visit your dentist – just for cheery check-ups, not to any sessions where actual work or drilling is done. They can lie on your lap and let the dentist look in their mouth at the end of the visit as practice.

You can tell your kid just before you take them or that morning so there's no time for some idiot to scare them about the dentist. Don't ever use the dentist as a threat ("You can't have any lollies because you'll get holes in your teeth and the dentist will have to drill your teeth and it hurts"). If your kid is apprehensive, find a dentist who specializes in children and has a drawcard such as a fish tank in the waiting room or special things to look at in the surgery, and plan to come back a couple of times if your kid refuses to open their mouth. (See "More Info" at the end of the this chapter for a kids' book about going to the dentist.)

TEETH ON THE MOVE

Some teeth may naturally grow in odd spaces or at different angles: check with a dentist if you're concerned. Little teeth are sometimes moved by dummy or thumb sucking. In some cases this makes a difference to chewing or speech. The teeth will often travel back slowly to the right position if the habit is broken (do this gently – see the previous chapter, "Dummies and Thumbs").

Your dentist will probably have all manner of pamphlets, free toothbrushes and other paraphernalia tucked away in the cupboard.

Later: Losing teeth

The milk teeth begin to drop out when kids are about 6 years old. Check with other parents to see what the going rate is with the Tooth Fairy. If a baby tooth is knocked out, don't worry about replacing it, but see a dentist as soon as you can to check that it's all out and there are no complications. When your child is older, get a fitted mouth guard for sports.

more info

Children's teeth and their care seem to occupy small corners of much larger websites devoted either to dental care as a whole (**www.dentalhealth.org.uk**), health in general (www.nhsdirect.nhs.uk), or baby and parenting (**www.babycentre.co.uk**). It can take a bit of time to find what you want to know, but the parenting ones often allow you to ask questions in forums.

Harry and the Dinosaurs Say "Raahh!"
by Ian Whybrow, Puffin, 2003
A boy and his dinosaurs go to the dentist and open wide. More fun than instructive but nicely diverting.

food

You might be an expert whizzer in the kitchen already, able to conjure up a family supper from some stale cumin, an artichoke and half a packet of freeze-dried mackerel. Or you might be serving a toddler truffle-oil bavarois of nutkin fern imported directly from a family-run vineyard in Sardinia. On the other hand you might be shocked – *shocked* – to find that not all food comes from McDonalds or, after kettle involvement, from a polystyrene cup. Even if you're a gourmet dinner-party

Behold, the fish finger

And yonder lies the mango yoghurt

bib

cook, you might have no idea how to feed a family with those pesky nutrient thingies. This chapter aims to soothe you as effectively as half a packet of chocolate HobNobs. (You didn't think I was going to get through a book without mentioning *them*, did you?)

cooking for your baby and toddler

Most people start off having to learn everything about feeding babies and toddlers and so they begin with lots of books, worry about it all the time, compare notes with other parents, freeze little ice cubes of colour-coordinated puréed things, and then a few months later find the kid is eating whatever the grown-up department is having that night and the books are propping up the wobbly end of the kitchen table.

It's in your interest to introduce a wide range of food to your baby and toddler from the get-go, but there's never any guarantee this will result in a child who will eat everything (even tripe-flavoured spinach sticks). Lots of babies love all they're given and then gradually get sterner about the whole caper. (You may be interested in the earlier chapters on eating in the babies and toddlers parts of the book.)

Do ask your health visitor or GP for the latest nutritional guidelines. Lots of grandparents and older books recommend using honey to sweeten things, but dentists and some nutritionists disagree with this – it must be awfully rare, but honey *can* be a cause of botulism in babies – so remember that "expert" advice changes over time, especially in this area. (Which is another reason not to worry too much: I mean, if they don't know what they're doing, why should you?)

Several books are given in "More Info" at the end of this chapter but be beware of child-

carrot rocket

centred cookbooks that are full of pictures of children's food shaped into fishes with carroty fins, and boats with tuna flags – you know the sort of thing. (Miriam Stoppard's book *First Foods* has Merry Meatball Pony and Liver Log Cabin.) This way lies MADNESS, I tell you. Plus, frankly, they're written by aliens.

> *"I told my 3-year-old daughter that mung bean shoots were called mung bean lollies. She loves them."* AHEM, ANONYMOUS AUTHOR

DRiNKS

Commercial fizzy drinks, colas, lemonades and other flavoured drinks that come with bubbles in cans and bottles are a bit of a disaster for little kids. Along with undiluted fruit juices, they're the largest cause of tooth decay and a big contributor to children being over a healthy weight. They have also been implicated in other health issues, which is hardly surprising when you find out there is the equivalent of several tea-spoons of sugar in most of them. Also, it's not a good idea to give little kids energy drinks or colas, with stimulants such as caffeine or guarana.

So avoid fizzy drinks whenever you can – if your kid doesn't have them as a habit, they won't ask for them all the time unless they're watching TV ads for them. Milk, water, and fresh fruit juice diluted 1:1 with water are much better for kids than expensive soft drinks. Fizzy drinks for special occasions can be the non-sugar ver-sions. Kids won't know the difference!

If a toddler has constant access to water in, say, a little pop-up-top bottle that can be taken on travels and left on the table or the floor during playtimes, or maybe from a filter system or a cold tap, they should be getting enough fluids on a self-serve basis. Refill com-mercial water bottles with tap water – it's a lot cheaper! Milk and other drinks can also be offered through the day. (Horlicks or cocoa mixed with other malted drinks may be a good source of iron: check the labels for what else is in there, possibly lots of sugar.) If a child is constipated, drinking more water may help.

cooking for the family

Many mums (and some dads) come from the full-time workforce to full-time or part-time parenthood and house executeering (I don't know what that means but clearly the word "housewifery" is out of the question). People are sometimes amazed to find that cooking becomes fun – or at least one of the more creative and rewarding parts of homemaking life. You may find you have time for experiments and waiting for things to rise, cook or marinate – at least once in a while. And in all but the most alarming cases, you get to eat your mistakes.

Of course you may still hate cooking, but even so the next few years are going to be a lot more pleasant if you learn ways to get it done efficiently. From now on money will probably be tighter than usual, unless you've just cracked onto Prince Harry, so eating in may be your only option most of the time.

My cooking skills rivalled those of an enraged marmoset before I was pregnant. With the help of some books I am now approaching snappy chimp status. Have a rummage about in "More Info" at the end of this chapter to find a basic Brit bible to suit your cooking style, whether or not you enjoy somebody's attitude (or TV cooking show!). If you're just starting out, begin with some family classics and feel-good guaranteed results, such as Nigella's banana cake. Don't try to do a Moroccan banquet for visitors or you'll end up hurling the hummus at them.

food allergies and intolerances

Many children have allergies or intolerances to various foods, which can include milk, wheat, peanuts, strawberries and oranges. Allergies are relatively rare and many children grow out of them or turn out to have been misdiagnosed. An allergy is a reaction by the immune system against something, such as a food, that most people don't have a problem with. Children usually don't grow out of an allergy that causes a violent reaction. You'll probably start with suspicions and instincts or the food allergy will suddenly become obvious because of a reaction.

Food intolerances arise when the body is unable to process a certain kind of food because of, say, enzymes not working properly to break down the sugar (lactose) in milk (this intolerance is often avoided by having kids use soya, rice or oat milk, goat's yoghurt and other lactose-free stuff; some lactose intolerant kids can eat normal yoghurt – with live cultures – with no problems). Some babies are unable to process the lactose in breast milk and need to go on a soya-based formula or alternate breast and bottle for a period recommended by their GP – but this is rare and usually temporary.

Your doctor will help you isolate an allergy or intolerance. It's very important to have your suspicions professionally confirmed. Support groups on the Internet and specialized books can help you manage any lasting problem. Unfortunately some people are airy-fairy and dismissive of allergies and may try to give your children the wrong food in the belief that you or your child is just fussy – you will need to explain the allergy and what's required calmly and firmly to the child as well as to others looking after your kid or running a party.

Children should not be given peanuts until they are over 4 years old (some people say 5), and then watched carefully for a reaction. Any violent reaction that involves breathing difficulties means you need to call an ambulance immediately – that's anaphylactic shock. Other substances that can cause anaphylactic shock include eggs and shellfish (and latex on skin contact).

See "More Info" at the end of this chapter for books on the effects of food, and cooking for children with allergies and food intolerances.

> *"My kid screamed and was in pain for the first 18 months of his life. We were told he had really bad wind and colic. Finally my doctor suggested we try an elimination diet. He's now great unless he eats something on the no-go list, when he gets stomach cramps, diarrhoea, cries a lot and often gets hyper and uncontrollable."* DANI

veGeTaRiaN aND veGaN KiDs

Many vegetarian parents allow their young children to eat meat and many vegan parents give their kids meat, dairy products and eggs because they see this as the best way for their kids to grow and develop in the early years. Many will seek out organic meats, free-range eggs and other products that are aligned to their philosophy. Rather than impose their beliefs, these parents are usually content to allow their kids to make up their own mind later about whether or when to become a vegetarian or a vegan, which is most likely to happen in the teenage years.

Any form of vegetarian or vegan diet you are on during pregnancy and breastfeeding, or you are giving your baby or children, needs to be okayed by an independent nutritionist who knows your individual needs. A paediatric nutritionist or a dietician at your nearest hospital or health centre will help you make sure you're meeting the special needs of babies and kids.

Vegetarian kids

Vegetarian children have very special needs. Because vegetarian food is high in fibre, kids often feel full before they've had enough nutrients and calories. This can mean that they're smaller than they would otherwise be and don't fulfil their growth and brain potential. They need energy-dense foods as well, such as dairy products, fruit, chopped nuts (but not peanuts before 4), seeds, avocado, protein such as eggs, and soya products. They will also need special care to get iron, calcium, fat and nutrients such as B_{12} and zinc. See "More Info" at the end of this chapter for recipe books for vegetarians.

Should kids be vegans?

Of all the children whose families insist its members follow strict dietary rules, vegan kids are the most at risk of damage or deficiency. Avoid any vegan websites and books that simply apply the principles of adult veganism to children as this is dangerous. Many vegan websites have suggested diets for pregnant and lactating women and for babies and kids, but don't forget to check these with an independent nutritionist who can adjust them to you and your child's special needs.

If you are very committed to being a vegan, you will need to take great care during your pregnancy and entire period of breastfeeding to ensure that your intake of various nutrients is enough for your baby to thrive. Babies who aren't breastfed *must* be given a commercial baby milk formula based on cow or soy milk, not soya milk, rice milk or some combination you mix yourself.

Vegans need to address the very real risk of a vitamin B_{12} deficiency in a foetus or a breastfed baby, and in vegan children. A B_{12} deficiency causes serious damage to mental and neural development. It's probably safest for pregnant and breastfeeding vegans to take a daily supplement that contains B_{12} as any B_{12} stores are rapidly used up. Although many vegan writings on diet suggest that B_{12} is in many foods, this is not always the case. Vitamin B_{12}-fortified soya milk is a good source, but other often-recommended foods such as mushrooms don't always contain absorbable B_{12}. Make sure you are getting the recommended daily dose for you and your baby.

Children on a vegan diet who appear well ("His height and weight are okay according to the charts, and he's happy") can in fact be deficient in iron, vitamins, calcium and calories, and not be as tall or as heavy as they would be otherwise. Vegan babies, toddlers and children who fill up on bran, grains and other high-fibre items will feel full but are not growing to their full potential, physically and mentally. To be honest, even among committed vegans themselves, only a minuscule minority of people advocate veganism for babies and small children and I could find very little detailed information about how to achieve optimum health for them on such a diet, even on vegan websites.

"UNDERWEIGHT" AND "OVERWEIGHT" KIDS

Babies need those roly-poly thighs and "rolls": they are not too fat. Many toddlers grow into a rangier shape, losing their "baby fat", while others maintain that cute sticky-out tummy. Remember that genetically your child may not be like you, your partner or any of your other children. They may resemble Great-Uncle Feargal and be just the shape they are meant to be. One of the greatest and most useful gifts you can give your child is to lead by example and help them maintain a healthy body image. Try not to use terms or voice tones that carry a sense of disapproval or judgement to describe your body, their body or anyone else's. If you say "I'm so fat" or "He's so scrawny", your kid will learn to think badly of themselves, whatever they look like.

Underweight kids, especially babies, need their problem corrected quickly so they can continue to thrive. See your GP straight away if your child is losing weight – kids in the under-5 age group should not consistently lose weight unless they are above their healthy weight. Some will not have a buffer zone of adorable extra chub and observable weight loss is often a sign of illness. Having said that, try not to panic about it – kids will go up and down a little all the time and you don't need to weigh them. Just know them well so you'll notice a big change. (Toddlers who are fussy eaters can go for days on a cheese stick and glasses of milk. I think they secretly do it to mock us.) If you are really worried, make sure you are referred to a specialist child nutritionist.

Children should not be fed too much fast or junk food (as opposed to fresh, home-cooked food) because it can be very filling, with few nutrients, and full of salt, sugar and saturated fats. Too much salt isn't good for the health of babies and toddlers in the short or long term; they're not able to process or get rid of it it as efficiently as adults can. It's okay to add a pinch of salt when cooking a whole family meal or a cake, but it's not okay to add it to, or sprinkle salt on, kids' food.

Kids who are above their average weight need to continue to eat a filling, nutritious diet and, most importantly, exercise each day. The diagnosis of "over-weight" must not be made by a relative or parent who thinks everyone should look "thin", but by a paediatrician. Kids who are in a healthy weight range should never be deprived of full-fat foods. (Low-fat foods are almost always for adults, unless prescribed by a paediatric dietician.) It can be hard to change a whole family's habits, but a nutritionist can help you. Ask your GP for a referral to find out what your child needs and the easiest way to achieve it.

See also the "Being Active" chapter coming up soon.

kitCHeN safety

As well as generally making your house safe, you'll need to look hard at the safety of your kitchen, particularly once your kid is able to walk and climb and is ready to enjoy "helping" you to cook and wash up (see the "Home Safety" chapter for what to do with sharp knives and poisonous cleaning liquids and powders).

Teach kids from the earliest age about hobs and ovens being hot. But don't expect small children to remember this applies every time – they've seen you touch or clean

---

THINGS KIDS SHOULDN'T DO IN THE KITCHEN
(UNTIL THEY'RE WELL TRAINED, SUPERVISED AND AT LEAST 8)

* Stir hot things.

* Go near the hob.

* Put things into or take things out of the oven.

* Operate any electrical appliance, including the toaster.

* Taste things without direct permission (it could be chilli powder).

---

a cold hob and oven. They also can't necessarily make the connection that somebody else's cooker might sometimes be hot too. Perhaps you can institute a rule that kids have to have their hands behind their back when looking at the hotplates or through the glass door of the oven, or when a cake mixer is going, for example. Balance this taboo with lots of things they *can* touch, pour, stir and measure.

Don't let children near an urn, a coffee maker (or any other heating appliance with those child-height easy-push taps!), a kettle or some other stay-hot device, and be vigilant when anything is on the cooker. And make sure there are no dangling electric cords. Most children's scalds are from hot liquids such as tea, coffee and water and usually on the hands, or on the face and chest when they pull a container down on themselves. Crawlers and toddlers are at special risk.

If you have a really inquisitive toddler and a dangerously designed kitchen, try cooking during their sleeptime and serving something cold or warmed up in a microwave oven (we'll get to the dangers of microwaves) in the evening when you can't be as vigilant because of everything else going on.

The cooker

Always turn saucepan and frying-pan handles away from the front of the stove so they can't be grabbed or knocked. Avoid cooking that's likely to cause burns or a fire. Why risk boiling things in oil? Chips can be done in the oven on trays brushed with oil. If your kitchen is badly designed or your child is really into everything, check out safety guards for cooker available from hardware or children's shops. These prevent toddlers from pulling things down on themselves.

If you are cooking on the hob and have to leave the kitchen, turn it off. It's better to be delayed than on fire. (What a splendid motto.)

Ovens

A microwave oven will heat random bits of the food to scalding temperature, yet often leave the container cool to the touch, so anything cooked or warmed in a microwave must be thoroughly stirred, rested, cooled and tested before being given to children. Don't put glass bottles in a microwave: they can break. Some microwave ovens heat more strongly and more quickly than others so be careful with unfamiliar ones.

If your ordinary oven is hot to the touch when it's on, try to rig up some sort of barrier, such as a bit of a playpen, so that the oven is out of bounds then. With food cooked in either kind of oven, be careful when taking lids off as steam can scald severely.

Water

Kids love splashing about in the sink and this can sometimes incidentally even be helpful with the washing up. Start the little ones on a low stool or a chair in front of a sink full of plastic things and lots of suds, and don't worry about splashes unless they're slippery. Always stay in the room with them when water is involved. If children visit or live in your house, make sure the hot-water service has been adjusted so the maximum possible temperature is 50 degrees Celsius so that it takes longer for the water to scald. (Schools and child-care centres are usually required to have their water set to 45 degrees.)

moRe iNfo

COOKING FOR YOUR BABY AND TODDLER

Annabel Karmel's New Complete Baby and Toddler Meal Planner
by Annabel Karmel, Ebury, 2008
The reigning queen of child feeding, Ms Karmel's book is a beautifully designed, cartoon-studded one-stop shop for knowing about vitamins and minerals, first foods and family eating. Little icons show which things you can freeze, and by circling a smiley or frowny face provided after each recipe title, you can record whether your child liked it or not. (But remember that sometimes a food has to be offered up to 9 times before a toddler gives in, agrees it's edible and loves it.) Meal planners would send some people bonkers, others may find a schedule useful, especially in the early days.

Baby and Toddler Cookbook
by Rachael Anne Hill, Ryland Peters and Small, 2008
Cheerful book with photos of the food as well as kids eating it that you could use as propaganda: "Look! This big boy's loving it!C" Ms Hill is a cookbook veteran, and here she balances sweets and treats with savoury lunch and tea suggestions, and useful "finger foods" (read "mash-into-face foods") for beginners.

Babies and Toddlers Good Food (Australia Women's Weekly)
by Susan Tomnay (Ed), ACP, 2006
Common-sense recipes for 4 months to 4 years, with good suggestions for portable food

and snacks, as well as sensible ideas for adapting family meals.

COOKING FOR THE FAMILY

Complete Perfect Recipes
by David Herbert, Penguin, 2007

Oh Mr Herbert, marry me. Basic, simple, sensible modern classics and old-fave recipes for anything you're likely to want, one easy-to-read recipe per page, organized alphabetically and ranging from apple pie and Christmas pud through pesto to lemonade, tomato relish and zabaglione.

How to Eat: The Pleasures and Principles of Good Food
by Nigella Lawson, John Wiley, 2002

I love you too, Nigella! Another basic book with loads of ideas and info on techniques, and handy headings for parents about feeding babies and small children, cooking in advance, quick food and cooking for one or two. Written in a chatty but dignified style.

How to Be a Domestic Goddess: Baking and the Art of Comfort Cooking
by Nigella Lawson, Chatto and Windus, 2003

Excellent tongue-in-cheek title and a book full of baking recipes and ideas including a fabulous kids' section. Important asides come from experience: here is someone who cooks with as well as for children, and for the school fete – someone who knows that one batch of cupcakes can give you superparent status instantly. Full of comfort food for rainy days.

Jamie's Dinners
by Jamie Oliver, Penguin, 2006

The cheeky-chappie scooter-revving heart-throb has grown up into a family bloke whose exposure of the atrocious quality of school dinners in the UK actually changed government policy virtually overnight. Like many modern chefs, his emphasis on fresh, quality produce and a simpler, healthier style makes his recipes accessible and ideal for family life. His enthusiasm is genuine, although his "you're my mate" style may annoy some.

Real Fast Food
by Nigel Slater, Penguin, 2006

"Real Food" guru Slater gives you tons of ideas to sling together in less than thirty minutes. He's not too sniffy about using things like tinned fish either, so this book is handy for those times when you've completely forgotten that you were meant to cook dinner – and mop the kitchen floor, and empty the bin, and ... GODDAMMIT!

The Australian Women's Weekly series of cookbooks
Australian Consolidated Press, Aust.

The shelves are chock-a-block with these low-priced cookbooks, which have every possible permutation from budget recipes (make that mince go FURTHER!) to lip-pursingly colourful birthday cakes, bikkies, roasts, pasta, low fat, big fatty fat, you name it. The bonus: the recipes are almost always literally "tried and true" – made with easily found ingredients and tested in the *Women's Weekly*'s Own Kitchen, which I am imagining does not have a toddler on the floor trying to poke a plastic giraffe into their ear.

FOOD ALLERGIES AND INTOLERANCES

The Allergy-Free Cookbook
by Alice Sherwood, Dorling Kindersley, 2007

This popular family cookbook is handy for feeding everybody; allergy-free folk won't know the difference, especially when it comes to chocolate cake. Symbols show which of the "Big Four" common culprits are avoided in each recipe (gluten, diary, nuts and eggs).

www.eatwell.gov.uk/healthissues/foodintolerance/

UK Government site with a fantastically comprehensive list of fact sheets covering all sorts of allergies and intolerances, info on where to have an allergy test, and shopping hints.

www.fedupwithfoodadditives.info

Australian author Sue Dengate's website helps parents with newsletters and updates on food additives and their effects, and by displaying a recommended diet for children whose behaviour and health may be affected by additives – but don't forget it's important to get a professional diagnosis and recommendations on your child's individual problem.

www.foodsmatter.com

Foods Matter magazine's UK site for people with food allergies and intolerances has info on common problems and natural and medical treatments, links, an archive of research studies and articles suggested reading and recipes, including cookbooks by the site's editor.

www.foodallergy.org
Has lots of useful info about many kinds of allergies and their effects, how to cope with them, recent relevant research, strategies for school and social life, food alerts (mainly relevant to the US) and allergy-free recipes, including a milk-free, egg-free cake.

allergies.about.com
It's a US central site providing links to sites on different allergies, cross-referenced with other common problems such as asthma: includes dust mites, mould, peanuts, cats, lactose and many more. (The prayer link isn't for people allergic to prayers. It's for people who think prayer might help.)

VEGETARIAN KIDS

While recommending some more info, it's important to acknowledge that it can be very hard to give small kids what they need on a vegetarian diet. I admire the parents who do the required lots of research about the special needs of kids on a veg diet, rather than just cutting out meat and hoping for the best, which can result in serious health deficiencies. This book does not recommend a vegan diet as I believe it's not adequate for children's physical growth and brain development. Don't write in if you think otherwise, we'll just have to agree to disagree.

Raising Vegetarian Children: A Guide to Good Health and Family Harmony
by Joanne Stepaniak and Vesanto Melina, McGraw-Hill Contemporary, 2002
Addresses the social and emotional aspects of vegetarianism, whether you're a parent concerned with imposing your decision on a baby, or head of a meat-eating household with a vegetarian child. Contains nutritional information and recipes.

www.vegetarian.co.uk
Newsy site with info on how to source vegetarian food and cosmetic products, holidays, clothing and the like. Various veggie blogs too.

www.bbc.co.uk/food/vegetarian_and_vegan/children
This site carries a round-up of where a vegetarian diet falls short and how you can supplement it to make sure your children are getting what they need. It's important to remember that supplements (such as a vitamin and mineral tablet) are not absorbed as easily by the body as with food itself.

HeaLtH

When people used to tell me that they couldn't come to work because their kid was ill, I thought that was nice of them to stay home with their kid. I imagined a cherub sitting up in bed in a pair of freshly ironed pyjamas, quietly doing a jigsaw puzzle on a tray, with a box of tissues and a small posy of pansies in a short, bulbous vase on the bedside table.

Say 'aaarrgh!'

For some reason I didn't imagine a kid projectile vomiting over 24 surfaces just after you'd put new sheets on the bed; the shock of feeling your child's forehead and it almost burning your fingers; the effect of three nights of randomly broken sleep on a parent trying to make smart decisions about health care; the listless misery of a child who doesn't understand why they feel bad; the fundamental need of a sick child to have their parent in sight at all times. I was, quite frankly, not even in the vicinity of a clue.

Kids get ill. It doesn't mean they're unhealthy or sickly; it's how they build up their immune system. And kids have accidents. So this chapter will tell you about injuries and first-aid kit essentials as well as about lots of common complaints and their treatment.

first aid

Going to a first-aid course and regularly practising is the only way to be proficient at stuff such as resuscitation. The St John Ambulance Association and the Red Cross both have courses specific to children as well as general lessons. These can be run as a one-off at a playgroup, child-care centre or school at a minimal charge if there are several participants. See the "More Info" section at the end of this chapter for contact details.

You should know how to:
* revive a child
* treat a broken bone until you get to a doctor or the ambulance comes
* get a child away from an electrical charge without being injured or knocked out yourself

★ recognize when you can move an injured child and when you shouldn't

★ recognize and treat clinical shock.

First-aid kit

Keep a first-aid kit anywhere the child often goes – home, car, grandparents' house and so on – and always out of their reach. Safety experts recommend you store your home first-aid kit 1.5m off the ground in a locked cupboard but I don't know anyone who has such a thing. Just be as safe as you can – perhaps a plastic tool box with a child lock, on top of a high cupboard so adults need to stand on a chair to reach it, and there's no way a child can climb up. Make sure any medicines that need to be in the fridge are safely out of toddler or kid reach. Strictly observe dosages, use-by dates and doctor's instructions on the label.

A home first-aid kit should include the following.

★ **Painkiller:** you can get baby and kid versions of paracetamol and ibuprofen, but check with your doctor first about which to buy (see the "Painkillers: Paracetamol and Ibuprofen" box later in the chapter). Both may also be used to bring down a fever (but see the "Fever and High Temperature" section later in the chapter). Children shouldn't be given aspirin or soluble aspirin because of a slight chance of developing a serious illness called Reye's syndrome. Annoyingly children's painkiller medication often comes in heavy, dark brown glass or has a label all the way round and you can't tell if a bottle is nearly empty – so it's always good to have a spare. There are paracetamol tablets that are to be put up a baby's bottom so they work faster: frankly I wouldn't bother unless your doctor recommends them for a specific reason, such as liquid medicine would be vomited up.

★ **A medicine measuring cup, dropper and no-needle syringe:** for giving medicine.

★ **Cotton-wool balls or squares:** these are good for cleaning cuts or infected skin because they can be thrown away afterwards.

★ **Antiseptic cream or liquid:** lightly apply it to a cleaned cut or sore.

★ **Sterile adhesive strips, or sticking plasters:** use these for minor cuts and sores.

★ **Sterile gauze dressings:** these are useful for larger cuts and sore areas.

medicine dropper

Baby Paracetamol

POISONS INFORMATION

Ring NHS Direct on 0845 4647 (England & Wales) or NHS 24 on 08454 2424 24 (Scotland).

Put this number in your home first-aid kit, car first-aid kit and on the wall under your other emergency numbers. You will get immediate advice on whether there is a problem needing medical help.

Keep the container or packet of what you think your child may have swallowed with you, so you can tell the advice line, doctor, or hospital what ingredients were in the liquid or tablets. The unfamiliar or horrid taste may have deterred too much from being swallowed. Stay calm, as that's what your child needs most from you in this situation.

Ipecac syrup was used in the past to induce vomiting. It's now considered likely to do more harm than good. Don't do anything such as trying to induce vomiting unless advised by NHS Direct.

★ **Bandages:** you can wrap one firmly around, say, a big cut, and fasten.

★ **Waterproof tape:** to keep on bandages or eye patches.

★ **Optional thermometer:** many doctors now say decisions about whether to give paracetamol, or to go to the doctor, shouldn't rely on the level of temperature but on other symptoms (see the "Fever and High Temperature" section a few pages on). If you decide to keep a thermometer, the old-fashioned style with mercury is the most reliable; forehead strips the least so.

★ **Saline solution and an eyebath:** these are useful for washing eyes or getting something out of an eye.

★ **A wheat pack or a hot-water bottle:** these can be used warm, not hot, for sore ears or tummies.

★ **An ice pack:** these should always be wrapped in a tea towel or other fabric before being applied to bumps and bruises.

You might like to keep handy an illustrated first-aid book (see "More Info" at the end of this chapter). A steam vaporizer to place in your child's room at night to keep down sniffles and coughs is also useful.

CHOOSING a DOCTOR

You'll need to find a good local doctor called a GP (general practitioner), which can save you lots of worry. Ideally you'll be wanting a doctor who specializes in kids or lives in an area where there are lots of kids – they'll know what's "going around". See the second chapter, "Your Support Team", in *Part 1: Babies* for info on how to choose one.

There is nothing wrong with going to another GP for a second opinion or insisting on a referral to a specialist.

> *"I recommend that dads take the children to the doctor. The medical profession treat a sick child and the dad totally differently than if a woman presents with a sick child."* CHRIS, HOUSEHUSBAND

> *"Always have baby Panadol in the fridge."* ANONYMOUS

iNJURieS

When to see a doctor with an injury

See a doctor straight away if your child has:

- ★ concussion. Signs and symptoms following a head bang or injury include amnesia, headaches, floppiness, tiredness, difficulty concentrating (hospital policy before discharging a patient after a bad knock to the head is usually to watch them carefully for a few hours – a doctor may get you to do the same)
- ★ a severe cut or a deep wound
- ★ something inserted into an eye, ear or other body opening
- ★ a blistered burn larger than a pea.

Small injuries: DIY

The best remedies for minor accidents are antiseptic cream and perhaps an adhesive strip (for small cuts and very small burns), ice packs (for small bumps and bruises), sympathy and kissing it better.

WHEN TO CALL AN AMBULANCE WITH AN INJURY

Ring the general emergency number: 999.
Call an ambulance if your child has:

* ✱ been unconscious or is unconscious

* ✱ a convulsion (a fit)

* ✱ stopped breathing and needed or needs resuscitation

* ✱ a suspected injured neck or back (don't move the patient)

* ✱ a serious head injury

* ✱ a suspected broken bone – support it with your arm and hand or a pillow and keep the patient still until the ambulance arrives

* ✱ had an electric shock

* ✱ gone into clinical shock after a trauma (usually caused by bleeding or a burn) – a quiet child, perhaps with staring or glazed eyes, is probably in shock

* ✱ anaphylactic allergic shock – very rare and usually triggered by an insect sting, a drug or a food.

"Acknowledge that it does hurt instead of jollying them out of it. Be truthful: 'Oh, darling, I know it's really hurting a lot now, but it will start getting better and it will stop soon'. " JILL

BURNS aND SCaLDS

These first-aid steps for scalds and burns are based on standard advice. Move quickly and get through the list as fast as possible.

1 If there is a scald, whip off any wet clothing because the heat of the liquid can continue to burn; and any clothing around a burn unless the material is sticking to skin.

2 Immediately run cold water over the area. Use the nearest cold tap. Keep the burn area under running water for at least twenty minutes or until the ambulance arrives. This will help alleviate pain and stop the area burning deeper, and applies to all scalds and burns. Keep the child warm.

3 Call an ambulance as soon as the burn or scald is under running water or get someone else to if ✳ the burn area is bigger than the child's palm (about one percent of their body area) ✳ a serious burn is on the face or head ✳ the burn area is whitish and not hurting (signs of charring and nerve damage) ✳ the child is quiet despite a bad burn ✳ the burn was caused over some time (for example, a hand on a heater wasn't taken away immediately) ✳ you are really worried and the GP's surgery is closed or you can't leave the house quickly because you're, say, looking after a bunch of kids or your other child or baby is asleep.

Follow the instructions the ambulance service gives you over the phone while you wait for the paramedics to arrive.

4 Cover the area with a clean cotton or non-fluffy cloth, such as a non-flannelette pillowcase or a flat tea towel, not a towel: you don't want threads or fluff sticking to the wound. Don't use ice on the burn or put the child in a chilled bath. Don't put butter, oils or anything else on the burn – these will only have to be removed by paramedics, doctors or nurses, often painfully, so they can see the wound, and they don't have any beneficial effect.

5 Take the child to hospital or your nearest doctor. You'll need medical advice for anything more than a very small scald.

CHOKING

Choking risks include long, stringy things such as bacon rind, soft pliable foods such as a marshmallow, hard lollies and any object such as a shell or a whole nut that can act like a stopper, as well as a bit of food or small pieces of a Barbie doll. Choking kids can always do with three hefty blows in the middle of the back between the shoulder blades. If that doesn't dislodge the object, try to remove it gently with your fingers. Turning the baby or small child upside down can also work.

If the object doesn't come out, encourage the child to be calm and call an ambulance on 999. Follow the instructions the ambulance service gives you over the phone while you're waiting for the paramedics to arrive.

getting iLL

The first six to twelve months of major contact with other kids (siblings or kids at child care, nursery or school) means it's germ free-for-all. This is one of the reasons it's so hard for a parent to work outside the home during the child's early years, even if it's part-time. Luckily very few of the things kids are developing immunity against are going to kill them, especially in the UK where we have almost universal immunization and our hospital staff are all generally wonderful (even though our politicians don't give nearly enough money to hospitals, the filthy swine). Kids usually get ill suddenly, although after a while you might be able to recognize when they're "fighting off something".

When a kid gets ill their immune system works to develop antibodies to provide future protection. Healthy kids under 5 can pick up a minor viral infection, which they fight off without treatment, every couple of months (a head cold, being quiet and "off-colour" – meaning pale – or an unidentified rash might be clues). As well as that there are minor sniffles and assorted "tummy bugs" that kids tend to pick up and get rid of over a day or so here and there.

THE IMMUNE SYSTEM

The immune system recognizes and repels many viruses and bacteria you've had before, preventing you from getting sick again. Having an immune system in good shape helps kids recover more quickly. But even the best immune system won't stop all germs or prevent all illnesses.

Good immune system boosters:

* breastfeeding

* fresh air

* exercise

* enough protein and carbohydrates

* being calm and happy.

450

If your kid has a chronic or very serious illness, make sure you get all the medical opinions you can and insist on seeing a specialist with the widest possible experience in the area. Enquire about any and all services available to you, from accommodation if you've travelled a long distance to support groups, tax breaks and equipment sharing.

What causes illnesses?

Childhood illnesses are usually caused by viruses and bacteria, which are both germs. Viruses are "bugs" that need to live and multiply in cells to survive, so they live in us and reproduce themselves by being passed on to other people, who then get ill and pass them on, and so it goes. Bacteria are little organisms that can live and grow independently (such as germs on a loo seat), with the side effect of infecting people.

When are illnesses contagious?

Illnesses are most contagious when the germs are multiplying the fastest. This often happens when you first "catch a bug", before any symptoms appear, and in the first few days of symptoms. Sneezing and diarrhoea are really efficient ways of spreading the germs, so while these symptoms continue, whatever the stage of the illness, the bug is probably still contagious. It usually takes three to five days for the incubation of a common cold, meaning from catching it to the end of symptoms. Despite the fact that parents often say "It's not contagious any more", they're often just guessing.

Should kids go back to playgroup, child care or nursery?

Child-care centres usually say kids with a tummy bug should be kept home until 24 hours after their last vomit or bout of diarrhoea.

Kids should be kept home from group care while they continue to have symptoms of an illness and until they're feeling bouncy again – not only because the bug is still contagious, although that's a big issue, especially with more serious illnesses, but because kids with symptoms are almost always below par or even miserable. It's harder for them to get one-on-one care in a child-care centre, even though I know staff do their very best. It isn't fair to the child, and they want to be at home with a parent. Many parents who work outside the home eat up their own sick-day allowance (if they have one) looking after their kids.

451

When to see a doctor about an illness

Keep the phone number of your GP's surgery near the phone. If the surgery is closed a recorded message should give you the number of your local out-of-hours service, which you can ring for a telephone consultation with a doctor. They may do a home visit, but if they think the problem is really serious they will probably tell you to get to your nearest hospital. My Cousin Suze, a paramedic, says "as well as getting better quickly, kids can often deteriorate quickly". She says parents need to keep a careful eye on an ill kid: "It's always suspicious if a child is quieter than usual. It's generally better to have a screaming one than a quiet one."

See or contact a doctor in any of the following situations.

★ Your kid has been in contact with an infectious disease that they haven't been immunized against.

★ Fever is accompanied by worrying symptoms such as misery, listlessness, repeated vomiting or an inexplicable rash (see also "When to Call an Ambulance with an Illness" opposite).

★ You're worried because your child is "not themselves", too quiet, uninterested in anything or "floppy".

You know your child best so take your own uneasy feelings seriously. All parents have these: some call them "instincts" and act on them, others mistrust them and are unsure whether they're worrying unnecessarily, but they're the same feelings so start calling yours instincts. The only way to check them out is to take your child to a doctor. Even if nothing is revealed, keep on trusting your instincts – you may need to try another doctor or the kid may have just beaten a bug.

★ Your child develops wheezing.

★ There's unexplained crying that isn't helped by the usual methods, especially in kids who can't tell you what's wrong.

Sometimes the only symptom of a kid's illness is listlessness, whingeing and a pressing need to be right next to Mum or Dad, or at least in the same room. A nurse I know always tested her post-toddler-age children by asking them to jump three times – if they couldn't, she knew they were really sick and not faking it. Kids under 5 are not likely to fake being sick unless it's learned behaviour (they can often suddenly say they have a sore back if you have one, for example, and will learn from you how to react to hurts and pains).

For books on recognizing and dealing with illnesses see "More Info" at the end of this chapter.

When to go to hospital accident and emergency with an illness

If you're very worried about your kid and you can't go to your local doctor because it's late at night or a weekend, you may need to go to the nearest A&E (casualty) department. Please be aware, though, that casualty areas are only for emergencies, and that you may have to wait many hours in a brightly lit area and then see an overworked doctor or nurse. So if you are anxious about, but not freaked out by, your child's symptoms, a good alternative to the almost certain hell of waiting in casualty can be to ring your your local GP's out-of-hours service requesting a home visit. Call and see how quickly the doctor can come: sick children will be a priority.

Looking after a sickie

★ Sick babies can be carried in a sling or wheeled about with you in a pram.

★ With a toddler help the patient camp out in the room you're working in. Make up a bed on the sofa with toy friends and settle the patient in for the day so they're not isolated; or move an armchair into their bedroom with some reading, the phone or work you can do there. If disgusting vomiting or pooing is not a possibility, the parental bed can be a good haven.

WHEN TO CALL AN AMBULANCE WITH AN ILLNESS

Ring the general emergency number: 999.
Call an ambulance if your child:

✱ has a convulsion (a fit)

✱ has difficulty with or stops breathing

✱ can't be roused

✱ has fever, repeated vomiting, a stiff neck and their eyes are sensitive to light (the symptoms of meningitis, a brain inflammation). You need to get your child to a hospital *straight*

away so call an ambulance if you're too stressed to drive safely.

✱ is miserable, has fever and a stiff neck, their eyes are sensitive to light and they have a spotty rash that starts as red but turns purple and doesn't fade when you press it (the symptoms of meningococcal disease).

★ Sick kids often sleep a lot as a natural defence or because of the sedative effect of medicines such as painkillers or cough suppressants. Don't use painkillers to sedate: it's not good for kids to have too many painkillers (see the "Painkillers: Paracetamol and Ibuprofen" box a few pages on).

★ Don't insist on games or activities – sometimes kids are too ill to do anything but lie about.

★ Read them a favourite book or two or play favourite sleepytime or relaxing music.

★ Don't let them veg out for ages in front of TV or new DVDs. The younger the child, the more it can addle their brain when they're sick – too many new sights and concepts to take in. Tried and true, quieter, old favourite programmes can be useful.

★ Offer simple food and healthy favourites. Old-fashioned comfort food such as custard or mashed potatoes can be good, depending on the illness. Upset tummies usually mean a very restricted diet (we'll get to that), and kids with stuffed-up noses can't taste anything. Sore mouths and throats often mean food rejection.

★ Don't forget to change the sheets after an illness to freshen up, and get some outside air into the room during an illness if possible and definitely after.

★ You want to be able to be as sympathetic as possible without making being ill a great adventure preferable to being up or going to nursery.

★ If you've had to cancel work or something else important to be at home, make sure you plot against the illness in partnership with your kid ("I can't wait to go to the park! Let's go as soon as you're better!") rather than resenting your child for being ill ("I hope you're better tomorrow because I missed some important things at work today").

★ Put your kid in a tepid bath if the weather is horribly hot, or a warm one can be relaxing if it's cold. If your child doesn't want one, try a flannel or "sponge" bath. The patient can try a dry wash of teddy first.

★ Reality check: you may have to re-establish your child's sleeping routine after an illness.

"Forget commitment, housework and cooking – cuddles, cuddles, cuddles." ANN

"Take them seriously about their illness. If you are seen to be concerned they can worry less themselves, and should recover sooner." ROBERTO

Giving medicines

Most children's medicines come as a liquid that can be sucked up into a dropper or syringe (without the needle bit, obviously) and squirted into the child's mouth; or it can be given on a spoon or in a tiny measuring cup. The dropper, spoon or measuring cup may come with the medicine or you can buy them separately at the chemist.

It's always handy to teach your kid how to take medicine from a dropper as soon as possible. Try to make it a game.

In cases of full-on, arched-back rebellion, when taking the medicine immediately is imperative, hold the child's nose so they have to open their mouth, squirt it in and then hold the mouth closed until it's swallowed. This is of course an absolutely last resort and can usually be avoided by reassurance or sneakiness.

If you have to disguise medicine in a mouthful of something, use a tiny amount of breast or formula milk for a baby or food such as ice cream for older kids. It's no good putting medicine in a glass of juice because they'll only drink 56.78 percent of the juice and then you'll have no idea how much of it was medicine. Unfortunately pharmaceutical companies seem to insist on over-flavouring and colouring children's medicines, which is guaranteed to make any baby or fussy toddler deeply suspicious.

Some parents have success with bribery – you take your medicine, you get a sticker or a star on a chart.

Never leave a bottle of medicine where kids can reach it.

"Try putting your baby's medicine into an upturned teat and let them suck it like it was on a bottle." SAMANTHA

"My kids will take medicine off the 'magic spoon' (we got it out of the kids' Nurofen packet)." PRUE

Complementary therapies

Many people see an alternative practitioner – yours should understand when it's necessary to have a medical diagnosis before natural treatments. Just treating symptoms might allow an underlying cause to go unnoticed. Complementary therapies are good

PAINKILLERS: PARACETAMOL AND IBUPROFEN

✱ Ask your doctor for advice on paracetamol and ibuprofen for babies and kids and keep a supply on hand (they come under different brand names). Although entirely safe for most babies and toddlers, painkillers containing ibuprofen can cause side effects in individual kids, including some who have asthma. As well as dulling or removing pain, paracetamol is commonly used for bringing down a temperature, although both will do this (but see the section "Fever and High Temperature" later in the chapter).

✱ Paracetamol isn't designed to be used all day every day, for several days in a row, without medical supervision: a whacking great paracetamol overdose can cause permanent liver shutdown. Long-term use or longer-than-recommended doses of ibuprofen cause tummy upsets and bleeding. Both should be kept out of reach and locked away.

✱ Don't ever exceed the dose – more will not kill pain quicker or more efficiently. The recommended dose should do it within 20 minutes. If it doesn't, you'll be needing medical advice.

✱ If you do accidentally give too much medicine, don't panic. Ring NHS Direct immediately (0845 4647) and let them know how much you've given. It's almost certainly fine – it's more likely that you would harm your child by giving consistently too-high doses or for too long a time.

✱ Aspirin or soluble aspirin shouldn't be given to kids as in rare cases it can contribute to Reye's syndrome, a liver failure and brain inflammation leading to convulsions and coma with a high death rate (10 to 25 percent).

for minor ailments when the cause is indisputable. Your practitioner should be both qualified and experienced in children's remedies, and the cause of the ailment should be fully medically established. Herbalists should be told about any medications the child is on, and doctors told of any herbal remedies the kid is taking as well. Sensible herbalists and naturopaths will not recommend their remedies alone for serious illnesses or injuries. So far, there have been no accepted scientific studies which show homeopathic remedies work better than a placebo, while some traditional, naturopathic or herbal remedies do have scientific backing. As with medical treatment, parents will have to make themselves aware of specific latest research.

Mindful of the long list of powerful and complicated aromatherapy essential oils, I should say that small children should probably only be given drops of eucalyptus oil on their hanky or pillow (to combat the sniffles) or drops of lavender oil in their bath for relaxation. Don't use aromatherapy candles or burners for children, and never leave these (or anything else with an unprotected flame) untended in a room that a child is in.

When you get ill as well

This is when you find out who your real friends and actually helpful relatives are. Many people want to stay away when there is illness in the home. It can be especially daunting, even frightening, when you are a sole parent and have been literally laid out by something really serious. Don't be afraid to ask friends and family for help, insisting if necessary.

Carer fatigue

I never used to understand what people meant when they said that having an ill child was difficult. Now I understand it can mean hours and hours of grinding exhaustion and sacrifice, the kind of worry that makes you realize you never really had a worry before, and the total inability to do anything at all apart from tend to the patient, get them to and from the doctor and wash mega kilos of sickie bed linen, jarmies and towels. Most children who are ill wake up a lot, distressed, and even if *they* go straight back to sleep *you* might lie awake until the next "alarm". If you have a partner, try to alternate the sleepless nights. One partner can wear earplugs or sleep in the furthest room when it's not their turn on shift.

If your child is in childcare or nursery, use the first few days they're well and back there to get some sleep during the day. Otherwise see if you can get help from a friend or relative so that you catch up on your sleep. The more tired (or the sicker) you are, the harder it is to have good judgement and stay patient.

The common illnesses and conditions given in the following sections of the chapter are in no particular order except that they start with the more temporary and common ones and end with the more long-term conditions.

feveR aND HigH temperatuRe

We are all so attuned to the idea that fevers are scary, it can be a horrible shock to pick up your baby or toddler and realize they're "burning up". It's comforting to know that most fevers are a friend: they have a sensible purpose – it's the body's way of "burning off" germs. Your kid's immune system is doing its job.

One of the quickest ways to see if a baby has a fever is to put the back of your hand against their tummy (their forehead and extremities may have been in a cold wind or near a heater and are not as close to the body's core temperature). If it feels very hot, there's probably a fever.

A febrile convulsion

It's rare, but a rapid rise in temperature can cause a "febrile convulsion", or fit, which causes the eyes to roll back and the baby or kid to shake and jerk. A fit is scary but usually takes only a few minutes and has no lasting effects, and doesn't cause brain damage or death. (A tendency to have fits sometimes runs in the family.) Call an ambulance if you're freaked out (let's face it, who wouldn't be?) but it'll probably all be over before they get to your place, with no harm done except to your nerves.

Doctors say it's likely that the rate of the temperature rise causes a fit rather than a magic high number such as forty degrees Celsius. So by the time you know your kid has a high temperature, if they haven't had a fit they're probably not going to. Remember: the vast majority of kids never have a febrile convulsion and those who do are not harmed by it.

Ways to treat a fever

★ If your baby or child has a convulsion, call an ambulance on 999.

★ Don't keep the kid too bundled up, and don't use ice or anything else sudden to "bring down" a temperature.

★ If the kid is in pain or miserable, give them a dose of paracetamol, according to the label. If they're jaunty, let the fever fight the illness.

★ See a doctor if your kid has other worrying symptoms, such as being "not themselves", cranky, listless, confused, off their food or having a rash, repeated vomiting or breathing changes. You'll probably want to take a baby under 6 months to the doctor if you feel they have a high temperature to rule out anything worrying.

★ If you're frightened by the high temperature or it's 4am and you're feeling exhausted, you can use a dose of paracetamol to bring down the
fever and see a doctor the next day.

The more old-fashioned advice is that a baby under 6 months with a fever over
37.5 degrees should be seen as soon as possible by a GP. For a baby older than that,
if the temperature is over 38.5 for more than 4 hours, or comes and goes at that high
level, also see your doctor.

gastro

*"When they say they have a tummy ache and turn a shade of green they ARE going
to vomit."* TRACEY

We're talking here about an upset tummy – the vomiting and diarrhoea associated with a
short-term bug rather than something longer term such as a tummy parasite, or the one-
off vomiting caused by stress, coughing or getting a chunk of apple caught in the throat.
The throwing up is often very upsetting for a baby or kid, especially if it wakes them or
they don't know what's happening.

Generally vomiting plus diarrhoea plus fever means you need to see your doctor, although it's almost certainly a short-term bout. The main danger, to babies in
particular, is dehydration if they're too sick to keep down or keep drinking fluids.
This can happen quite quickly to babies: 24 hours of vomiting and diarrhoea can
be enough. If you can't rehydrate them, they need to go to hospital to be sedated
and go on a nice drip of fluids and mineral salts for a day or so. Scary for you, but
standard procedure.

Gastro is caused by a virus picked up anywhere really, but often in a place where
there's a concentration of other kids; by bacteria, perhaps in contaminated food (food
poisoning); or, in rare cases, by a rather violent allergic reaction. Symptoms are usually
most full-on for the first 24 hours, and the diarrhoea often lasts longer than the vomiting. There may be only throwing up or only diarrhoea.

A viral case usually comes on suddenly: the kid complains of feeling nauseated
or goes quiet, then suddenly vomits. It may be accompanied by other charming

SIGNS OF DEHYDRATION

* The baby or kid has repeated runny poos over the course of 24 hours.

* Their skin feels dry and papery or cold and clammy and is paler than usual.

* The skin on a baby's fontanelle looks sunken.

* The kid has a dry mouth, lips and tongue.

* The face and eyes look sunken.

* The baby or kid has a spaced-out, glazed look.

* There's less wee than usual or fewer wet nappies.

* The wee is darker coloured than usual (this is sometimes hard to see when the child is wearing a nappy).

* The kid's breath is foul.

features such as runny poo and sniffly cold symptoms. This is the most common, catching kind.

A bacterial gastro such as food poisoning usually comes on within about 12 to 48 hours of contact. The food involved can be anything from a tiny bit of old milk not jooshed out of an otherwise clean formula bottle to something that touched a surface contaminated by raw chicken. Tummy cramps and explosive poo usually come first, followed by vomiting. It normally lasts two to three days.

Treatment for gastro

There's not much in the way of medication you can give for gastro – usually you have to ride it out by doing the following.

★ Help your baby or child and be with them while they are vomiting, then clean up as soon as you can.

★ Give them reassurance and cuddles. Throwing up is an unpleasant experience and they need comforting and soothing.

★ Rest your child's tummy from rich foods (see "What Not to Feed a Kid with Gastro" further on). Do this for a day – more if it seems to be still upset.

★ Rehydration is the important issue. Give your kid lots of fluids. Basically keep offering the breast, bottle or cup as often as you can to babies. Keep a drink next to a child who is old enough to help themselves and also offer it to them often.

You can get a rehydration formula from the chemist (you may need a prescription for some, others can be bought in bottles or sachets over the counter). It needs to be appropriate for your child's age and contain the right mineral salts as well as fluids. Some can even be frozen as icy poles to make them more attractive to kids. This is what you need, not flat lemonade. Remember that many chemists will home deliver.

★ Keep cross-infection to a minimum by washing all utensils, sick bowls, towels and jarmies in hot, soapy water.

★ Always take a child to the doctor if you're worried or there are any signs of dehydration.

BABIES UNDER 6 MONTHS WITH GASTRO

★ Off to the doctor with you, just to make sure it's all okay: ask for advice about rehydrating.

★ If the baby is breastfed, keep offering the breast regularly.

★ If they're a formula-fed baby, ask your doctor whether you should try a special rehydration formula for their age from the chemist in their bottle for a day, then their own formula at half-strength for a day, before going back to normal. Some babies come good suddenly and can probably go straight back onto their formula.

OLDER BABIES WITH GASTRO

★ See your doctor if the vomiting and diarrhoea last longer than 24 hours or if you're worried.

★ The baby should go back on breast or formula milk as soon as possible.

TODDLERS WITH GASTRO

★ Keep giving plain water and clear fruit juice diluted 1:1 with water or rehydration fluids or "icy poles" from the chemist.

★ Never assume a toddler knows what's going on. Explain why you're offering different foods and drinks, why you're going to the doctor, why it's good to stay quietly at home.

★ A kid old enough to understand (but who may have forgotten what throwing up is) should be reassured that the situation will end soon, that they have a germ that is making their tummy have a tantrum and that you're trying to fix it as fast as you can but sometimes it may take until tomorrow (anything longer is virtually incomprehensible).

★ If a toddler or a with gastro wants to eat, feed them bland things and don't worry too much – they will be getting a few nutrients even if they throw up everything soon after (see "What to Feed a Kid with Gastro", which follows).

★ See your doctor if the vomiting and diarrhoea last longer than 48 hours.

WHAT TO FEED A KID WITH GASTRO   Don't force feed – start food when your child is ready. Try:

★ plain cooked rice and pasta

★ rice pudding

★ fingers of dry toast and bread

★ plain dry biscuits, with reduced salt

★ porridge made with water

★ mashed potatoes

★ puréed, mashed or sieved frozen blueberries and raspberries or little bits of fresh fruit

★ plain soya milk

★ grated or paper-thin apple slices

★ stewed pear

★ banana

★ mashed carrot or courgettes

★ junket, flummery or jelly

★ finely chopped steamed chicken breast

★ plain home-made chicken soup.

WHAT NOT TO FEED A KID WITH GASTRO

- ★ Only plain water for longer than 24 hours: the body needs more nutrients than that.
- ★ Full-strength fruit juice or full-strength lemonade because both are too sugary and can stimulate diarrhoea – water it down to at least 1:1.
- ★ Flat lemonade or sugar dissolved in water – it's much better to get a rehydration formula from the chemist.
- ★ Bottled electrolyte and sports drinks: they're for adults.
- ★ Spicy, acidic or rich foods, chocolate, junk foods, sweets, cake and other sugary things: these can make the diarrhoea worse.
- ★ Salty things: these can increase dehydration.
- ★ Anti-diarrhoea medicines unless your doctor prescribed them specifically for this bout of illness (these medicines are rarely given and hardly ever to babies).
- ★ Milk and other dairy food because they're too fatty – soya milk can replace cow's milk until the child is better.

SNiffLes aND COLDS

Home remedies

- ★ A steam vaporizer can be bought from a chemist. You fill them with water and they keep pushing steam into the child's room at night – this helps keep the airways open and greatly reduces a stuffed nose and coughing. Some people put eucalyptus drops in but that's not necessary for them to work effectively.
- ★ A vapour rub (from the chemist) on the chest for toddlers may help clear the schnozz.
- ★ Add a few drops of eucalyptus oil to the bath.
- ★ Eucalyptus drops on the pillow, underneath the pillow case, might help too.
- ★ Elevate the head of the bed with a few *Yellow Pages* volumes – the mucus will drain down.
- ★ Books or music on a tape can be soothing.

PRACTICAL TIPS FOR LIVING WITH THE VOMITS

Sick bowl
Protect yourself and bedding from sudden vomits by teaching your child as soon as possible to use a sick bowl. Make sure you have a couple of non-metal sick bowls or buckets (who wants to see their reflection at that point?) and plenty of layers of towels to avoid getting vomit on the bed or furniture. The towels will have to be washed in very hot water and an antibacterial washing powder such as a nappy one. The bowl the child uses will have to be disinfected with boiling water at intervals too, with the spare kept in circulation in case there's a need while the other one's being washed.

Stripping the bed
When a kid throws up in bed, it's all hands on deck. This is why you never throw out old, threadbare towels – keep all the towels you can.

Soothe the kid thoroughly first, then completely clean them with a nice warm flannel and a soap substitute, paying special attention to their face, hands and hair. Rinse off the soap substitute, wrap your darling in a clean towel and prop them in a corner or on a beanbag where they can't fall over (but never leave a baby on a beanbag while you go into another room). Dress them in loose clothes that you'll be able to get off easily if they're sick again. Don't assume they won't vomit again or that there's "nothing left to come up": protect the immediate area.

Coughs
* ★ A wheezy cough: this could indicate asthma and should always be checked by a doctor.
* ★ A cough that ends in a heaving sound (a "whoop") as the baby or child tries to take in air: this should also always be checked by a doctor.
* ★ A croupy cough (one with lots of rattly phlegm in the chest): this can often be suddenly improved by placing a steam vaporizer in the bedroom at night.

Pharmacy shelves are chockers with expensive cold, cough and sniffle remedies for kids but doctors are dubious about their effect on illness. A honey and lemon

Strip the bed of all the sheets and any bedding with vomit on it and soak up any extra vomit with old or used towels. Clean any vomit-touched surfaces with antibacterial spray (or similar) and another towel. Explain that you're putting all the bedding, jarmies, towels and vomity stuffed animals in the washing machine, or leave everything in a pile to take away later.

Come back; have a cuddle and remake the bed: if you don't have a waterproof mattress protector use a couple of layers of old towels. Make up a top sheet with a bath towel that folds back to protect the top layer of sheet, duvet or bedspread. Have the sick bowl ready next to the bed before the child gets back in. Prop an older child up with pillows and make sure the only toys that stay are washable. (We've had to have Pinky re-upholstered twice and it's quite undignified.) Explain that the vomiting might happen again but it might not, and what's causing it. Offer them a drink of water. Reassuringly tuck them in and send them off to sleep.

Before loading the washing machine rinse off anything chunky, do a short but adequately cleansing washing-machine load with antibacterial powder in hot water.

If you're unlucky, do it all again.

Of course if there are two adults divvying up the actions just described it will work even better.

drink could well be just as good. Remember that children's cough medicines must be literally made for children – never use a smaller dose of an adult cough mixture – and that most have quite a strong sedative as well as a cough suppressant in them. So generally they are most helpful at night to let a kid get some sleep (and you too) if that's what's become necessary.

Babies under 1 year mustn't have off-the-shelf decongestant cough mixtures: these must be prescribed for them by a doctor.

> *"Mums tend to see changes in a condition where dads see variations from the normal state. Listen and act on both concerns."* GRAHAM

ear PROBLems

Lots of babies and small kids get ear trouble, usually after a cold or other virus. Although unusual in a tiny baby under a couple of months old, after that it can be a battle, with some kids having constant problems for years. Most kids will have at least one ear infection before school starts. The three main types of ear condition are given below. (If you want to have your child's hearing tested call your GP's surgery.)

Outer ear infection

This is often caused by "picking something up at the pool". You can see the ear is red, with maybe a discharge – older kids may say it feels blocked or sore. It may go away by itself but should be seen by your GP and may need antibiotics or steroid medicines.

Middle ear infection

Inside everyone's ear is a thing called a eustachian tube that drains any fluid from the middle ear, which is protected from the outside world by the eardrum. In kids under about 3 the tube is often rather horizontal before developing a downward angle so fluid can drain

away. If the fluid doesn't drain and sits there, it can get very infected and yucky and can eventually burst out of the eardrum, causing sudden pain (or it can cause "glue" ear – the third type of ear condition listed).

The symptoms are usually bad earache and a lack of interest in food (because it hurts to swallow). Unfortunately a little baby or toddler may not be able to understand and articulate the pain or show you where it is. The early signs may be listlessness, tears and deafness that might be obvious or not.

The first treatment is pain relief – usually the label dosage of paracetamol for the correct age. If the yuck has burst through the eardrum, the pain of the pressure will be released and the drum will probably heal nicely by itself (not that you'd want this to happen repeatedly). Antibiotics can be used to clear up the infection behind the ear, but the problem is likely to recur until (or if) the tube starts draining properly.

EARS

★ See a doctor if there is ear pain, redness, pulling at an ear associated with pain (not the typical baby "What's this thing on my head I've just discovered?" behaviour), perceived or suspected hearing trouble, or a discharge from the ear.

★ If you need to give ear drops, have your child lie down with their head sideways on your lap and let gravity help you. Say it won't hurt (if that's true) but might feel wet or tickly while the drops are draining into the ear.

★ Don't push anything, even a cotton bud, into a baby's or a kid's ear. Clean the bit you can reach with a flannel.

"Glue" ear

The ear becomes blocked when fluid can't drain away or doesn't burst through the eardrum, but it's not necessarily infected. There's no pain, but there is significant partial to total hearing loss. Quite often someone else notices it first – a child-care worker or a relative. Kids can get very good at lip reading and finding other ways around their deafness. Parents often first realize when a child has their back to them and doesn't respond to questions, or keeps asking for the music or TV to be turned up.

In persistent cases or where the alternative is a partial or complete deafness in one or both ears that would lead to learning and social difficulties, the kid may have to have an operation under general anaesthetic to insert "grommets". These are little eyelets holding open holes in the eardrum so that the fluid can drain out. Kids can swim with grommets in, but not dive or jump in the pool or ocean waves in case water pounds into their inner ear. After a few months grommets drop out of the ear naturally and the drum heals itself.

Incidentally those candle things that people burn outside a kid's ear that are supposed to draw out a blockage are completely useless. Even if a candle could draw out material from an ear, there's an eardrum in the way, making it impossible. "Natural" remedy ear drops should only be used when your doctor is certain the eardrum has not been perforated.

CHICKEN POX

Chicken pox usually starts with a fever, listlessness, loss of appetite and a rash, which are followed by the tell-tale spots, usually ten days to three weeks after catching the virus. It is when the spots erupt that it's contagious, but sometimes the early ones are hard to see. The spots keep appearing for a few days and they all go through a process of becoming blistered, then itchy, before finally drying up. Scratching them may cause a wee scar. It is very contagious until the last sore has dried up.

Chicken pox is not usually life threatening, but it is very miserable and irritating for most kids – some get nasty sores inside their mouths, down their throat and on their genitals. While there is a vaccination against it, this is not part of the UK childhood immunization programme. (It may occasionally be given to high-risk patients or to siblings of very sick children.) You will have to ask for and pay for a chicken pox immunization if you want one, because it is not part of the free UK childhood immunization programme or routinely suggested. Ideally, it should be administered by the age of two before your child gets out into the world and comes into contact with it.

A few advances have been made in chicken pox treatment. Nothing "cures" it – it has to run its course – but a special bath oil (ask your chemist) will help cut down the irritation of the itchy sores. Rather than the traditional calamine lotion, many pharmacists and doctors now recommend a cooling, less drying gel to put on the spots.

TOO MUCH SUN

Because running around in the fresh air and sunshine is one of the bonuses of living in a temperate climate, we have to find a happy medium between toasting our children and making them move slowly in the shade dressed in head-to-toe bee-keeping outfits. The main risk factor for later cancers is getting burned a lot when you're a kid.

Time in the sun

It's ultra-violet radiation (UV rays) that are the problem. UV rays are most intense between 11am and 3pm: basically the hours when the sun is highest in the sky, especially between May and September when the UV levels get very high. Kids should be indoors, in the shade or very well protected during these times. It can take as little as 15 minutes to get sunburned, depending on the time of year and lots of other factors.

Weather

UV rays themselves don't feel hot so sunburn is very common on days when people don't expect it. Cloudy days? Yes, you can be burned on cloudy days. And on cool days with sun and on windy days that feel cool. And in the snow where there's lots of intensifying reflection. Most people get burned in temperatures between 18 and 27 degrees Celsius. The biggest factors are time of year and time spent outdoors. Even if you're making sure your kid only goes out in the sun in the early morning and later afternoon, you should still slap sunscreen on them.

Skin type and sun care

While fair-skinned blondies and darling freckly ginger nuts are most in danger from sunburn, kids with olive or dark skin do get sunburn and can get skin cancer too. A tan or freckles are evidence of sun damage – of the skin trying to protect itself. A tan does not protect kids against further damage or cancer.

Sun care for babies

Sunburn for a baby can be very serious, causing blisters and rapid dehydration. They shouldn't be exposed to direct sun, as in sunbathing. They'll get plenty of vitamin D and sunshine without being directly exposed. Babies lying on a rug in the park or at the beach should be in the dark, sharp-edged shadow cast by trees, those pop-up tenty things or an umbrella. They will still need to be protected from reflected or "scattered" UV rays by being covered up (see the info about clothes and sun further on). Sunscreen alone should not be relied on to protect a baby, even in the shade. A baby in direct sun must always be covered up, have infant sunscreen on the small bits that can't be protected any other way and wear a hat that shades their face and neck. If they are being wheeled around, they must have serious shade covering. Remember UV rays can get through mesh netting. All the above stuff about babies applies for toddlers, but they should use a toddler sunscreen.

Sun protection

SUNSCREEN This should be broad spectrum (which means it absorbs both kinds of relevant UV rays); sun protection factor 30 (usually labelled as SPF 30+), which provides the most protection, especially for infants and toddlers; and water resistant. Most sources recommend an SPF of at least 15. SPF15 will protect against about 95 percent of the damaging sun rays, and 30 will only get you one percent or so more protection, so SPF 15 is fine. No sunscreen guarantees full protection, as thousands of lobster-coloured Brit tourists in Queensland so glowingly attest.

You can test a little bit of sunscreen on the back of your kid's hand to see if it causes a rash. If it does, talk to your pharmacist about a replacement: rashes are usually a reaction to perfumes or preservatives rather than the sun protection part. Remember that a thick layer of sunscreen lotion will make a kid hotter: it's better to cover large areas of skin with loose protective clothing.

Sunscreen should be applied about 20 minutes before going outdoors (there's a complicated chemical reason that will put you to sleep) and should be reapplied at least every 2 hours. Some people burn within that time even with sunscreen on. And it should be applied more often than that if it is likely to have been wiped, washed or sweated off. Apparently sunscreen, particularly as a spray, is usually not applied thickly enough or rubbed in sufficiently, although nobody seems to be able to explain exactly how much you should put on kids. And it's recommended that if your child (or you) are in the sun for 2 hours, more protection, from hats and clothing, will be needed as well.

Sunscreen ingredients cost about the same so if you pay more, it's for perfume, moisturizer or a brand name. Check the use-by date and don't apply the sunscreen beyond it.

SUNHATS These should be legionnaire-style (like a baseball cap with a flap at the back and sides) or broad-brimmed (the recommended brim size is 8–10 cm). They should not be mesh or have holes in them that let sun through. A lot of UV rays are reflected from below by water, sand or concrete.

SUN CLOTHES Kids in the sun between May and September should be dressed in loose clothes that cover as much of the body as possible. Cancer Research UK says if you hold a fabric up to the light and the light passes through, UV rays will too, so choose materials with a close weave. Tags showing UPF (ultraviolet protection factor) 50+ have the most sun protection. Most cotton has about UPF 20+. All fabrics have less UV protection when they're wet. I'm starting to think we should live underground.

SUNGLASSES Intense sunlight can make babies and toddlers squint, get cranky and even long term lead to the development of cataracts as the eyes try to protect themselves. Shade your baby's eyes by not having them in the direct sun. Look for sunnies for your toddler: they need to meet British standard BSEN 1836: 1997, which only relates to the lens, and to block out all UV (check the tag). Groovy toy sunglasses will probably offer no protection. Wrap-around styles will protect the eyes from sun coming in at the sides. Some toddlers won't have any truck with them, but others when told they look cool may wear them proudly.

SUN ON WHEELS Most baby and car shops sell screens you can stick on a car window to shade a baby or toddler. If you can find them get stick-on ones that will peel off later if your toddler pulls off the more temporary ones held on with little suckers. There are also retractable (roller blind style) ones as a further alternative. Prams and strollers should have a shade roof. Drape a solid cloth over the pram or stroller to get complete protection if you can't get into the shade, but make sure the baby is cool and well ventilated. A soaked, then wrung-out muslin square can be very cooling draped over a pram top, but not on the kid's skin.

LEADING BY EXAMPLE Little kids won't be bothered about sun-care issues if you don't have a hat and sunscreen on. They love to do what older kids and adults do.

Head Lice

Lice is the plural of louse (as in lousy); they're the little critters that can invade a child's hair, lay eggs (called nits), which are "glued" onto the base of hairs with icky, lousy secretions. The first sign of nits or lice is usually your child scratching their head, or an alert from playgroup, child care or nursery. The itchiness is caused by the lice – euwwwww! – sucking tiny amounts of blood from the scalp. You will, on close inspection, probably be able to see the tiny, yellowy white eggs, like dandruff, on the hair shaft near the scalp and maybe some little browny grey lice disporting themselves. If an egg is a centimetre or more away from the scalp it's either dead or hatched. The live eggs are down nearer the scalp.

Don't be embarrassed and don't faff about making your kid feel like they've got something appalling. All kids get lice and will continue to. It has nothing to do with personal hygiene. Lice can't jump and they can't live on pets. Chemical companies say lice can live for up to a week without their human host; natural treatment advocates say lice rarely survive this for more than a day or so.

A louse can lay several eggs a day. Eggs hatch after 7–10 days, and and 10–14 days after hatching the babies are laying their own eggs. This is no time to feel the kinship of motherhood. It's time to kill, kill, kill.

Lice-killing stuff
Get from the chemist these three things:

1 conditioner – the gloopier the better and the more gaudily coloured so the eggs are visible against it

2 a fine-toothed metal, not plastic, lice comb – the placcy one is a bit bendier and so not as efficient

3 lice-killing lotion – depending on your philosophy either the full-on poisonous chemical stuff or the natural stuff.

The usual chemical ingredient is malathion, an organophosphate pesticide solution used up to 90 to 95 percent pure on farms and in mass mosquito spraying – but at a concentration of only one per cent in lice shampoos. (Anything more than two percent requires them to be behind the counter in the chemist and only sold with instructions from the pharmacist.)

Here's what sources in the industry have said about malathion: "Less than ten percent is absorbed through the skin where it is rapidly detoxified (approx ten times faster than other organophosphates) and excreted, therefore it is much safer for human topical use. It is not recommended for infants under 6 months of age, and caution is advised when using in children under 4 years, and pregnant and breastfeeding women."

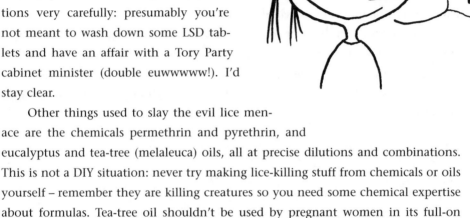

I'm not sure exactly what caution means, apart from following label instructions very carefully: presumably you're not meant to wash down some LSD tablets and have an affair with a Tory Party cabinet minister (double euwwwww!). I'd stay clear.

Other things used to slay the evil lice menace are the chemicals permethrin and pyrethrin, and eucalyptus and tea-tree (melaleuca) oils, all at precise dilutions and combinations. This is not a DIY situation: never try making lice-killing stuff from chemicals or oils yourself – remember they are killing creatures so you need some chemical expertise about formulas. Tea-tree oil shouldn't be used by pregnant women in its full-on incarnation. Other preparations now on the market kill the lice by having a different physical effect on them from pesticides, effectively making them either shrink or swell (depending on the type of liquid used) so that they die.

To kill lice my Nanna used to put her three girls through the sheep dip in the 1950s (full of now-banned chemicals at eye-popping concentrations) and they've survived. Mind you, they're all completely mad. But Mum says their hair was very shiny.

Resistance to the pesticides used in the lice-killing lotions is evolving all the time, so ask a pharmacist (not a shop assistant) which is the currently recommended preparation. Also read the fine print (which can be virtually unreadable), especially on the chemical treatments, in the pharmacy before you buy; it may tell you that the treatment is not suitable for children under a certain age. Babies and very small children shouldn't be treated with strong chemicals: all the manufacturers say babies under 6 months should not be treated with their product.

Some of the chemical lotions are supposed to be left on for twelve hours: make sure you don't get one of those. You'd either get it all over the bedclothes and your child's face or you'd have them in a shower cap keeping hot, poisonous chemicals next to the scalp for 12 hours. That's called *not* recommended.

Wet combing or "bug busting"

Some people don't use any lotion except the conditioner, preferring to comb out all lice and eggs and squash them rather than use chemical or other killing agents. This method may be more reliable than using special lotions, either because of chemical resistance (see above) or because these preparations don't always kill the eggs (despite what they claim), requiring a repeat treatment a week later.

Wet combing with loads of conditioner is often called "bug busting" because it aims to break the life cycle of the lice by ridding the head of them before they are mature enough to start laying eggs. It will need to be done every three days for at least two weeks to be sure of removing all the lice, which may be too much for your child to bear.

How to get the lice out

Babies are usually pretty easy to inspect for eggs and lice, which you can remove yourself, because they have less hair.

It's important not to use lice-killing treatment unless someone is definitely infested: this can only be decided after a thorough inspection. Follow the instructions on the label. It's essential not to get any of this stuff in eyes or mouth.

Do not put a kid in front of a heater or use a hair dryer. The chemical lotion may be flammable. (Gawd.)

Rub conditioner or a lice-killing lotion gently but thoroughly through the kid's hair. Sit the child on your lap on a towel, divide the hair into sections, and comb their hair meticulously with the metal lice comb. Get out all the dead lice and drag out all the eggs. This can take a very long time. Older children can be kept amused by pretending you are a family of chimps. (Do not go so far as to eat the lice. Please.) Wash your hands and wash the towel in hot water.

Wash all the bedclothes, fluffy toys and clothes the child has been using in hot water. Woollen jumpers and other things that will shrink in hot water can be treated with an anti-lice soaking solution available at the chemist.

And that's it. But keep checking your kid's head regularly to see if the critters have come back. Keep the lice lotion safely out of reach and keep an eye on the use-by date. If swallowed, call NHS Direct (0845 4647) immediately .

See "More Info" at the end of this chapter for resources.

Hiccups

Hiccups are quite common in babies and nothing to worry about. Painless hiccups that go on for a while in toddlers and children are also not a problem. Don't try to give the kid a fright. And don't give them an adult preparation such as an antacid.

But if your child seems unable to stop and is affected by the hiccups, try getting them to:

- ★ hold their breath – you may need to show them how
- ★ drink upside down – again you may need to show them
- ★ drink from a cup while you put your fingers gently in their outer ears
- ★ breathe in and out of a paper bag – for one minute only.

eczema

Itchy, dry skin can develop a red rash and flaking known as eczema, which can affect babies and kids. It's more common in kids who have allergies, and sometimes pet fur or a certain food can make it worse. Most kids grow out of it before they start school.

Moisturizing creams to help with red, dry skin are sold in supermarkets and chemists, but check which ones can be used on a baby's or an older kid's face and hands (in other words the bits most likely to be sensitive or that can easily transfer cream to the mouth). You may need to apply moisturizing cream to your child before and after they go swimming, after baths and hand washing, and perhaps morning and night or whenever it's needed. See your doctor if the dry skin becomes rashy and doesn't respond.

Like bad nappy rash, if the eczema rash breaks the skin, or the skin is scratched, it can become infected: see your chemist or doctor for info about a therapeutic cream or antibiotics.

Babies usually get eczema on the face, especially the cheeks and around the mouth. Factors that make eczema worse include wetness, such as in high-dribble places, heat and dryness. Avoid woollen clothes or hats, "non-breathing" unnatural fabrics, and soap and detergents, which dry the skin. Keep the car and pram as cool as possible with shade devices. We often take off one layer for while we're in the car: don't forget to do this for your baby or kid as well.

Car and home heaters can be very drying, particularly those that blow hot air. Better for you all to put a jumper on than to turn the heater up. There's not much you can do in a windy, drying, harsh environment or a humid, sticky one, but try to adjust for the weather as much as you can. Duvets can be too hot (and mustn't be used for babies anyway): try using a combination of cotton blankets and woollen ones (away from the skin) or, in the case of babies, a cotton sleeping suit (like a sleeping bag with arms, available at baby clothes shops and department-store baby sections). Washing-machine detergents can be too harsh: it's best to use gentler wool or hand-washing mixes. Chemically treated water, such as swimming-pool water, can also be very drying.

Baths should be tepid (but not cool or chilly) and short and a soap substitute used. Two to three baths a week will do.

For extra help see "More Info" at the end of this chapter.

astHma

Asthma is caused by the little tubes in the lungs being squeezed or inflamed so it's harder to get big, full breaths in and out. The mildest symptom is usually wheezing, stepping up to asthma attacks or "respiratory distress", which in very severe cases results in the child not being able to breathe at all.

Not all wheezing is asthma: it can be caused by bronchitis or another virus, so it's important to get a proper diagnosis. Other causes of wheezing include the kid swallowing something that gets stuck; an infection in a baby under 1 year old (bron-chiolitis); and smaller airways than normal.

It's not known why some people get asthma and others don't, but the incidence is rising and known trigger factors include a smoker in the house; having allergies; the house-dust mite in dust; pollen; mould; and pet fur. It's held that breastfed babies are statistically more likely to grow up asthma free, but many children who were breastfed for years have asthma and many formula-fed children don't. Asthma UK can give you a checklist so you can rejig your home to avoid triggers and can keep you in touch with the latest research results and treatments. Painkillers containing aspirin, which should never be given to children, or ibuprofen (under various brand names) can cause a reaction in some kids who have asthma, so ask your doctor about what

MANAGEMENT OF ASTHMA

1 Take asthma medications as directed.

2 Monitor the asthma.

3 Stay active and healthy.

4 Avoid triggers such as allergens whenever possible (but most kid asthma is triggered by unavoidable viruses).

5 Have a written asthma action plan to refer to.

6 Visit the doctor regularly.

Sources: Australian Asthma Foundation and Dr Michael Harari

to use (and see the "Painkillers: Paracetamol and Ibuprofen" box earlier in the chapter).

Asthma is not so much cured as managed or controlled so that it has as little effect on someone's life as possible. The main medications used are liquid ones and inhalers – some are preventative and some are used for an asthma attack. Asthma doesn't mean a kid should stop being outdoors or playing sport.

A child who suddenly has an asthma attack should be taken to a doctor or hospital straight away, where they can be treated and you can be given a plan for managing any further attacks. Shortness of breath or an obvious asthma episode mustn't be ignored as a severe attack can cut off breathing entirely.

Current medical thinking is that preventative steps and medication are much better ways of managing asthma than intermittently having to use heavier drugs to treat severe attacks. Specialized slow-breathing techniques have helped some people.

Part of the trauma of an asthma attack for a kid is the panic that goes on around them. Let the professionals do their job, while you concentrate on keeping your kid calm.

Your kid's babysitter, child-care centre or nursery needs to be told about your kid's asthma status and about any regular or emergency treatment or procedures. Their fridge can hold a spare inhaler, with instructions attached. See your doctor about any instructions these places should be given, provide them in writing, talk through the action plan with at least two staff members and keep copies for babysitters, relatives and friends.

Spare inhalers should be kept in your toddler bag; in your handbag; at homes you regularly visit; in the holiday first-aid kit; and anywhere else sensible, but not the car glove box (too hot). And check the use-by dates.

autism spectrum disorders, including asperger's syndrome

Autism is often referred to as the autism spectrum because it covers many levels of related disorders, including a subgroup called Asperger's syndrome. Autism is diagnosed much more commonly than in the past. Basically it is believed to be caused by problems in the brain that have some kind of genetic basis (boys are more likely to have autism and so is the twin of a child with autism).

Autism and its variation Asperger's syndrome should be diagnosed by a specialist. Because medical services and special programmes have long waiting lists and because great improvement commonly occurs when treatment is begun early, don't hesitate to see your GP the minute you feel any unease about your baby's or child's development, and a specialist if that's needed.

If autism is diagnosed, aggressively seek special programmes that can help your child. Hassle your local members of parliament if necessary. Symptoms of autism and Asperger's syndrome are most often seen from 18 months onwards, although many parents say they saw earlier signs but did not then have the information to be suspicious. (See "More Info" at the end of this chapter for resources.)

It's probably needless to say, but many development problems have nothing to do with autism and are in the normal range.

Why is the autism rate rising?

The area of autism is still under intense study, there are lots of theories, and variations of the syndrome are being described more thoroughly and applied as a diagnosis more than ever before. For a while there many parents were concerned that the MMR (measles mumps and rubella injection) was associated with autism. It is now known that there is no link. Doctors and mainstream autism organisations worldwide are convinced there is no link, and MMR immunization rates are starting to recover. (See the Immunization chapter for more). Doctors say that the rise in cases is explained by the fact that autism syndrome is now usually viewed as a spectrum – a diagnosis of autism or Asperger's syndrome is made where in the past a child with mild autistic symptoms or Asperger's syndrome would just have been described as "difficult", "different", "retarded" or simply "not good with people".

Meanwhile in the computer-industry-dominated Silicon Valley area of California, there has been a very sharp rise in the number of autism-type cases, and especially

---

SOME SYMPTOMS ASSOCIATED WITH AUTISM DISORDERS

A child:

* has a delay in speech development

* is unwilling to make eye contact

* doesn't like to be cuddled

* seems detached

* has rages caused by frustration

* has repetitive, obsessive movements or pursuits

* does not engage in imaginative play

* is anxious if there's a change to routines or something expected

* has difficulty communicating or conversing.

People with autism rarely understand jokes, feelings, body language or how to behave in many social situations.

---

of Asperger's syndrome. It is thought by some in the field that the "intermarriage"of people affectionately known as computer geeks, many of whom had variations of Asperger's syndrome, has led to the passing on of other variations to their children.

attention-Deficit Hyperactivity Disorder (aDHD)

Attention-deficit hyperactivity disorder, sometimes called attention deficit disorder (ADHD), is a clinical diagnosis that has been given to the sort of kid who bounces off the walls. The commonly recognized symptoms include:

* a short or no attention span
* fidgeting
* being "hyperactive" – always on the move
* aggressive behaviour
* boredom.

It's not a diagnosis that should ever be made by a parent, a teacher or a GP as commonly happens. There is a fierce debate in medical circles about whether ADHD is a real medical disorder or a name given to a wide range of behaviours that are not necessarily medical at all. There is also much dispute about whether children diagnosed with ADHD should be given the strong brain-chemistry-affecting drugs associated with the medical treatment of ADHD, the long-term effects of which are unknown.

Many people believe that ADHD can be used as a convenient label for kids who have short attention spans, or who are easily bored and often disruptive in class, or who have psychological problems and are more controllable when drugged. There is some evidence of this. Western Australia, for example, has a vastly higher rate of both diagnosis and drug treatment than other states, and this has led to accusations of a disturbing over-diagnosis of ADHD.

Some of the symptoms of what might seem like ADHD at first glance can actually be treated with family counselling, behaviour strategies, diet changes or even a change of school or parenting philosophy. Many of the symptoms, unless absolutely out of control, are the sorts of outer-edge-of-normal, rambunctious behaviour shown by intelligent children – often boys. In very severe cases diagnosed as ADHD some doctors say there are neurological (brain) differences. (See "More Info", which follows, for resources.)

ADHD must be diagnosed by a paediatric specialist and should only be treated with drugs as a last resort.

moRe iNfo

FIRST AID

First Aid Fast for Babies and Children

Dorling Kindersley, 2006

Produced by the British Red Cross, this is a handy first port of call for basic first aid through to life-saving procedures. Clear illustrations and colour-coded for when you're in a hurry.

St John Ambulance

Helpline: 08700 10 49 50

www.sja.org.uk

Website has everything you need to know about learning first aid and becoming a volunteer. Life-saving first aid information can be downloaded onto your MP3 player for use wherever you are.

Red Cross

Helpline: 0844 871 11 11

www.redcross.org.uk and there is also www.redcrossfirstaidtraining.co.uk

The British contingent of the international humanitarian mob we all look to in a crisis.

COMMON CHILDHOOD ILLNESSES AND CONDITIONS

None of the following handy reference books and websites should be considered a substitute for individual, face-to-face medical diagnosis and advice. As with all books that involve medical information, get the latest edition. Don't forget to check for these at your local library if they're too expensive for your budget.

When Your Child Is Ill: A Home Guide for Parents (BMA Family Doctor)

by H. B. Valman, Dorling Kindersley, 2008

This is the "official" British Medical Association book on how to manage your sick child. Very easy to use and well illustrated. It has a great development chart and some useful but rather graphic photos of disgustingly erupting things you'd normally not want to see unless there are some already on your kid and you need to know what they are. Contains everything from limping and sniffles to whooping cough and muscular dystrophy. It also includes rudimentary first aid and has sensible flow charts that direct you to the right action required in an individual case.

Baby and Child Healthcare: The Essential A-Z Home Reference to Children's Illnesses, Symptoms and Treatments

by Miriam Stoppard, Dorling Kindersley, 2001

Dr Stoppard has written a whole string of books on baby and child care, so if you like her style, this is the one.

Natural Health for Kids: How to Give Your Child the Very Best Start in Life
by John Briffa, Penguin, 2007
Comprehensive and accessible "natural" health care guide for common childhood
conditions such as asthma, allergies, bee stings and the dreaded nits. Remember to have
a diagnosis confirmed by a doctor, and consider the doctor's advice, before treating
with a natural remedy.

Natural Health for Kids: Complementary Treatments for More Than 50 Ailments
by Sarah Wilson, Hamlyn, 2006
Draws on a range of holistic therapies such as aromatherapy, reflexology, herbalism
and nutritional therapy to treat minor ailments and maintain good health. Again, get a
medical diagnosis and advice before proceeding.

www.bbc.co.uk/health
This is an excellent general health website with plenty of advice relating to young
children, and a good section on asthma.

www.ich.ucl.ac.uk
The joint website of the Great Ormond Street Hospital and the Institute of Child Health,
University College London includes factsheets on various common childhood health
problems, handy hints on bringing a child to hospital, a roundup of support groups
for families with kids who have certain conditions, advice from child health experts
(including an alphabetical archive of "Dr Jane's" down-to-earth advice on everything
from pidgeon toes to hayfever) and a glossary of terms you may need to understand.

www.kidshealth.org
A website established by a philanthropic foundation, which has info on common
ailments, kids' feelings and a preventative lifestyle. There's a glossary of medical terms
and stuff for kids with disabilities. Very American – British kids are unlikely to have to
deal with a chigger bite (I have no idea). The advantage is that all health problems are
explained at a kid's level – it may help you explain things to a toddler (and yourself!).

TOO MUCH SUN

www.canceresearchuk.org

Great advice on sun care for yourself and your children. Also has details of their "SunSmart" Campaign.

www. nhsdirect.nhs.uk

From the home page, search sunscreen or sun, for a wealth of relevant info. And remember when on other sites that kids with very dark skin need more sun than those with pale skin, so they can make enough vitamin D and cover-up advice on most sites seems to assume you're a pale-face.

HEAD LICE

Good information is available on **nhsdirect.nhs.uk** or **bbc.co.uk/health** (search headlice or nits from the home page of either). Be aware that while **www.headlice. co.uk** has some useful info, it's a commercial site owned by one brand of lotion.

ECZEMA

www.eczema.org

Helpline: 0800 089 1122 (Mon–Fri 8am–8pm)

The website of the National Eczema Society has comprehensive information.

ASTHMA

www.asthma.org.uk

Tel: 08456 03 81 43

Helpline (an asthma nurse specialist): 08457 01 02 03

Asthma UK's site provides info for parents on asthma triggers, treatments and management (click on "all about asthma") as well as details of its fundraising and lobbying activities, camps for kids with asthma, and more. You can ask questions of an asthma nurse specialist on the helpline or email questions from the site.

AUTISM SPECTRUM DISORDERS, INCLUDING ASPERGER'S SYNDROME

www.autism.org.uk

Helpline: 0845 070 4004

The website of the The National Autistic Society. There is good general information, and it tells you about the branches all over the country, with separate pages for Wales, Scotland and Northern Ireland.

www.nationalautismassociation.org

The US National Autism Association has plenty of info on the condition, latest medical thinking and more, but all the stuff relating to the US health and medical insurance system is of course, irrelevant to the UK.

Ten Things Every Child with Autism Wishes You Knew

by Ellen Notbohm, Future Horizons, 2007

Families seem to find this book very helpful.

A Real Boy: How Autism Shattered Our Lives - and Made a Family from the Pieces

by Christopher Stevens with Nicola Stevens, Michael O'Mara Books, 2008

This is a highly personal account of life viewed through the eyes of someone with autism. Not everyone's bag, but great if you like this kind of thing.

The Complete Guide to Asperger's Syndrome

by Tony Atwood, Jessica Kingsley Publishers, 2008

Comprehensive analysis of this complex condition based on this specialist's clinical experience and correspondences with families. Its level of detail might make it more suitable for professionals, but it is nevertheless accessible for the "lay" person.

Asperger's Syndrome, the Universe and Everything

by Kenneth Hall, Jessica Kingsley Publishers, 2000

Fascinating book by a 10-year-old Irish boy with Asperger's syndrome. Suitable for children and adults.

www.wired.com/wired/archive/9.12/aspergers.html

The Silicon Valley gene theory is explored in a *Wired* magazine article, "The Geek Syndrome".

ATTENTION DEFICIT HYPERACTIVITY DISORDER (ADHD)

www.addiss.co.uk

Tel: 020 8952 2800

ADDISS stands for ADHD Information Services. There is a disappointing amount of out-of-date stuff on the site, but there are useful pointers to other sources of information.

hi2u.org.uk

Website for ADHD, Asperger's syndrome, dyslexia and other "hidden" impairments. **adhd.org.uk** is a subsection of this website. Lots of different people have contributed to the content, so it's neither all professional nor all "lay" in its approach.

www.attentiondeficitdisorder.ws

A website of links to all things ADHD.

The Pocket Guide to Understanding A.D.H.D.: Practical Tips for Parents

by Dr Christopher Green and Dr Kit Che, Vermilion, 2004

This is easily the best and most accessible book on ADHD around.

The ADHD Parenting Handbook: Practical Advice for Parents from Parents

by Colleen Alexander Roberts, Taylor Trade Publishing, 1994

Highly regarded and not as out of date as its publication date might make you think.

Being active

Unfortunately almost every book about kids has pages and pages on what to feed them and pages and pages on what development stages they're supposed to be at, and almost nothing about appropriate exercise for toddlers.

Exercise is a crucial part of preventing kids from developing an unhealthy body. Exercise in this context just means being active. An added bonus: kids sleep better when they're physically tired. Kids in the past were outside a lot more and stood, walked and played more, using up energy. Now they tend to play indoors and to

Let's play!

eat more calorie-rich food than kids used to twenty years ago, yet do less exercise. Some of the reasons for this include parents themselves not getting outside or exercising as much, kids watching more TV and back gardens becoming smaller or non-existent.

All health professionals stress that unless the whole family is willing to get involved in a more healthy and active life, it's almost impossible to help a TV-addicted kid this young learn to enjoy pottering about the garden, climbing trees, playing sports and having other outdoor fun.

exercise tHat's good foR kiDs

Dr Elizabeth Waters, a child health specialist says people can get too uptight and formal about exercise for little kids: "The best thing for parents to do is get out there with their kids and make walking and playing in the park part of normal life . . . The worst thing is to put kids through their paces at clubs or organisations where it isn't family fun and natural play together." (I just love it when an expert says something sensible like "Oh, just go outside and play and talk and do stuff that makes you laugh".) Dr Waters suggests that parents aim to have a chat and a fall-about with their kids every day, but not to freak out if they miss a day here and there. Dads and other blokes can often get special joy from passing on important ball and balancing skills.

★ Babies who can't walk can roll balls and move to music.

★ Toddlers can do fun stretches, kick a ball and start to learn to catch (try a balloon first and work up to soft balls).

★ Little kids can throw a large, light ball with two hands (throwing with one hand began the first time they dropped something on the floor).

★ Kids who can run can start doing obstacle games and football.

Exercise doesn't need to be structured. But to keep it interesting, and to develop different muscle groups and skills, choose one or two age-appropriate activities from the list "Good Exercise Stuff to Do with Kids" (next page) to concentrate on each day.

Instead of taking an adult angle and saying kids must exercise for a certain time each day, be guided by your kid: how long are they interested in this exercise or game? When they sit or lie down, get cranky, yawn or want to do something else, that's the time to stop. Have another go later or the next day. It's important to remind everyone that it's all about fun and experience, not setting goals: anything that isn't fun is guaranteed to fail.

Keeping exercise varied will give a kid a chance to find out what they like and what they're good at. Training or concentrating on one sport is not good for young children: it is too restrictive mentally and physically and can lead to injury and underdevelopment in other physical areas. I heard recently of some parents who encourage their 3-year-olds to do laps of a pool equivalent to swimming a kilometre: I would like to slap them. That kind of "achievement" is not applicable to toddlers. "The notion of winning doesn't need to emerge at this age", says Dr Waters. (Or at least until they're 32, if you ask me.)

iNfo oN BeiNg active

★ Local councils often have information about hidden opportunities in your area. You might find that even in the inner city, tucked behind a block of flats, there's a ramshackle adventure playground with a real pony in one corner, some live chickens, a trampoline and lots of things to fall off and climb under. These and some other adventure playgrounds can be more dangerous than the pristine, rounded, almost guaranteed no-injury, plastic-moulded climbing equipment made only for the youngest children. (A child of 3 on a flying fox will need to be very closely helped, for example.) But if you're prepared to take a few risks, and supervise properly, they can be so much fun for kids.

★ Toy libraries may have activity equipment such as balls, trikes, and mats to roll on.

GOOD EXERCISE STUFF TO DO WITH KIDS

✱ Ball throwing and catching.

✱ Riding a trike, a bike or other wheelie device.

✱ Running with paper streamers.

✱ Exploring the garden or park, and perhaps having a picnic.

✱ Doing exercises in the garden or park.

✱ Flying a kite.

✱ Balancing.

✱ Doing "acrobatics" (somersaults and cartwheels) on the lawn.

✱ Mucking around at the adventure playground.

✱ Going to the local swimming pool.

✱ Walking to the shop (take the stroller for sudden fades).

✱ Playing variations of football, dodge ball, tennis, rounders or cricket.

✱ Playing kick-to-kick with a football.

✱ Going on a nature ramble or treasure hunt to collect things (find a red leaf, an acorn, a bent stick).

✱ Playing in the sandpit.

✱ Making patterns in sand or dirt with a rake, shells, stones or sticks.

✱ Dancing.

✱ Playing chasey.

✱ Running through the sprinkler (but not when there's a drought).

✱ Jumping in puddles, wearing wellies.

✱ Pottering in the garden, doing some weeding, planting and picking.

✱ Running around with the dog (but always supervised).

✱ "Painting" the fence with water.

✱ Sweeping the paths.

✱ Climbing trees or other things.

✱ Decorating trees.

✱ Playing hide and seek.

★ Parenting magazines and newspapers often have ads for kids' physical activity programmes, frequently held during school holidays. These are usually for older kids so be careful.

toDDLeR gyms

Movement-based groups such as these can be fun for kids and can be a sort of parents' group as well. They are held in many areas and can be for babies aged 1 month up to school age. A trained coordinator uses songs, bubbles, climbing equipment, exercise mats – all sorts of things – to develop coordination, muscles and physical capabilities. Movement programmess aim to promote intellectual development also, which makes sense. But rather than thinking of them as "hothousing" or "training" your child to "get ahead", it's much nicer to think of them as good fun and good for children.

An organized, gym-style programme will not suit many children, especially the ones who don't like being regimented, and equipment that must all be used and in a certain way can curb creativity. Sometimes a programme is held in too small a space, which can be restrictive for kids who need to explore. Gym-style routines shouldn't be a replacement for kids just having active fun with their family and friends. You can make a DIY physical-fun session: see "More Info" below.

moRe iNfo

Moving to Learn: Making the Connection Between Movement, Music, Learning and Play (Birth to 3 Years)
by Robyn Crowe and Gill Connell, book/ music CD set, Caxton Press, 2003
This Aussie–Kiwi collaboration between two early-childhood professionals presents all sorts of info and ideas for fun physical activities. Ideal for parents, playgroups and child-care centres. The accompanying website is **www.movingtolearn.com**.

GARDENING

Great Gardens for Kids
by Clare Matthews, Hamlyn, 2002

Wonderful ideas to show that gardens are for getting about and into, not just something to look at. Simple instructions for making a daffodil maze, a living "tent", a rope spider web, and ideas for Easter egg hunts, halloween lantern fun, a CD wind chime – all illustrated with photos so kids can choose what takes their fancy and help with creating the projects.

Kids Container Gardening: Year-Round Projects for Inside and Out
by Cindy Krezel, Ball Publishing, 2006

A roundup of a few small-scale projects such as terrariums, veggie hanging baskets, and seed germination for young ones and parents to do together, or for independent older kids, many of which can be tackled even if there's only a balcony or no garden at all. Divided into ideas for each season.

PHYSICAL ACTIVITIES FOR TODDLERS

Your local authority can provide you with a list of your nearest leisure centres, many of which will run toddler gym classes, either supervised by you or more formally with specially trained instructors.

www.all4kidsuk.com
The Activity Groups section of this general site will help you locate gym and other physical activity classes in your area.

www.tumbletots.com
Commercial site supporting organized movement classes for kids, from babies through to age 7, with instructors trained in fun activities tailored to age-specific development. This can also be a good way to meet other parents with similar age kids to help socialize the offspring and get to meet some potential new pals (or swap babysitting offers).

immunization

In developing countries where parents can see the effects of crippling and fatal diseases around them, they eagerly attend government and charity clinics, desperate for their children to be immunized. In the developed world, many parents were confused by now discredited stories of the dangers and side effects of vaccines. The confusion and misinformation led to a fall in UK immunization levels, and inevitable outbreaks of measles and other illnesses. Thankfully, the vast majority of Britons do have their kids fully immunized, and this chapter looks at why it's necessary.

This has gotta be worth a chockie frog

immunization overview

All UK kids under the age of 5 should have been given the list of recommended immunizations (also called vaccinations) to protect them against a range of infectious diseases with symptoms that can include a severe fever and spots, a miserable few days, a scary cough, paralysis, permanent physical disability or brain damage and death. These diseases include diptheria, tetanus, polio, whooping cough (pertussis), a bacteria called Hib that used to be a common cause of meningitis, pneumoccal disease, measles, mumps, german measles (rubella) and meningitis C. No doubt other vaccines will go into the mix in future.

The immunization programme has two aims: to protect individual children from these "old-fashioned" diseases; and, in some cases, to have a public health campaign to eradicate a disease altogether. It isn't compulsory to have the vaccinations, but it is urged by all doctors and the vaccines are provided free by the government. Kids are given injections by a GP or a nurse at the surgery or health centre.

The World Health Organization (WHO) says that almost three million people a year are alive because they've been vaccinated against diseases. It's a calculation based on the pre-vaccination death rates of various diseases.

There are some very heated debates about vaccinations. At the extremes there are doctors who say it isn't worth discussing the fact that a relatively tiny number of kids are damaged by vaccines because it's far fewer than those who would have died from the diseases if there had been no vaccinations; and at the other end there are some nutty anti-vaccinators who say extremely dodgy stuff, often on their websites, including this: "Children who were breastfed and are well looked after have an immune system which will protect them against diseases". (This, frankly, is a big fat fib.)

Parents don't always look at the big picture and I think doctors need to understand this. We are usually more worried about what effect a vaccine might have on our individual tiny person than thrilled to participate in a disease-eradication public health programme. When doctors say there's less than a one-in-a-million chance of a serious vaccination reaction such as inflammation of the brain, they should remember we're all worried that our baby might be that one in a million. (For the vast majority of parents, it gets easier by the second lot of scheduled shots because the first ones caused no problems at all.)

Parents with legitimate questions can be treated like rabid twits by both sides. On the one hand the "information" given them in anti-vaccination books and on websites is most often a shocking mix of lies, twisted statistics and accusations totally irrelevant to UK vaccines. On the other hand a few worried parents have been bullied by doctors instead of being given information respectfully. (Time to find another GP if that's the case: the majority will talk to you sensibly about concerns.)

Most people have already made up their mind about what they think of vaccines by the time they have children. Some get whatever's on the schedule, no questions asked. Others vehemently oppose vaccinations and won't be swayed by any facts presented. The following is really for people who want more info before closing their eyes, crossing their fingers and jumping (a time-honoured, metaphorical parent-decision-making technique).

Despite the claims of many anti-vaccine lobbyists, the dedicated medical staff who immunize children are, hey, *probably not* part of some bizarre, worldwide, shifty-eyed conspiracy to make money for drug companies, and *probably not* brainwashed, robotic devotees of weird science. And it seems equally evident that sadly a very, very small number of individual children among millions may be harmed by a vaccine. In a perfect world each child's reactions would be perfectly predictable, each child with a medical predisposition would have obvious symptoms, and each vaccine dose would be individually tailored to the levels of immunity in each child without needing blood to be taken with yet another injection. Ultimately parents will have to weigh up the tiny statistical risk for their child against the protection from diseases.

CURReNt ROUtiNe CHiLDHOOD immUNizatiON SCHeDULe

Although the list of vaccines at each scheduled age looks daunting, they'll be combined in "cocktails" so there probably won't be more than two jabs at any appointment, except at four months when there'll be three. The following schedule operated at July 2008:

★ **two months** – diphtheria, tetanus, pertussis, polio, Hib, pneumococcal infection

★ **three months** – boosters for diphtheria, tetanus, pertussis, polio, Hib; meningitis C

KEEPING A RECORD

All immunizations administered to children are logged in the Personal Child Health Record (the "red book"), which is issued at birth for all babies and kept by the parents. The book also contains a consent form for you to sign prior to the jabs. Nurseries and schools in the UK do not usually require proof of immunization, but you may be required to show some record when entering another country.

★ **four months** – boosters for diphtheria, tetanus, pertussis, polio, Hib, pneumococcal infection, meningitis C
★ **around twelve months** – boosters for Hib, meningitis C
★ **around thirteen months** – measles, mumps, rubella; booster for pneumococcal infection
★ **three years four months to five years old** – boosters for diphtheria, tetanus, pertussis, polio, measles, mumps, rubella

The next scheduled jabs are adolescent boosters.

Children considered "at risk" may be targeted for extra, free vaccines such as tuberculosis or hepatitis B: ask your GP if you are eligible. Vaccines that may be required for travel are not on the pharmaceutical benefits list and many must be paid for.

See also the table "Diseases and Their Vaccinations" coming up soon in this chapter.

How Does a Vaccine Work?

Vaccines against bacterial disease usually contain a form of the bacteria or toxin that causes the disease it will protect against. A tiny bit of, let's say, Hib bacteria has been treated so it can't actually cause the disease itself but prompts the body to produce antibodies – protection against the disease. In some cases an inactive component of the bacteria (for example, its sugar coating) is mixed with a protein known to help it produce the required reaction in a young body.

A vaccine might also contain a preservative and barely detectable traces of formaldehyde, used to kill the contagious bit of the bacteria or virus in the lab. Some vaccines that protect against viruses are "live" but have been altered so that they are a very weak form of the virus. They produce immunity but don't cause the disease. Initially a vaccine is tested on laboratory animals, then larger animals, then finally on human volunteers. Results are reported, published and checked by government licensors.

getting an immunization

If you have a lot of questions you'd like answered, it's probably best to go to your doctor or health visitor. They should ask you some questions to make sure the vaccine is safe for your child and your family, and that there are no previous illnesses or allergic conditions that mean your child should see an immunization specialist at your local hospital.

If you buy a vaccine from the chemist on prescription and take it back to the doctor for the injection, make sure you keep it at the right temperature – usually refrigerated but not frozen or it will lose its potency. After the injection hang around with your baby or toddler for fifteen minutes to ensure there is no anaphylactic shock (see the section "Reactions" later in this chapter).

If your kid is quite sick and has a fever, it's probably best to postpone the immunization in case it's harder to spot any side effects of the vaccination. If your kid has sneezes, sniffles or an ordinary old cold it's almost always fine to go ahead with the immunization, but ask if you're worried.

How to help a child on injection day

Babies usually just look momentarily horrified and accusing when they get their injections, and cry briefly until they're cuddled and distracted, perhaps by a breastfeed or bottlefeed. Older kids usually are stoical or cry a little and they too forget the pain moments later, especially when cunningly distracted. You

Teddy's had 27 injections

may be surprised to see how slender and quick the disposable needle is these days.

Have on hand tissues for tears, two special treats for an older baby or small child, a comforting toy or other item. The following things should help with toddlers and nursery-age children.

★ There is usually no point in describing the scene to a kid or building up anticipation (which is likely to be fearful) – but be guided by your specialist knowledge of your child. Jennifer Irwin, an immunization nurse, says "Think about how much preparation your child needs before any new experience. Sometimes it is good to have a story or two a day or so before or perhaps some play with a toy medical kit to prepare." You can ask your playgroup or child-care centre to have a group chat about it.

★ You can use a pretend or toy syringe to give injections to a teddy or dolly, but it's probably not a good idea to "train" kids to pick up real-looking syringes.

★ At the actual time be matter of fact about having an injection; don't build it up to be important or scary.

★ Never say "Don't cry".

★ Explain (even if it's been explained before) that the nurse or doctor is going to put some very special medicine inside them to stop them from getting bad sicknesses, and that the nurse or doctor is going to use a needle and it will only take a second.

★ If asked, don't pretend that it won't hurt. Say it might sting for a short time but you'll have a special surprise treat ready for them straight afterwards.

★ You will be asked to hold the kid firmly to help them be very still. Try to make this feel cuddly rather than restraining.

★ Distraction is the key. Most kids prefer to look away, but some like to watch: either is fine. Some like a cartoon adhesive strip over the injection spot.

★ Immediately afterwards ask the kid to make a choice between, say, a sticker or a jelly bean: a choice of treats is very distracting and will usually stop any crying.

★ Praise them for sitting still during the injection and having it. Make a fuss of them.

★ You can press on the injection site afterwards to dull the stinging, but don't massage it.

DISEASES AND THEIR VACCINATIONS

Disease	Symptoms and effects	How it can be spread
Diphtheria	A growth in the throat can lead to suffocation. Rarer effects include paralysis; and death in seven percent of cases.	Sneezes, coughs, contact with bacteria on hand or hanky.
Tetanus	Muscle spasms; breathing problems; convulsions; the nervous system shuts down; and, if untreated, often leads to death.	A common micro-organism in dirt and manure, which will produce a toxin if it gets into a deep cut or puncture wound.
Pertussis (whooping cough)	Distressing coughing fits and inability to draw breath until spasm ends, when desperate intake of breath causes "whooping" sound – the coughing can continue for months; more rarely, convulsions and coma; often fatal in babies under 1 year old and a death rate in under-2s of one in 200; survivors may have permanent lung or brain damage.	Coughs, sneezes. The bacteria is highly contagious – three vaccine doses by the age of 6 months are needed to give high protection to a baby.
Poliomyelitis (infant paralysis, "Polio")	Fever; vomiting; muscle stiffness; nerve damage; five percent who get it will die from their breathing muscles being paralysed and half of the survivors will have permanent paralysis of the legs.	A virus spread by saliva and poo (for example, due to a nappy-changing hygiene problem).
Haemophilus influenzae type b (Hib)	Not actually anything to do with flu virus but a bacteria. Can cause meningitis (inflammation of the brain); swelling in the throat that can suffocate; pneumonia; joint and tissue infection; and death. A severe problem for the under-5s.	Coughs, sneezes, contact with bacteria on hand or hanky.

Possible side effects of the vaccine	Why we need the vaccine	Alternative to the vaccine that would guarantee safety from infection
See "pertussis" (below).	One of the most deadly infectious diseases at the start of the 20th century. Now virtually eradicated in many Western countries. (The former Soviet Union still has outbreaks: one in the 1990s, when immunization rates had fallen, saw more than 150,000 cases and 4000 deaths.)	None.
See "pertussis" below.	Tetanus is rare in the UK and almost exclusively strikes older, under-vaccinated people. The death rate of patients is about ten percent. About 800,000 babies a year in developing countries die each year because of low or no vaccination.	None. Unimmunized people need a tetanus immunoglobin (jab has side effects) and vaccine after a wound.
The modern vaccine causes far fewer side effects than the old one. Possible sore arm from jab and, rarely, low-grade fever, irritability, redness at jab site, brief fit in the 24 hours afterwards, with no long-term effects. The vaccine lasts about five to ten years.	Whooping cough, before there was a vaccine, killed thousands of children, especially smaller and more vulnerable babies. Even if it is not fatal, the illness is very distressing and frightening for babies and their parents.	None.
Now usually added to diphtheria, tetanus and pertussis	While many people believe polio has been eradicated, in fact it is still a serious problem in many places in the world, including India. Without immunization, another outbreak of polio here and elsewhere would be inevitable. Polio, like other diseases, doesn't respect borders or need a passport.	None.
Low-grade fever, sore injection site (the thigh in babies up to age 1, and the arm for older kids because the muscle is bigger then), nausea, joint pain.	Before Hib vaccine was introduced in 1992, around one in six hundred children developed some form of Hib disease by their fifth birthday, resulting in about thirty deaths every year and leaving about eighty children with deafness and permanent brain damage. Since the vaccine cases of the disease in young children have fallen by 98 percent.	None.

499

DISEASES AND THEIR VACCINATIONS *continued*

Disease	Symptoms and effects	How it can be spread
Pneumococcal infection	Fever; fussiness or listlessness; sensitivity to bright light; headache. If there's also a rash and neck stiffness it may mean meningitis.	Sneezes, coughs, dribble. From contact with the bacteria to symptoms may be less than 24 hours.
Meningitis C	A bacteria present in many healthy carriers causes flu-like symptoms that worsen within hours. Symptoms may include muscle pain; fever; stiff neck; aversion to bright lights; later development of a serious red or purple rash. Can be very quickly fatal.	Sneezes or other way of droplets being transported from the throat.
Measles	High fever; cough; conjunctivitis; feeling miserable; irritability; exhaustion; a red rash usually begins on the face after a week. One in 25 previously healthy kids with measles gets pneumonia; one in 2000 gets encephalitis (inflammation of the brain): of those with encephalitis ten per cent will die and up to forty per cent will have brain damage.	Sneezes, coughs or other contact. Astonishingly contagious virus, active for four days before and after the first appearance of the rash.
Mumps	Fever; headache; big puffed-out cheeks caused by infection of salivary glands. Rarer side effects include deafness; swollen testicles in post-puberty males, which in a few cases causes infertility; brain inflammation in one out of two hundred kids.	Sneezes, coughs.
Rubella (German measles)	Swollen glands; joint pains; a two- to three-day rash on the head and neck. It's easily recovered from, but if transmitted to a pregnant woman in the first eight to ten weeks there's a ninety percent chance of severe birth defects, including blindness, deafness, mental retardation; the risk continues to twenty weeks of pregnancy.	Very contagious: coughs and sneezes.

Possible side effects of the vaccine	Why we need the vaccine	Alternative to the vaccine that would guarantee safety from infection
Rarely, fever, redness at the jab site. Even more rarely, vomiting or diarrhoea.	Pneumococcal disease results in serious infections of lungs, blood and ears and is a major cause of meningitis in kids (mostly under 2). The vaccine stops the seven types of bacteria that cause most cases here.	None.
Injection site inflammation, temporary crankiness in babies, temporary headache in adults.	Before the introduction of the vaccine in 1999 the type C strain accounted for around forty percent of meningococcal cases in the UK.	None. A person exposed can take an antibiotic to reduce the chance of catching it. See your doctor immediately.
Sore arm; in ten per cent of children a mild fever and non-catchy rash five to twelve days after the injection. Up to one in a million children may develop encephalitis. A case of measles itself is much more likely to cause encephalitis.	Measles used to be a common childhood disease in the UK millions of people worldwide. In 1987 (the year before the MMR vaccine was introduced in the UK), 86,000 children caught measles and sixteen died.	None. The MMR (measles, mumps, rubella) vaccine given within 72 hours of contact, or an immunoglobin injection given within seven days, may or may not prevent or modify the disease.
Low-grade fever, which is related to the measles component, and in about one percent of cases slight facial swelling.	Before the MMR vaccine was introduced, about 1200 people a year in the UK went into hospital because of mumps.	None.
Slight fever and sore arm are the most common; some women develop transient joint pain.	Before immunization it was a very common cause of deafness.	None. Women need to be immunized up to one month before getting pregnant.

actual
size

★ If the injection site is red and sore afterwards, a cool pack can be held gently on it and a usual dose of baby or child paracetamol (see label) could be given.

★ Children will appreciate a "debriefing" so have a chat about why they had the injection and how they're protected against special sicknesses now. Keep up the praise.

★ The site of the injection may be sore to the touch for a few days. This is because injection into soft tissues can cause low-level bruising.

★ Ask your doctor or nurse for any side effects you should keep an eye out for and what to do if they appear.

Reactions

Most children show no reaction at all, apart from being a bit affronted and up for a major bribe straight after the injection. Breast or bottle milk or drinks can also be comforting. If there is a fever a trip to your doctor is a good idea: it might not be the immunization that is causing the high temperature. (Young children pick up new infections often but usually fight them off.) Don't give paracetamol to bring a fever down, but only if your kid is in pain or miserable. A sudden high fever can cause a brief fit (look up "convulsion" in the index). Fever does not cause brain damage. If there is a convulsion, call an ambulance on 999 immediately: it's best to be safe.

In extremely exceptional cases, vaccination can cause anaphylactic shock, an immediate allergic reaction. Because babies and small children rarely faint after an injection, a loss of consciousness should be assumed to be anaphylaxis – a life-threatening emergency because it can cause throat swelling leading to suffocation. If it's going to happen, it will almost certainly do so within ten to twenty minutes of the injection. Treatment is usually a swift adrenaline injection, possibly extra oxygen and always a trip to hospital for observation. (A nurse giving one hundred immunizations a week for 52 weeks a year would see one of these reactions once every two hundred years. And she'd be very wrinkly by then too.)

If your child has had a reaction such as fever to an injection, talk about it with your doctor, call the immunization clinic at your local hospital for a chat and maybe schedule the next injections at their clinic where they're specialized at this sort of thing.

aRguments about immunization

Additives
The argument against the MMR (measles, mumps, rubella) injection used to be that mercury in the injection was causing health problems. As there is no mercury (thiomersal) used in this or any of the other UK injections on the schedule for kids now there's little point in arguing the issue here, although a link was never proved. Despite the claims of most anti-vaccination books and websites, you can be assured their MMR jab and almost all other childhood vaccines are free of mercury. If you're worried, ask your doctor to get out the list of ingredients from the packet and take you through them. If there is anything in the mix that bothers you, talk about ordering another brand if that's possible.

There is a tiny amount of pork gelatin in one brand of MMR vaccine. However, the Muslim Council of Britain advises Muslims they are "duty-bound" to use life-saving preventative measures and the WHO on its website has posted a statement endorsed from many Islamic medical scholars to the effect that the transformed gelatin can be considered "pure" and "permissible" to consume.

Autism and vaccines: no proven link
Various anti-vaccine activists have accused various vaccines of causing various things, including autism, in the past. Largely because of publicity over a controversial piece of research in the UK, the triple MMR (measles, mumps, rubella) injection has been accused of causing autism and intestinal problems.

Basically it's a disagreement between all of the medical doctors in the world except for a tiny, tiny handful, versus many parents of sick children who say they are worried about whether damage was caused by the MMR vaccine, ranging from worries about mercury additive (no longer relevant to UK, USA or Australian vaccines for children), or in opposition to the idea of giving three vaccines in one jab, preferring three injections spaced over time.This is because they believe that the immune system is too challenged by a multiple vaccine: another theory that doctors say has no supporting evidence and is disproven by the vast number of successful "triple" jabs (more on this coming up). In the 1990s a UK digestion doctor called Andrew Wakefield urged a boycott of the MMR (measles mumps rubella) vaccine because he claimed it was linked to, or may cause, autism. This study has now been totally discredited by every other study on MMR and autism rates, and all reputable immune system and infectious diseases specialists. Dr Wakefield currently faces charges of professional misconduct from the General Medical Council (charges which he is contesting) concerning ethical questions and accusations of research irregularities. Sadly, much damage was done to parents' confidence and MMR immunization rates though improving in the wake of the revelations concerning the research have yet to fully recover.

Dr Nigel Curtis, an immunization expert says he understands why parents might blame an illness or condition on immunization when it is not actually the culprit. Like other doctors, he points out that most kids who get autism do have the MMR injection – and most kids who don't have autism have it too.

"In any given day there are hundreds of babies having their MMR jab or pre-schoolers having the booster. That means any cold, cough, fever or dribble could be mistakenly blamed on the MMR even though it is probably not associated at all. One child in the queue here the other day had a fit just before his injection. If it had been 5 minutes after, it would have been blamed on the injection. There is no connection between MMR and autism except that parents usually first notice signs of autism around the same age as the MMR injection is given," he says.

No study or doctor can prove that vaccines don't cause autism in a tiny number of cases, say, one in a million, because that's impossible to prove. But it is also true to say that absolutely no link between autism and MMR has ever been proved despite exhaustive checks of all the relevant research going back decades, and new studies following up kids in many countries who have had the MMR vaccination (see "More Info" at the end of this chapter).

For info on other theories of why the autism rate may be rising, see the section on autism in the "Health" chapter.

"The oldest inhabitants recollected no period at all at which measles had been so prevalent, or so fatal to infant existence; and many were the mournful [funeral] processions . . ." CHARLES DICKENS, *OLIVER TWIST*, 1837

Usual reasons for opposing immunization

Religious reasons Many people who oppose vaccination do so from a religious point of view: some Christians because of their idiosyncratic interpretation of the Bible.

It isn't natural If you look at it that way, neither are tampons, anaesthetics, aeroplanes, men without beards, or HobNob biscuits. But they can all be quite useful on occasion.

The diseases don't exist any more Yes they do. Whooping cough cases are in many hospitals at any given time; measles and many other diseases are just an incoming plane away. Measles is so contagious that you can just walk past someone (with measles) in the street and come down with it.

Vaccines don't work Vaccines have been remarkably successful in reducing or eradicating diseases, but a very few vaccinated people can still contract a less virulent form of some of the diseases such as whooping cough. The medical establishment has always acknowledged this.

It is too much of a challenge to the child's immune system to give so many vaccinations, especially triple whammies Millions of children have taken the vaccine "load" without incident or injury. A very small number of children may have had a problem, but this is not provable. Some doctors say kids could take thousands of vaccines without a problem, and that's not provable either because it's a stupid and unnecessary suggestion. Doctors should just admit that they're offering a vast improvement on the past, when your child ran a much, much higher risk of pain, suffering, damage and death from preventable and rampant childhood diseases. As my Grandma used to say "You pays your money and you takes your chances".

There are alternatives, such as breastfeeding and organic food Several anti-vaccination lobbyists claim that you can protect your child from childhood diseases by breastfeeding and giving your child love, fresh air and organic food. This is a cruel and stupid lie that encourages some parents to think their dangerously sick or dying child wasn't given enough love, fresh air, unsightly carrots or breast milk when it has nothing to do with any of that. Some of the vaccine-preventable diseases are so wildly catching that an infected person walking into a room full of unimmunized people is likely to infect 90 percent of them, regardless of whether they were or are breastfed or how healthy they are. It is true that all those things will help build a better immune system. But that won't stop you from getting a very infectious disease.

There are homeopathic and herbal "alternatives" to vaccination   These have been discredited by responsible herbalists and the British Homeopathy Association itself which says "There is no evidence to show that homeopathic medicines can be used instead of vaccination. The Faculty of Homeopathy recommends that immunization is carried out in the usual way, unless there are strong medical contraindications."

Childhood diseases are mostly trivial, just requiring a couple of days in bed   Oh, poop (see the "Diseases and Their Vaccinations" table earlier in this chapter). The World Health Organization reports irregular outbreaks of all these diseases, including polio, whooping cough and diphtheria. Measles still kills hundreds of thousands of kids worldwide. It is certainly not true that childhood diseases are trivial for everyone, especially among children who are already at risk, such as babies in Third World countries and whom we also want to protect.

Pro-vaccination contacts
Your health visitor and GP will have all the official info on your immunization schedule and can provide pamphlets and info about individual vaccines and the diseases they protect against.

Most pro-vaccination books are heavy-going medical bricks that are only understandable to people in cardigans covered by white coats who use words such as "histocompatibility antigen specificities" in their lunch hour, and the books concentrate on the wider issue of public health rather than helping you to make an individual decision (for the more accessible books see "More Info" at the end of this chapter).

Anti-vaccination contacts
I totally understand the parents of autistic children wanting more research done on vaccines. I tried to find an anti-vaccination book or website that seems perfectly sober and reasonable. God knows I tried. But to be brutally candid, I only found nutty ones.

This is one of the reasons why the writings are almost always self-published – big publishing houses and magazines won't touch them. Most of the authors fervently claimed that immunization doesn't prevent disease – which is demonstrably not true. Almost all books, websites and articles in "alternative" magazines quote the same handful of self-described "researchers" or "experts".

You should be aware that many anti-vaccination websites and books repeat as facts claims that have been disproved, such as that vaccines cause sudden infant death syndrome or cancer and germs do not cause disease, or are unprovable. Most give lots of statistics, often obviously quoting from each other rather than primary sources, but on further investigation the statistics are selectively used or plain wrongly interpreted. Their info is almost always irrelevant to the UK. They have said immunization causes (variously) shaken baby syndrome, asthma, attention deficit disorder – in fact anything that has statistically risen since the introduction of vaccination, including (there is a whole book on the theory) criminal behaviour. Sometimes it seems a bit like saying that because a lot more bicycles have been manufactured since the Dodo became extinct there must be a link.

more info

You may like to know that many anti-vaccination websites and books have authoritative-sounding titles which make them sound "official". And that "reviews" on sites such as Amazon praising them to the skies and saying they're "backed up" or "with medical facts" are not necessarily reliable. (Lynne McTaggart, author of the *Vaccination Bible* has also written a book on how the power of the mind can change the bacterial content of water, believes in faith healing and conducts "experiments" to try to prove that "thought intentions" sent by people concentrating can lower the crime rate in another country.) Also, be aware if reading American books (such as *The Vaccine Book* by Dr William Sears) or info on US sites that there is a different immunization schedule for kids over there and different vaccines, and the information can be entirely irrelevant to the medical situation here in the UK. Here are some recommended medical and other useful sites.

www.immunization.nhs.uk

The best "official" website about all aspects of immunization. You can download a schedule, and there is clearly laid out statistical detail about cases of diseases, lists of FAQs and all the latest research on MMR.

www.dh.gov.uk

The Department of Health's site has a downloadable copy of the "Green Book", the professional bible of UK immunization (click on Public Health, then Health Protection, then Immunization), but it's massive and cannot be updated as fast as the immunization website can. However, it's useful if you want more detailed info on a specific aspect of immunization or a particular disease.

www.path.org

View the key achievements of the children's vaccine programme worldwide. The Vaccine Resource Library looks at the arguments surrounding immunization and gives guidance on diseases.

www.who.int

From the home page of the World Health Organization, search disease outbreak news to see where diseases on the UK immunization schedule pop up elsewhere in the world, or search immunization programme to see the work still going on to combat global diseases.

www.polioeradication.org

This is the website of the Global Polio Eradication Initiative (comprising WHO, Rotary International, the US Centres for Disease Control and Prevention and UNICEF). The organization was set up to try to wipe polio out worldwide, with the help of massive vaccination campaigns run by volunteers in the developing world. The website has factsheets and answers to the most frequently asked questions about polio, as well as moving photographs, important stories and hornswoggling statistics.

www.skeptics.com.au/journal/anti-immune.htm

The Australian article "Anti-immunization Scare: The Inconvenient Facts" takes on some of the many misleading statements by the anti-vaccination lobby.

www.briandeer.com/wakefield-deer.htm

A respected British investigative reporter wraps up the Dr Wakefield anti-MMR campaign story.

www.thelancet.com

The *Lancet* medical journal's website has information on specific issues and worries about vaccination such as those about the measles, mumps and rubella jab and autism controversy. Some of the info is very "medical" and in researcher language, but some of it is not so mystifying.

A Field Guide to Germs

by Wayne Biddle, Doubleday, US, 2002

An entertaining, almost fun history of diseases and germs, with sections on polio, diphtheria, whooping cough, measles, mumps, rubella and hepatitis so you can see what you are protecting your kids from and how many people used to die from them before immunization. Plus entertaining stuff on the plague, rabies and other disgusting matters to keep slightly older children saying "Euwwww!" for hours.

Vaccine: The Controversial Story of Medicine's Greatest Lifesaver

by Arthur Allen, Norton 2007

Mr Allen uses his long experience as a journalist to detail the history of vaccines including a clear-eyed cataloguing of the problems and covers the fight against polio, the eradication of smallpox , the anti-vaccination movement and the autism controversy.

multiples

More and more twins, triplets and other multiples are being born in developed countries due to better nutrition and health care, and there's a suspicion that women who have their babies from their late thirties onwards tend to have twins more often than younger mums. Some twins and triplets are due to the IVF process (because fertility drugs increase egg production and more than one egg is implanted in the womb to get the best chance of a pregnancy).

HOW People React

Luckily when you have multiple babies, and especially if you already have older children or a toddler, you are too tired to shout at people who say silly things to you. Don't forget the golden rule of parenthood: while it's interesting to hear what people say, some of them are no more intelligent than a trout, although most mean well. Here are some comments you've probably already heard and some handy replies.

"Oh, my God!" "Yes, thanks, we'll put you down for an hour of housework and bringing over dinner every Thursday, shall we?"

"You'll go mad." "Well, I've had lots of practice."

"You're kidding." "Yes, I love a jolly jape about a multiple birth – oh how we laughed."

"Are there twins in the family?" "There are now!"

"Were you on IVF?" "I have no idea. I must ask my husband." (Even if husband fictitious.) Or "Were you?".

"They must be a handful." "No, I hardly notice they're around the house really."

"Are they identical?" "I'm not sure. I've never looked."

"Wow, double (or triple) trouble!" "So they tell me [*stifled yawn*]."

"How much time are you taking off work?" "I'm not sure yet." Or "Oh, a couple of hours, I expect."

"Well, I see you are eating (have eaten) for three!" "Come over here and let me strike you on the nose with a rolled-up newspaper." (Some people put on lots of weight with twins, others don't.)

your feelings and fears

There are fears and issues around having more than one baby at once, just as there are about having one. A pregnancy with multiples is likely to involve more exhaustion, more hormones running around your system, often a greater weight gain, and worries about whether your bubs might come early, be underweight or need special medical care.

Because you will have an extra dose of pregnancy hormones that "turn off" after the birth, and you face the possibly daunting task of being mum to twins or more, you may be likely to go through a period of feeling depressed or freaked out. You'd be mad if you didn't feel at least a bit apprehensive about how you'll manage everything. (See "Feeling Overwhelmed or Depressed" in *Part 1: Babies* if that's how you feel.)

Here are some things to remember.

★ Lots of people have had twins or more and managed it really well.

★ None of them tried to do it without help: don't try to be a martyr and go it alone. There are people you can talk to and places if it all gets too much (see "More Info" at the end of the second chapter, "Your Support Team").

★ If you are loving and kind to your babies, it doesn't matter if the washing isn't done – but ask a friend to do it anyway.

★ It doesn't matter if everything is not perfect. In fact it doesn't matter if NOTHING is perfect!

team effort

Ideally parents of twins, and especially of more babies, will initially have a project manager: a sister, mum, close friend or partner who can take at least a month or two off work and set in place rotas for helpers and food bringers and do other sensible things such as answer telephones, organize meals and keep visitors away unless they're actually assisting the process of settling the newies into the home.

People often don't offer to help because they don't know what to do: assign tasks based on capability and ability to learn rather than waiting for people to work out what to do. This makes them feel needed and wanted instead of all at sea.

Ask for help from strangers as well as family and friends. "Here, feed this baby with a bottle while I do the other one" said a mother of twins to my friend once in a public place: he was thrilled. People are almost always happy to help with prams and hold doors open as long as you let them know you won't bite and you actually want the help.

If it's at all possible, get someone to pay for a cleaner for at least a while. If it isn't, try a rota of friends and family.

REASONS TO BE CHEERFUL

* That weird fashion of dressing twins in exactly the same clothes has long gone.

* Fingers crossed, multiples will play together so you can get things done.

* You may have produced a whole family all at once, like an efficiency expert. (Oh, try to look like you did it on purpose.)

* You have a ready-made excuse not to do anything else, such as bring a plate to a family do (try to make this last until the babies leave home).

* You're not alone. There are parents like you and support groups everywhere.

* Each child will gradually have their own special interests, ideas and possessions, but in the meantime they can share equipment and toys (although one mum informed me this honeymoon period ended at six weeks).

* Most people will be cluey enough to refer to your children by their individual names rather than "the twins" each time.

See the contacts in "More Info" at the end of this chapter for support and help. (If you come across the term "super twins" it means a multiple birth with more than two babies.)

"If you have twins get a hands-free telephone that clips onto your clothes, and a headset that allows you two hands so you can chat while doing things. Always record a good TV show to watch while feeding because it makes you feel like you're doing something for yourself at the same time, and can take your mind off your worries." JENNIFER

stuff to keep in mind

The first eighteen months are likely to be really intensive. Apart from finding time for feeding, changing and washing (and that's just the grown-ups), you'll be getting to know two new people with different personalities.

Some twins fight and will need to be separated or distracted; some will always want to hang out together. Some may benefit from being in separate rooms at their child-care centre or nursery; others will want to be together.

feeding

This is probably the biggest early issue for mums (and dads) of twins. Bosoms, bottles or a mix of both? Don't make a decision before you have the babies and then stick to it no matter what. The most important thing is to change if you need to. And use all the help with feeding you can get.

Feeding one baby while the other cries is very difficult emotionally as is not being able to spend one-on-one feeding time with each baby. But if you have other one-on-ones with them, don't stress about feeding times being sacred for this. Better to have two happy, fed babies to play with afterwards. Some mums use expressed breast milk in bottles for one bub during the day and breastfeed that twin at night. For ideas on how to breastfeed two (or more!) as a routine, get in touch with the La Leche League which has articles on its website for the multiple feeder – that's you, my multi-skilled goddess of plenty (contact details are given in "More Info" at the end of the "Bosoms" chapter in *Part 1: Babies*). Or talk to some mums who've breastfed two armfuls – you can find them through the parenting websites listed below in "More Info" below. See also p.93 for La Leche League and NCT details for support and guidance.

more info

www.multiplebirths.org.uk
Tel: 020 8383 3519
Independent charity with an emphasis on information for medical professionals working
with families who have twins or triplets, as well as loads of pamphlets for parents on
everything from feeding and sleeping issues for little ones, to special info on individuality,
school and teens (there is a nominal cost for these).

www.tamba.org.uk
Helpline: 0800 128 0509 (10am–1pm and 7pm–10pm); call 0870 770 3305 out of hours
Twin and Multiple Birth Association charity (TAMBA) has a parent-friendly site for families
with twins, triplets or more, with FAQs and factsheets on important issues including
breastfeeding more than one baby, clothes and equipment swaps, forums for a chinwag,
notification of social events, book recommendations for kids and adults, special section for
doctors, parenting advice on everything from logistics to developmental stages and more.

www.twinsonline.org.uk
www.twinsclub.co.uk
www.twinsuk.co.uk
These specialist parenting websites are for all numbers of multiple births, despite their
names. They are all advertising-driven online shopping sites, some with large parent
forums.

www.mostonline.org
For parents of triplets, quads and more, the Mothers of Supertwins US-based international
website is a non-profit outfit. It has sections including "Breast Leakage Inhibitor System"
(lordy) and relevant resources, support volunteers and books on the subject.

Twins: A Practical Guide to Parenting Multiples from Conception to Two Years Old
by Katrina Bowman and Louise Ryan, Orion, 2007
This book is a good resource for parents of twins. It acknowledges their range of
feelings – euphoria, fear, shock, regret, relief and joy. Some expectant parents have found it

reinforced the idea of having twins as frightening and intimidating, so perhaps don't read it all at once like a novel, but look up bits as you need them.

It's written by two Australian mums of twins, including one of whom on IVF treatments. They give their honest assessments of the feelings and fears involved and the practicalities, from finding out and pregnancy right through to after the birth and the equipment you'll need, plus lots of quotes from other mums, info for dads, contacts and sections on breastfeeding, bottlefeeding, the early weeks and all the nuts and bolts of sleeping. It's the only book I've seen that has a parent-centred, sensible and understanding section on having a preterm baby. It also has a glossary of terms used by doctors, nurses and other baby industry folk.

Double Trouble: Twins and How to Survive Them
by Emma Mahony, Thorsons, 2003
A twin herself, and the mum of twins, Ms Mahoney takes a practical approach to managing your pregnancy, what to eat, and knowing your rights when it comes to birth options, which equipment you'll need lined up, putting support systems in place ready to go; and what to anticipate in case of an "early" birth. Then after the birth she launches into crucial areas such as deciding what extra help you need and are entitled to and how to get it from friends, family and government services; working out a routine that will let everyone get a rest; bosom wrangling if you're breastfeeding; how to cope with multiple crying or sleeping problems and sibling issues. Thankfully, it's both realistic and optimistic.

iNSiDey activities

There are some days when it would be a thrill to be visited by a nomadic troupe of performing kids' entertainers who also clean the bathroom and give you a facial. In lieu of that, here are some ideas for insidey activities on rainy days, very hot days and middle-of-the-days when the UV rays are beaming down fiercely.

The play ideas are compiled and edited parents' answers to the survey done for this book. If your kid says "I'm bored", get them to close their eyes and jab a finger onto one of these pages.

You might also like to ask your child-care centre staff for their inside-play ideas. And get your kid to brainstorm a list of activities for this kind of day, which stays on the wall so you can refer to it easily. Boredom can be just the lull before another burst of creative energy.

iDeas from Parents

◎ Bubble spooning for littlies: fill a saucepan with lots of detergent in a bit of water; froth it up with a hand beater; spread towels around your kid, then give them other saucepans, bowls, cups and spoons and they'll sit for hours transferring bubbles from one container to another (you'll have to froth the water up again every so often) ◎ put down cheap, large cheap rolls of paper, ask your kid to lie down, then draw a line

READING TO BABIES AND TODDLERS

Here's the main reason to read to your baby or toddler: they LOVE it. It sparks all sorts of questions, drawings and games, and at bedtime it can prepare them for sleep. And it's a ready-made bonding activity wrapped up in educational phoofery: experts say that kids who are read to regularly get a huuuge start in learning to read.

The best thing you can do to encourage a love of books is to introduce your child to the world of imagination and experiences they offer. Point to words as you read them, talk about what's happening in the pictures, pause for questions, and don't be afraid to do some ham acting when reading. Kids love all sorts of books: ones with rhymes and repetition, ones that have pop-ups or flaps you lift. But perhaps the best books for kids are the ones that work on an adult level too, so that you will enjoy reading them time and time again – chances are they will also become your child's favourite.

It's never too early to start reading to a baby. In the early months they will enjoy focusing on strong images, and you can guide their hand in "touch and feel" books. Later on they will learn to lift the flaps or anticipate pop-ups themselves. Part of the fun of reading to older children is rediscovering your own childhood favourites as well as finding new ones together. Don't be afraid to start reading books that are a little beyond their capability – they may not understand every word but they'll love the additional challenge. Here's a short list of books to whet your appetite.

FOR BABIES
Peepo!, by Janet and Allan Ahlberg – a baby's-eye view of the world.
Dear Zoo, by Rod Campbell – learn the names of animals with this favourite lift-the-flap book.

around their body and let them put in eyes and mouth and create a full-length self-portrait, using paints, crayons or pencils (felt-tip pens tend to lose their lids and are harder on clothes) ◎ cut out pictures from magazines and catalogues and have them make scrapbooks ◎ fill in the baby book or memory book together ◎ unroll a ball of string or wool around the house and have a small present at the end ◎ have a puppet show, with bought puppets, your child's stuffed toys or sock ones with button eyes that you've made ◎ cook a cake or muffins and clean up the mess together ◎ watch a DVD ◎ sing songs together ◎ go through or compile photo albums and

The Very Hungry Caterpillar, by Eric Carle – munch through this brightly-illustrated book as the caterpillar turns into a butterfly, with bright colours!

Orange Pear Apple Bear, by Emily Gravett – just four words swapped around create different layers of meaning.

Kipper, by Mick Inkpen – the quirky world of an engaging dog.

The Bear in the Cave, by Michael Rosen and Adrian Reynolds – babies will love the splishy, vroomy noises.

FOR TODDLERS

Handa's Surprise, by Eileen Browne – even the youngest children will understand the joke.

Mr Gumpy's Outing, by John Burningham – repetition and anticipation are the key elements to this tale of an outing on a river.

The Gruffalo, by Julia Donaldson and Axel Scheffler – bestselling rhyming book in which an improbable monster is outwitted by a mouse.

Elmer, by David McKee – (nearly) everyone's favourite patchwork elephant.

Owl Babies, by Martin Waddell – the mummy owl goes out hunting for food, but she always comes back.

AND FOR THE QUICKER LEARNERS

I Will Not Ever Never Eat a Tomato, by Lauren Child – a hip fable for fussy eaters.

Pumpkin Soup, by Helen Cooper – a splendid wonderfully colourful treat of a tale about three animal friends learning to change roles and to share.

All About Alfie, by Shirley Hughes – charming day-to-day toddler antics.

discuss holidays and other family events ◎ make a den with boxes, cushions and blankets ◎ cook bread and have a nap while it rises ◎ mix food colouring with shaving cream to make pictures in the bath and on the walls around the bath, then splash it off ◎ cut out fish shapes from coloured paper and attach a paperclip to each, then tie string with a magnet at one end to a stick (or similar) and let your kid try to pick up all the fish with this "rod" ◎ make a clock from a paper plate and cut out pictures from magazines that resemble things we do at that time of the day ◎ draw roads on a large piece of cardboard (or a flattened cardboard box) and get your kid to place cars, street signs and shops and houses of blocks around the roads ◎ blend fruit with yoghurt to make ice-lollies and put them in the freezer ◎ get something out of the "presents cupboard" where you keep bargain toys and games picked up over the year ◎ cover the floor with a few old sheets (you can get them from charity shops) and do finger and foot painting ◎ have a picnic or tea party on a rug with toys and real cakes ◎ keep cardboard boxes for these times and give your kid the lot, plus sticky tape, coloured paper and paints to construct whatever they want to ◎ make up a story that goes around: you say a bit, they add to it, and so it goes on ◎ read books ◎ kids' CDs can really do the trick (MP3 players or personal CD players shouldn't be given to preschoolers as the earphone cords are a risk, and toddlers are hard on electronics – best for you to put music on at a central position, which means, sadly, you'll have to hear it, too) ◎ make pictures, letters or postcards to send to friends and relatives and end with a trip to the postbox ◎ blow bubbles in the bathroom ◎ make your own thunder and lightning with pots and pans ◎ do jigsaw puzzles (jigsaws must be for the right age group) ◎ bring out the dress-up box and have everyone in the family join in ◎ clean out your kid's wardrobe, decide which of their clothes is ready to be handed down, talk about growing up and present the stash of bigger clothes you've been buying at sales for them to try on ◎ dress up in someone else's old gear ◎ put on some music and dance ◎ play musical statues: when the music snaps off everyone has to freeze (best with a remote control) ◎ look through magazines for pictures of animals, cut them out and your child can paste them on cardboard to make up a "zoo" or a wildlife park ◎ make goop (just add water and a few drops of food colour to a cup of cornflour, mix it until it's thick and creamy, pour it onto a tray with sides so that it doesn't run off and they can get their fingers into it); it feels great, is non-toxic and washes out of clothes ◎ cook "speriments" (very popular) ◎ make up and mould papier-mâché over a blown-up balloon to create a mask or round animal ◎ invite a friend over to play ◎ build a world for toy cars to use ◎ go to an indoor-play centre ◎ let them help to sort out the little basket of junk (or third drawer down) that accumulates in

ART AND MUSIC

Kids can start drawing and painting from the time they can hold an implement in their hand. At first they need large coloured crayons and chunky paintbrushes that are easy to hold. Don't insist on your idea of what they draw and paint – you can suggest, but let them lead the way. Allow them to enjoy colours, lines and shapes without worrying too much what it (or your house) looks like. As they get older they will enjoy cutting and sticking to create collages, and a chalk-board easel is a great idea for larger scale work. They will also love a long roll of paper to make footprints or a mural on. Don't forget that your kids can always draw with chalk on safe footpaths or concrete areas, with a stick in packed earth or sand, and with water on patios, sheds or brick walls.

Art box supplies * painting apron * fat paintbrushes * poster paints * chunky crayons * big coloured pencils * little sponge shapes for printing with paint * coloured chalk * children's scissors * glue * collage material: old wrapping paper, glitter, snippets of fabric and ribbon, feathers, felt shapes.

Babies make their own music with their cooing, by shaking a rattle, or banging a block on the side of the cot and it's all fun from there on. There are endless recordings of music made for children of varying quality (and some of them are very dire indeed) but kids also will enjoy adult music that's lively and catchy – just beware of any dodgy lyrics. The point of making music is participation and fun. Young children are very rarely able to play a tune without scary repetitive coaching, so you'll need to go along with a bit of a cacophony caused by shaking, banging and blowing and tuneless bellowing. What you add to your box of musical instruments will depend on the age and capabilities of your child – just don't give them an expensive one and expect them not to break it, and be careful of ones not specifically made for children which may have bits that could fall off and be put in mouths (or worse).

Music box supplies * plastic containers filled with dried beans to shake, or shop-bought maracas * a drum * wooden tapping sticks * a child's tambourine * bells * a whistle * a xylophone * cymbals (saucepan lids are good) * a triangle.

most homes and is usually out of bounds ◎ give them special permission to kick and throw a blow-up beach ball, play loud music, run or play hide-and-seek in the house ◎ supply blocks that stick together ◎ bring out the fabric box that holds materials, ribbons and some fabric glue and make a fabric poster ◎ pretend to go camping in the house ◎ go shopping together ◎ set up a shop with items from the

TV AND DVDS

Watching TV or children's DVDs affects each kid in a different way. Some become slack-jawed zombies. Others jump about and follow all the instructions of a perky presenter. Kids who are scared by what they see might scream and cry, or they might watch silently, feeling confused and frightened on the inside. And the big decision for parents is whether or not to allow viewing of commercial channels, where the ads are designed to make your kids whinge for things that aren't good for them or you can't afford.

According to statistics, the more TV kids watch, the more likely they are to be above their healthy weight, unfit and falling behind at school, so you may want to think about setting some time limits, say half an hour every second day for kids of eighteen months, increasing to an hour a day for a three-year-old. DVDs have the advantage of being divided into short sections, which provide a logical break to turn off. Some TV programmes can be beautiful and educational, others are of very poor quality, so sit with them at first to decide which ones you both like. Most shows for young children have male leading characters, although the newer ones are beginning to redress this balance. Here are some toddler TV favourites.

FOR YOUNGER TODDLERS
In the Night Garden – happy toy characters love and care for each other.
Miffy – the adventures of a little white girl rabbit.

pantry and some pretend money they draw themselves and play shopping ◎ dress up and act out a play ◎ sing all the rain songs you know ◎ make and decorate gingerbread people ◎ visit friends with larger houses ◎ make a cubby house with cardboard boxes and decorate it ◎ make up stories for your child to act out as you narrate them – they can be the hero ◎ get them to help chop up veggies with a safe knife for dinner or freezing ◎ collect all the old Christmas and birthday cards and let the child cut and paste them ◎ thread buttons, beads or cotton spools on string (make sure there are no choking hazards) ◎ help clean the house ◎ they tell you what shapes to cut out of adhesive coloured contact paper and then put them on windows (older toddlers can use children's scissors to do the cutting out themselves) ◎ go to the library ◎ sort the washing into piles and fold it ◎ use playdough or real dough for cutting out shapes with biscuit cutters ◎ cut greeting cards with a strong image into simple jigsaws ◎ start a treasure box or dress-up box ◎ play dominoes

Pingu – expressive sounds but no real language make the slapstick antics of this mischievous penguin easy to follow.

Pocoyo – a lively little boy with a big personality.

Teletubbies – toddler-speak with four colourful, nappy-bottomed friends and their vacuum cleaner, the Nu-nu.

FOR OLDER TODDLERS

Bill and Ben – learn about the seasons and growing things with this revamped duo of tricksters.

Bob the Builder – slightly hapless construction worker and his anarchic machinery are kept in check by organized Wendy.

Fifi and the Flower Tots – the adventures of forgetful Fifi and her garden friends.

The Hoobs – muppet-style madness from these psychedelic creatures.

Noddy – politically correct version of Enid Blyton's old classic.

Peppa Pig – the life of a playful and slightly bossy little girl pig.

Postman Pat – gentle rural tales of this village postman, his cat Jess and a range of country folk.

Thomas the Tank Engine – unimaginative, barely animated stories about a range of engines with attitude that boys seem to love.

or cards (surprisingly good fun even if the rules aren't yet grasped – invent or go with the flow) ◎ make your own wrapping paper and cards for birthdays that are coming up ◎ make chocolate crispie cakes – messy, quick, creative, cheap, delicious ◎ make hats (feather ones are fun) ◎ face painting (you'll need the special paints in advance) ◎ make tunnels with sheets and chairs to crawl and walk through ◎ have a bath with bath bubbles and lots of things to pour, squirt and play with ◎ take blocks into the bath ◎ let a littlie cook while sitting in their high chair ◎ visit a free museum (kids of any age love them) or a gallery ◎ run around the house screaming (them not you – they love it too!) ◎ one parent plays the guitar or another musical instrument while the child sings the songs with the other parent ◎ let them tear a newspaper to bits ◎ change the rooms your kid can play in ◎ make a feely box – put a heap of different-textured things in a box and get your child to put their hand in and guess what they are feeling ◎ keep some toys hidden away so when you bring them out they seem like new ones ◎ let them get into the container cupboards ◎ chase Dad or be chased by Dad ◎ play with water at the kitchen sink ◎ paint egg cartons ◎ play computer games ◎ go to the website of a favourite TV show ◎ add blue food colouring to the bath so they think they are at the pool ◎ use an umbrella under the shower ◎ play hopscotch ◎ go to an indoor swimming pool ◎ play Snakes and Ladders ◎ go to a café for a warm drink ◎ make yourselves morning or afternoon tea and have a grown-up chat ("How are you?" "What's been happening?") ◎ go through recipe books together with bookmarks or tags and mark things that look like they'd be fun to make or eat ◎ go through the toy box to make up a bag for the charity shop or friends – the kid has the final decision ◎ watch the rain through a window and hunt for a rainbow ◎ blow up balloons and play volleyball with them ◎ test drive the tricycles and fancy cars that live at the big toyshop ◎ place stickers into plain scrapbooks or sticker books ◎ bang anything that makes noise ◎ wrestle ◎ allow them to ride a bike indoors ◎ tie scarves onto bangles and wear them to dance to music ◎ roll on the bed ◎ let them play with that noisy train or car set (if they can't run around the garden and scream their heads off, you're going to have to be prepared for noise inside) ◎ children love anything that you take time to do with them, especially creating something or cooking ◎ purchase a little table-and-chair set (littlies will spend hours sitting at them with playdough, paper, pencils and books) ◎ put their favourite CDs on while they are doing activities ◎ dance to *Carmen* or something loud and wild ◎ make a band using the kitchen pots ◎ make a hiding place with a sheet over the table ◎ get your kid to help with vacuuming and folding washing ◎ lie on the floor and let your baby roll around on top of you ◎ get a little trolley and go for rides in it up and down a passage (you push) ◎ give your child glue, scissors, scrap paper, streamers and pompoms to decorate tissue boxes, then get them to wear them as slippers ◎ have a teddy bears' picnic using a plastic tea set and a blanket – Barbie can come too if she behaves herself ◎ sail boats in the bath ◎ bring out the trusty shape sorter for a littlie ◎ tidy the bedroom ◎ get them to decorate a pizza base to make it more individual ◎ set up a hospital: use dolls and teddies as patients and tear up old sheets for bandages ◎ supply a bucket of pegs and a licence to peg anything ◎ make the room really dark and play with a torch ◎ make the whole house a shopping centre with different goods available at varying prices (you could use Monopoly money); the kids could even have special offers such as buy this packet of two-minute noodles and receive a complimentary glass of rasp-berry cordial ◎ read a favourite book and get them to act it out ◎ devote a corner in the garage to painting or chalk drawing on the concrete floor ◎ do some potato printing: cut out shapes from a potato, dip the shapes in paint and stamp them onto paper ◎ blow up balloons and hit them around with fly swats ◎ finger paint on a window ◎ play indoor skittles ◎ put all the plastic toys and cars in the bath for your child to give them a good scrub ◎ set some special housework activities; for example the kid sprays and you wipe ◎ teach the kid about how things grow by making a terrarium: cut the top off an old soft-drink bottle about a quarter of the way down and make holes in the bottom; "plant" some seeds on damp cotton wool on a small plate and cover them with the bottle; leave the terrarium in a warm, sunny place – in a couple of days shoots will appear ◎ construct Fuzzy Felt pictures ◎ let your kid dress up in your and your partner's clothes for a good laugh ◎ tape a lot of the children's TV programmes for when you are desperate ◎ make jelly and eat it ◎

make a book – they draw the pictures and tell you the story and you write it down, put their name on it and most importantly KEEP IT ◎ create shadow pictures on the wall ◎ make sandwiches and cut them into shapes with biscuit cutters ◎ put on some classical music and make up a story to go with it as it plays ◎ get out your button tin so that your child can group the different colours or sizes, then design patterns, make pictures, thread necklaces ◎ together make an absent relative or friend a big book of pictures of what you've been doing ◎ get dressed up in rain coat and wellies and go outside and jump in puddles!

BiRtHDay PaRties aND PRESENTS

If your kid's only a bub, you won't need to read all this stuff now; plenty of time for operatic, cast-of-thousands, four-weeks-in-the-planning extravaganzas later – but only if that takes your fancy. A bit of colour and movement, some streamers and balloons, a cake and lots of fuss on the morning of the birthday make for a great day. You don't have to get Nanna to do water ballet in the garden.

If you're the sort of insane person who wants a patting zoo, industrial-music circus and modern mime performance for your baby's first

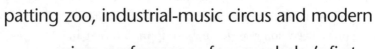

birthday, I suggest you have a good lie down. The kid won't remember any of it. And that old rule about "It's not a great party unless the police arrive" definitely doesn't apply to the under-5s.

If you're not sure what's a good present to take to a party, see the lists provided for kids aged 1 to 5. It's best to steer clear of anything that might create a blood feud between you and other parents – such as a live animal, a toy gun or "little girl" make-up and high heels. Or a nice bottle of chardonnay.

PLANNING

Try to start planning early to minimize stress: before you got pregnant would be a good time. And rope in as many people to help as you can – this is a great event for special uncles, aunties, friends and babysitters, especially ones who don't have their own children, to help with. "Bring a plate" is a good maxim, as is "plan one game", but coordinate this so nobody doubles up. A party's a dud if the hosts are frazzled out of their minds.

Ask your kid what kind of party they would like and who they'd like to invite, but feel free to use a power of veto. Brief your kid about the behaviour expected of them as host (but don't expect them to necessarily get it together).

Sometimes the birthday child behaves very badly at their party or gets hysterical. Time Out may help, but don't treat it as a punishment. The birthday is more likely to be relaxed if you keep your child (and yourself) calm the day before and perhaps only remind your little person it's their birthday on the actual morning rather than creating a "thirty-three more sleeps" anticipation (or not much sleep actually).

TO-DO LIST

Make yourself a list of what you'll
need to do. For example:

✱ make or buy and write
invitations with your kid

✱ check camera battery is charged

✱ buy decorations, candles and
matches

✱ plan and buy the party food
and drinks

✱ organize the birthday cake

✱ move anything breakable or
dangerous

✱ stock the first-aid kit with cute
sticking plasters

✱ decorate the party room

✱ find someone to mind the pets

✱ explain to the birthday kid how
to behave at the party.

Old-fashioned games that involve
participation, simple party food and rituals seem to work best for toddlers.

Just in case the party falls apart
or the entertainment gets eaten by the
dog, rained out or goes missing, have a
DVD ready as a back-up. One that will
appeal to all ages, has episodic bits and
incorporates music is best, instead of
one long narrative story. The kids will
be slack-jawed and zombified in seconds
as long as they haven't eaten their body
weight in mood-altering additives.

See "More Info" at the end of this
chapter for books and websites with good
ideas and hints for parties.

iNVitatioNS

Sorry to be crushingly obvious but when you're busy things do get overlooked.
Invitations should go out at least two and preferably three weeks in advance, and
should be written, at least to people you don't know well such as the parents of your
kid's child-care friends. (And it's always nice to keep an invitation for your baby
scrapbook as a souvenir.) They should be posted or given privately to avoid hurting
anyone else's feelings at the child-care centre or nursery.

A party invitation should give:

- ★ the reason for the party ("Francine's third birthday")
- ★ the day and date
- ★ start and finishing times
- ★ the address of the venue
- ★ the theme of the party and any special instructions, especially if costumes are required ("Please wear old clothes and bring a smock", "Please wear a yellow outfit", "Please come dressed as a jungle animal")
- ★ an "RSVP", meaning please reply (by a certain date if that's important) and your telephone number
- ★ any other relevant details ("Parents welcome to stay", "Brothers and sisters welcome" – unfortunately you can't say "Leave that bossy big brother at home").

venue

The local park always seems like a great idea for the party venue if the weather's good enough because the squashed cupcakes and sticky drinks go on the grass or in the park bin, but a park party is difficult to supervise, especially when parents drop their kids off at the start and collect them at the end. Keep this kind of party small and make sure that one of the adults arrives early to "bags" the area and that there's a rain shelter nearby. (After three false starts for park parties in winter, I gave up.)

Avoid a pool or beach party if you can't ensure strict supervision. Better not to have to worry about drowning.

Some fast-food chains and other places hold pay-per-head parties. The advantages are obvious – you don't have to prepare the house or clean up afterwards. But the drawbacks are equally clear: a high set fee for each invitee and hell to pay if you lose someone's kid on the way.

If your party is at home, keep your pets out of the way. You don't want them tortured by strange kids, and some children may be afraid of them. Also put away anything breakable and check for safety risks. Enlist help from the older kids, cousins or whoever you can for the clean-up afterwards.

Again to save yourself worrying about safety, avoid a party involving anything with wheels or unrestrained animals.

It's not usually a good idea to take young children to a theatre production or a film, or even to show them a full-length DVD at home. Kids who are the same age will be at different levels of development and concentration. One person's favourite film can be another's terrifying experience or a dull "been there, done that" time.

tHeme

Many parties have a theme: fancy dress, a single colour or a character from a book or TV show. The theme can be carried through a few aspects or everything – from clothes, the colour of the streamers and the pictures on placemats to the design of the cake.

Party shops, organizers and entertainers (check in the *Yellow Pages* or online) will supply helium balloons, decorations, hats, tablecloth, napkins and paper plates to suit a theme, whether it's generic (such as dinosaurs) or specific (TV-show licensed products). But honestly kids won't notice the difference if it's DIY and will have fun helping to make things and put up the decos.

DecoRatioNs

A few balloons and streamers should do the trick. A bunch of balloons tied to the front gate on the day will announce the party venue. If the party is in a park or other outdoorsy place, signs or balloons will help people find you.

Hired entertainment

Please remember that some young kids will scream the house down if they see a giant animal, and it's no use explaining there's a person in it! (You don't ever see this in a magazine or online article about birthday parties because the party entertainment firms advertising wouldn't like it.) Characters such as fairies and magicians are likely to be more successful, at least with older toddlers. Face painters are always a hit. If you do hire an entertainer, try to get one whose good reputation precedes them, and a written quote beforehand.

Length of the party

Parties for the under-5s are generally an hour and a half or 2 hours maximum (otherwise it's too much for kids and party givers). Mid-morning or early afternoon is a good time, ideally starting at 10.30am or 2pm. This allows for naps and avoids the late afternoon arsenic hour. A morning party avoids hours of anticipation and excitement fatigue. A weekend party is easier for everyone and most people prefer Sunday because Saturday is often a chores or sports day – but suit yourself. A sleep-over party at this age is complete insanity and no correspondence will be entered into.

Numbers

One theory for 1– to 3–year-old parties is to keep the number of child guests to the kid's age plus one; in other words, for a 3–year-old's birthday party have four children. Some families have a tradition that the birthday child asks only two or three friends. Others invite ten, fifteen or more, but it's doubtful whether your child will remember them all the next morning so why put yourself through the chaos? Of course this won't apply if you feel like an extravaganza or have stacks of helpers, or lots of friends and family with young children. (Even so, the kids themselves might find all the colour and movement too much.)

Encourage other parents to stay rather than just drop their kids off, and have some adult food and drink for them (but perhaps not whisky sours).

HeLP aND SUPerViSioN

Marshal all the able-bodied friends and rellies you can to help on the day. Some people like to hire a babysitter who is well known to the kids. You might want to assign special tasks, including taking photos or a video, making sure the little ones are being included, and being in charge of coats or toilet trips.

The younger the kids, the more adults you'll need. One adult to four children isn't a bad ratio, but there's nothing wrong with one adult for each kid, especially tinies.

Make sure you make the party area safe for the youngest person there. For example, burst balloons are a choking hazard so need to be carefully cleaned up straight away.

If you are taking your child to someone else's party, you may want to stick around for the whole time. You may feel especially strongly about this if the party involves a park or water or you don't know the parents.

Some people combine adult frolicking with a children's party so several people may need to be Designated Carers (sober and alert). Even a small amount of alcohol can result in liver and brain damage in a small child: kids this young should never, ever be given even a "sip" of a drink with any alcohol in it. So if you're all having a droi whoite whoine, put it up somewhere hoi.

fooD

Personally I think only lunatics try to serve tofu cake and bran granola at a kid's party (unless a child has allergies), but you can serve sugar-free lemonade to keep the sugar level down (forget soft drinks with caffeine in them). One mum suggests magic lemonade, using several food colourings. A drop of each colour is put at the bottom of an individual clear plastic cup, then sugar-free lemonade is poured into every cup and the different colours appear like magic.

It's probably the excitement of the event that revs kids up the most, but serve protein and carbo things such as little sausages and party pies as well as the sugary stuff with chemical additives. You can get some ideas from your party theme (jungle = tiger = Marmite stripes on bread, for example).

Parents should let you know in advance if their child is allergic to common party food ingredients. Try not to use that food if possible and ask the child's parent to come to supervise. (Parents of kids with allergies should have some suggestions of what party foods they can eat and in extreme cases can BYO.)

Individual cupcakes can be easier for littlies to handle than a large slice of birthday cake and easier for you to distribute. The birthday kid's cupcake can be at the top of a stack with a candle in it.

Parties for littlies shouldn't include choking hazards such as marshmallows, whole nuts, popcorn and crisps.

Kids under 4 don't always eat a lot of the party food. Don't take it personally.

Presents

Often the birthday kid will open the presents as soon as they are offered and they can get overexcited and under-appreciative. You can set aside a special time for opening presents after the party has begun or dispatch an older child or helper to follow the flow of presents and keep a list of givers so that the birthday kid can write thank-you letters later. (You might like to use photos of the party as thank-you postcards.) Some party planners say your child should wait until everyone has gone home before opening their presents. You'll have to judge whether this is acceptable to your kid or whether the very thought would send them into orbit.

Some people will give inappropriate presents, especially well-meaning relatives. If a toy is too fragile for your child or not right for their age group, explain this in a kindly way privately later. Some people give expensive presents, but discourage this because it sets a difficult precedent. A kid will be just as happy with a packet of crayons or some brightly col-oured discount plastic bath toys as with an elaborate toy.

If you're not sure about your idea for a present, check with the birthday kid's parent or caregiver. Always check safety labels on toys – and if an item looks dodgy, then it probably is.

PaRty games

Games need to be age specific and are best reserved for older toddlers if introduced at all before age 6. Group activities are always less likely to cause violence, tantrums or jealousy because nobody "wins" or "loses". Games that require high levels of dexterity or are set up for the fastest to win are bound to get out of hand and result in disappointment for many young children (see the "Games and Activities Without Winners" list coming up soon).

> *"Don't ask the children what they want to play. Just tell them what the next game is."* KIDS' RETAILING WEBSITE

PaRty Bags

Party bags, also known as booty bags, are a souvenir of the party given to each child guest. They can be as simple as a greaseproof bag with a piece of birthday cake in it or as artful as a party theme bag full of relevant goodies. Parents will appreciate it if the lolly quota is low. (Maybe keep a couple of spare bags for potentially tearful unexpected guests such as siblings.)

Party shops have ready-made party bags, but you can create your own. They can be sewn from felt or calico, or made by decorating ordinary brown-paper bags or a takeaway-food box. One with handles is good. Buy either random or themed items from a toyshop such as a few pages of stickers, a packet of plastic animals or something similar from the pound shop, then throw in some lollies from the newsagent or supermarket. Spread the loot equally between the bags. Always give the party bag to the child or their parent as they are walking out the door and not a moment sooner.

PaRty iDeas foR 1-yeaR-oLDs

The consensus of opinion among parents is that a party for a 1-year-old is a ludicrous proposition likely to result in maximum stress for minimum impact on your kid.

That doesn't mean you don't take a few nice photos, have a family lunch or invite some friends over for tea, just that major games, decorations, themes and berzillions of guests is more about what *you* want than about what the baby will get out of it. The most common suggestion from the survey done for this book was: keep the first birthday to family only or extended family. But if you're keen, suggestions include ◎ bubble blowing ◎ a picnic ◎ afternoon tea ◎ lots of crunching of wrapping paper ◎ playing with boxes.

PReseNts foR 1-yeaR-oLDS

◎ A book ◎ a balloon ◎ clothes ◎ something to ride on such as a trike with a pole for the parents to push it with ◎ plastic bath toys ◎ toys that encourage hand–eye coordination such as hammering toys (a plastic hammer on its own will do) ◎ activity toys such as push-down pop-up things ◎ shape sorters ◎ toys that make a noise (but will the adults like the noise quite as much?) ◎ stackable rings, cups or blocks ◎ soft, squeaky toys ◎ simple, safe musical instruments (clap sticks, not a tuba) ◎ balls with different sounds and textures ◎ mobiles and wind chimes ◎ a baby pram or mower to push ◎ a tree that you can plant together and then take a photo of with your child in front, every birthday afterwards ◎ touchy-feely textured cloth books ◎ anything bright or musical that the baby can have an effect on (It opens! It squeaks!).

See also the "Toys and Games for Babies" chapter in *Part 1: Babies*.

"Keep it short, otherwise it's too overwhelming for them."
CAROLYN

PaRty iDeas foR 2-yeaR-oLDS

Now that their kid is mobile, many parents are keen to introduce races with winners and games that are likely to result in a lot of adults yelling indecipherable

GAMES AND ACTIVITIES WITHOUT WINNERS

✱ Statues: play bursts of music and each time the music stops everyone has to freeze.

✱ I'm with the band: put on some kid-friendly music, give each child an instrument and let them march about. Simple dancing to the music is also an option.

✱ Bubble blowing: give everyone a wand to dip into a bowl (or old hub cap) filled with bubble mixture.

✱ A piñata: let everyone have a go at whacking a brightly decorated hollow papier-mâché shape, hung from a tree or a corner of the rotary clothes line, until it breaks and showers down lollies and trinkets. Traditionally long sticks have been used, but a toddler-sized cricket bat is a good whacker. You can make a piñata yourself with a balloon and papier-mâché (although you'll need to get the thickness right otherwise the kids will be whacking all day or it will break at the first hit),

or you can buy a ready-made one at a kids' party shop. This game has to be very closely supervised so no one gets hurt and each child has one go at a time (perhaps with some hefty adult whacks to the piñata every now and again to start it breaking open).

✱ Create a banner or a tablecloth: provide an old sheet or a huge length of paper, some pre-mixed paints, felt-tip pens, crayons, glitter glue and whatever else takes your fancy and let them at it. Perhaps kids can take their shoes and socks off and make hand- and footprints (make sure an art-party invitation says to wear old clothes and why).

✱ A treasure hunt: hide the treasures – stickers and small but non-hazardous toys and lollies are good – before the guests arrive and keep a few emergency ones in your pocket to sprinkle near a kid who hasn't had any luck.

encouragement to a bunch of confused, harassed 2-year-olds, but it might be better to wait until after the fifth or even sixth birthday for this. Suggestions included ◉ a family day ◉ a teddy bears' picnic (everyone brings their teddy – don't let them go home without them!) ◉ an indoor picnic (always a good option in winter) ◉ the sandpit ◉ the local playground ◉ playing with special toys from the toy library.

* Paint your own: buy some cheap white T-shirts, pillowcases or hankies and let the kids decorate them with fabric paints. This is best done in summer when their creations can dry on the line before the party ends.

* Story time: have a good storyteller or actor (every family should have one) read a book to the kids. It could be one that matches the theme of your party.

* Pass the Parcel to music: make a parcel with many layers of wrapping and put a little novelty gift (one for every child) between each. You'll need someone good on the music control to make sure each child gets a present.

* Pass the Treasure Chest (a good alternative to Pass the Parcel, at the end of the party): when the music stops the kid with the small chest opens the lid, takes a lucky-dip prize and passes the chest on.

* Other old-fashioned games: teach the kids hopscotch, Simon Says, Follow the Leader or very simple charades ("What's this animal?"). No penalties or prizes for getting it "wrong". Lots of traditional games for young kids can be sourced on the Internet (see "More Info" at the end of this chapter) or learned from older rellies.

* Dens and tunnels: put up a tent for a den and make tunnels (perhaps from sheets) the kids can crawl through.

Not-so-good games for toddlers parties include hide and seek ("Oh, there you are, in the poisons cupboard!"), sack races, any game with more than one or two rules and anything that requires a helmet or changing clothes quickly.

PResents foR 2-yeaR-OLDS

◎ A book ◎ large plastic click-together blocks ◎ simple musical instruments ◎ a *Teletubbies* or *Thomas the Tank Engine* DVD ◎ a plastic clamshell sandpit ◎ an easel ◎ big crayons ◎ playdough and plastic biscuit cutters ◎ a wee umbrella and wellies ◎ a soccer-type ball ◎ a bubble-blowing kit ◎

a tip truck ◎ something that squirts in the bath ◎ a tea set ◎ pull-along toys ◎ a library book with a library card and an explanation of what it's for ◎ toddler crockery and cutlery ◎ a plastic tool set ◎ simple large puzzles ◎ a bucket and spade set.

See also the "Toys and Games for Toddlers" chapter in *Part 2: Toddlers*.

> *"Don't try to organise them – just let them be together."*
> LISA

Party ideas for 3-year-olds

◎ Themes based on video or TV shows or characters such as Bob the Builder ◎ butterflies ◎ playdough ◎ Winnie-the-Pooh ◎ an indoor playground ◎ fairies and pixies ◎ a single colour (for example, purple costumes and decorations) ◎ the local playground ◎ under the sea ◎ a music or dance party ◎ face painting (you'll need the special non-poisonous paints from a craft or toyshop – or you can hire the painter).

Presents for 3-year-olds

◎ A book ◎ big snap-together blocks ◎ dress-up outfits ◎ crayons ◎ trikes or ride-on wheeled things ◎ an age-specific jigsaw puzzle ◎ a creative kit with crayons, glue and coloured papers, in a bucket with a lid ◎ a plastic tool set ◎ playdough ◎ a rolling pin and plastic biscuit cutters ◎ stickers ◎ a personal tape player with ear-phones and music or story tapes ◎ little cars ◎ a beach ball ◎ character dolls from TV or video shows they already love ◎ a backpack ◎ a tea set ◎ a kite.

See also the "Toys and Games" chapter in *Part 2: Toddlers*.

more info

Free local parenting magazines distributed in child-centred venues such as play-groups, libraries and leisure centres, as well as the *Yellow Pages* and Internet search engines carry loads of listings of party entertainers for hire and online shops featuring "partyware" (paper plates, cups, streamers, and other stuff that strikes terror into the heart of environmentalists) – everything from a simple matching colour scheme to the latest book tie-in, fairy extravaganza, and kids' TV show or movie merchandise. Ask other parents to get a recommendation. Beware that some pre-filled sweet bags and party favours may originate in places where health and other regulations regarding additives are not tough, or as well observed as they are in Britain. You may wish to buy your own sweeties or party favours when making up gift bags.

Children's parties
by Charlotte Packer, Ryland, Peters and Small, 2006
Budget-saving and stress-reducing ideas for one- to ten-year-olds, with suggestions for age-appropriate themes, party invitations, party bags and games. Useful party planner for each age group.

Creative Crafts for Kids
by Gill Dickinson, Hamlyn, 2006
Huge hardcover with ideas for gifts and projects that toddlers and older kids can help make for little friends, relatives and holiday celebrations, including costumes, masks, cards, gifts, whacky gourmet delights and delightfully shonky homewares. All projects come with a list of materials needed, time required and age suitability.

Kids' Birthday Cakes ("Australian Women's Weekly")
by Susan Tomnay (ed), Australian Consolidated Press, 2006
This award-winning new version of the classic UK best-seller Children's Birthday Cake Book has several basic cake and icing recipes, and lots of fresh decorating ideas for lurid, big-impact cakey constructions.

Practical Parenting's Party Games
by Jane Kemp and Clare Walters, Hamlyn, 2003
Ideas on fun, safety, chill-out strategies and catering for kids' parties up to five years old.

Annabel Karmel's Complete Party Planner
by Annabel Karmel, Ebury Press, 2000
As you'd expect from the recipe wrangler, there's loads of party recipes, plus suggestions for invitations, games, and giveaways.

extra RESOURCES

CHILDREN'S HOSPITALS

ENGLAND

Birmingham Children's Hospital
Steelhouse Lane
Birmingham B4 6NH
(0121) 333 9999

Bristol Royal Hospital for Children
Paul O'Gorman Building
Upper Maudlin Street
Bristol BS2 8BJ
(0117) 927 6998

Derbyshire Children's Hospital
Uttoxeter Road
Derby DE22 3NE
(01332) 340131

Evelina Children's Hospital
St Thomas' Hospital
Westminster Bridge Road
London SE1 7EH
(020) 7188 7188

Great Ormond Street Hospital for Children
Great Ormond Street
London WC1N 3JH
(020) 7405 9200
Great Ormond has a special focus on dealing with children with multiple health issues, rare congenital conditions and life-threatening or terminal illnesses. It offers a national rather than local service, taking referrals from other hospitals, and has no Accident and Emergency section. (It does have an excellent website in partnership with the Institute of Child Health at **www .ich.ucl.ac.uk** which has useful health fact sheets and more for parents, reviewed in "More Info" at the end of the "Health" chapter in this book.)

Royal Alexandra Hospital for Sick Children
Eastern Road
Brighton BN2 5BE
(01273) 696955

Royal Liverpool Children's Hospital
Alder Hey Hospital
Eaton Road
Liverpool L12 2AP
(0151) 228 4811

Royal Manchester Children's Hospital
Hospital Road
Swinton
Pendlebury
Manchester M27 4HA
(0161) 794 4696

Sheffield Children's Hospital
Western Bank
Sheffield S10 2TH
(0114) 271 7000

NORTHERN IRELAND
Royal Belfast Hospital for Sick Children
180 Falls Road
Belfast BT12 6BE
(028) 9024 0503

SCOTLAND
Royal Aberdeen Children's Hospital
Cornhill Road
Aberdeen AB25 2ZG
0845 456 6000

Royal Hospital for Sick Children
9 Sciennes Road
Edinburgh EH9 1LF
(0131) 536 0000

Royal Hospital for Sick Children
Yorkhill
Glasgow G3 8SJ
(0141) 201 0000

WALES
Children's Hospital for Wales
University Hospital of Wales
Heath Park
Cardiff
CF14 4XW
(029) 2074 7747

DOWN SYNDROME ASSOCIATIONS

Down's Syndrome Association
Langdon Down Centre
2a Langdon Park
Teddington TW11 9PS
England 0845 230 0372
Northern Ireland (028) 9066 5260
Wales (029) 2052 2511

Down's Syndrome Scotland
158/160 Balgreen Road
Edinburgh EH11 3AU
(0131) 313 4225

FAMILY AND PARTNER ABUSE AND VIOLENCE

24-hour National Domestic Violence Helpline
0808 2000 247
Immediate help and practical advice, this is run by the Refuge and Women's Aid (see below).

Women's Aid
www.womensaid.org.uk
Helpline: see above
Excellent site of the national charity offers fact sheets on what to do if you or a friend needs help, answers frequently asked questions, lots of information about violence and abuse, and how to get help in your area. Make sure you include "UK" at end of the address.

Refuge

www.refuge.org.uk

This charity site offers help for women and children in a violent or abusive situation. Links pages, info on prevention, how to work to change a family situation, and on where to go if you need to get away.

National Centre for Domestic Violence

www.ncdv.org.uk

A free service that helps domestic violence victims secure legal injunctions or non-molestation orders to protect them from further abuse.

National Society for the Protection of Cruelty to Children

Adult Helpline: 0808 800 5000

www.nspcc.org.uk

The NSPCC campaigns to put an end to cruelty to children.

www.carelineuk.org

Helpline: 0845 122 8622 (Mon–Fri 10am-1pm & 7–10pm)

Confidential telephone crisis counselling service.

SEVEN-STEP ESCAPE PLAN

✻ Ring one of the helplines listed above to find out how the police or a women and children's refuge can offer you protection. ✻ Have a secret signal arranged with a friend, or more than one friend, for use in an emergency – a special word or sentence that means to come and help or call the police. ✻ Have an excuse ready about why you need to leave quickly and rehearse it so the abusive partner won't be suspicious. ✻ Always carry change for phone calls and keep your mobile phone charged. ✻ Leave a list of emergency phone numbers with your friend, or somewhere else so that it's hidden but easy to get to. ✻ Organize a safe place to go to in an emergency. Ask your friend to show you where they hide a key to their house. Or it may be safer to use a house that your partner does not know about – that of a friend's relative or a friend's friend. ✻ Prepare an escape bag and hide it somewhere safe, or at a friend's house: it could have emergency cash, spare car and house keys, and copies of legal documents and ID.

HELP FOR MEN IN VIOLENT OR ABUSIVE RELATIONSHIPS

www.mankind.org.uk

01823 334244

The website of the ManKind Initiative has advice and help for men suffering from domestic violence.

www.mensaid.com

Helpline: 0871 223 9986 (8am–8pm)

Men's Aid is a charity providing free practical advice to men who have been abused.

www.respect.uk.net

0845 122 8609 (Mon, Tues, Wed, Fri 10am–1pm, 2–5pm)

Help for those who want to stop being the abuser or the violent partner.

GAY FAMILIES

www.pinkparents.org.uk

For information, advice and support for lesbian and gay parents or children of lesbian and gay couples.

Pink Parents UK

Unit 29 Hillier Road

Devizes

Wiltshire

SN10 2FB

01380 727 935

GOVERNMENT SERVICES

www.dwp.gov.uk

The government Department for Work and Pensions is responsible for a range of benefits and services for families. Check if you are eligible for any of them. These include:

Child Benefit Enquiry Line

0845 302 1444

Child Support Agency National Enquiry Line

08457 133 133

www.dh.gov.uk

Department of Health's website, with information on NHS services, links to the latest surveys and publications on women's and children's issues.

ww.nhsdirect.nhs.uk

Helpline (24-hr): 0845 4647

For general health advice, support and enquiries. The website has some self-help tools and health glossaries but the core of the service is the 24 hour health helpline.

www.direct.gov.uk

Lists all the government services available in the UK, with clear information and links to other public service organizations. Leaflets include subjects such as Breastfeeding and Work and Bottlefeeding. Links to regional equivalents in Wales, Scotland and Northern Ireland.

www.hse.gov.uk/mothers

This special part of the Health and Safety Executive's government website covers rights and entitlements for pregnant women and new mums at work. Lots of FAQs, a roundup of legal rights for workers and bosses, as well as the health and safety advice you'd expect to find.

www.taxcredits.inlandrevenue.gov.uk

The majority of families with children in the UK are entitled to tax credits. Find out your entitlements and apply online.

CHARITIES

www.familyandparenting.org

The Family and Parenting Institute is an independent charity working to support parents in bringing up their children to promote the wellbeing of families and to make society more family friendly. Gives answers to common questions and referrals for more help.

www.parentlineplus.org.uk

0808 800 2222

Parentline Plus is a charity which offers support to anyone parenting a child – the child's parents, step-parents, grandparents and foster parents – runs a free helpline and courses for parents, develops innovative projects and provides a range of information.

LOSS AND GRIEF

When a fetus is lost before it would have been able to live on its own, this is usually called a miscarriage. If a "viable" baby dies before it can be born or is born dead, this is usually called a stillbirth. Other even less thoughtful words may be used by medical professionals.

The Child Bereavement Trust

Aston House

West Wycombe

High Wycombe

Buckinghamshire HP14 3AG

0845 357 1000

Offers support to families who are experiencing loss and grief.

MISCARRIAGE

Because early miscarriage is so common (believed to be up to one in five pregnancies), many people, including some GPs, suggest you simply try again. But it's important to talk to your obstetrician or another medical specialist in fertility or pregnancy and request any blood tests or surgical procedures that may help determine whether you have a problem (for example, with blood clotting, or your uterus or cervix) that could cause recurrent miscarriage before trying to become pregnant again. You may be able to take preventative steps next time.

The Miscarriage Association

Provides information and support for those who have suffered the loss of a child in pregnancy.

www.miscarriageassociation.org.uk

Clayton Hospital

Northgate

Wakefield

West Yorkshire WF1 3JS

01924 200 799

In Scotland contact Miscarriage Support 0141 552 5070 (www.miscarriagesupport.org.uk)

Websites Use a search engine such as Google to find websites that are relevant to any diagnosis you may have had of the cause of your miscarriage. For example, if you have been diagnosed with a "factor V Leiden" problem (a blood clotting disorder), you can search variations on the name to find sites such as **www.fvleiden.org** and **www. naturalchildbirth.org/natural/ resources/prebirth/prebirth35.htm**.

COUNSELLING AND HELP
Stillbirth and Neonatal Death Support (SANDS)
www.uk-sands.org
28 Portland Place
London W1B 1LY
Helpline: 020 7436 5881

SANDS provides support for parents and families whose baby is stillborn or dies soon after birth. They have many publicatons you can order by telephone or online, including the booklet *Saying Goodbye to Your Baby*. They also produce useful factsheets that cover a range of practical and emotional issues, such as advice for bereaved fathers, grandparents, and other children in the family and topics such as sexual problems following a stillbirth and coping with the next pregnancy.

BOOK
Coming to Term: Uncovering the Truth About Miscarriage
by Jon Cohen, Houghton Mifflin, 2005

A well-respected US science writer decided to investigate the subject after his wife's fourth miscarriage. He clearly explains the common and not-so-common reasons for it, the treatments and suggestions often given, includes the stories of real women and families who've been through it, and provides hope for the future.

RELATIONSHIPS

Relate
www.relate.org.uk
Local offices can help with relationship counselling, sex therapy and other relationship support services.
Relate Central Office
Herbert Gray College
Little Church Street
Rugby
Warwickshire CV21 3AP
0845 456 1310

Relationships Scotland

www.relatescotland.org.uk

18 York Place

Edinburgh EH1 3EP

0845 119 6088

Relate Northern Ireland

www.relateni.org

3rd & 4th Floors

3 Glengall Street

Belfast   BT12 5AB

028 9032 3454

Relationship Counselling for London

0800 652 2342

Part of the Tavistock Centre for Couple Relationship organization provides practical help for Londoners with relationship difficulties. They have two centres: one in Camden and one in the City of London.

www.ukcouplescounselling.com

Network of specialist counsellors for couples "at any stage" in their relationship.

www.bonusfamilies.com

For separated parents and others with so-called "blended families" this is a useful US website. You'll have to dodge Halloween questions, but this non-profit site answers lots of questions on etiquette, step-parenting dilemmas and more.

SINGLE, SOLE AND SHARED-CUSTODY PARENTS

One Parent Families/Gingerbread

www.oneparentfamilies.org.uk

This newly merged outfit is now *the* organization of first resort for lone parent families in the UK. It also publishes a *Lone Parent's Survival Guide*, a useful downloadable resource. Call the phone number or search online for details of your local group and activities.

One Parent Families: Gingerbread
255 Kentish Town Road
London NW5 2LX
020 7428 5400
Lone Parent Helpline: 0800 018 5026

SCOTLAND
One Parent Families Scotland
13 Gayfield Square,
Edinburgh EH1 3NX
Helpline: 0808 801 0323
Tel: (0131) 556 3899

SPINA BIFIDA AND NEURAL TUBE PROBLEMS

www.asbah.org
Helpline: 0845 450 7755
Association for Spina Bifida and Hydrocephalus (ASBAH)
ASBAH provides information about spina bifada and hydrocephalus, as well as specialized advice on health and educational matters. It also aims to improve services and opportunities for people living with spina bifida or hydrocephalus.

SCOTLAND
www.ssba.org.uk
Helpline: 08459 111112
Scotland's Spina Bifida Association provides help and info on spina bifida, hydrocephalus and related issues.

SUDDEN INFANT DEATH SYNDROME (SIDS)

The Foundation for the Study of Infant Deaths (FSID)
www.sids.org.uk
Artillery House
11-19 Artillery Row
London SW1P 1RT
Helpline: 020 7233 2090
General: 020 7222 8001

The FSID provides counselling and practical help in the case of a baby's death for any reason. It is a centre for research and information on SIDS, as well as campaigning for greater awareness of the issue. Their booklet, *When a Baby Dies Suddenly and Unexpectedly*, explains what happens, answering some of the most frequently asked questions concerning post-mortem examinations, funeral arrangements, grieving, keepsakes, seeking and giving support and having another baby. Their most popular publication, *Babyzone*, offers advice on protecting babies from cot death, accidents and infections.

Scottish Cot Death Trust
www.sidscotland.org.uk
Royal Hospital for Sick Children
Yorkhill
Glasgow G3 8SJ
0141 357 3946
This Scottish trust can help with information and support, online, by phone or in person. They also run a "befriending" scheme and advice if you are thinking about having another baby. It also supports education and research programmes.

TEENAGE MUMS

Most of the major women's hospitals have special help for teenage mums. Community health centres, women's health centres, Family Planning Clinics, your GP and churches often have young mum groups or can point you in the right direction for somewhere to live and looking after the baby, government financial help and finding work in the future. Brook Advisory Centres across the UK (0800 0185 023) offer young people advice, counselling and medical help on pregnancy.

WOMEN'S HOSPITALS

There are two dedicated women's hospitals in the UK.

Birmingham Women's Hospital
Edgbaston
Birmingham B15 2TG
(0121) 472 1377

Liverpool Women's Hospital
Crown Street
Liverpool L8 7SS
(0151) 708 9988

All other major hospitals have women's health departments and many also have maternity units and obstetric and gynaecology departments. To find a hospital in your area, check out one of the following resources.

www.nhs.uk/servicedirectories
An online search facility where you can look up your local health-care practitioners, from GPs, dentists and opticians to walk-in clinics and hospitals.

Dr Foster Good Hospital Guide: A Good Hospital Guide: A Unique Guide to Getting the Best Out of the Health Care System in the UK
by Dr Foster, Vermillion, 2002
"Dr Foster" isn't a person, but a joint venture by an NHS offshoot called the Health and Social Care Information Centre and "Dr Foster", a company that sells reports and other information to clients in the medical industry. This book is a listings guide to hospitals in the UK, whether NHS or private, but you'll probably find more recent info on the matching website, below.

www.drfosterintelligence.co.uk
Run by the same joint NHS-private venture this site complements the book (see above) with more up-to-date info on hospitals, birth centres, and medical and alternative health special-ists. Click on "Information for the Public" to use the search facility and remember, the details will have been provided by the centre, doctor or practitioner themselves: this is not an inde-pendent review or recommendation.

index

Kaz Cooke is an author, cartoonist and mum, with a background in journalism, dancing on tables (well, okay only that once, at a party) and sleeping in. She lives in Australia and divides her time between the keyboard and the couch. Her remaining ambitions include finding a flattering hairstyle before she dies and finishing a hot cup of tea before being interrupted. *The Rough Guide to Pregnancy and Childbirth* was her first book with Rough Guides.